MISHA GLENNY

Misha Glenny is a distinguished investigative journalist and historian. As the Central Europe Correspondent first for the *Guardian* and then for the BBC, Glenny chronicled the collapse of Communism and the wars in the former Yugoslavia. He has won several major awards for his work, including the Sony Gold Award for outstanding contribution to broadcasting, and is the author of five books, including the acclaimed *McMafia* and *DarkMarket*.

MISHA GLENNY

McMafia

Seriously Organised Crime

VINTAGE

For Kirsty

1 3 5 7 9 10 8 6 4 2

Vintage
20 Vauxhall Bridge Road,
London SW1V 2SA

Vintage is part of the Penguin Random House group of companies
whose addresses can be found at global.penguinrandomhouse.com

Penguin
Random House
UK

Copyright © Misha Glenny 2008

Misha Glenny has asserted his right to be identified as the
author of this Work in accordance with the Copyright,
Designs and Patents Act 1988

First published in Vintage in 2009
First published in hardback by The Bodley Head in 2008

penguin.co.uk/vintage

A CIP catalogue record for this book is available from the British Library

ISBN 9781784706746

Printed and bound in Great Britain by Clays Ltd, St Ives plc

Penguin Random House is committed to a sustainable future
for our business, our readers and our planet. This book is made
from Forest Stewardship Council® certified paper.

MIX
Paper from
responsible sources
FSC
www.fsc.org
FSC® C018179

CONTENTS

ILLUSTRATIONS

MAPS

FOREWORD TO NEW EDITION OF *MCMAFIA*

McMafia is both a book and a TV series. The book is non-fiction, the TV series is fiction; but the two are intimately linked. Although the protagonists of the TV show are entirely made up, as are many of the plot lines, they are nonetheless an entirely authentic projection of the characters I got to know both during the research for the original *McMafia* and also in subsequent years, when I have gone on to investigate other aspects of global crime.

Most non-fiction authors do not embark on a book in the hope that it will be optioned as a film or a TV drama. Real life that is well and faithfully reported tends to have too many weird kinks and meandering cul-de-sacs to be squeezed into the parameters of those other media, especially in the form of fiction. Indeed, I believe non-fiction writers harbour a quiet resentment towards novelists. Where we are bound to stick to the facts, however awkward they may make the narrative, novelists can just make stuff up.

As I wrote the book, *McMafia*, I did think the finished product might attract some interest as the source material for a documentary. In fact, on several occasions production companies attempted to sell the idea to broadcasters but for one reason or another, the ideas never quite took off. Even with this earlier interest, it was to my surprise that, soon after its publication, the book was optioned by a major British film production company. The option means that you get paid a modest sum of money not to hand the film or TV drama rights to another company.

Meanwhile, the option owners explore whether it will be feasible to find a suitable writer, a good director and, most importantly, sufficient funding to turn the project into a real film or TV drama.

I had been well prepared by friends, colleagues and agents that from the base camp of the 'option' to the peak of Everest, where a film or TV show is actually made and broadcast, is a long and arduous journey. It is like a game of Snakes and Ladders in which snakes outnumber the ladders by about 15 to 1.

And, yes, many of the clichés of this new world I was getting to know are true – there is much LaLa in this land. I lost count how often I was told that the book was 'incredible', 'wonderful' or 'path-breaking', and how much everybody loved me. And yes, on one occasion I was flown to LA, dined at a spectacular restaurant and told solemnly that *McMafia* was about to become a major TV show in the United States. And that was the last I heard of it. Like many others with a fleeting acquaintance of this industry, I am at a loss to understand the economics of it.

Working on the assumption that the series would never happen meant that I was never disappointed when project after project fell at one hurdle or another. In early 2013, yet another American TV channel were in touch dangling a chunk of money, in exchange not just for the option but for all rights to the book in its entirety and in perpetuity. It was not a great deal, but as I had never believed that the book would be transformed into screen fiction, I was on the verge of signing.

At this point, two Brits, the writer, Hossein Amini, and the director, James Watkins, approached me and asked if I would like to collaborate with them on a TV series based on the book. They both had considerable experience in feature films and were highly sought after by studios. Hoss was nominated for an Oscar for his screenplay of the Henry James novel, *The Wings of the Dove*, and had also written *inter alia* the extraordinary Hollywood movie, *Drive*. James, meanwhile, was the writer and director of *Eden Lake* and the director of *The Woman in Black*. This was serious pedigree. Like many creative workers with a background in film, the two were interested in branching out into television.

Television is the new Hollywood. At the moment, we are witnessing what some refer to as 'The Battle of the Platforms', where HBO, Showtime, Netflix, Amazon, the BBC, Canal+, and diverse Scandinavian broadcasters, to name a few, slug it out to see which model will seduce the most viewers and garner the greatest acclaim. As a consequence, for the moment broadcasters are sinking huge sums of money into high-end television drama to such an extent that it is sometimes hard for the viewer to choose what to watch next.

But there is also a significant difference in the production of television compared to film production. In Hollywood, the director is king; in television the writer is the most important part of the team. If Hoss and James were to fashion a major television series, they would be the decisive members of the team.

Within five minutes of meeting the two men, I was convinced that whether they succeeded in convincing a broadcaster to take on the idea of *McMafia* or not, these were the people I wanted to work with. Helped along by Nick Marston, my agent who had nursed the idea of *McMafia* as a fictional series from the beginning, and Dixie Linder at Cuba Productions, a London film company, it didn't take long before the BBC grasped the vision that Hoss and James had laid out. I knew that any fictionalisation of *McMafia* would involve the creation of new characters. But what impressed me so deeply about Hoss and James was how they understood and appreciated the world that I had been attempting to map in the book. It was immediately clear that the authenticity of any TV show involving them was of paramount importance. To this end they wanted me to act not just as a nominal consultant but a real one.

Since the BBC initially commissioned the series, I have been involved in the realisation of Hoss's and James's extraordinary vision. I have participated in the writers' room where Hoss and James were joined by three other great screenwriting talents, Laurence Coriat, David Farr and Peter Harness, to thrash out the narrative and emotional journey of the main characters. It was an exceptional privilege to watch a masterclass in the art of television writing.

I am pleased to say that some of the stories in the original book have indeed made it into the TV series in various forms. What you will read in this book is not the gripping fictional story created by Hoss and James. *McMafia*, the book, is the true story. With real people and real lives.

INTRODUCTION

It was the evening of April 30th, 1994, and spring had settled on Woking in Surrey. The Barnesbury Estate is not quite middle-management, but there is no shortage of aspiration in this part of southern England. And as dusk fell on Willow Way, a quiet road of terraced housing, cars had already been garaged and families sat down for dinner and Saturday-night television.

At nine o'clock, a man emerged from his red Toyota outside No. 31. Carrying a flat blue-and-white box, he strolled up to the front door and tapped on it. Inside Karen Reed, a 33-year-old geophysicist who analysed seismic data for a living, was enjoying a glass of white wine and a chat with a friend when they heard the man's muffled voice through the window. 'Have you ordered a pizza?' he enquired. Karen opened the door, whereupon the pizza deliverer drew a .38 pistol and shot her several times in the head with calm deliberation. The killer then ran back to the car and drove off.

Karen Reed was not the intended victim that night. There was a reason for the murderer's confusion, however. His real target was Karen's sister, Alison Ponting, a producer at the BBC World Service who was living with Karen at the time, but happened to be out that evening. The killing had probably been carried out at the instigation of Djokar Dudayev, President of the Republic of Chechnya.

In 1986, Alison had married a chubby Armenian charmer, Gacic Ter-Oganisyan, whom she had met a couple of years earlier while studying Russian at university. The marriage triggered a chain of improbable events, which eight years later unleashed the whirlwind of death, imperialism, civil war, oil, gangsterism and nationalist struggle that is otherwise known as the North Caucasus upon the sleepy commuter town of Woking.

Eighteen months before Karen's murder, two brothers, Ruslan and Nazarbeg Utsiev, had arrived in London as envoys of President Dudayev, with a brief to arrange the printing of passports and banknotes for the new Chechen state. Ruslan was the volatile Dudayev's most trusted adviser and a hardliner in the faction-ridden administration. His brother was a martial-arts expert and general muscle-for-hire. Along with their public mandate to print the documents of the putative Chechen state, they had a number of other missions: to secure a $250 million loan from an American businessman for the modernisation of Chechnya's huge oil refineries; to conclude negotiations with the German energy company, Stinnes AG, for the quick sale of Chechen oil at world prices; and, as investigators later discovered, to purchase 2,000 ground-to-air Stinger missiles. To embark on such complex negotiations, the Chechen Government representatives needed a skilled interpreter and fixer. Ruslan remembered that he was once interviewed by a BBC producer, Alison Ponting, and he turned to her for help. She suggested her husband, Ter-Oganisyan, hoping, perhaps, that he would find gainful employment.

During his time in London, Alison's Armenian husband had developed into the consummate chancer. Ter-Oganisyan was ducking and diving: smuggling, setting up fake companies for money-laundering and also doing menial work when his tentative criminal activities dried up. Initially the macho Caucasian trio hit it off, holding raucous parties to which a stream of call girls were invited. Not surprisingly, Alison was increasingly unhappy at the behaviour of her husband and the two Chechens, as were the wealthy occupants of Bickenhall Mansions, the apartment block a stone's throw from Sherlock Holmes's reputed domicile at 221b Baker Street, where the Utsiev brothers had found a flat.

At some point, relations between the Armenian and the Chechens soured. Later, England's Crown Prosecution Service insisted that Ter-Oganisyan had discovered that the Stinger missiles were destined for Azerbaijan to be deployed in the war against his home country, Armenia. There was a second theory – that the Stingers were indeed bound for Chechnya, and that the Utsiev brothers and Ter-Oganisyan fell out over money. What is certain is that Ter-Oganisyan alerted senior members of the Armenian KGB to the Utsiev brothers' activities and a couple of hitmen were dispatched from Los Angeles, the centre of the Armenian diaspora in the United States, to London.

The Utsiev brothers were murdered in gruesome fashion (Ruslan's body was dismembered and only discovered when it fell out of a packing case en route to the north-London suburb of Harrow). Ter-Oganisyan is now doing life for their murders, while a co-defendant, an officer of Armenia's KGB, hanged himself at Belmarsh prison while awaiting trial.

I was appalled when reading about this case at the time, not least because I discovered that Alison and Karen's father was David Ponting, a lecturer in drama at Bristol University, where I had been an under-graduate. His one-man show about Dylan Thomas had made a great impression on me when I studied there. David had taught me radio production, skills I would later employ as the BBC's Central Europe correspondent.

After Karen's murder, Alison accepted an offer to go into a witness-protection scheme. Deprived of his children, David moved to the United States, where he worked for a while as an actor. Later, he, too, went underground.

The Pontings were gentle and unassuming. It is hard to imagine a family less likely to be involved in a political mafia killing from the former Soviet Union. But as one of the officers involved in the Utsiev brothers' case pointed out at the time, 'We were suddenly dealing with crime and politics from a part of the world that, to be honest, none of us in the Metropolitan or Surrey police had ever heard of. We knew nothing about the wars, about the crime and about the politics – we were, frankly, all at sea.'

Around the world, a new type of country was emerging – the failing state. And the fallout was visiting Britain for the first time.

The post-Second World War order began to crumble in the first half of the 1980s. Its dissolution followed no obvious pattern, occurring instead as a series of seemingly disparate events: the spectacular rise of the Japanese car industry; communist Hungary's clandestine approach to the International Monetary Fund (IMF) to explore a possible application for membership; the stagnation of India's economy; President F.W. de Klerk's first discreet contacts with the imprisoned Nelson Mandela; the advent of Deng Xiaoping's reforms in China; Margaret Thatcher's decisive confrontation with Britain's trade-union movement.

Individually, these and other events seemed to reflect the everyday ups and downs of politics; at most they were adjustments to the world order. In fact, powerful currents below the surface had provoked a number of economic crises and opportunities, especially outside the great citadels of power in Western Europe and the United States, that were to have profound consequences for the emergence of what we now call globalisation.

There was one development, however, that had its roots firmly in America and in its primary European ally, Britain. The world was taking its first steps towards the liberalisation of international financial and commodity markets. American and European corporations and banks had begun to prise open markets that had hitherto maintained strict controls on foreign investment and currency exchange.

Then came the fall of communism in 1989, first in Eastern Europe and then in the mighty Soviet Union itself. Out of ideas, short of money and beaten in the race for technological superiority, communism fizzled out in days rather than years. This was a monumental event, which fused with the processes of globalisation to trigger an exponential rise in the shadow economy. These huge economic and political shifts affected every part of the planet.

Overall there was a significant worldwide upsurge in trade, investment and the creation of wealth. That wealth was, however, distributed very unevenly. Countless states found themselves cast into the purgatory that became known as 'transition', a territory with ever-shifting borders. In these badlands, economic survival frequently involved grabbing a gun and snatching what you could to survive.

The fall of communism was, of course, a great victory for the West, demonstrating the superiority of the world's democracies over communist dictatorship in every respect. Europe celebrated the unification of Germany and the liberation of many Eastern European countries. The new Russia was quite content, it seemed, to give up its military dominance of the region, disbanding NATO's erstwhile rival, the Warsaw Pact. Initially reluctant, Moscow then allowed the other peoples of the dying Soviet Union to form their own independent states, fulfilling their national aspirations.

Looking back, this was the high point of my own life. In my teens, I had become involved in Western organisations supporting the beleaguered opposition throughout Eastern Europe, such as Poland's Solidarity and Czechoslovakia's Charter 77. I had done everything from translating documents to smuggling dismembered photocopying machines across the Iron Curtain to the dissidents. And so when I stood five yards behind Czechoslovakia's great moral leaders, Vaclav Havel and Alexander Dubcek, as they addressed their public from a balcony above Prague's Wenceslas Square in November 1989, I felt both a sense of real achievement and cautiously optimistic about the future of Europe and the world.

However, the initial euphoria was soon dampened by indications, admittedly in rather obscure places, that the new world of peace and democracy might face some teething problems. In the Caucasus along Russia's southern border, sporadic reports emerged of fighting in obscure pockets of the region. In parts of Africa, such as Angola, wars that had started as proxy conflicts between American- and Soviet-backed forces did not end like the Cold War – if anything, they intensified. Then the former Yugoslavia dissolved into a murderous civil war, presenting the new united Europe with a challenge that it was entirely unable to meet.

The new circumstances bewildered old international institutions. Everybody had to improvise and nobody quite understood the implications of their actions.

One group of people, however, saw real opportunity in this dazzling mixture of upheaval, hope and uncertainty. These men (and occasionally women) understood instinctively that rising living standards in the West, increased trade and migration flows, and the greatly reduced ability of many governments to police their countries combined to form a goldmine. They were criminals, organised and disorganised, but they were also good capitalists and entrepreneurs, intent on obeying the laws of supply and demand. As such, they valued economies of scale, just as multinational corporations did, and so they sought out overseas partners and markets to develop industries that were every bit as cosmopolitan as Shell, Nike or McDonald's.

They first became visible in Russia and Eastern Europe, but they were also exerting an influence on countries as far away from one another as India, Colombia and Japan. I spotted them in the early 1990s when I was covering the wars in the former Yugoslavia as the BBC's Central Europe correspondent. The booty that paramilitary units brought home with them after destroying towns and villages in Croatia and Bosnia was used as capital to establish large criminal empires. The bosses of these syndicates became rich very quickly. Soon, they established smuggling franchises that conveyed illicit goods and services from all over the world into the consumer paradise of the European Union.

As a writer on the Balkans, I was invited to many conferences to discuss the political issues behind the disastrous wars in the region. It was not long before I received invitations to gatherings discussing security issues. Politicians, policemen and non-governmental organisations (NGOs) were all hoping to learn what lay behind the immense power of organised crime in the Balkans and beyond. However, most knowledge of the new wave of global crime was anecdotal at best. Nobody had joined up the dots.

Initially I looked at the networks and motives of criminal groups in the Balkans, but quickly realised that in order to understand crime there, I would have to extend my research to other parts of the world: the regions that produce criminal goods, like Russia, South America, Africa, India and China; as well as the regions that consume them, like the European Union, North America, Japan and the Middle East.

Among the many consequences of the Soviet collapse was the emergence of a thick belt of instability that began in the Balkans and stretched all the way across the Caucasus, the so-called *stans* of Soviet Central Asia, and on to the western edge of China and the north-west frontier of Pakistan.

This was the New Silk Route, a multi-lane criminal highway that linked the belt with other troubled regions such as Afghanistan, and which permitted the swift and easy transfer of people, narcotics, cash, endangered species and precious hardwood from Asia to Europe and further to the United States.

This clutch of uncertain new states on the southern periphery of the former Russian empire was born as the pace of globalisation accelerated. And as the scramble for power began along the New Silk Route, the need for money to buy political influence became ever greater. Those harbouring ambition in the failing states needed this anarchic swathe of territory for three related transactions: to transfer cash to the sanctity of Western banks and real estate; to sell illicit goods and services into the European Union, the United States and eastwards to Japan; and to buy and sell arms within the former Soviet Union and export them into the world's trouble spots.

'In '93/94 I started working in law enforcement, knowing that globalisation was beginning to have an impact on a whole range of issues,' Jon Winer told me in his plush office a couple of blocks from the White House. The architect of the Clinton administration's organised-crime strategy, Winer had spotted these new developments earlier than most. 'The paradigm was El Salvador,' he continued. 'After the war, people decided to use their arms caches to make money in criminal gangs. And then we saw that the right-wing paramilitaries and left-wing guerrillas began *working together*! Burglary, car-jacking plus kidnapping, car theft . . .'

Winer had stumbled across something that still plagues peace initiatives aiming to stop wars that engulf failed states. When diplomats succeed in bringing the fighting to a halt, they are confronted with a wrecked local economy and a society dominated by testosterone-driven young men who are suddenly unemployed, but have grown accustomed to their omnipotence. If you want lasting stability, you have to find useful jobs to occupy them. Otherwise these people find irresistible the temptation to retrain themselves as organised criminal units. In retrospect, Winer argued, the extent of this problem in El Salvador and other conflicts from the 1980s was a stroll in the park compared to what the 1990s had in store: 'The main sources of revenue in Salvador were not car-jacking or drugs. But when you got to the Balkans or the Caucasus, the main source of revenue in society *was* criminal. Now you had a very different model!'

The deepening links in a globalising world magnify the impact of immense disruptions to the international order, like the collapse of the Soviet Union. And for the first few years after the event, nobody had the slightest notion what the sudden injection of huge sums of mineral wealth and criminal profits into the legitimate and shadow economies actually implied. And those who did observe some changes in the way the world worked were frequently baffled by it. What was a cop on the beat in leafy Woking expected to know about the internecine struggles of the Caucasus?

Academics and researchers have channelled considerable energy into understanding the process of 'licit' globalisation, a process that is largely regulated and quantifiable. But since the liberalisation of international financial and commodity markets, on the one hand, and the fall of communism, on the other, the shadow economy has shot up as a percentage of global GDP. According to figures culled from the IMF, from the World Bank and from research institutes in Europe and North America, it now accounts for between 15 and 20 per cent of global turnover.

Of course, this includes a multitude of sins, like tax avoidance, which cannot be ascribed to a growth in trans-national criminal conspiracies. But given that the shadow economy has become such an important economic force in our world, it is surprising that we devote so little effort to a systematic understanding of how it works and how it links into the licit economy. This shadow world is by no means distinct from its partner in the light, which is itself often far less transparent than one might suspect or desire. In both banking and commodity trading, the criminal operates much closer to home than we think.

That vast unregulated economic area is a swamp that contains protein-rich nutrients for a host of security problems. International terrorism certainly feeds in these same grounds, but in terms of the death and misery caused, terrorism is a primitive and relatively insignificant species. Crime and the pursuit of money or political power have proved incomparably more damaging over the last two decades. The concentration of huge resources on fighting terrorism to the neglect of other security problems is the consequence of chronic mismanagement, especially under the administration of President George W. Bush. It is striking how all opinion polls in Iraq since the invasion have placed corruption and crime in equal first place with terrorism as the major concern for citizens. The impact of the former

– not just in Iraq alone, but across the Middle East – will last long after the latter has diminished.

From the Balkans, which I knew well, I embarked on a journey around the world in an attempt to trace the history of the astonishing growth in organised crime and the shadow economy over the last twenty years. On my travels, I met fascinating characters of great intelligence, vitality, courage, wit and spirit. Many were criminals, some were victims, others were politicians, policemen or lawyers. Almost all were happy to tell their strange, frightening and even funny stories. The nature of the topic means that many were only willing to speak anonymously and for that reason names have sometimes been changed.* I would like to thank all those I interviewed and consulted for their time and their profound insights.

I hope their stories contribute to solving the puzzle of how organised crime fits into a globalised planet. I also hope they offer some clues as to how politicians and police might address these problems to prevent men and women, like Karen Reed, falling victim to this shadow world.

---

* Indicated by the italicisation of a name on first appearance.

PART ONE

THE FALL OF COMMUNISM

DEATH OF AN AMERICAN

The bells tolled uninterrupted for fifteen minutes as they carried the coffin into St Nedelya's Cathedral. At the head of the procession was Patriarch Maxim, head of the Bulgarian Orthodox Church, and behind him several thousand mourners. It seemed as if *le tout Sofia* had come on that blustery cold Friday in March 2003 to pay their final respects to Ilya Pavlov, the man who had defined the 1990s for them.

At the end of the service, thirty brothers from the dear departed's Masonic Lodge, the Antient Free and Accepted Scottish Custom, closed the doors of the Cathedral. Dressed in jet-black suits and clasping bouquets of white flowers, the men performed a secret ritual to speed 'Brother Pavlov to the Eternal Orient'. His overall, gloves and the Lodge's crest then 'accompanied Brother Pavlov to the Grand Architect of the Universe'.

A government minister bore a message from the Prime Minister, Simeon Saxe-Coburgotski. Formerly the King of Bulgaria, the lean and elegant Simeon had relinquished his claim to the throne in order to lead his country and its government out of the morass of the late 1990s after his political party had won a landslide victory in the elections of 2000. 'We shall remember Ilya Pavlov,' read the King's telegram of condolence, 'because he created jobs for many families in a difficult period for the people. We'll remember him for his spirit as a businessman and for his extraordinary energy.'

MPs, artists, the bosses of the most important oil companies and banks, two former Miss Bulgarias, the entire CSKA soccer team (to Bulgarians, a fusion of Manchester United and the Yankees) all joined

Pavlov's grieving family. There, as well, was another prominent group of his acquaintances, better known to the Bulgarian public by their nicknames: 'The Skull', 'The Beak', 'Dimi the Russian' and 'The Doctor'.

The most conspicuous absentee was the American Ambassador to Bulgaria, Jim Pardew. The Embassy had made urgent enquiries a week earlier, on March 7th, when a single sniper bullet had felled Ilya Pavlov at a quarter to eight in the evening as he chatted on the phone outside the headquarters of his mega-corporation Multigroup. The death of such an eminent and wealthy American citizen on foreign soil would naturally raise serious concerns for the US and its representatives.

Pavlov would never have made it to the White House as he was not born in America. But he was still a proud foot soldier in that mighty army of naturalised immigration to the US. The only curious aspect about Pavlov's aspirations to American citizenship was that two consecutive US ambassadors to Sofia vigorously opposed them. Both diplomats made personal representations in Washington to try and prevent Pavlov entering the country, let alone having US citizenship bestowed upon him. But Pavlov also had his supporters in the United States. Despite an FBI investigation into his past activities, not to mention heightened security concerns after 9/11, Pavlov received his American passport.

In the 1970s and 1980s, communist Bulgaria was only topped by Romania and Albania as the most miserably depressing place to live in Europe. I recall tramping through the fog-bound streets of Sofia, drifting from one shade of grey to the next in search of a restaurant or café to alleviate the boredom. As a foreigner and journalist, my personal hospitality pack always included at least two minders from the DS (the Bulgarian equivalent of the KGB State Security) who tracked my every footstep. Their presence ensured that on the rare occasion I persuaded ordinary folk to engage in conversation, the best I could hope for was a little chit-chat about the weather.

But slowly I understood that beneath this moribund conformity there were eddies of activity, some quite vigorous, which nourished more interesting lifestyles – not the pained martyrdom of intellectuals and dissidents who fought courageously against the injustice of communism, but those who through serendipity or good fortune found ways to mould parts of the system to their advantage.

As a teenager growing up in the 1970s, young Ilya Pavlov had one particular skill that marked him out from most of his peers – he was an accomplished wrestler, indeed the champion of Bulgaria in his weight class. Had he been very smart or a gifted rock guitarist, Ilya might have landed in trouble, as these talents usually led youngsters to a life of rebellion and disobedience. But in Bulgaria, the greatest heroes were not soccer or tennis players, but muscle-men. Before the fall of communism, weightlifting, wrestling and boxing were dominated by Eastern Bloc states, which routinely pumped their promising sportsmen and women with gallons of steroids in the search for Olympic glory.

A pro in all but name, the successful wrestler could expect public acclamation (and fringe benefits such as casual sex on tap), money, an apartment and a car (the last two being out of the reach of all but the most fêted youngsters). Pavlov would have anticipated this when he was picked out to attend the Institute for Physical Culture in Sofia, Bulgaria's elite breeding ground for future Olympians.

Ilya was doubly advantaged because his father ran a restaurant and bar in Sofia, where his tough young son worked. 'At that time, being a barman or waiter conferred considerable social status on you,' explained Emil Kyulev, a graduate of the Police Academy and Pavlov's contemporary. 'He hung out with a lot of tough guys, and people looked up to him. That way he also came into contact with the security services.'

For an uneducated young steer like Pavlov, the DS was not the Orwellian instrument of repression that people in the West perceived. For some Bulgarians, it was an avenue to status and influence. If, as many claim, Pavlov worked as an informant for the DS, then he could expect rewards. His most important came in the shape of a pretty young woman, Toni Chergelanova, who accepted his proposal of marriage in 1982. A greater catch than the girl was her father, Petur Chergelanov, who worked for State Security. Ilya had wed into secret-police royalty.

The Bulgarian State Security Service was held in special regard by its Soviet masters for its efficacy and reliability. Usually invisible, it never disappointed on those occasions when it did catch the public eye – the DS masterminded the death of the Bulgarian dissident Georgi Markov, who, when working for the BBC in London, was struck down by a poison-tipped umbrella as he strode across Waterloo Bridge in 1978.

The business of eliminating enemies of the state Le Carré-style was mere icing on the cake. The most important and lucrative trade of the Bulgarian secret service was smuggling – in drugs, in arms and in high tech. 'Smuggling is our cultural heritage,' Ivan Krastev, Bulgaria's leading political scientist, told me. 'Our territory has always nestled between huge ideologies, between Orthodoxy and Roman Catholicism, between Islam and Christianity, between capitalism and communism. Empires riddled with hostility and suspicion for one another, but home, nonetheless, to many people who want to trade across the prohibited boundaries. In the Balkans, we know how to make those boundaries disappear. We can cross the roughest sea and traverse the most forbidding mountain. We know every secret pass and, failing that, the price of every border guard.'

Fortified by the might of the totalitarian state, the DS took full advantage of this romantic tradition. As early as the 1960s, it established a company called Kintex, which enjoyed a monopoly on the export of arms from Bulgaria and sought out markets in trouble spots like the Middle East and Africa. At the end of the 1970s, the DS expanded Kintex by setting up the 'Covert Transit' Directorate. Its primary role was to smuggle weapons to African insurgent groups, but soon the channels were also being used for illegal people-trafficking, for drugs and even for the smuggling of works of art and antiquities.

Other companies specialised in the sale of an indigenous Bulgarian amphetamine, Kaptagon, to the Middle East, where it was a hugely popular drug due to its alleged aphrodisiacal properties. In the other direction, some 80 per cent of heroin destined for the Western European market would cross into Bulgaria from Turkey at the Kapetan Andreevo border point and into the hands of the DS. Not only did Bulgaria make big money out of this, but the trade helped to undermine capitalist Western Europe by flooding it with cheap heroin.

The DS enabled Bulgaria to play a pivotal role in the distribution of illicit goods and services between Europe, the Middle East and Central Asia. But it was resolute in preventing anyone else from muscling in on the trade. Bulgaria's border force was ruthless, and severe punishments were meted out to anybody caught smuggling drugs or weapons without authorisation. This resolve was not born of a commitment to uphold the rule of law (a concept that was anathema to the Security Service), but to underscore the DS's economic monopoly.

According to the dictates of the Soviet Bloc's unwieldy trade association, COMECON, which determined the 'socialist international division of labour', Bulgaria was to be the heart of the electronics industry, while Moscow ordered Czechoslovakia to concentrate on producing turbines for power stations and Poland to produce fertiliser.

As a consequence, in the late 1970s, Bulgaria (the most rural of all Eastern European economies) flowered into an unlikely centre of the magnetic-disk and computer industries. The *Pravets* was born – Europe's first socialist PC, which was manufactured in the eponymous little town twenty-five miles north-east of Sofia that (not coincidentally) was the birthplace of Todor Zhivkov, Bulgaria's long-standing dictator.

Moscow charged the DS with breaking the COCOM regime – this was the regulatory body set up by the United States, which included Western Europe and Japan, to prevent sensitive high-tech equipment with possible military usage from making its way through the Iron Curtain and into the Soviet Union.

The DS conscripted some of Bulgaria's most senior scientists, with the goal of supplying Bulgaria and the Soviet Union with advanced technologies over which COCOM had imposed an embargo. Two years later, it established clandestine companies abroad into which revenues of about $1 billion flowed from the illegal sale of technology.

The most important spin-off from this was the Memory Disks Equipment company (known as DZU), where Bulgaria began to build a team of gifted hardware and software engineers. It was a profitable business. 'According to our clients' estimates,' a former intelligence boss later admitted, 'between 1981 and 1986, the annual profit of technological and scientific intelligence activities was $580 million – i.e., this would have been the price of technologies had we bought them.'

All three industries – drugs, arms and high tech – were deemed of immense strategic value to the Bulgarian state. At the heart of the smuggling operations lay Military Counter-Intelligence, the 3rd Directorate of the DS, which controlled all of Bulgaria's borders. And the head of Military Counter-Intelligence was General Petur Chergelanov, father-in-law to Ilya Pavlov.

In 1986, as Mikhail Gorbachev consolidated his authority in Moscow, Western leaders were unaware that the Soviet Union's hegemony over its Eastern European allies was coming to an end. The Bulgarian State Security Service had no such illusions about the system it policed. An experienced observer of the Soviet scene, the DS's leadership calculated that communism did not have long to last.

Under pressure from Gorbachev, the Bulgarian Communist Party had passed Decree 56, which overnight permitted the opening of private enterprises in Bulgaria and allowed the creation of joint-stock companies. Many in the Party, still hardliners, were shocked by this development as it looked like the thin end of a capitalist wedge. But the Security Services, which habitually subordinated ideology to the love of power, took it in their stride.

'When I looked at the trade register for 1986, it struck me,' explained Stanimir Vaglenov, a Bulgarian journalist who specialises in corruption and organised crime, 'that the Security Services founded the first company a week after Decree 56 came into effect. And within the first year, members of the DS had founded 90 per cent of the new joint-stock companies!' While the bulk of Bulgaria's long-suffering population was still being force-fed the rhetoric about socialism's bright and eternal future, the regime's most senior representatives were teaching themselves how to make money. Big money. Having spent forty-five years expounding the theoretical evils of capitalism to ordinary Bulgarians, the secret police were now keen to demonstrate those evils in practice.

In 1988, a year before the collapse of communism, Ilya Pavlov himself registered Multiart, a company dedicated to the import and export of antiques and high art (using the secret channels established by the DS for selling arms through Kintex's Covert Transit Directorate). Business flourished, and before long Pavlov had become the talk of the town, bursting into one of the new private restaurants with a team of stunning young women swinging behind him – the lizard had acquired a tail. 'Multiart was in fact a big mess,' Pavlov later conceded in describing his early days. 'We developed a whole string of businesses without any structure.' One of Multiart's co-directors was Dimitur Ivanov, boss of the 6th Directorate of the DS. Ivanov introduced Pavlov to Andrei Lukanov, the country's leading reform communist. Ilya Pavlov, one-time champion wrestler, all-round toughie and glitzy playboy, was on the verge of a new career.

Andrei Lukanov beamed mischievously as we surveyed the chaotic parliamentary proceedings in the last days of 1989. 'This is all going rather well, don't you think?' I was perplexed. 'But aren't you worried about ordinary people's reaction towards communists like you?' I asked him. 'Oh no, Misha, you mustn't be alarmist,' he retorted in impeccable English, 'I have always wanted to change, and things are about to get much better.'

Despite his slightly gnomish face, Lukanov was charm personified (in stark contrast to most other influential communists). People, including me, took an instant liking to him. A polyglot with the smoothest political patter, Lukanov was born in Moscow, where he maintained a dense web of connections. He had assumed the role of Prime Minister after the overthrow of the dictator, Todor Zhivkov, in November 1989 and, together with Ilya Pavlov and their friends in the DS, he was planning to hijack the Bulgarian economy. Almost all their bases were covered – Lukanov controlled the political machine; Dimitur Ivanov mobilised the Security Services network; Ilya and his wrestler friends provided the muscle.

The only thing missing was support from the democratic opposition. The newly formed Union of Democratic Forces, with unstinting financial and political backing from the American Embassy, had seized the moral high ground in Bulgarian politics after the 1989 revolution. It was bitterly hostile to the communists for the destruction they had wrought on the country. Pavlov and his colleagues were all closely associated with the communist regime, and so they needed to neutralise any opposition attempt to foil their business plans.

In 1990, Ilya came up with the solution. A good friend was the deputy head of Podkrepa, Bulgaria's fiercely anti-communist independent trade union, which also received strong support from the American Government. Pavlov persuaded Podkrepa's bosses that the real enemies of ordinary workers were the communist-appointed directors of the big state-owned factories.

'Ilya's game was simple.' Boyko Borissov speaks with authority. In his mid-forties, the former General Director of the Interior Ministry is a black belt in karate. He also used to be involved in the insurance industry before joining Prime Minister Saxe-Coburgotski as his body-guard. The quintessential poacher turned gamekeeper, he has inside knowledge of the criminalisation of Bulgaria. 'It was called the Spider Trap. Ilya walked into the office of the director of Kremikovtsi, one of the biggest steel works in Eastern Europe. He was accompanied by a boss of the most powerful trade union, and then sitting there is Dimitur Ivanov, the man who until recently was head of the 6th Directorate. And these guys tell the director of the enterprise – "You have a choice . . . Work with us or we will destroy you!"'

Pavlov told the Director that from now on he would be buying raw materials not directly from the Russians at a subsidised price, but from one of his companies at the world market price. And then, instead of selling the end product directly to the consumer, the Director would have to sell it at a knock-down price to another of Ilya's firms, which would then sell it on the open market. He controlled the entrance and exit to the factory – the Spider Trap.

The simplicity and efficacy of this system delighted Pavlov. The government run by Lukanov continued to provide subsidies to the company over many years. 'The enterprise doesn't collapse immedi-ately,' said Emil Kyulev, one of Bulgaria's richest bankers before his assassination in October 2005. 'You hang a goat on a hook and cut it at its foot and it will expire very slowly as the blood leaves its body, drop-by-drop – it agonises over the years. Pavlov and friends created these holding companies in virtually every branch of the Bulgarian economy, in agriculture, in transport, in industry, energy – you name it. The holdings were parallel to the branch organisations of Podkrepa – wherever Podkrepa was, Ilya would create a holding company.'

After the revolution of 1989, Bulgaria's social-security system collapsed, leaving a trail of poverty and destitution in its wake. The country had been hit hard as it emerged from the cave-dwelling existence of socialist economics into the blinding sun of free-market capitalism. Under communism, factories had survived thanks to massive state subsidies, while the Soviet trading bloc ensured their shoddy products a guaranteed sale on Eastern European markets. When the Berlin Wall fell in 1989, Bulgaria's markets crumbled with it.

With industry in near-terminal crisis, agriculture – the economy's traditional mainstay – assumed ever greater importance, but this sector, too, ran into trouble. The European Union was unwilling to increase its minuscule imports of Bulgarian agricultural produce, as this would undermine its protectionist racket masquerading grandly as the Common Agricultural Policy (CAP). As the world's major powers began to trumpet the revolutionary significance of globalisation in the early 1990s, they skimmed over its inconsistencies. When countries opened up in the hope of greater cooperation with the mighty Western economies, the EU, the US and Japan demanded that these emerging markets accept the sale of European, American and Japanese goods. At the same time, they insisted on low corporate tax rates in exchange for new investments as the vogue for 'outsourcing' production to keep down labour costs took hold among Western corporations.

Within months of the end of communism, Snickers, Nike, Swatch, Heineken and Mercedes had begun their irresistible march eastwards, conquering in a matter of weeks those parts of Europe that had defied even Napoleon and Hitler. Entranced by the novelty and quality of these must-have Western goods, the peoples of Eastern Europe (and Africa and Asia for that matter) dug deep to spend what little money they possessed to acquire the new status symbols.

It is a universally acknowledged truth of international trade that if you import goods and services into your country, you need to export others in order to pay for them (the poorer the country, the more urgent the need – it is much cheaper for rich countries like the United States to run up ludicrous debts). Bulgaria's high-quality soft fruits, cotton, roses, wines and cereals could have played a vital role in restoring this battered little economy – such goods could perhaps have offset some of the cost of the new Western products flooding the market. Unfortunately, the opportunities were severely limited by arrangements like the CAP, blocking the sale of agricultural produce. Bulgarian consumer goods were still socialist in design and durability (that is, they were ugly and did not work) and therefore no competition for Western consumer products. So the problem of how to pay for the growing number of Western imports remained.

While most Bulgarians experienced a sudden collapse in living standards, a small minority was taking advantage of the chaos. By 1992, Ilya Pavlov had become a multimillionaire and on his way to becoming a billionaire by transferring the assets of the state into his private liquid capital using the Spider Trap. Still in his early thirties, he soon created a sister company in Vienna, Virginia, just outside Washington, DC. Through Multigroup US, he bought two casinos in Paraguay.

Back home, Pavlov employed several PR firms to project an image of dynamic success and patriotism – he became the face of the new Bulgaria. The most high-profile businessman in the country, his exploits were slavishly followed by newspapers and TV shows. Invitations to social events like his birthday party on August 6th – traditionally held at one of the most opulent hotels in the Black Sea resort of Varna – became prized possessions, as recipients had the opportunity to mix with the grandest members of the country's economic and political elite. A photo taken with Ilya was enough to secure large loans on easy terms. At first hundreds, then thousands, then tens of thousands of Bulgarians desperate for money and employment became dependent on the commercial operations of Multigroup and similar mega-corporations springing up around the country. Naturally, many disapproved of Pavlov's methods. Many others were jealous competitors who conspired with and against him in the demi-monde of Bulgaria's nascent market economy, where it was usually impossible to distinguish between the legal, the grey and the outright criminal. But others regarded him as a genuine, energetic and likeable entrepreneur with the interests of Bulgaria at heart, providing jobs in areas where the state had unexpectedly and calamitously fulfilled Marx's prophecy by withering away.

The headquarters of Multigroup, his new corporation, was located outside Sofia in the mansion on Bystrica Mountain where Bulgaria's top trade unionists had once spent their holidays. The building had been bought for a song by Robert Maxwell, the British media magnate who had been cultivating both the Soviet and Bulgarian communist leaders for several years. The Maxwell connection demonstrated how quickly some predatory Western businessmen linked up with proto-oligarchs from Eastern Europe to internationalise the asset-stripping of the new democracies. Maxwell was in the vanguard of a criminal industry that would run out of control in the 1990s – money-laundering. Together with Prime Minister Lukanov, Maxwell arranged the transfer of $2 billion from Bulgaria into Western tax havens – subsequent Bulgarian governments were unable to trace what happened to this cash, although we do know that it did not end up in the *Daily Mirror*'s pension fund from which Maxwell was also stealing hundreds of millions of pounds at the same time.

For most Bulgarians, the early 1990s looked grim: the country had lost its markets; Pavlov and friends were skinning the economy of all its valuables; nobody wanted to buy Bulgaria's goods; and furthermore, now that Bulgaria was a fledgling democracy, the United States and the IMF wasted no time in demanding that Sofia meet its obligations and start paying off $10 billion worth of debt run up by the profligate communist regime.

At the same time, in a bid for popularity, successive governments started sacking thousands upon thousands of policemen. All manner of operatives lost their jobs – secret police, counter-intelligence offi-cers, Special Forces commandos, border guards, as well as homicide detectives and traffic cops. Their skills included surveillance, smuggling, killing people, establishing networks and blackmail. By 1991, 14,000 secret policemen were kicking their heels and looking for work in a country where the economy was contracting at an alarming rate. One sector, however, was experiencing an unprecedented expansion and it was a line of work that was ideally suited to unemployed and dis-affected policemen. This sector was organised crime.

Another recently disenfranchised group found themselves in a similar situation – the wrestlers, boxers and weightlifters. As a budget-ary crisis combined with the zeitgeist of freedom to reduce the state police to a skeletal force, sports societies throughout the country were transformed into small private security forces. With their superior muscle and high levels of mutual trust, they embarked on a violent spree of intimidation, gradually incorporating petty thieves and street gangs into their protection rackets. By 1992, the wrestlers enjoyed a near-stranglehold on Bulgaria's major cities, although in some areas they faced competition from ex-policemen and security officers. The brighter sparks among them combined the skills of the two professions: sportsmen for muscle, policemen for networking. The hybrid organis-ations grew to dominate the economy, and two groups, known by the acronyms SIC and VIS, became the overwhelming market leaders.

SIC and VIS presented themselves as insurance companies. 'I took possession of my Mercedes in June 1992,' one Sofia taxi driver explained, 'and naturally I took out insurance with the state company to reduce the bribes paid to the traffic cops. At the time, we were stopped every few miles and the cops just demanded cash for no particular reason. But if you were in violation of traffic laws, like driving without insurance, you'd have to pay double. Before long, however, I was approached by a bunch of hard guys – you know, cropped hair, tattoos, leather jackets – and they told me I had to take out insurance with SIC. So I did – I wasn't going to mess with them. But some of the drivers refused – within hours their cars were stolen. And they could only get them back when they had paid up their SIC premiums . . . with interest, of course!'

This was not just extortion. If your vehicle was stolen when already insured with SIC, the thugs would work hard to get it back. They were providing a genuine service (albeit with menaces) and they took a dim view of smaller operations trying to muscle in on their turf.

SIC, VIS and later TIM became huge operations, diversifying into many branches of the economy, licit and illicit. It often seemed as if these people, and not the Government, were in charge of the country. 'We are not just talking about these thick necks with gold chains taking the best seats in one's favourite restaurant,' exploded one European diplomat unable to contain his disgust. 'They had the cheek and the confidence to block off entire thoroughfares in the centre of Sofia just because they wished to lunch undisturbed by the traffic!'

Some oligarchs running companies like Multigroup outsourced part of their security requirements to SIC and VIS. Others preferred to build up their own in-house goon squad. Later on, Ilya Pavlov was careful to dissociate himself from the racketeers. But earlier on, he was close friends with several of the most prominent gangsters. Most notably, he worked with one of SIC's bosses, Mladen Mihailev (known to all as Madzho), not least because Madzho started his career as Ilya's chauffeur. To blame Ilya Pavlov for choosing this life, which veered between gross corruption, grand larceny and organised crime, would be unfair. He was not an especially moral person. But he took his opportunity at a time when the Bulgarian state had all but collapsed. People were discovering all over Eastern Europe that when the country goes into freefall, the law is the first thing that is crushed under the rubble of transformation. Capitalism had not existed until 1989, and so the hopelessly weak states that emerged throughout the former Soviet Union and Eastern Europe had simply no capacity to define what was 'legal' and what was 'illegal'. They had neither the money nor the experience to police the novelty of commercial exchange. Those who positioned themselves well in the first three years after the end of communism were often in a position to make up the rules of their brave new world as they went along.

* * *

It was a bright, warm spring day in 1991 as I pulled up in front of the Hotel Esplanade on Gajeva Street in central Zagreb. The four-hour drive from Vienna had been a breeze in my black Audi Quattro. Without question the spiffiest car I had ever driven, it was a cut above the standard BBC issue, but I had insisted on a four-wheel drive after several hair-raising journeys accompanied by snowstorms on the ever-unpredictable tarmac of Eastern Europe during the revolutions of 1989. As I got out of the car, a new, slightly nervous porter asked for the keys so that he could valet-park the car. This was a regular procedure at the Esplanade and so I handed them over.

Everyone swung in and out of the Esplanade – mediators like Cyrus Vance and Lord David Owen, and various ministers from the region, from the EU and from the US. They would dine next to mercenaries who were filling the rooms in anticipation of a profitable war. Or next to young diaspora Croats from Edmonton or Cleveland, Ohio, who were ready to risk their lives for a fatherland they had never before clapped eyes on.

Next morning, I went to find the Audi in the car park. It wasn't there. I didn't yet know it, but my car had embarked on a mystery tour that would end several weeks later at a used-car market 200 miles away in Mostar, the capital of western Hercegovina. By then I had collected the insurance (fortunately the Austrian insurance companies had not yet scrapped cover for Yugoslavia, as they had done for Poland, Romania, Bulgaria and Albania) and so I never saw again my dear Audi, which would almost certainly have then been commandeered by one of the emerging militias in Bosnia–Hercegovina.

Thus did I fall victim to Europe's fastest-growing industry – car theft. Every month thousands of cars would be stolen from the streets of northern Europe in preparation for their illegal export to Eastern Europe and the Balkans. In 1992, I watched a huge container ship regurgitate the contents of its hold into the decrepit Albanian port of Durres. Onto a quay of chipped stone and rust rolled dozens of BMWs, Peugeots, Hondas and above all Mercedes, Mercedes and more Mercedes, mostly the 200 series beloved of taxi drivers in Germany, the Low Countries and Scandinavia. Customs officers barely awoke from their slumber as excited, dusty and dirty men took possession of vehicles still with their original number plates, with their anti-odour Christmas trees and family photos dangling from the mirror, and with old cigarette packets on the seats.

Cars were banned in communist Albania except for official use – the roads were designed to accommodate a few trucks a day, while nobody except the small band of state chauffeurs learned how to drive. In the chaos of collapsing communism, the flood gates opened and anyone able to get their hands on a (stolen) car hit the public high-ways with Mediterranean gusto, despite never having sat behind a wheel. Mayhem! The country was transformed into a huge and deadly dodgem ride, while any vehicle was fair game for thieves (given that they were all stolen anyhow, it was difficult to construct a morally watertight case of ownership). The cars that did not stay in Albania were sold in Macedonia, Bulgaria, Russia, the Middle East, the Caucasus and former Soviet Central Asia.

At the time, I didn't appreciate the significance of my car being stolen. I could not see the iceberg of crime that was rapidly forming below the swirling sea of revolution, freedom, nationalism and violence that had engulfed Eastern Europe. Many people were engaged in settling old scores. Others were working hard to preserve the privileges they enjoyed under the old system, but in a society where 'communism' was suddenly a dirty word.

Protection rackets like SIC and VIS were deeply involved in car-smuggling. And the cross-border nature of the trade ensured that the emerging Bulgarian syndicates established links with similar groups in other Balkan and Eastern European countries. Each country developed a reputation for being especially good in the trading of particular commodities. In the former Yugoslavia, for example, it was arms and cigarettes. In Bulgaria, it was cars. In Ukraine, it was the trafficking of migrant labour as well as women. Everyone shifted narcotics.

Hungary and Czechoslovakia had a special place in the new crime networks, thanks to the close economic and commercial links they had established over the previous decade with their neighbours, Germany and Austria. But as former socialist countries, they still maintained a visa-free regime with the rest of Eastern Europe. Kazakhs, Georgians, Bulgarians, Moldovans, Yugoslavs and Latvians could all settle temporarily in either country without difficulty.

So, of course, could the Russians.

An especially lively currency-exchange market emerged in Hungary, which became an early centre for major money-laundering operations. Such was its appeal as a base for trans-national criminal operations that it was not long before the most powerful Russian mafia groups selected Budapest as their forward base in Central Europe as they sought to expand their activities westward. The Bulgarians were forced to operate elsewhere. 'When the Russians came, they pushed the new Bulgarian mafia into Czechoslovakia,' explained Yovo Nikolov, Sofia's leading expert on Bulgarian organised crime. At first it was simply more car-smuggling. 'But then the guys noticed something else.'

That something else was the *silnice hanby* or Road of Shame – the highway that linked Dresden and Prague via the heart of Czechoslovakia's heavy-industry complex, northern Bohemia. In a depressed and chaotic economic climate, young Czech women began selling themselves for pocket money on the E55. For the price of a modest meal, the teenagers would satisfy the desires of the ceaseless column of sweaty BMW drivers and overweight truckers cruising between Bohemia and Saxony.

'People are coming from all over Eastern Europe to the "affluence border" in order to offer young prostitutes to ageing German men,' noted *Der Spiegel* at the time. The national aspect to this sexual *Drang nach Osten* gave the sordid trade an added frisson, as many punters were East German (so there were a few sweaty Trabant drivers among the BMWs).

Women working on the Road of Shame were, on the whole, exercising choice – to be sure, their economic circumstances compelled them to work as prostitutes, but they were not physically coerced. A minority was forced into the trade by individual pimps, but a majority worked voluntarily in order to earn a living in this way. A large percentage was made up of young gypsy or Roma women, who faced a double dose of prejudice as prostitutes and as Roma.

The Bulgarian heavies milling around Prague and northern Bohemia noticed the virtual absence of any effective policing of this spontaneous sex trade. The potential market was huge – it was well known how thousands of German men travelled every year to South-East Asia and the Caribbean to indulge in sex tourism. Why not take advantage of that demand by offering them beautiful young women at low, low prices just over the German border, in slightly more relaxing surroundings than the lay-bys of the E55? So Bulgarian gangs bought up, built or rented cheap motels in northern Bohemia. With the aim of maximising their profits, they needed pliant women who were not so well connected with the local community. So they sought out their compatriots. In contrast to the local Czech women, however, these Bulgarian women did not enter the trade voluntarily – they had no idea what awaited them. Nineteen-year-old Stanimira shared a dingy apartment in the polluted Danubian port of Ruse in northern Bulgaria when her flatmate suggested breaking out. 'She told me she had a great job as a shop assistant, and I could get one too with a wage of about 3,000 Deutschmarks a month.* From Bulgaria we went straight to Dubi in the Czech Republic via Hungary and Slovakia. The first thing I noticed about the apartment building when we got there was that all the windows were barred.'

The building in the northern Czech town of Dubi belonged to a former Bulgarian muscle-man and it was positioned just off the Road of Shame. In his early forties, Tsvetomir Belchev had trodden the familiar path of graduating from a Sports Academy in Razgrad, Bulgaria, before drifting into a life of crime. At nineteen, he was sentenced to twelve years' imprisonment for attempted murder and, not long after his release, he was back in prison. 'From his prison cell, he then founded the political party "Renewal" in defence of the rights of prisoners,' his file at the Bulgarian Interior Ministry explains, suggesting that he was an extremely intelligent inmate. 'In this capacity, he organ-

---

* About £1,000 at the time – a fabulous salary for any unemployed Bulgarian.

ised prison strikes, riots and protests throughout 1990. He then stood for President the following year.' As his political career petered out, Belchev moved to the Czech Republic to investigate business opportunities away from the prying eyes of the Bulgarian police. His mother acted as a scout for girls back home.

On arrival, Stanimira was told that she would not be working as a waitress, but as a prostitute. At first she refused point-blank to cooperate. 'Belchev beat me black and blue, hitting and kicking me, in the pavilion opposite the Sport Hotel. He kicked me with hobnailed shoes. He kicked my back, and used a chair too. He summoned his mates, Krassi and "Blackie", on the walkie-talkie, and ordered them to beat me too. I was taken down to the cellar, where the two went on kicking and hitting me, mainly in the abdomen. Blackie clasped my head and struck me with fists. When I passed out, they poured water over me, and when I came round they handcuffed me by one hand to the radiator pipe. I was in excruciating pain. I was handcuffed there all day. Belchev then raped me in one of the rooms in the country house.'

Belchev and his henchmen had tortured and raped each of the forty women who were rescued by police when they finally raided the Dubi brothel in the summer of 1997. During their imprisonment, the women were required to earn a minimum of £2,000 per month (naturally they never saw any of this money). Failure to do so resulted in beatings, as did any hint of insubordination (Belchev ran a system of informers among the women). A refusal to sleep with any of the gang led to both rape and beatings, and the Czech investigators' suspicion that at least one girl had been murdered was confirmed a few years after Belchev's arrest when they found a corpse buried in the brothel grounds. Invariably young and frightened, deprived of their passports, unable to speak the local language and ostracised in any event as prostitutes, the women were entirely dependent on their tormentors.

The Belchev case was a rarity because he was actually busted, the racket broken up and the women freed (astonishingly, Belchev continued to manage three brothels from his prison cell using a mobile phone that his lawyer smuggled in to him). But elsewhere, before the dust from the Berlin Wall had even settled, gangsters and chancers were laying the cables of a huge network of trafficking in women that reached into every corner of Europe. Bulgarian gangs quickly assumed a pivotal role in this industry due to their country's strategic position. Every border offered a lucrative trade. South to Greece represented the quickest route into the European Union – once across that border, the women could be transported anywhere in the EU (except Britain and Ireland) without having to pass a single police control. The south-eastern route to Turkey was reserved for the burgeoning sale of women to the Middle East, in particular the United Arab Emirates. The road west led to the traffickers of Macedonia and Albania (and later Kosovo as well), where the demand grew exponentially as soon as the first peacekeepers were deployed in 1994 as part of the UN Preventive Deployment (the bulk of the internal Balkan trafficking is based on UN peacekeepers and international civil servants). Travelling north, the gangs would transport women to the Czech Republic and Germany before making the return journey in a stolen car.

There was some overlap between the traffickers of women and the car-smugglers. They certainly shared routes and expenses, but police have since identified them as separate enterprises. As a general rule, trafficking in women is performed by small cellular groups who pass their commodity on from region to region, unaware of where their buyer is taking them. Wide-scale car theft is more complex, requiring the direction of larger and better-organised syndicates. Despite the overlapping of most commodities and services (especially regarding the routes they travel), it is the commodity, its geographical origin and its destination that usually define whether it is traded and distributed by large or small syndicates.

Women are attractive as an entry-level commodity for criminals. They can cross borders legally and they do not attract the attention of sniffer dogs. The initial outlay is a fraction of the sum required to engage in car theft; overhead costs are minimal; and, as a service provider, the commodity (a trafficked woman) generates income again and again. Just one woman can make £3,000–6,000 per month for her trafficker. These calculations do not take into account the frightful reality of multiple rape and unspeakable exploitation. But neither the supplier (the gangster) nor the consumer (rich Western Europeans) understands this relationship in anything other than economic terms. The former lives in an environment that is scarcely regulated or policed

– if he does not sell this woman, somebody else will. The latter is apparently able to leave his conscience at the cloakroom with his hat and coat.

Police forces throughout Eastern Europe found the transition to capitalism exceptionally hard. Many people reviled them for their previous complicity in repressing opponents under communism. The drudgery of policemen's lives in the new democracies contrasted with the playboy lifestyle that some former colleagues enjoyed as they helped to build huge criminal empires. In the new market conditions, a policeman's pay cheque was risible – every time I drove through Bulgaria, Yugoslavia or Romania in the years immediately following communism's collapse, I would be forced to pay at least £30 in informal fines levied by impoverished traffic cops. The rule of law, so crucial for building confidence in these embattled societies, was a fiction.

Then – and not for the last time – the West did something really, really dumb. On May 30th, 1992, the UN Security Council in New York passed Resolution 754, which imposed economic sanctions on Serbia and Montenegro. The Balkans – war-ravaged, impoverished and traumatised – were about to be transformed into a smuggling and criminal machine that had few, if any, parallels in history. While the world wrung its hands and fretted over the terrible nationalist urges of the Yugoslav peoples and their leaderships, the Balkan mafias started putting aside their ethnic differences to engage in a breathtaking criminal collaboration.

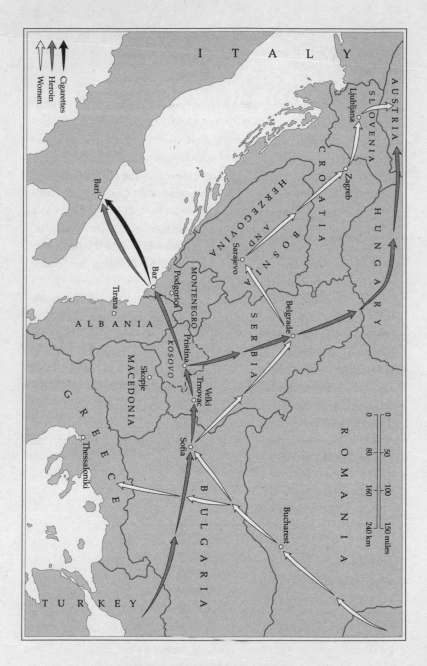

Balkan smuggling routes in the 1990s

2

BLOODY LUCRE

'Five minutes, Dick,' snapped Sandy Berger, National Security Adviser to Bill Clinton. 'He gets five minutes with the President and no more.' Dick Sklar was disappointed. He felt the President of Montenegro, Milo Djukanovic, deserved more time with his US counterpart. But Berger was unequivocal.

Sklar had worked for several years behind the scenes as an indefatigable fixer on behalf of Clinton. He knew the President's views on the Balkans well, but he was taken aback by the short shrift given to the youthful Djukanovic. Admittedly, the President of Montenegro represented an obscure mountainous statelet in the Balkans, the butt of fictional jokes from John Buchan to Agatha Christie. But he had been NATO's most courageous supporter during the Kosovo campaign. And victory in that war was why Clinton and his team were in such a sunny mood that mid-June 1999 when they arrived in Slovenia, the Alpine state nestled between the Balkans and Central Europe.

A couple of weeks earlier the Yugoslav military had sued for an armistice, to the palpable relief of Clinton and his closest advisers. It had been a tough war – not the one-week pushover that some senior Administration officials had predicted in advance of hostilities. Now the President had travelled to Europe to express America's gratitude to its eighteen NATO allies and to other supporters for staying the course.

Montenegro was younger sibling to Serbia's capriciously violent elder brother in the dysfunctional federal family called Yugoslavia. But although Montenegro's airports, harbours and borders were controlled

by the Yugoslav military during the Kosovo war, the willowy pro basket
player turned Montenegrin President had emerged as a thorn in the
flesh of Serbia's dictator, Slobodan Milosevic. Not only did Djukanovic
support Western policy (despite having suffered since 1992 under the
UN's stringent economic sanctions), but he provided a safe haven for
Milosevic's opponents, ensuring that dissent in Serbia was not stifled.
Milosevic bullied and threatened Djukanovic, but the Montenegrin
held his nerve – and that took guts.

Djukanovic's war had been uniquely awkward. NATO had bombed
dozens of targets in Montenegro during the campaign, and yet he
supported these attacks on his own republic by a foreign aggressor.

These risks taken on behalf of the West, Dick Sklar felt, had earned
Djukanovic more than five minutes' chit-chat at the Brdo Castle north
of the Slovene capital, Ljubljana. But as soon as the two presidents sat
down, Sklar was able to relax: Clinton warmed to Djukanovic immediately, and they cast protocol aside and spent over an hour talking on
all manner of subjects: on Milosevic, on the war, on Kosovo and on
the future of the Balkans. Djukanovic later expressed his pleasure at
Clinton's knowledge of Montenegrin history – as ever, the US President
had done his homework. But there was one subject they touched upon
about which Djukanovic was uncharacteristically coy: cigarettes. An
odd subject, perhaps, for a non-smoker like Clinton to raise. But then
he had been informed that cigarettes were Djukanovic's biggest vice
and he felt compelled to issue his Montenegrin counterpart with a
health warning.

Throughout most of the 1990s Djukanovic's country, Montenegro,
with a population of just 600,000 (regarded by the rest of the Balkans
as a legendarily indolent people), was the focal point of a multi-billion-
dollar criminal industry that generated income from America through
the Middle East, Central Asia, the Maghreb, the Balkans and Western
Europe.

Week after week, several tons of illegal cigarette shipments would
land at the country's two main airports, before being swiftly transferred to the port of Bar. In the spring of 1996, I recall speeding along
empty Montenegrin roads in keen anticipation of the view that would
greet me when I hit the Adriatic coast just north of Lake Shkoder. The
bright-yellow cliff fell sheer hundreds of feet to the dramatic coastal

road. The sea in this part of the Adriatic is a deep crystal-blue, free from the green-black gunge that Italy's industrial behemoths spew out along the Adriatic's north-western coastline. But when I looked down at the port of Bar on this occasion, I also saw hundreds of tiny little speedboats cluttered closely in the marina. Packed with contraband cigarettes, they were all revving up for the short 130-mile hop across the Otranto Strait to their sister port of Bari, where the Italian mafia was waiting to unload them.

Each carton of smokes was subject to what Milo Djukanovic styled a 'transit tax'. Milosevic in Belgrade had throttled the flow of federal funds to Montenegro to a trickle and so, Djukanovic argued, the 'transit tax' was the only way to keep his little state on its feet and free from Serbian pressure.

Everybody in the Balkans knew their region was a centre of the illicit trade in cigarettes. Soon after the outbreak of war in the former Yugoslavia in 1991, little boys as young as six would sneak in and out of restaurants in Zagreb, Belgrade and Sarajevo, wooden trays hanging from around their necks neatly stacked with the best-quality Western cigarettes. On the sidewalks, old men with the craggy features born of a lifetime of committed puffing were positioned every twenty-five yards offering Winston and Marlboro in cartons of ten packs. In London these would cost $75, in New York maybe $40. But all over the Balkans, they cost just ten bucks a time. That price differential made smoking an entirely affordable bad habit, even in the harsh conditions of war. More than half of the people in the Balkans smoked – this was a rich market.

I had a regular supplier, a cheeky lad from Belgrade with tousled brown hair called Micko. (Dear reader, rest assured that I have since rid myself of the addiction.) It was important to build a relationship of trust with your smoke supplier because there were two types of illegal cigarettes, indistinguishable to the naked eye, but very different. One was produced with low-grade local tobacco and then packaged as a Western product. It looked like the genuine article, but it tasted like sawdust mixed with goat's droppings.

The second cigarette was high-quality, produced by Western tobacco companies as a Duty Not Paid (DNP) item, designated for export. Purchased direct by wholesalers from the factories in America, Europe and Japan, the merchandise was then sent to Europe's two free-trade zones, Rotterdam in Holland and Zug in Switzerland. From here, it would be sold on to a third country with high levels of corruption – perhaps Egypt, perhaps Uzbekistan. Officials and organised-crime syndicates levied a tax at every subsequent step of the journey, and those aimed at the European Union market would make their final stop in Montenegro before re-entering the EU by speedboat. Even with everybody taking a cut in this fashion (the customs officer in Egypt, the Director of Ports in Romania, and so on), the cigarettes were nonetheless more than 50 per cent cheaper when sold on the black market in Italy or Britain because taxation on tobacco in these countries is so high.

After an eight-year investigation into the trade, prosecutors finally filed a lawsuit in October 2002, accusing two US firms, R.J. Reynolds and Philip Morris, of complicity in the trade, although in 2004 Philip Morris struck a deal with the EU releasing the company from any liability. It also agreed to work with the EU against Mafia penetration of the tobacco trade. R.J. Reynolds denies any complicity.

The charges levelled in 2002 were wide-ranging, including the claim that the Balkan cigarette trade was linked to the money-laundering of Colombian drugs money. The lawyers included a detailed breakdown of how the Montenegrin state made hundreds of millions of dollars from smuggling. Two Montenegrin companies, both controlled by Djukanovic and the secret service, levied £20 on each case transited through the country. 'This money was divided up among various Montenegrin officials involved in this business and who controlled the licences to ship cigarettes through Montenegro,' stated the EU court submission. The second company, with the disarmingly frank name of Montenegrin Tabak Transit (MTT), was co-owned by Italians who have subsequently come under EU, Italian and Serbian investigation. 'MTT was created by certain members of organised crime in conjunction with Montenegrin government officials. The company was officially sanctioned by the Montenegrin Foreign Investment Agency and operated under the special protection of Milo Djukanovic,' the EU document claimed.

As early as 1994, the EU had learned that the cigarette mafia with whom Djukanovic did his business was costing it an estimated £4–6 billion annually in lost tax revenue alone, largely in Italy and the United

Kingdom. Italian prosecutors were desperate to indict Djukanovic on charges of smuggling. Yet at the same time, the United States sent discreet messages to the Italian Government in Rome, requesting that the Italians lay off Djukanovic. Washington needed the Montenegrin President in their battle against Milosevic.

Djukanovic claims that the annual revenue from the tobacco trade was £20 million and that with this he was able to pay for most of the state's running costs. In 1998, when the Italians were looking to indict Djukanovic, Dick Sklar was sent to Rome to negotiate on behalf of the West's Balkan ally. Sklar posed the eminently logical question, 'Why don't you just pay him the £20 million and then he'll close down the trade?' The Italians refused (quite illogically), but by the time Clinton met Djukanovic in the summer of 1999, the Kosovo war had been won and so the Montenegrin President was no longer quite so valuable as an ally. Washington was now telling him that if he wanted closer relations with NATO and the EU, it was time to get out of the cigarette business. 'After the meeting with Clinton, I told Milo that he had now better put on a clean starched shirt and he had to stop getting those shirts messed up by the nasty company he had been keeping,' Dick Sklar explained. By October 2001, British intelligence finally reported that Montenegro had reined in the speedboat traders. Djukanovic had got the message and acted upon it.

During the 1980s and 1990s, a huge discrepancy in wealth had emerged between Western and Eastern Europe. Never before had so many Western Europeans (about 75 per cent) lived not only above the poverty line, but in secure comfort. In the second half of the 1990s, there was much debate about whether the affluent countries of Western Europe could maintain their expensive welfare systems in the face of a rapidly ageing population and a fatal antipathy towards labour migration into the EU. The appearance of dynamic young economies in Eastern Europe then put this problem in an even starker perspective as Poles, Czechs, Hungarians and others proved willing to put in longer hours for less money as they sought to make up for half a century of consumer misery under communism. Growth rates in Eastern Europe began shooting up after the fall of the Berlin Wall. Germany was busy outsourcing its industrial base throughout Poland, the Czech Republic,

Slovakia and Hungary, while the European Union accession programme meant that huge sums in regional development funds were fighting poverty and assisting in the development of democratic institutions in Eastern Europe. Ordinary people there still moaned about how difficult life was economically under capitalism, but after an initial dip, living standards began to pick up.

But thanks to the war, sanctions and ill-conceived reconstruction and development plans, the Balkan peoples had experienced a grinding, debilitating collapse in their incomes and lifestyles. Culturally, they not only felt like Europeans, they were surrounded by other Europeans. They watched their television programmes and movies, they listened to their music, and they were fully aware of how rich their neighbours were. Furthermore, on those rare occasions when they were allowed to travel to their Western neighbours, they faced frequent humiliation at the hands of immigration officers. Finally, they had to run the gauntlet of Balkan stereotyping, which presented them as natural-born killers and only happy when slitting the throats of their neighbours. Set this miserable desert, characterised by unemployment, stagnation and violence, next to a boundlessly rich fertile paradise, and should we wonder how powerful the temptation is to become involved in organised crime?

Montenegro's entanglement with the mob was the rule, not the exception. More than in any other communist country, politics and organised crime were tightly intertwined throughout the former Yugoslavia as it descended into the most frightful fratricidal civil war at the beginning of the 1990s. Organised crime controlled dictators, opposition politicians, liberals, nationalists and democrats alike.

Most shocking of all, however, is how these men fuelling war between their peoples were in private cooperating as friends and close business partners. The Croat, Bosnian, Albanian, Macedonian and Serb money-men and mobsters were truly as thick as thieves. They bought, sold and exchanged all manner of commodities, knowing that the high levels of personal trust between them were much stronger than the transitory bonds of hysterical nationalism. This they fomented among ordinary folk, in essence to mask their own venality. As one commentator described it, the new republics were ruled 'by a Cartel which had emerged from the ruling Communist Party, the police, the military, the mafia, and with the President of the Republic at the centre of this spider web . . . Tribal nationalism was indispensable for the Cartel as a means to pacify its subordinates and as cover for the uninterrupted privatisation of the state apparatus.'

As a consequence of war, sanctions and corruption in the Balkans during the first half of the 1990s, the states of the former Yugoslavia turned to and nurtured mafias to run the logistics of their military effort, and it was not long before the criminals were in control of the economy, the government and the war. Anyone with any serious political ambition had no choice but to get mobbed up.

In February 1991 I was sitting with friends in the elegant baroque centre of Croatia's capital, Zagreb, before the term 'ethnic cleansing' had been invented, and before the outside world had heard of Kosovo. Anxiety was written on their faces, as credible rumours were spreading that the Yugoslav military was about to launch a coup to stop Croatia from declaring independence. The anxiety turned to fear when the authorities in Yugoslavia's federal capital, Belgrade, announced the suspension of normal TV programming for two hours that evening. Instead, the main state channel would broadcast a film alleging a major criminal conspiracy inside the country. Along with Yugoslavia's frightened fragmenting peoples, I watched a concealed black-and-white camera catch three men on film mumbling inaudibly across a sparse wooden table in a modest kitchen. Subtitles had helpfully been added by Yugoslavia's Military Counter-Intelligence Service (KOS), making clear that one of the three men was the new Defence Minister of the proto-Croatian state and a close collaborator of the Croat nationalist President Franjo Tudjman. The other two were supposedly Hungarian arms dealers. The man selling large amounts of illegal weaponry to the Croats was not a Hungarian arms dealer, as he claimed, but a Serb and an agent of KOS.

Yugoslav military intelligence had tasked the same man with infiltrating Multigroup, Ilya Pavlov's mega-company in Bulgaria, and the agent was indeed an early member of its board. In Eastern Europe, KOS had no peers – the fact that KOS had penetrated the new criminalised structures of neighbouring countries like Bulgaria as early as 1990 was ample demonstration of its power and reach.

The film was a piece of KOS propaganda designed to prove that President Tudjman was planning an armed uprising. Milosevic's Serbia and Tudjman's Croatia were heading for a major conflagration. But in their wars for independence from Yugoslavia, first the Croats and later the Bosnians faced one huge challenge: Yugoslavia boasted the Serb-dominated Yugoslav People's Army (JNA), the fourth biggest military in the world, which possessed a sizeable, if ageing, arsenal. The great majority of Croat and Bosnian officers in the JNA went over to their local governments to fight for secession. But their nascent armed forces desperately needed weapons. This became all the more urgent when the United Nations imposed an arms embargo on all the Yugoslav republics three months after the fighting broke out in June 1991. In order to stand a chance of winning the war, first Croatia and then a year later Bosnia had to find ways of importing weapons despite the international ban.

The Croat diaspora in the New World has never been as prominent as that of its Mediterranean neighbours, the Italians, the Greeks or even the Albanians, but it is quietly effective and fiercely patriotic, notably in central Canada, Ohio in the US, Australia and above all in South America. The South American community is regarded as the most nationalistic of all, as many Croatian fascists fled here at the end of the Second World War. Immediately after the UN imposed the arms embargo in 1991, the Argentinian state permitted the sale of 6,500 tons of weaponry to Panama under the terms of a secret decree. The shipment was in fact diverted to Croatia on vessels of the state-owned Croatia Line. Menem followed this up with a second secret authorisation for the sale of £40 million worth of arms to Bolivia. An official investigation in Argentina later revealed a secret clause, rerouting to Croatia '8,000 automatic rifles, 18 155-mm cannons, 2,000 automatic pistols, 211,000 hand grenades, 3,000 Pampero rockets, 30,000 rifle grenades, 3,000 mines, 60 mortars and several million rounds of ammunition'.

When, a year after this, the Muslim-dominated government of Bosnia–Hercegovina found itself squeezed between the two Christian armies of Croatia and Serbia, it appealed to Muslim countries to break the UN weapons embargo and supply it with the means to defend itself. Between 1992 and 1995, Saudi Arabia, Iran, Turkey, Brunei,

Pakistan, Sudan and Malaysia deposited some $350 million into the bank account of a Muslim charitable organisation in Vienna, and the money was then used to purchase weapons.

The arms embargo played a key role in establishing the smuggling channels to Croatia and Bosnia, and soon drugs were accompanying the guns along the same routes. But this was nothing compared to the Balkan-wide impact which the comprehensive UN *economic* sanctions imposed on the rump Yugoslavia, comprising Serbia (including the troubled province of Kosovo, with a large Albanian population) and Montenegro. The UN imposed the sanctions in July 1992 because Serbia was aiding the Bosnian Serb military in violation of earlier Security Council resolutions.

Unlike the Croats and Bosnians, Serbia and her allies in Bosnia were not short of weaponry. But with the sanctions in place, Belgrade needed to guarantee oil supplies and it needed to find goods to export to pay for the business of waging war. Just as Serbia allowed weapons from Romania and Bulgaria to reach its enemies in Croatia and Bosnia via Serbian territory, so were the Bosnians, Croats and Albanians more than happy to sell oil to their Serbian enemies because of the extraordinary profits that a sanctions regime generates. These profits were then split between the state, which purchased more weapons with them, and the deep pockets of a growing mafia, which included men like Vladimir 'Vanja' Bokan.

In a darkened café, I listened to a former business partner of Vanja Bokan, the man who as a 30-year-old had opened Hannibal, Belgrade's first private clothes boutique, in 1985. My interlocutor warned me that if I identified him, he would soon be dead. 'And they'll probably kill you, too,' Mr X added for emphasis. After this sombre introduction, however, he warmed to his subject. 'At first we would travel to Italy and buy designer clothes in bulk, which we sold in Hannibal. But then Vanja had a better idea – we called it the Dazzle,' he explained. 'He'd order the clothes from Romania: the dazzle. They were perfect – you couldn't tell them apart from the Italian original – and then he'd sell them as originals for an enormous mark-up in the shop. In order to get goods like these previously, people had to go on an expensive trip to Italy.'

Bokan was restless, dynamic and intelligent. His mother was a paediatrician and his father had worked as an engineering consultant to the United Nations, so Vanja had grown up in such exotic places as Indonesia and South America. He was a talented linguist who spoke Greek, Italian and English alongside Serbo-Croat. Full of ideas, Bokan was a natural-born entrepreneur. When he opened his boutiques in Belgrade and Novi Sad, and later his workshops across the Balkans, he was a model capitalist seizing the opportunities that the collapse of communism and the embrace of the West enabled. Even before the outbreak of the wars in the early 1990s, he had diversified the company, importing and exporting all manner of goods to and from Yugoslavia. His business was entirely legal; he was forging economic ties between a former communist country and the European Union; and he was creating both revenue for the state and employment.

But in 1992 the war with Bosnia and UN sanctions intervened, altering his business environment. The vote imposing an embargo on Yugoslavia immediately rendered all Bokan's trade illegal in international law, as Serbia was the centre of his trading empire.

Sanctions had a negligible impact on the European Union and America. Most Western companies could afford to stop trading with Belgrade, especially as their governments threatened tough penalties if anybody violated them. Serbia lies at the heart of all Balkan trading routes – its roads and its markets are almost as essential for its neighbours as they are for Serbia itself. The UN, of course, issued warnings to the surrounding countries that they must break off all links with Serbia and Montenegro. For Balkan countries, the sanctions were a catastrophe, and it was inevitable that they would be violated.

Even though the Bulgarian Government could no longer officially buy and sell to Serbia, businessmen like Ilya Pavlov felt less constrained. Yugoslavia's Military Counter-Intelligence, KOS, used its influence in Multigroup and encouraged Pavlov to borrow railcars from the Government in order to send millions of gallons of petrol into Serbia by train. They were accompanied by members of the SIC, one of the two largest protection rackets in Bulgaria, and were waved through by customs officers whose measly pay-packets meant that their allegiance was easily purchased. The then US Ambassador to Sofia, Bill Montgomery, remembers how the Bulgarian state was in fact deeply involved from the start: 'An embassy officer was passing the western border by chance at night when he noticed there were a lot of police around with flashlights. He pulled over and just watched what happened. Along came 100 oil tankers – he counted them – rumbling through the night before being directed across the border by the Bulgarian police.'

Bulgaria's main route to the rest of Europe was through Serbia. The UN Security Council had already told Sofia to kiss goodbye to the $1 billion it was owed by Saddam's Iraq when it imposed sanctions on Baghdad. Now the UN was telling Bulgaria it could not send its trucks through Serbia. This was devastating, as the country's most important exports to Western Europe were perishable. 'Bulgaria had a GDP of $10 billion and on the fruit and vegetables alone they lost $1 billion of income annually,' explained Bill Montgomery. 'I proposed that we allow the Bulgarians to send a weekly convoy through Serbia, which would be accompanied by a UN vehicle at the head and a UN vehicle at the tail. They would not stop, but travel straight through. The UN signed off on this; the Europeans signed off on this; but Leon Furth, adviser to the Vice-President, Al Gore, was opposed and he blocked it. He was not to be moved and it was very frustrating.' Frustrating and, further- more, a cheering boost to organised crime, which thrived on the economic distress that such myopic policies promoted.

Not a penny of assistance or compensation was offered to Yugoslavia's neighbours – they were all expected to shoulder the costs of the international community's moral indignation. So the only way they could pay pensions, wages and health care was by allowing the mob to shore up its control of the country's main trading routes and claim ignorance, helplessness or both. As the crisis deepened, so did this damaging symbiotic relationship between politics and crime.

In Serbia itself, Vanja Bokan, the clothing entrepreneur, was quick to arrange shipments of oil and metals into Yugoslavia. Criminals and businessmen throughout the region worked feverishly to create a dense web of friendships and networks to subvert the embargo. Virtually overnight, the vote at the UN Security Council ordering sanctions created a pan-Balkan mafia of immense power, reach, creativity and venality.

Some inside the US administration had warned President Clinton of serious consequences. One senior member of the US Treasury told me that 'We made it plain to our colleagues in the White House that you could never break Serbia with sanctions. The Serbs were self-sufficient in food and, given its centrality to the regional economy, the neighbours were bound to continue trading with them.' Like so many warnings about the deleterious impact of sanctions, this one was ignored.

Soon everyone was following Vanja Bokan's example by selling oil to Serbia from wherever they could get their hands on it. The Romanians floated barges almost sinking under the weight of their appallingly low-grade oil. 'In Albania,' a US intelligence report noted, 'imported oil was shipped via pipeline across the northern border, by boat across Lake Shkoder, by caravans of cars with extra fuel tanks added, by donkeys carrying barrels of oil across mountainous regions . . . The total oil flow was estimated to have brought Albania more than $1 million per day during 1993–1994.' Despite being one of Serbia's harshest critics, Albania played a key role in supplying Belgrade with oil. 'Barges were used to bring oil products from Ukraine,' the report continued. 'The volume of shipments along the Danube River attracted the interest of Serbian pirates who would cruise the Danube looking for fuel shipments to hijack . . . Romanian oil products arrived by highway, by ship, and by an underground pipeline from the Romanian oil facility at Timisoara. Cars were refitted to carry as much as 500 gallons of fuel.'

The sanctions-busting carnival was also, of course, an opportunity that Russian business could not let slip through its fingers. Their oil companies agreed to a barter arrangement with Serbia. Using its surplus grain stocks, Belgrade was able to exchange $100–250 million of oil a year.

By the time the petrol reached the consumer in Belgrade, it was four times the price of fuel elsewhere in Europe. I would buy it by the side of the road in the district of Zemun. Petty traders sat on their jerrycans and buckets full of petrol (lit cigarettes hanging out of the mouth as a matter of course). Vehicles just pulled up beside them and the driver purchased two or three gallons of whatever was available. I developed a business relationship with a certain Stevo from Zemun who, for a consideration, ensured that I only got high-quality petrol from Hungary or Bulgaria and not the explosive mix from Romania, which, legend had it, would lead to your engine seizing within hours.

The economies of the fragmented republics of the former Yugoslavia had been devastated – firms were often dependent on suppliers in countries they were now at war with; the export of industrial products to Eastern and Western Europe had collapsed. But still they were purchasing billions of dollars of weapons, oil, food, consumer goods and luxury goods every month. Although the majority of the population was becoming poorer by the day, a hugely wealthy new class of entrepreneurs and gangsters was visible on the streets of all Balkan cities. Ferraris, Porsches, armoured Mercedes and SUVs clogged up Zagreb, Belgrade and elsewhere. Occasionally, the thick-necks with shades would emerge from behind the smoked-glass windows. I well recall a terrified restaurant owner in Skopje, the capital of Macedonia, asking me to pay my bill and vacate my table in a hurry as some special guests were arriving whom he did not wish to disappoint. As I saw the platoon of lobotomised bodybuilders stride into the establishment while I exited, I noticed that they weren't even Macedonian, but Bulgarian – they treated foreign countries as their own.

These men carried guns with impunity and would sport the nationalist insignia of their particular tribe – the four Cs of Serbia, the lily of Bosnia, the eagle of Albania or the chequered board of Croatia. Because although they were quite happy to trade with their equivalents in enemy territories, most were hooked up with the vile militias that were busy slaughtering civilian populations in the war zones of Bosnia and Croatia. In Bosnia, the Serb forces who had locked Sarajevo in a siege were not the only thugs in town. Bosnia's own Muslim warlords controlled the entire economy of the city, trading with the Serb besiegers and then squeezing every last penny out of their compatriots by ratcheting up the price of basic foodstuffs, many of which were stolen from the United Nations and other humanitarian organisations.

Somehow this orgy of war and consumer excess had to be paid for. The former Yugoslav republics were no longer in a position to balance the books with their traditional exports, and so they decided to finance the war by other means. And because the industry of sanctions-busting had now created a huge pan-Balkan network of organised crime (whose members had no sense of ethnic loyalty when it came to trade), the easiest way of underwriting the affairs of state was through mafia business: drugs, arms, oil, weapons, women and migrants. The foundations for a factory of crime had been laid.

Life as a sanctions-buster and dodgy entrepreneur entailed risks, as Vanja Bokan discovered. Competition for the illegal markets in the former Yugoslavia was tough, and spectacular assassinations of gangsters and businessmen became a regular feature of life in the capitals of Croatia, Serbia, Bosnia and Montenegro. Bokan's wealth and market share were sufficient of themselves to make him a target. But he was still more vulnerable for another reason – he did not like Slobodan Milosevic, the big boss of Serbia, and furthermore he was not afraid of telling people.

Bokan's former partner, Mr X, recalled how one summer day in Belgrade, 'We were driving down Revolution Boulevard when a black Jeep drew up beside us. The passenger pulled out a semi-automatic and just started firing at us.' Three of the five bullets lodged in Bokan's shoulder. It was time to lie low for a while, and so Bokan and his family moved to Greece. This proved an ideal base – Greeks were sympathetic to Serbs and the country's northern port in Salonika was by now one of the most important pivots of the growing sanctions-busting operation. 'The Greek authorities did everything in their power to facilitate the violation of the embargo,' Vanja later admitted. 'For example, they never asked for Letters of Discharge . . . They believed the embargo was unjust.' Bokan secured citizenship in record time by using his contacts in Greek intelligence, and quickly established himself as a sparkling social light on the cosmopolitan stage that Athens had become since the fall of communism. The Greek capital teemed in the early 1990s with Georgians, Hungarians, Albanians, Russians, Balts and more. All were loaded, all were attracted by Greece's corruptible civil servants, and many claimed a Greek heritage and thereby an automatic right to a European Union passport.

He also now turned his attention to Serbia's sister republic, Montenegro. In a curious echo of the Bulgarian Ilya Pavlov's experience, Vanja Bokan's Montenegrin father-in-law was one of the top three generals of KOS. He introduced Bokan to Montenegro's leading politicians and businessmen, including the ambitious young Prime

Minister, Milo Djukanovic. Linked by an entrepreneurial spirit, the two men were soon exploring possible areas of cooperation. The Black Pirate, as Bokan had become known, had recently acquired two Ilyushin-76 transporter planes. At first, this looked like a poor investment, as NATO had imposed a no-fly zone over Serbia and Montenegro. But Bokan had uncovered a loophole that allowed planes to land in Montenegro 'for technical purposes'. With help from his new Montenegrin friends, Bokan came up with his billion-dollar idea – selling untaxed cigarettes to the Italian mafia.

Bokan worked it like this. He would fill his cavernous Ilyushins with cigarettes imported legally to one of the free-trade zones in Europe (Rotterdam and Buchs in Switzerland) direct from the factories of all the major tobacco manufacturers in America and Western Europe, although sometimes the planes would pick up the merchandise from airports in the Middle East or in Central Asia, where their export paperwork was easily lost. They would then fly on to Malta or other apparently innocuous destinations in Europe, but would be permitted the 'technical landing' in Montenegro. 'I get the cigarettes from America and dispatch them to Rotterdam using entirely legal channels,' Bokan explained in an interview in 2000. 'The cigarettes are formally destined for Romania, but I divert them to Montenegro and then sell them to Italy,' he added frankly. 'The planes are on the ground for the shortest time. They land, unload, and then take off again, while the cigarettes are taken off to storage or directly to the port.'

At the harbour, they were packed onto the speedboats, and every night a swarm of tiny vessels buzzed across the Adriatic to the Italian province of Apulia. The province was home to one of the youngest, more chaotic, but undoubtedly more pugnacious Italian organised-crime groups, the Sacra Corona Unita (SCU). 'Initially, the Italian police and customs were in a hopeless position,' said a Serb journalist who investigated the trade closely. 'From the port of Ancona way to the north down to Bari – i.e., 300 miles of coastline! – they possessed just *two* high-speed vessels capable of catching the Montenegrin speed-boats, of which there were dozens and dozens making the crossing every night!'

'Since 1992, Montenegro has become one gigantic marketplace for smuggled cigarettes,' wrote the German State Prosecutor who has been looking into the entire trade since 1994. Of course, the reason why this impoverished state became involved is because men and women in the European Union do not like paying high taxes on cigarettes and are prepared to break the law themselves by buying them off the street. In north London one could buy stocks of untaxed cigarettes from a group of Kurdish and Kosovo Albanian sellers, just outside Safeway's supermarket on the Holloway Road, a busy thoroughfare. A pack cost between £1.50 and £2.00, a saving of almost £3.00 on those sold with the tax included. Despite the tortuous journey these cigarettes had taken, from the United States via Rotterdam, on to the eastern Mediterranean and then back through the Balkans, the dozens of people involved in the smuggling had all made a handsome profit as the cost of cigarettes at the factory gate was a mere £0.30 a pack. For many in the Balkans, this was the ultimate victimless crime – there is no opprobrium attached to the smoking habit in the Balkans, and the only people who lose out are the Finance Ministries of Europe. So who cares?

Bokan could only run the cigarette business with the approval of the Government in Belgrade, which meant Slobodan Milosevic himself signed off on it. 'He approved everything,' Vanja's father-in-law, the KOS general, later admitted. So of course did Yugoslavia's mighty secret-police forces, UDBA (civilian) and KOS (military). Unlike in all other Eastern European countries, the establishment of nationalist dictatorships and the collapse into war in the former Yugoslavia meant that there was no campaign to strip the secret police of its power, as happened in Bulgaria. Organised crime and secret police worked hand in glove throughout Yugoslavia; indeed, it was often impossible to distinguish one from the other. The criminalisation of Yugoslavia thus surpassed that of all other countries in Eastern Europe. The consequences were violent and damaging.

Croats, Albanians, Macedonians, Montenegrins and Serbs cooperated splendidly in shifting contraband, narcotics and women from territory to territory. 'Licensed' by governments and the security services, these were effectively horizontal cartels that stretched across several countries. One of the largest combined Turkish heroin gangs with Bulgarian, Serbian, Macedonian and Albanian syndicates to shift the bulk of the heroin originating in Afghanistan into Western Europe. The cartel functioned smoothly during both the Kosovo and Macedonian wars at the turn of the millennium, even though the front lines cut right across the smuggling route.

While collaboration with national enemies proved easy, the criminals faced serious threats from competitors on their home turf. In the hundreds of mob-associated murders between 1990 and 2007 in the Balkans, most were commissioned by compatriots of the victims – Serb-on-Serb or Croat-on-Croat violence was an everyday phenomenon.

One of the bloodiest episodes in Serbia was triggered by the 'cigarette wars', which broke out when two new guys on the block decided they wanted to muscle in on Vanja Bokan's action. Both were very dangerous men. Stanko 'Cane' Subotic, who had started as a lowly tailor and an employee of Bokan, eventually became the most powerful smuggler in Europe, residing in Switzerland with offices in Dubai. Cane exploited Bokan's reputed stinginess to muscle in on the Montenegro cigarette trade by offering co-conspirators higher cuts from his profits.

The second man was an amateur racing driver who built Bambiland, a *faux* Disneyland, in his home town of Pozarevac, Serbia. He also happened to be Slobodan Milosevic's son, Marko, and as a result commanded a certain respect. The Anti-Organised Crime Unit in Serbia has detailed how Milosevic Junior ordered the bulldozing of duty-free shops (a pivotal retail outlet for cigarettes) belonging to his competitors on Serbia's borders. It has also uncovered how Milosevic's wife, Mirjana Markovic or the Lady Macbeth of the Balkans, persuaded the chief of customs to allow her son's contraband goods in and out of Serbia with impunity.

The emergence of these two competing syndicates was quickly followed in 1997 by the outbreak of political warfare between the presidents of Serbia and Montenegro, Milosevic and Djukanovic. Both men ruled over republics where organised crime had usurped key positions in political and economic life, and where politicians used the security forces and gangsters to intimidate opponents. But Djukanovic realised that Milosevic's strategy of continually goading and challenging the West was unlikely to result in long-term dividends. Deploying his brisk, modern approach, Djukanovic announced that he wanted to emulate the other republics in the former Yugoslavia by leaving Serbia to become independent.

Within weeks, close associates of both presidents and almost all leading figures in the cigarette trade were being whacked in broad daylight. Serbia's Deputy Interior Minister was holding court in Belgrade's nouveau restaurant, Mamma Mia, just a few yards from the British Embassy when he was pumped full of bullets from the sub-machine gun of an unknown assailant. An unreconstructed thug of whom Milosevic was especially fond, the Deputy Interior Minister was murdered as he guarded a bag containing DM 700,000 in cash (believed to be cigarette profits). 'He just got greedy,' one of his colleagues in the Serbian Security Forces lamented. 'He wanted to grab too much for himself and didn't cover his arse.' Next it was the turn of Djukanovic's security chief, who was up to his neck in the business, assassinated at his home. As his pistol was still in its holster (it was otherwise always cocked and ready to fire), most concluded that he fell victim to someone he trusted. 'People were ordering murders like they were ordering cups of coffee,' recalled one Serbian Government minister after the fall of Milosevic. But while the roll call of corpses grew longer, the cigarettes kept moving and the money kept rolling in – and even though Milosevic and Djukanovic became the most bitter enemies, their representatives still managed to find a *modus vivendi* over distributing profits from the cigarettes, although arrangements were occasionally complicated by unexpected funerals.

A mobbed-up country like Serbia is inherently unstable. Huge discrepancies between rich and poor become extremely visible; inefficiencies plague the economy; corruption becomes endemic; and leaders like Milosevic are easily persuaded to engage in military adventures that eventually prove self-defeating. Defeat in the Kosovo war in 1999 unsettled Milosevic's criminal backers. There were signs that some major oligarchs and underground figures were tiring of the uncertainty which their own mob rule perpetuated. And the rise of Milosevic's wife and son as the bosses of a major cartel generated widespread resentment among ordinary people and competitors alike. Then six months after the Kosovo war had ended, an assassination took place in Belgrade whose consequences were immense.

*   *   *

The cold in January 2000 would break records and on Saturday 15th, freezing fog had smothered the city for most of the day. Night had fallen and the temperature had begun a downward slide past zero. The blackness was pierced by the intense dark-green light emanating from the Hotel Intercontinental, a desolate rectangular block that stands lonely over the Sava river in New Belgrade. Just inside the building, a group of tough-looking men were slouched in the reception area's hideous 1970s leather-sofa enclaves, discussing football and filling out betting slips. At 5.04 p.m. a former Belgrade cop, Dobrosav Gavric, emerged from the elevator and walked towards them. But as he reached reception he pulled out a gun and started shooting. Pandemonium reigned for about two minutes as the men sitting down returned fire. Gavric was hit in the back, but was saved from certain death by an accomplice who appeared from nowhere, hauled him through the entrance's revolving door and into a car, which the thick fog soon swallowed up as it sped towards a rendezvous with a second getaway vehicle.

Back inside the Intercontinental, amidst blood and wailing, one of the men was dying. Known to his many admirers as the Commandant, he was breathing his last. He had received three bullets to the head, one of which had gone straight through his left eye into his brain. This was the predictably inglorious end of Arkan, the most notorious crime boss in Belgrade, who was wanted throughout Europe on charges of murder and armed robbery – 'aggressive, armed and extremely dangerous', as the Interpol warrant described him. The Hague War Crimes Tribunal was also preparing a case against him for genocide, and even the thoroughly immoral Serbian dictator, Slobodan Milosevic, had a year earlier dubbed him 'my greatest enemy', despite the fact that during the Yugoslav wars of the 1990s Arkan had soaked himself in blood on Milosevic's behalf.

But Arkan had many friends, and indeed countless Serbs venerated him as the country's most glamorous celebrity. At the time of the killing, Zoran Djindjic, the opposition leader beloved by the West as a scourge of Milosevic and later as Serbia's first democratic Prime Minister, reacted to the assassination by declaring Arkan a close friend. 'It was Arkan who warned me to flee to Montenegro during the Kosovo war because Milosevic intended to murder me,' Djindjic later explained. (Indeed, with an eye to Serbia's democratic political future, Arkan had

organised and paid for Djindjic's evacuation.) Gangsters, opposition-
ists, entertainers, supporters of Milosevic, opponents of Milosevic,
soccer hooligans and the business fraternity mourned Arkan in their
hundreds of thousands. His reputation even extended to Italy. He had
brokered the sale of some of Serbia's best soccer players to Lazio, and
so fans of the Italian side had once rolled out a huge banner proclaiming
'Honour to Arkan and his Tigers'.

In 1995, Arkan had married Ceca, a buxom singer who had popu-
larised Turbo-folk, the indigenous rock genre favoured by Serbia's
dissolute nationalist youth. The wedding saw Arkan emerge from St
Sava Cathedral in the full dress uniform of a First World War general.
This image proved almost as popular with photo-editors around the
world as when he had posed in front of a tank in paramilitary outfit
holding a baby tiger (Milica, on hire from Belgrade zoo) and presenting
his cut-throat comrades from the Serb Volunteer Guard, the 'Tigers'.
The latter picture was carefully framed to instil admiration and war
fever in the Serbian masses and fear in the villagers of Bosnia and
Croatia whom he intended to kill or 'cleanse'. Early in the Bosnian
war, I remember being holed up in a hotel close to Sarajevo airport
under sustained, although relatively harmless, attack from Serb forces.
During this siege, we noticed that all the Muslim villagers were packing
their things and preparing to flee. 'We've been told that Arkan and
the Tigers are on their way,' they explained to us hurriedly. Nothing
was more effective in the business of ethnic cleansing than the mere
possibility of Arkan's imminent arrival.

Arkan was born Zeljko Raznatovic in 1952, the son of a Yugoslav
air-force pilot. He enjoyed a relatively privileged upbringing, but developed a reputation as a tearaway in his teens, receiving his first prison
sentence for theft in Belgrade aged just seventeen. Unlike other Eastern
European countries, which were allied to the Soviet Union as members
of the Warsaw Pact, Yugoslavia professed neutrality in the Cold War and
permitted a small degree of capitalist enterprise in its socialist system.
Moreover, whereas most citizens of the Soviet Bloc were imprisoned
in their own countries, unable to travel to the West, Yugoslavs enjoyed
free access to Western Europe. Hundreds of thousands travelled to
Germany, Switzerland and Scandinavia to take up menial jobs, and
this provided a milieu in which less salubrious Yugoslav characters

could take refuge and disappear from the police if necessary. After his release from Belgrade prison in the early 1980s, Raznatovic decided to try his luck in the wider world. Throughout that decade, his notoriety blossomed as he robbed, extorted and murdered his way across northern Europe. For these crimes, he was imprisoned in Sweden, Holland, Belgium and Germany, escaping at least three times, often with the aid of false passports.

'When Bulgarian organised-crime groups were emerging in the early 1990s, they came into contact with their Yugoslav counterparts for the first time at the beginning of the war. And when they did, they had a big shock,' explained General Boyko Borissov, the General Director of the Bulgarian Interior Ministry. 'Our guys were just playing at being gangsters – the Yugoslavs had been thieving and killing in Europe for real over decades. They were seriously tough and to this day, if you want to kill somebody in Bulgaria and you want the job done reliably and cheaply, then you hire a Serb. They are the best assassins.'

In 1983, Arkan was charged with the attempted murder of two Belgrade policemen. Under normal circumstances, this would have meant a lifelong lock-up. But at his trial it emerged that he was an agent for UDBA, one of the most feared secret-police operations in Eastern Europe. Arkan, it seems, had sold his outlaw's soul to Mephistopheles. The attempted murder charge was dropped and the two parties began a deep and fruitful relationship, which over the next seventeen years would bring Arkan great riches, beautiful women, power and fame. Until, that is, Mephistopheles came to claim his soul on that cold winter night at the Intercontinental.

Arkan's killers were found, tried and imprisoned, but they were simply hired hands. To this day, nobody has discovered who ordered the murder or why. But the consequences were profound, as the events that January afternoon triggered an unprecedented internecine battle among Serbia's gangs, known as Bloody Spring 2000. Less than a month after Arkan's death, the Yugoslav Defence Minister was exterminated while dining in a Belgrade restaurant. Thereafter assassinations and executions occurred on a weekly basis as Milosevic's final months began to resemble the fearful denouement of an Elizabethan revenge tragedy.

As he emerged from his Mercedes 500 in front of his villa in

Athens early on the morning of October 7th, 2000, Vanja Bokan's face
was obliterated by twenty-nine bullets fired from a couple of semi-
automatics. He was a victim of uncertain times. Two days earlier, the
thirteen-year rule of Slobodan Milosevic had ended in the flames that
engulfed Yugoslavia's parliament as half a million Serbs took to the
streets of Belgrade in support of the opposition. Frustrated by the way
he had been excluded from business in Serbia and Montenegro, Bokan
had started to talk to the Greek press. In unprecedented detail, he had
begun to reveal secrets of the cigarette trade, and he hinted that he
was preparing to spill all the beans and name names. Gangsters are
reluctant to wash their dirty laundry in public for understandable
reasons – but Bokan had chosen an especially bad time to break the
omertà.

Much of the killing that took place between Arkan's death in January
2000 and Milosevic's fall was in anticipation of the latter event. The
leading mobsters, oligarchs and secret-police operatives were hedging
their bets against a change in the regime. As Zoran Djindjic, the
incoming democratic Prime Minister, admitted, several top bosses
established discreet contact with him and his fellow opposition leaders
in advance of Milosevic's demise. Like all influential politicians, whether
democratic or not, Djindjic commuted regularly between the grey and
the black zones of the economy to fund his political activities – although
his ultimate declared intention was to lead Serbia into the light. He
was aware that a pair of clean hands and honest features were not
sufficient to beat Milosevic and his criminal networks. So in the run-
up to Milosevic's political collapse, Djindjic made deals with a number
of criminal bosses who were not only involved in dirty business, but
were also stained by complicity in war crimes in Bosnia, Kosovo and
elsewhere. The new Prime Minister was perfectly frank about these
events. 'The mafia,' he explained, 'had lost the Milosevic state and so
it was looking for a new one.'

The rising kingpin in Belgrade was an extremely violent thug called
Dusan Spasojevic, leader of the Zemun gang, named after a fashionable Belgrade suburb where he had built a preposterous nouveau-riche
mansion. Spasojevic hailed from south Serbia near Veliki Turnovac, a
town with a majority Albanian population which had for decades been
the Balkan pivot for the heroin-smuggling industry. During the 1990s,

Spasojevic had established a monopoly on the heroin trade in Belgrade so that, according to the local police, 'He was processing about 100 kilograms of hard drugs monthly – this was bringing him in tens of millions of dollars.'

The chaos in Serbia at the turn of the millennium was mirrored by instability elsewhere in the former Yugoslavia. With a decade of brutal wars coming to an end, the region was now full of testosterone-fuelled unemployed young men, often well armed. The conflicts had also created hundreds of thousands of refugees, a majority of whom went to Western Europe, establishing efficient distribution networks.

Naturally, cigarettes were not the only commodity traded across the Balkans and into the European Union. Nor did the Serbs and Montenegrins have a monopoly on these activities. Situated just below and across from the soft underbelly of Europe, the Balkan Peninsula has developed into the ideal transit zone for illicit goods and services from around the world seeking access to the most affluent consumer market in history – the EU. Europeans could choose from a glittering array of consumer goods to ease their lifestyle and fill their leisure time. Despite the boundless choice of licit consumer goods, a significant section (including both the wealthy and the poor) sought to satisfy its needs outside the legitimate market. Organised crime is such a rewarding industry in the Balkans because ordinary Western Europeans spend an ever burgeoning amount of their spare time and money sleeping with prostitutes; smoking untaxed cigarettes; sticking €50 notes up their noses; employing illegal untaxed immigrant labour on subsistence wages; admiring ivory and sitting on teak; or purchasing the liver and kidneys of the desperately poor in the developing world.

With no wars left to fight, former paramilitaries became engaged full-time in the transit of heroin, cigarettes, labour migrants and women into Western Europe. The Keystone Cops' regime of the UN and NATO in Kosovo had no resources to combat the Albanian fighters from the Kosovo Liberation Army, who had consolidated Kosovo as a new centre for the distribution of heroin from Turkey to the European Union. Elsewhere, Bosnia–Hercegovina was mired in an early scandal involving UN peacekeepers and trafficked women, as well as developing a reputation as a regional money-laundering centre. Macedonia was about to dissolve into a civil war that was provoked almost exclusively by a dispute between mafia groups over control of the illegal cigarette routes through the country.

Spurred by his success in moving heroin, Spasojevic wanted to expand his operations by trading in another drug: cocaine. 'Cocaine is a rich man's drug – rich people, bigger profits, and Spasojevic wanted a piece,' said Milos Vasic, Serbia's leading expert on organised crime. Spasojevic soon realised that he had hit a goldmine. Cocaine usage in Europe was rising everywhere, with significant new markets opening up in the former communist countries of the East. Spasojevic quickly understood that he was not alone in wanting to exploit the Balkans' collapsing infrastructure. Another group of people had begun to monitor it very closely. These people lived far away in Colombia.

The 300-mile railroad ride west from the Brazilian border through dense Amazonian jungle in eastern Bolivia is known as *El tren del muerte* because it is repeatedly targeted by bandits with scant regard for human life. Thieves perpetrate all manner of scams on this route – most notoriously they pass themselves off as Interpol officers in their efforts to mug unsuspecting foreigners. The relief on arrival in Santa Cruz is combined with shock, as much of the housing in Bolivia's eastern capital resembles the middle-class suburbs of Texas or California. Fuelled by large gas deposits, which, since the mid-1990s, have attracted a host of multinationals into the region, the opulence of Santa Cruz seems a million miles from the desperate inert poverty that affects most of Latin America's poorest country.

Apart from the energy sector, Santa Cruz is the centre of Bolivia's commercial farming industry, which distributes vegetables and oils throughout the world. In late July 2003, managers of an import–export business in Santa Cruz were finalising the departure of two consignments, one of which was bound for a clinic in Madrid and consisted of seventy-eight containers of medicinal clay. A second cargo, made up of some 770 boxes of powdered mashed potato, was being loaded onto trucks that were headed for Chile.

At 9.30 in the morning, dozens of police from Bolivia's Special Force against Narco-trafficking surrounded a Varig plane destined first for Brazil and then for Spain. A few hours later, they stopped the trucks. The two tons of cocaine hidden amongst the medicinal clay

was relatively easy to find. But it took two or three days for government chemists to discover that the mashed potato was infused with
three tons of cocaine. Even more baffling for the Bolivians was its
destination – from Chile it was due to sail to the Black Sea port of
Varna in Bulgaria.

The Santa Cruz bust was the culmination of Operation Moonlight,
which included the cooperation of British intelligence, the Bulgarian
police, Washington's Drug Enforcement Administration (DEA), the
Spanish police and the Bolivian Special Force. Interestingly the
Bulgarian and Bolivian Interior Ministries had no idea of each other's
role in the operation until the arrests were made. 'This is the biggest
trans-national trafficking group we have ever monitored in Bolivia,'
said the government minister Yerko Kukoc at the time of the operation, 'and the largest amount of cocaine ever seized.'

The affair had begun just under a year before when a British-
intelligence officer passed on a mobile phone number to the Bulgarian
police. 'Frankly, it wasn't much to go on,' said the officer in Sofia in
charge of the case. But gradually the Bulgarians pieced together an
extraordinary story. A Colombian cartel (almost certainly from Medellín)
arranged to smuggle a top chemist into Bulgaria, where he lived for
several months. 'The Colombian arrived in Greece using his real passport, then somebody from the group picked him up and brought him
across the border illegally. His job was to train the Bulgarian chemists,'
added the policeman, 'and he did a good job.' It later emerged that a
year before the mashed potato, the chemists had extracted 200 kilograms of cocaine from a shipment of soya oil that had arrived in
Plovdiv via the same Santa Cruz–Varna route.

Ever since the collapse of Francoism, there had been two main
centres for the import of cocaine into Europe: Spain and the
Netherlands. Spain had been the entry point of choice for South
American coke-smugglers as they cashed in on the habits of Europe's
yuppies during the boom years of the 1980s. The reasons were obvious
– the linguistic and cultural connections between Latin America and
Spain allowed the establishment of a strong host community to receive
and distribute the drugs. Spain also had a huge coastline, which was
difficult to police. However, an improvement in cooperation between
European police forces and the DEA, combined with a vigorous increase

in the use of cocaine in Europe during the 1990s, meant that the Spanish route could no longer satisfy the demand.

Amsterdam, with a significant Colombian community, remained the pivotal distribution point for northern Europe, with the drugs arriving largely from Spain, Italy and West Africa. However, a new gate was opening.

By the late 1990s, the American cocaine market had reached super-saturation, notwithstanding the billions of dollars pumped by successive US governments into eradicating the coca industry. The price to the US consumer dropped year on year and so, in response to these depressed market conditions, the Colombian producers sought out new marketing and distribution strategies. Not only did their research establish that the European markets were still underdeveloped, but they realised that with the collapse of the Berlin Wall, a new middle class, young and dynamic, was springing up in Eastern Europe and Russia. They wanted to increase their access to these markets by improving distribution, and the poorly policed coastlines and corruptibility of Croatia, Albania and Bulgaria represented a superb opportunity. In addition, the Colombians could make use of the high levels of education that were the legacy of communism in the Balkans to outsource production. Yugoslavia and Bulgaria abounded in highly qualified chemical engineers and so the processing of cocaine could now be completed much closer to its final destination.

Since the end of the Kosovo war in 1999, the Balkans' role in the industry had been transformed. 'Spain still accounts for almost half of the coke imported into Europe,' the Bulgarian officer explained, 'but in the past four years the Balkans has absorbed most of the rest of the traffic.' The three tons of cocaine headed for Bulgaria in the mashed potato was a vast quantity, and altogether Operation Moonlight's catch was worth more than $300 million.

This was a truly trans-national operation. The British and Italian police uncovered three tons of acetone on a ship harboured in Trieste en route to the Albanian port of Durres. 'There's only one thing you use acetone for in those quantities,' said the head of the Balkans unit of the National Crime Intelligence Service in London, 'and that's processing coca paste.'

Then, in 2003, a leading Bulgarian gangster had his head blown off in the crowded foyer of the five-star Sonesta Hotel on the Caribbean island of Aruba. The murder was caught on the hotel's CCTV, revealing the killer to be Latin American in origin, according to the Oranjestad police. Bulgarian police suspected that the gangster had been killed for having stolen 600 kilograms of cocaine in 1999 and that this belonged to one of the Serb coke bosses. Evidently it had upset some Colombians on Aruba as well.

In the Balkans itself, major gangsters from all the former republics were involved in the trade and either making huge amounts of money or getting killed. In the summer of 2002, French police and the DEA thought they were getting close to finding the main channel between Colombia and the Balkans when they set up a complex sting operation. But French and American officers looked on aghast when Spasojevic was taken off a plane about to leave Paris for Bogota because the Serbian Government had ordered his extradition on suspicion of murder. By now Croatian paramilitary generals, Slovene businessmen and half of the Bulgarian underworld had become involved in this wild new industry, whose profits outstripped the traditional Balkan narcotic contraband, heroin and amphetamines. Most made considerable sums from the trade, although most are now dead. The business, of course, continues.

Just fifteen years ago, contraband through the Balkans was limited by the ubiquitous communist police force. But although war and sanctions led to one of the swiftest and highest degrees of criminalisation in the world here, the underlying cause for this lay elsewhere – in Russia.

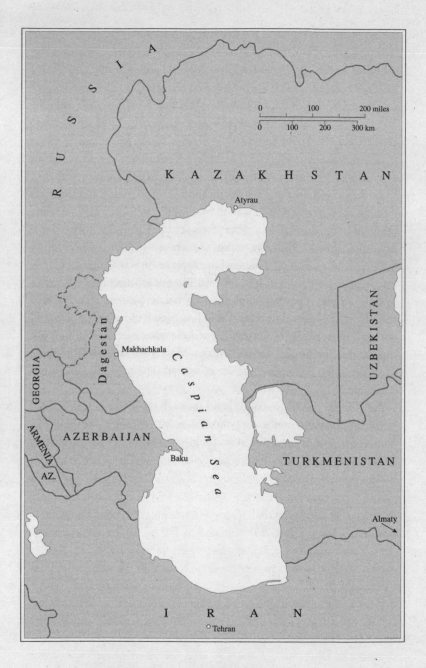

Atyrau and the Caspian – the centre of Kazakhstan's oil and caviar trades

3

THE *MAFIYA* – MIDWIVES OF CAPITALISM

Astride the great Ural River, the city of Atyrau is distinguished by the non-porous soil that lies beneath it, blocking all natural drainage. In winter, the river water rises, covering the paved roads and sidewalks in mud. For the first fifteen minutes of my visit to this town of 60,000 people, I tiptoe along the streets with trousers hitched, in the hope of keeping them clean. Then, like everyone, I yield to the gunk that has already plastered my shoes, socks, jeans and coat. The yellowy-brown walls of the Soviet-era housing appear to have been designed with the colour scheme of mud in mind. Inside, the grubby decaying hallways and elevators give off a powerful stink of urine.

This dilapidated architecture is common to hundreds of towns in the former Soviet Union, but in Atyrau it comes to an abrupt halt as one approaches the centre. Suddenly rows of pristine white houses stand in place of the socialist projects. Guards in slick blue uniforms patrol this displaced American suburbia laid out behind imposing fences. Opposite the gated community stands a postmodern office structure whose façade is dominated by glistening slanted windows. The district emanates efficiency, progress, cleanliness and wealth. Yet somehow the new Atyrau seems as soulless as the ageing Soviet slum it is replacing.

For all these bleak first impressions, Atyrau in Kazakhstan's far north-west is no ordinary post-Soviet wasteland. In economic terms, it is probably one of the ten most important areas in the former Soviet Union. The chief reasons for this (and for the invasion of Western offices and housing) are the huge reserves of oil and gas, about 50 per cent of Kazakhstan's voluminous capacity, that sit 100 miles and more away at the bottom of the Caspian Sea. The coast is a mere twenty miles distant at the delta of the Ural River. And yet, as most Atyrauans remind you, 90 per cent of the city's inhabitants have never seen the Caspian – the entire region around Atyrau was a restricted military and economic zone in the Soviet Union and remains one today.

Kazakhstan achieved its independence in 1991 through no effort, fault or desire of its own. The Soviet Union fell apart and Russia relinquished its direct political control over huge swathes of Europe and Asia. One such area was this little-known Central Asian country, which is larger than Western Europe, but home to a tiny population of fifteen million. To most people, the country's only claim to fame is Borat, the outrageous fictional Kazakh TV presenter invented by the British comedian, Sasha Baron Cohen. Borat's Kazakhstan is a land of donkeys and prostitutes. In reality, it is a land of great geo-strategic importance, wooed by Russia, America and China alike. Independence coincided with the dawning realisation that Kazakhstan's potential oil wealth might be immense, and it was not long before the great powers and great corporations were hovering over Atyrau, sniffing the riches and offering the technological know-how to extract as much of the energy resource as quickly as possible.

The question facing Kazakhstan today is whether its new/old elite (former communists turned Kazakh patriots) possess the wisdom to circumvent the 'curse of oil', or whether any nascent institutions of democratic accountability will be swamped by the tidal wave of human greed that accompanies the discovery of mineral treasure trove. The alternative to these institutions is a system that is regulated chiefly by corruption. Such has been the fate of countries like Angola, Nigeria and Indonesia, recently afflicted by the discovery of underground wealth, although Saudi Arabia remains the original, probably unbeatable model.

So far there are few signs that the electoral dictatorship of President Nursultan Nazarbayev has the capacity to distribute the money equitably, although with such a small population, he and his oligarchic friends have a real opportunity to do so.

The corrupt system of governance that the oil revenues have fostered also generates a permissive environment in which flourishes one of the world's most destructive criminal industries. I had not travelled to Atyrau to investigate the petroleum billions, but the other 'black gold' for which the city is renowned. The Ural River is home to the only remaining spawning grounds of the beluga sturgeon. As one approaches the river's delta, Atyrau quickly peters out and what remains of the road merges into a barren moonscape. Visibly poor fishermen shuffle glumly in their wading boots around the few desolate villages. They are reluctant to talk about the sturgeon trade, but one reveals how 'We receive three dollars per fish from the state when we sell them the caviar. But it gets more difficult each year. Fewer fish.' When the dead female's eggs have made the long journey from the Ural to the finest dining tables in New York or Paris, they will be worth $6,000–7,000 per kilo. This mark-up of more than 100,000 per cent is the sort of price hike that can tempt even the most law-abiding citizen. And there is no expensive drilling equipment involved. The only initial investment needed to harvest caviar is a net and a knife.

The decreasing availability of caviar in the Caspian has prompted the growth of one of the most profitable mafia operations in the former Soviet Union. In the last fifteen years, the Caspian Sea's sturgeon population has fallen dramatically. In 2004 just 760 tons of sturgeon were caught by the Caspian nations, down from 26,000 tons in 1985. This is a consequence of the frenzied programme of extermination that human beings have launched against an ancient species, which, until 1989, had faced with equanimity most evolutionary challenges since the dinosaurs. Before the collapse of communism, there were only two Caspian littoral states – the Soviet Union and Iran. But the break-up of the Soviet Union divided the coast among four new countries – Azerbaijan, Turkmenistan, Kazakhstan and the Russian Federation (which includes the frenetically unstable province of Dagestan). Unless Iran and these four new custodians of the Caspian introduce drastic remedial measures, the five main types of sturgeon of the former Soviet Union will be close to final extinction by 2010.

Officially, visitors to Atyrau are permitted to purchase 100 grams of caviar from the modest personal quota agreed between the Government of Kazakhstan and CITES, the Convention on International Trade in Endangered Species. Officers at the local Fish Protection Squad insist that it is impossible to find caviar for sale except in special shops regulated by the Government. Entering one of these is like stepping through a time portal that whisks me back twenty years to an authentic retail experience from the Soviet era. The paltry selection of goods projects a peculiar sadness – it is as if the merchandise is hiding from the attention of desperate-looking customers. In the display cabinets, a few sheets of parchment turn out to be desiccated carp scattered around four of five tiny pots of caviar. In the government shops, the system is clearly working – you cannot buy ludicrous amounts of top-quality caviar for next to nothing.

But one hundred yards away, I wander down the narrow channels of the city's main Bazaar. Here dozens of stalls boast richly coloured vegetables, sausages and cheese. Barking excitedly, traders extol the virtue of their goods as I am led into a bare room where five ageing Kazakh women sit and gossip. I ask the most craggy-faced of all if she has any caviar to sell. 'Sure,' she replies tersely as she lifts a cloth covering a table to reveal buckets of fresh, but illegal, caviar. 'What do you want? Fresh beluga, seasonal sevruga – we've got most in at the moment.' I gawp at her stocks, which are worth tens (if not hundreds) of thousands of pounds in the West. 'I'll take a kilo of the fresh beluga, please!' As she shovels my hoard of 'black pearls' into a square plastic salad container, I ask her, 'Can you give me a receipt to get this through customs at the airport?' She explains irritably that this is out of the question, but is busy writing down a number nonetheless. 'Here, call this man – he's called Nurlan, the Director of Customs at the airport.'

Later in the day, I transfer my contraband from its container into a sturdy glass jar with a tightly sealed lid. Like most internal Kazakh flights, my return to Almaty, the country's commercial capital 100 miles from the Chinese border, is scheduled inexplicably for two o'clock in the morning. Despite my exhaustion, I still want to discover what would happen if I do not invoke Nurlan's protection, so I place my luggage with the caviar through the X-ray machine before calling him.

The unfriendly policeman scanning the bags stops the machine as mine goes through.

'What's this?' he asks suspiciously, pointing at the caviar.

'It's some caviar I bought.'

'Wait here,' the policeman says, pocketing my passport and ticket.

He invites me into a back room and is on the verge of arresting me when I decide the time has come to call the cavalry: I dial Nurlan's cellphone. The policeman takes the call and smiles; seconds later, he hands me back my phone, passport and boarding pass. 'Have a nice flight, Mr Glenny,' he bids me farewell in his excellent English.

And that was it. Included in the price of 23,000 Kazakh tenge (about $175 for a kilo of the most sought-after caviar in the world – although note the mark-up from the river, $3 per kilo, to the market ten miles away) was a free, if corrupt passage through Atyrau customs, courtesy of its Director. And that is how it works – from the fisherman right up to the Parisian restaurant buyer: everyone is on the take except the wretched sturgeon.

My little kilo was a pebble on the Everest of caviar that the world had consumed since the early 1990s. (I say the world, but the United States accounts for one-third of the total, while Western Europe consumes some 38 per cent and the Middle East – especially the Gulf States – absorbs much of the rest.) Until the 1970s, the two Caspian states – Iran and the Soviet Union – were producing caviar at sustainable levels. Then, 'In 1977, the Soviet Government decreed a massive increase in the production and export of caviar because they desperately needed hard currency and this was an easy way to get it,' explained Artur Shakhnazarian. Gaunt, serious and with penetrating blue eyes, Shakhnazarian is an unlikely anti-mafia campaigner, although his courage should not be underestimated – he fought in two wars on the periphery of the Soviet Union as it was breaking up. Together with his energetic wife Oksana Martinuk, he has been fighting to prevent the extermination of the sturgeon for over a decade. 'They were over-fishing to such a degree that they ran out of rail trucks to export the stuff. To his credit, Mikhail Gorbachev put a stop to this overfishing and strengthened the Spetznaz [Special Forces] teams who were charged with protecting the sturgeon,' Oksana said.

In a short time, the armed protection and a new restocking programme had a demonstrably positive impact on sturgeon numbers. But after 1989 the police state that had cowed so many people for seven decades appeared to shrivel and die. 'At first the poachers came at night, shooting their way to the river. And then the boats started to appear off the coast and the fishing assumed an industrial scale,' remembers Artur. Gangsters began exporting caviar to Turkey, to the Middle East and to Moscow – truckloads, boatloads, trainloads, and even planeloads to Dubai. Azerbaijan was plunged into bitter conflict with Armenia and needed to finance its war effort. The Azeri oil fields were either underdeveloped or obsolete, and so caviar became the most important provider of foreign currency. The Republic of Dagestan in the Russian Federation descended into lawlessness, which saw the Russian customs and border guards fight a losing battle against one of the most ruthless branches of the caviar mafia; 20,000, 30,000 and then 40,000 tons of caviar were fished a year as the New Rich in Moscow gorged themselves on black pearls, selling on the excess to the West for huge profits.

In 1998, the oligarchs in Russia had been plundering the state and polluting the financial system to such a degree that the banks went into meltdown. Tens of millions of Russians found themselves below the poverty line overnight as their savings were eaten up by hyper-inflation. The rouble was worthless; the dollar was king, but was only available to those already bloated with wealth through criminal enter-prises or the stripping of state assets (if, indeed, these were discrete phenomena). Caviar, with its unsinkable hard-currency value, became even more prized.

Caviar seeps out of the Caspian region across every border and in every direction. At the port of Novorossiysk on the Russian Black Sea coast, the mafia sends hundreds of individuals by ferry to Samsun in Turkey every day. They all carry their personal entitlement of 250 grams of caviar. Once in Turkey, the caviar is recognised internationally as a legal *Turkish* product and can be exported without weight restriction. As a return ferry ticket costs about $10, there is plenty of profit for everyone and nobody is breaching the letter of the law. A little of this caviar finds its way to the fish restaurants around Istanbul's Taksim Square, but the bulk is sent on to the United Arab Emirates to be enjoyed by wealthy Westerners and Arabs in the preposterous hotels that have set new standards in unnecessary opulence. But the southern route pales in comparison to the real hub of the trade: Moscow. 80 per cent of illegal caviar is transported to the Russian capital for local consumption or export.

The collapse of the Soviet Union is the single most important cause of the exponential growth in organised crime that we have seen around the world in the last two decades. Almost overnight, it provoked a chaotic scramble for riches and survival. From the bitter wars of the Caucasus to the lethal shoot-outs in towns and cities, this was a deadly environment as a new class of capitalist exploited the vacuum of power by seizing whole industries and raiding the state coffers. Accompanied by an orgy of consumption and decadent behaviour, the like of which was last witnessed a century ago under Tsar Nicholas, it sucked almost every citizen into its vortex of violence. Even such mighty organisations as the KGB and the Red Army quickly became embroiled in this spectacular nightmare, whose repercussions travelled well beyond the Soviet Union's borders into all continents of the world, as money poured out of the country in the search for safe havens. Throbbing at the heart of these extraordinary events was Moscow.

Although shocking, terrifying and threatening, Moscow in the early 1990s was also thoroughly exhilarating – unless you got on the wrong end of a bullet. By 1993, when I made a short visit, the shootings had begun, the knock-out prostitutes were already soliciting in public with equanimity, the most exotic food and expensive wines were being piled high in the restaurants catering for the New Russians, the casino lights dazzled at night. I had by then become used to the chaos of the Yugoslav war, whose bloody logic was comprehensible, if repellent. But Moscow? I had been visiting the Soviet capital since the early 1970s, and was always struck by how joyless it seemed. Now it was unrecognisable – even since my last visit in 1991. The grandiose buildings were the same, but the sudden energy and the suppurating wealth were too much to grasp. This was a fantasy Russia. I spent an evening at a brand-new restaurant, eating food that would have garnered Michelin stars. I was flabbergasted by each mouthful, simply unable to conceive that this was indeed the reinforced-black-breaded, rubbery-boiled-egged and watery-souped Moscow that I remembered. Only the overweening brusqueness and a cheerful indifference to anything non-Russian remained constant. In two years Moscow. had been transformed into a breathtaking Babylon of guns, enterprise, money, violence and fun.

General Vladimir Rushaylo shook his head and smiled sympathetically at the businessman sitting opposite him.

'I can't pick him up, Artyom Mihailovich.'

'And why not?'

'For one thing, nobody's issued a directive telling me to, nor has anyone paid us to do so. And secondly, unless he were caught red-handed, then we'll have to carry out a long and tedious investigation, which would probably lead absolutely nowhere.' The head of Moscow's Anti-Organised Crime Unit, Rushaylo was apologetic, but couldn't see that it was any of his men's business to get mixed up in this case. 'When he shoots you or kidnaps you,' one of Rushaylo's subordinates chipped in helpfully, 'then we'll go after him!'

Artyom Tarasov understood the message clearly enough: blood on the pavement was sometimes enough to get the cops involved. But threats? If the desperately overstretched police had investigated mere threats in the bewildering circus that was Russia in the early 1990s, then they'd have had no time for anything else. Tarasov sighed. It seemed that he must continue unaided his uncomfortable dispute with a former business partner who was demanding a pay-off of several million dollars. He was just one among tens of thousands of Russians targeted by an extortion racket.

Looking back, Tarasov believes he was blessed with naivety. 'Sharks only move in for the kill when they can taste the fear of their victims,' he mused, 'and I don't believe I understood quite how serious things were with the gangsters at this time, so I wasn't as scared as perhaps I should have been.'

Tarasov's affable manner belies his exceptional business acumen, which transformed him from communist bureaucrat into Russia's first millionaire after Gorbachev's reforms had opened a window on private enterprise in 1988. 'Our first business was fixing Western television sets. There were no spare parts, so we had to improvise with Russian ones. And they worked – although if people had looked inside their sets, they would have seen a rather monstrous apparition: we couldn't get the genuine parts so we had to bodge them ourselves. After that I started a dating agency. I made thousands of dollars in a single week, but the police closed it down almost immediately for supposed immorality. It dawned on me that the market for these services was enormous.'

In 1988, the Soviet leader, Mikhail Gorbachev, introduced a Law on Cooperatives, which permitted characters like Tarasov to set up a business in Russia for the first time in sixty years. Entrepreneurs discovered that as soon as a business was up, running and making money, it attracted competition. 'And rivals would employ any method to muscle their way into your market,' he explained, 'including violence.'

Appealing to the police for protection was futile. As General Rushaylo's frankness in conversation with Tarasov demonstrated, the police (traditionally the imposing frontline of the Russian state's authority) were giving up the ghost. They had neither the intellectual nor the financial resources to adapt to the emergence of capitalism. And so the state, slowly but momentously, started to concede its monopoly on violence to the so-called *gruppirovki* or street gangs. But far from being harbingers of anarchy, these groups of men – Afghan veterans, street toughs, martial-arts experts, former KGB officers, and every one of them terrifying – were the indispensable midwives of capitalism.

Businessmen like Tarasov appreciated that the *gruppirovki* were in fact privatised law-enforcement agencies. In contrast to their state-run counterparts like the Interior Ministry (MVD) and the KGB, these flexible self-organised gangs had an instinctive understanding that there was a vibrant demand for their 'protection' or insurance services among the new business class. Instead of paying taxes to the state (which had no idea *how* to tax the new small-scale private enterprise), businesses willingly handed over 10–30 per cent of their turnover to local thugs, who would ensure in exchange that they could continue trading, free from the violence of *gruppirovki* working on behalf of their competitors. 'We are prepared to work with the racket because it charges ten per cent,' a businessman from Omsk noted at the time. 'The state takes ninety per cent in taxes and even more in fines.'

The emergence of the protection rackets was the first phase of a three-stage development that saw Russian organised crime steer a passage from petty-criminal origins to its position as a powerful transnational force that sought a fixed berth within the global economy.

With the state in collapse, the security forces overwhelmed and unable to police contract law, Tarasov explained that cooperating with the criminal culture was the only option. Above all, he stressed, most businessmen had to find themselves a reliable *krysha* under the leadership of an effective *vor*.

The words *krysha* and *vor* are as essential to understanding the Russia of the 1990s as *glasnost* and *perestroika* were to the Gorbachev era. *Krysha* literally means 'roof' and is the Russian word for a protection agency or racket, the purest meaning of the Sicilian word *mafia*. The *vor-v-zakonye* is a term that originated in the prisons of the Soviet period. It means thief-in-law, and refers to those criminal (as opposed to political) prisoners who were 'crowned' leaders by their peers. The *vory* were subject to a peculiar code of behaviour (they were not supposed to marry, for example), while subordinates considered their word final in the resolution of disputes between prisoners. 'Most of the *vory* were also run by the KGB, whether knowingly or not,' according to Peter Grynenko, a New York cop who specialised in Russian organised crime before setting up his own consultancy in Latvia. It was a means, Grynenko explained, by which the state monitored and controlled the criminal world, both inside and outside prison.

Some of the *vory* were tough, but others were there just for show. When the largest Slav protection racket in Moscow, the Solntsevo Brotherhood, was first emerging as a force in 1991, they invited a *vor*, Dzhemal Konstantinovich Khachidze, to join them. Nominally, Dzhemal was supposed to be Solntsevo's boss, but he brought little to the party apart from his status as a *vor*. 'This guy is a drunk and a drug addict, but they clean him up and teach him how to use a knife and fork, although they don't get him off the coke,' said Bobby Levinson, who ran the FBI's Russian Organised Crime desk in the 1990s. 'But they build him up for PR purposes and promote him as the *vor* behind the throne, as it were. And he begins to control the narcotics dealers on a protection-racket basis.' So the *vory* proved useful marketing for nascent protection rackets, but they were not necessarily effective operatives. 'All they'd ever done was sit around in prison being *vory*,' Grynenko said. 'None of them had actually done any serious killing or anything like that.'

And until the winter of 1991, it was indeed very tame stuff. The mob was largely a collection of inchoate street gangs, who still had to watch their backs for the cops and the KGB. However, the latter suffered a huge blow to their prestige and room for manoeuvre with the failure of the hardline coup in August 1991 that saw Gorbachev toppled in favour of an even more ambitious reformer – Boris Yeltsin. It was not long before Yeltsin was moving beyond even the most radical of his youthful team of disciples by announcing that on the eve of January 1st, 1992, the Russian Government would free all prices (with some crucial exceptions). With this single act, seventy years of centralist discipline, where the writ of the state penetrated the dustiest nooks of people's lives, went into hibernation for a decade. It took just months for Russia to descend into a surreal anarchic capitalism, the Wild East.

The pilots of Yeltsin's self-styled 'kamikaze cabinet' were two young economists, Yegor Gaidar and Anatoly Chubais. Guided by the watchword 'deregulate', they flew their planes into the engine room of the Soviet social contract, which had ensured a stable – if grim – course for seventy years. 'We dismantled everything,' explained Oleg Davydov, a key official at the Ministry of Trade, 'we began liberalisation in the absence of any controls.'

Price liberalisation, a dry economic term, was the starting gun for a roller-coaster ride into the unknown. For the American economists and advisers who swarmed to the Government in Moscow, this was a unique opportunity. Russia's economy became a giant Petri-dish of Chicago-school market economics, but among the cultures they were busy cultivating was a Frankenstein that slipped out through the door of their laboratory almost unnoticed.

This was partly because the reforms contained a number of catastrophic anomalies. The prices that mattered to millions of ordinary Russians – namely, bread and rents – were liberalised, while those prices that mattered to a tiny enterprising minority were not. In what Gaidar once referred to with gentle understatement as 'a mistake', the reform team inexplicably held down the prices of Russia's vast natural resources – oil, gas, diamonds and metals. A new class of traders could still buy these commodities at the old Soviet subsidised price, often as much as forty times cheaper than the world market value. This was a licence to print money.

At the same time, the Government agreed to privatise the state monopoly that the Soviet Union had imposed on the import and export of all goods and commodities. This monopoly compelled foreign companies to conduct their business with the Foreign Trade Ministry in

Moscow as an intermediary. When it came to settling the contract, foreign companies did not deal directly with the individual enterprises that were buying or selling. The Ministry would buy from the diamond mines or oil fields in Siberia at the subsidised prices, for example $1 a barrel of oil. It would then sell on to the foreign buyers at the price of diamonds or oil on the global market, pocketing the difference and channelling the profits back into the state coffers.

By exploiting the discrepancy between the high cost of raw materials on world markets, on the one hand, and their subsidised domestic prices on the other, this regime ensured that huge foreign-currency earnings afforded some compensation for the witless inefficiencies of the Soviet planned economy. The Ministry's monopoly was one of the few things about the Soviet Union that actually worked. It was a supporting wall of the economy: remove it without first installing a replacement and the house would collapse. The 'kamikaze cabinet' just removed it.

The coupling of a privatised foreign-trade mechanism with the retention of rock-bottom subsidised commodity prices gave birth within months to an entirely new species of robber baron – the Russian oligarch. The logic of this life form is simple: buy Siberian oil for $1 a barrel and sell it for $30 in the Baltic states and before long you become a very, very rich citizen. The state was no longer getting its cut from the deal. Instead that vast profit was going to a few individuals.

Within a matter of four years, a group of several hundred fabulously wealthy men and women had evolved, while an inner clique of mega-billionaires formed a cortex that exercised ever more decisive political influence over President Yeltsin. Between the oligarchs and tens of millions who had fallen into penury stood a small, fragile and exasperated middle class.

This process of enrichment was quite simply the grandest larceny in history and stands no historical comparison. As the New Russia dressed itself up to look like a responsible capitalist economy that was attractive to foreign investment, its most powerful capitalists were raiding its key commodities (mineral resources of almost incalculable value), trading them for dollars and then exporting these funds out of the country in the biggest single flight of capital the world has ever seen. As the IMF shovelled billions into Russia to stabilise the economy and prop up the rouble, the oligarchs sent even larger sums to obscure banks in every corner of the world, from Switzerland to the Pacific island of Nauru, to be swallowed almost immediately in bafflingly complex money-laundering schemes. The whole process was dramatic testimony to how venality and myopic stupidity are always likely to triumph in the absence of regulatory institutions.

The Soviet bureaucrats who still administered the state did not understand how to monitor, regulate or adjudicate the principles of commercial exchange. The result 'was that for all practical purposes the law-enforcement agencies themselves abandoned their task of safeguarding private commercial structures,' as Olga Kryshtanovskaya, the leading sociologist of the New Russia, explained. The police and even the KGB were clueless as to how one might enforce contract law. The protection rackets and mafiosi were not so clueless – their central role in the new Russian economy was to ensure that contracts entered into were honoured. They were the new law-enforcement agencies, and the oligarchs needed their services. Between them, the oligarchs and mafia groups defined the justice system of the New Russia. Between 1991 and 1996, the Russian state effectively absented itself from the policing of society, and the distinctions between legality and illegality, morality and immorality barely existed. In any event, there were no hard-and-fast definitions of organised crime, money-laundering or extortion and, by implication, all commercial transactions were illegal and legal at the same time. This applied as much to drugs and women as it did to cars, cigarettes and oil. Had the rule of law prevailed at the time, then there is no question that the oligarchs' behaviour would have warranted severe punishment.

Meanwhile, in an administration learning to cohabit with the new business conditions, some bad seeds were germinating. The old Soviet criminal-justice system may have had no capacity to regulate the rampant commercial activity that flourished from 1992, but individual bureaucrats could go a long way to facilitate it by rubber-stamping a timely loan from the Central Bank, or by granting a crucial export licence. The catchword at the time was 'resources' – the gangster's 'resource' was his ability to wield convincing violence. The oligarch could use his 'resources' to blag his way into the ownership of whole factories for a song, and then use this as leverage for further funds.

The bureaucrat's 'resource' was his rubber stamp, ever ready in the desk drawer. Each group sold its 'resources' to the other. 'In Soviet times,' explained Lev Timofeev, a mathematician and economist who was a prominent dissident in the Brezhnev period, 'the bureaucrat would initiate a deal. He well understood that he operated in a market – there were always shortages in the Soviet Union and a bureaucrat could sell his influence to help individuals overcome that shortage. The key shift in the 1990s comes when the individuals – that is, businessmen – approach the bureaucrat and offer a deal.'

This simple triangular conspiracy between oligarchs, bureaucrats and organised crime was happily concealed from most by the intense drama being acted out upon the streets of Moscow and other major cities: unbridled sexual activity, outrageous displays of wealth, and impenetrable political intrigues. Above all, it was hidden by the outbreak of violent mob wars.

'There were a number of *vory* who turned up that day – most of them Georgian. They had a clear mission: extract several million dollars from me or, failing that, kidnap me.' Artyom Tarasov smiled as he described one of his first *strelki* or gangster meets. *Strelki* were organized affairs whereby the *krysha* of one businessman would consult with the *krysha* of another in order to settle a contractual dispute. In 90 per cent of cases, the *strelka* would finish with an agreement, and both businessmen were obliged to follow the advice of their respective *kryshy*. On this occasion, however, Tarasov had a narrow escape.

'A veritable army emerged from both sides – thirty to forty men. This bunch of inveterate cut-throats had occupied the Club Volodya Cemago in Moscow's Taganka district. They were brandishing their weapons in a way that would have terrified any normal person . . .'

Tarasov was sent next door with his personal bodyguards to wait while his *krysha*, Malik and Shamad, negotiated with the *vory* from the other team. 'Suddenly there was this wild screaming:

– Why did you come here? What are you doing mixed up with this bastard?

Our boys were shouting at the *vory*:

– He's just dirt. And who do you think you are anyway?

– We are *vory-v-zakone*! they screamed back.

'Given that all were armed to the teeth, it was only a matter of minutes before they started shooting. I was brought into the hall. It was just like a gangster movie – totally unreal.'

Weighing up the situation, Tarasov made the right decision: he fled. Perhaps the first oligarch, or at least proto-oligarch, Tarasov was lucky to escape from this *strelka* alive. It was unusual for one of the businessmen at the centre of the unresolved dispute to be present at a meet. Meetings between protection rackets or *kryshy* to hammer out contractual difficulties between the businesses they represented were a daily affair. The vast majority of these meets were harmless – protection rackets were rational operations that sought to avoid unnecessary loss of their personnel. But by its very nature, there was a danger that the *strelka* might develop into a *razborka* or shoot-out.

Vadim Volkov, Russia's foremost student of 'violent entrepreneurs' as he describes them, explained, 'One cannot ignore or miss a *strelka*. Not only does failure to show up for a *strelka* automatically mean defeat; it also damages one's reputation . . . The most remarkable feature of the *strelka* is its semiotics. When setting up a *strelka*, participants do not negotiate many details, but there are subtle signs . . . All violent entrepreneurs are remarkably sensitive to these signs and know how to read them, since those who fail do not live long. Most important, one has to be able to predict the probability of a violent outcome and to prepare accordingly. How many people should be taken to the *strelka*? Should they all be armed and ready for a shoot-out? . . . Is it worth the risk?'

Tarasov's relationship with his *krysha* mirrored the links between oligarchs and organised-crime rackets in general. The millionaires and billionaires could not make and then hold on to their money without the protection of the rackets, and the gangsters flourished thanks to the oligarchs' demand for security. The richer the oligarch, the bigger and wealthier his protectors – mutually assured wealth creation.

The Russian protection rackets of the 1990s differed in three ways from the classic mob families of southern Italy or New York and Chicago.

a) They were indispensable for the transition from socialism
   to capitalism.

Despite the murders and the shoot-outs, the Russian mob actually ensured a degree of stability during the economic transition. Of course, by normal standards one might perceive extortion, kidnapping and murder as constituting a rather harsh policing regime; and most people would probably find it hard to approve of car theft, narcotics or sex trafficking as legitimate business enterprises. Yet Russia was not in a normal situation. No societies are free from organised crime except for severely repressive ones (and while North Korea has undoubtedly very low levels of organised crime, its state budget is decisively dependent on the trading of narcotics to criminal syndicates in neighbouring countries). But when you replace one set of rules (the Five-Year Plan) with another (free-market) in a country as large as Russia, with as many mineral resources and at a time of epochal shifts in the global economy, then such immense change is bound to offer exceptional opportunities to the quick-witted, the strong or the fortunate (oligarchs, organised criminals, bureaucrats whose power is suddenly detached from state control) that were absent hitherto. It is certainly true that the Yeltsin Government made some appalling errors. But they were under considerable economic pressure at the time as the crumbling Soviet system was no longer able to guarantee food deliveries to the people, and inflation (even before the freeing of prices) had hit at least 150 per cent and was still rising. Something had to be done.

By the mid-1990s the Russian Government estimated that between 40 and 50 per cent of its economy was in the grey or black sectors, and it is within this context that Russia and the outside world need to understand the phenomenon of organised crime: it emerged out of a chaotic situation and was very brutal, but its origins lie in a rational response to a highly unusual economic and social environment.

b) Unlike the traditional American and Italian mafias, members of the Russian gangs were not strictly bound by family loyalties. The codes of the *thieves' world* (which conferred honour and recognition on the *vory*) only survived a matter of months in Russia's primitive capitalism.

Before long the title of *vor* was up for sale. Instead of earning it by spending years in prison, you could simply buy it. This devalued the authority of the *vor*, and the strict hierarchy of thieves that had pertained in Soviet-era prisons crumbled in the face of street gangs and operational criminal networks.

One of the most violent and feared groups to emerge in Moscow and elsewhere was the Chechen mafia. Their mere reputation for being both fearless and gruesome was often sufficient to cow an opponent or persuade a businessman to take them on as his *krysha*. But their members were not drawn exclusively from the Caucasus, let alone from Chechnya: 'The Chechen mafia (who should not be confused with the guerrillas fighting in the Chechen war) became a brand name, a franchise – McMafia if you like,' explained Mark Galeotti, who has devoted the last fifteen years to studying the Russian mob. 'They would sell the moniker "Chechen" to protection rackets in other towns provided they paid, of course, and provided they always carried out their word. If a group claimed a Chechen connection, but didn't carry out its threats to the letter, it was devaluing the brand. The original Chechens would come after them.' So the Russian mafia as it developed was not guided by family loyalties, but solely by transactions. How much? Who for? What's in it for me? This meant that they were unpredictable, fluid and dangerous.

    c) In contrast to the five families of America's *Cosa Nostra*, there were thousands of these organisations in Russia.

By 1999 there were more than 11,500 registered 'private security firms', employing more than 800,000 people. Of these, almost 200,000 had licences to carry arms. The Russian Interior Ministry has estimated that there were at least half as many again that remained unregistered. Not surprisingly, this proliferation in arms translated into a proliferation in murders and assassinations. By 1995, thousands of murders were being committed throughout Russia every year, especially in Moscow, St Petersburg, Ekaterinburg and other major centres of commerce. The cost of taking out a rival in 1997 was '$7,000 for a "client" without bodyguards and up to $15,000 for one with bodyguards'. Paradoxically, if you were not involved in business or the protection industry, you were much safer in Moscow than in most other major cities. 'Solntsevo [a district on the outskirts of Moscow] was one of the safest places in Russia,' explained Alexei Mukhin, Moscow's most fastidious chronicler of organised-crime groups. 'You wouldn't get mugged there because that was the home base of the Solntsevo Brotherhood and they were genuinely proud of their origins.'

There were about twenty major gangs in Moscow and dozens of minor gangs, some of them Slav and others Caucasian. Although there were tensions between the so-called ethnic groups and the Slav groups, both sides were wary of each other's influence and firepower. Within the first five years, *Solntsevskaya bratva* (the Solntsevo Brotherhood) emerged as the biggest Slav organisation. Like its competitors, the Ismailovskaya and Lyubertsy, this Brotherhood started life in the early 1990s during the First Phase of Organised Crime – the Protection Racket – and rapidly brought about the Second Phase: Monopoly Control of Goods and Services. It shifted from being a privatised law-enforcement agency to becoming a fully fledged organised criminal syndicate.

Just outside the bleak centre of the Solntsevo (Sunnyside) district of Moscow, a small road leads to the village of Fedosinye – physically very near the buzzing metropolis, but spiritually closer to the peasant world of Tolstoy. Life here revolves around a modest but well-kept and brightly coloured church whose bells ring out with exceptional clarity. At the centre of the nine bells (a huge collection for such a small community) is the sonorous bass dome, on which is engraved, 'From the Senior Priesthood, the Charitable Foundation Uchastye, the Firm CB-Holding and the Solntsevo Brotherhood'.

The last three organisations were all the brainchild of Sergei Mikhailov, born into a modest working-class family in February 1958 and raised in the Solntsevo district. As a young man, Mikhailov trained to be a maître d'hôtel at the Sovietskaya Hotel in central Moscow, just south of the Dynamo Moscow soccer stadium. The job brought with it certain influence because, as a registered hotel for foreigners, it was one of the very few places in Moscow where alcohol could be purchased after 9 p.m. in the evening. 'Remember,' said an erstwhile colleague of Mikhailov, 'this was a country where collecting empty Western beer cans was considered chic. Actually having access to real alcohol after hours not only offered a certain prestige, it was a way to make money as well.'

In 1986, Mikhailov spent several months in custody for falsely claiming the insurance on his motorbike. After receiving a conditional jail sentence, he returned to Solntsevo and devoted himself to his other passion – wrestling. MVD reports from the time detail how he joined forces with another former prisoner, Viktor Averin, and together they began to take control of Solntsevo's streets. A map of Moscow shows how a majority of the most influential gangs emerged from the post-war working-class districts that sit immediately outside the M-KAT, Moscow's equivalent of the Beltway or the M25. Solntsevo grows like a wart off the south-west of the M-KAT. The cosmopolitan inhabitants of the city centre never considered these depressing zones an integral part of Moscow, nor were they particularly aware of their working-class inhabitants. But in the late 1980s the gangs started encroaching inwards as they sold their services of violence to businesses, or destroyed those who refused to purchase them. Areas like Solntsevo possessed the key resource for the development of protection rackets – lots of tough, unemployed, aggressive young males, easily identifiable by their beloved uniform of loose-fitting tracksuits (sometimes accompanied by a baseball bat), cropped hair and elaborate tattoos.

But Solntsevo offered more than just goons. One mile to the west lies Vnukovo, one of Moscow's biggest airports. A little further round the M-KAT is another airport, Domodedovo. And a little further still, and equally enticing, lies Southern Port (Yuzhny Port), the huge river docks through which goods from all areas of Russia pass into Moscow. The roads leading into Moscow via Solntsevo linked the Russian capital with Ukraine and the ports of the Black Sea. More commerce was concentrated here than in any other part of the city, and it was not long before the Brotherhood had established monopolies with allies at Vnukovo airport, a second airport, Sheremetyevo 2, as well as the Southern Port. This proved especially advantageous when the Brotherhood was developing its first enterprise outside of the protection business – the import of cars. As the oligarchs started to funnel huge amounts of cash into their pockets and organisations, there was a sudden rise in the demand not just for Western cars, but for luxury cars. In a short time, the Mercedes 600 had become the status symbol of the New Russians, and Solntsevo controlled much of the vehicle traffic into the capital.

By the mid-1990s, Moscow had the highest number of Merc 600s registered anywhere in the world.

In December 1989, Mikhailov, Averin and two other key leaders of the Brotherhood were arrested and held in custody for more than a year on suspicion of extortion. As in most similar trials of the time, witnesses just dropped their allegations or disappeared long before the case actually came to court. But the Solntsevo leadership had been imprisoned at a crucial time, just as the market was about to open up. On their return, they discovered that other groups were moving in on their territory. The Chechen mafia posed the greatest threat to Solntsevo. Hooked up to a network of tribal militias in the Caucasus, the Chechens had weapons, recruits, money and a reputation as fearsome fighters.

The Slav–Caucasian Gang War that engulfed Moscow for about two years from 1992 is often portrayed as driven by national antipathy between the two groups. According to this widely held view, the bloody shoot-outs between the Chechens and Solntsevo in particular (although there were also battles featuring other Caucasian groups, like the Armenians, Azerbaijanis and Georgians, as well as other Moscow Slav brotherhoods) represented an attempt by the Slav groups to demonstrate their patriotism at a time of rising tension between the Russian Army and insurgents in Chechnya itself.

There may have been elements of genuine nationalist ill will between the Caucasians and the Slav gangs, but behind the heady rhetoric there lay the predictable motive of economic interest. From 1988 to 1990, the Chechens had succeeded in wresting partial control of the Southern Port from the Solntsevo Brotherhood, as well as some of the key car dealerships. The most notorious clash between the two gangs took place in the summer of 1993 when Solntsevo became involved in a shoot-out with Chechen gangsters at the Kazakhstan Cinema. One of the Solntsevo legends, Cyclops, was killed in the battle, but slowly Mikhailov and his men were reasserting themselves as Moscow's top dogs. 'Solntsevo operated differently from other groups and here lies the key to its success,' said the FBI man Levinson. 'Every brigade with its own leader was autonomous, earning its own money. Each brigade organised their own protection rackets and their own scams. The cash was not funnelled up to the leadership – it was a loose confederation and allowed people leeway. The top leaders, who included Mikhailov, were known as the Big Four. They also ran their own businesses, but they split the profits four ways. But as membership dues, as it were, the smaller guys provided their services *gratis*. If there was a problem between brigades that required the intercession of one of the Big Four – then there had to be a split of profits between Mikhailov and those in dispute as the price of conflict resolution.'

The Solntsevo empire grew. From car showrooms and bars, it expanded into hotels and supermarkets. It also controlled three major markets in the centre of Moscow and at least three major railway stations. Mikhailov seemed to understand instinctively that he must distance himself from the group's overtly criminal activities. He refused to assume the crown of *vor*, insisting instead that he be described simply as a businessman.

As early as 1992, the organisation decided that it needed, like its competitors, to assume control of a financial institution. 'Most Russian banks at this time were not banks in any recognisable or meaningful sense,' explained Mark Medish, who under President Clinton worked at the US Treasury as an expert on the Russian economy. 'They did not take deposits or make credits; instead they made easy money by handling government transactions, borrowing state funds at low interest rates, then buying high-yield, short-term government bonds, making super profits.'

The move into banking brought Solntsevo and the top criminal syndicates still closer to the oligarchs. Together they set exuberant new standards in tastelessness as they celebrated their recent status among the world's super-rich.

One of the many ways they liked to flaunt their wealth was by throwing extravagant parties. A prominent oil executive threw a Soviet Union Nostalgia Party in a chateau outside Paris in the summer of 2004. It was a spectacularly ironic celebration of the system from whose downfall the oilman had garnered unbelievable riches. French peasants dressed as Soviet collective-farmworkers from the 1930s were driving their tractors around the fountain in front of the mansion. Heroic Soviet-era songs exhorting the working class to increase their production norms boomed out of loudspeakers. Underneath their fancy dress of greatcoats and Soviet Komsomol uniforms, the guests were clothed in the finest designer garb. Welcoming them into the main hall was an imposing hammer and sickle carefully positioned between two enormous red banners that covered most of the chateau's façade.

Inside, skipping between the fountains of champagne and lines of coke (carefully chopped and ready for use), women with miniskirts split to reveal their buttocks would writhe occasionally to the marching beat of 'Defenders at the Siege of Leningrad', or some such. Paintings and busts of Lenin, Stalin and Brezhnev glared down with staunch disapproval on the unproletarian bacchanalia that satirised their memory.

The party alone cost several hundred thousand dollars – a large sum to most of us, but an unimaginable fortune to all but a tiny clique of Russians. On top of that, there was the cost of two large passenger aircraft chartered to bring most of the guests in from Moscow that day and back two days later. There was a hierarchy within the party, with most guests having access to a variety of entertainments in different rooms, but only a privileged few allowed into the inner core. At the doors of this sanctum, the photographers stopped snapping and the videos stopped whirring as the oligarchs inside contemplated their billions and how to multiply them further.

The Soviet Union Nostalgia Party was a mere side-order in the movable orgiastic feast that was in constant preparation for the oligarchs and their entourages – family, friends, lawyers, heavies, PR associates, politicians, entertainers. To this day, they slide from Marseilles to Miami, from Athens to Ashkelod, and from Tokyo to Tahiti in search of ever more outrageous kicks.

The rape of Russia's assets enjoys pride of place in the boom of the global shadow economy during the 1990s. Not only did the oligarchs succeed in turning Russia upside down, but their actions had a huge economic and social impact on countries throughout Western Europe, in the United States, in the Mediterranean (above all in Cyprus and Israel), in the Middle East and Africa, and in the Far East. Unable even to claim that they were helping to police the transition to capitalism (as protection rackets undoubtedly were), their overall influence has been more destructive than most of Russian organised crime.

Those organised-crime bosses who survived the 1990s settled well into Putin's Russia. Several have Interpol red notices on them, wanted for crimes committed in Western Europe or the United States, but the government in Moscow shows no inclination to extradite them. Sergei Mikhailov, leader of the Solntsevo Brotherhood, has insisted that he is a legitimate businessman who now conducts much of his work in China. Chasing down alleged members of a global mafia is low on Beijing's priority list. Other mobsters now make their living brokering major gas and oil deals between Russia, its neighbours and Western Europe, recording handsome profits for their clients and themselves. Many remain in the opaque world of private security. President Putin has restored the power and prestige of the KGB (under its new acronym, the FSB), where he spent most of his career before his unexpected political elevation as Russia's Prime Minister in the late 1990s.

Under Putin, the Kremlin has clipped the wings of several of the most powerful oligarchs. From exile in the West or from inside prison, oligarchs like Boris Berezovsky and Mikhail Khodorkovsky warn that the new President is the reincarnation of Stalin. But he isn't. He has fashioned a novel system that brings together aspects of capitalism and Soviet socialism – market authoritarianism. The oligarchs' desperate attempts to portray Putin as the new Stalin seek to conceal the primary responsibility they bear for the mess in which they and Russia find themselves.

After the period of 'easy money', as the early 1990s were called, the oligarchs could offer such attractive rewards that they were able to buy whoever they wanted. When senior members of the KGB/FSB and MVD (Interior Ministry) observed how their influence was sinking as the wealth and power of the oligarchs grew, many decided to switch horses. The Russian Security Services have experienced fluctuating fortunes since the Gorbachev period. Some members established companies abroad as covers for industrial espionage and money-laundering. Others were less fortunate, and in 1992 the KGB's financial situation deteriorated to such an extent that officers were forced to sell light bulbs and toilet paper stolen from their headquarters in the Lyubyanka prison (as sacrilegious, surely, as nicking candlesticks from St Peter's in Rome).

Almost all major oligarchs and business empires started to employ former KGB men to advise them on security. Vladimir Gusinsky, the media magnate and one of the most influential early oligarchs (before he fell foul of Putin), appointed Filip Bobkov as the boss of his security. Bobkov achieved notoriety in the 1980s as the former head of the KGB's 5th Directorate, which was responsible for combating dissidents in the Soviet Union. 'These days everyone is doing it!' Artyom Tarasov told me in his Moscow office. 'I was talking to my old employee, Viktor Vekselberg – you know, the one who bought the Fabergé eggs for Russia – who is one of the men behind the oil consortium, TNK-BP. He was telling me the other day that he currently has twenty former KGB generals on his payroll!'

The death of Alexander Litvinenko, the former senior KGB officer poisoned in his London exile in late 2006, revealed how confused the relationship between the KGB and private Security Services had become. In the late 1990s, Litvinenko himself had been assigned to protect the oligarch Boris Berezovsky while still working for the KGB, and one of the prime suspects in his murder was another former KGB man who ran his own private security firm, and had once also provided protection to Berezovsky.

Through such characters, the oligarchs were in a position to exercise influence over the residual forces of law and order in what is known as the 'deep state', the mighty forces of political influence that operate behind the scenes even in ostensible chaos. It went further, though – the integration of high-ranking KGB and MVD personnel into the paid retinues of the oligarchs triggered the privatisation of Russia's security forces. During the 1990s, the two iconic institutions of Soviet power, the KGB and the MVD, became simply another competing private law-enforcement agency. In one fundamental sense, they were no different from the *Solntsevskaya bratva*: their services were available to the highest bidder.

As a consequence, different branches of Russia's Security Services would find themselves fighting against each other on behalf of warring oligarchs. On December 2nd, 1994, Vladimir Gusinsky noticed that he was being followed by a group of large, intimidating masked men as he drove to his offices on Novy Arbat. These also housed the offices of his chief political sponsor, Yuri Luzhkov, the Mayor of Moscow and a political rival to Boris Yeltsin. As the owner of NTV, the most popular independent television station, Gusinsky was among the most influential oligarchs and one who excited jealous outbursts among his peers.

Boris Berezovsky, the first among equals in the oligarchy, persuaded President Yeltsin that Gusinsky needed to be taught a lesson. In late November, an article called 'The Snow is Falling' in a pro-Yeltsin newspaper had claimed that Gusinsky's Most Company was 'planning to force its way into power'. If this was a shot across the bows, December 2nd witnessed a full-scale broadside. The masked men started roughing up Gusinsky's bodyguards in the oligarch's car park. Watching from his office and feeling increasingly alarmed, Gusinsky was calling his contacts inside the counter-intelligence service of the KGB. These guys turned up and a *razborka* (shoot-out) broke out. Before blood was spilled, however, one of the KGB men realised that their opponents were from the Presidential Security Service. They decided to withdraw. The more powerful the oligarchs became, the more damaging their rivalry. This both parodied and accentuated the rivalries that existed within Russia's security forces.

'All of us from the intelligence networks sat up when the shoot-outs between the KGB and the Interior Ministry began,' the former head of a Balkan intelligence service told me. He had grown up with a profound admiration for the KGB and observed the events in a state of shock. 'We then realised that the situation in Russia had run out of control. We could no longer rely on them – it was like losing a father.'

The KGB officers and networks who had outsourced their services formed the middle belt of a pyramid supporting the opulent oligarchs at the top. The Security Services provided a crucial link with the state. But at the bottom of the pyramid, bolstering the entire structure, was a diverse group of people known as the *zashchita*, or 'defence'. This included a host of professionals – lawyers, PR companies, journalists (and, in the case of a few oligarchs, entire newspapers or television stations) – and anybody who might contribute to the defence of the oligarch's interests. The core of the *zashchita*, however, remained the *krysha* – the protection racket or mob. 'Russian organised crime is thus characterised by at least three seamless webs,' explained Jon Winer, President Clinton's Deputy Assistant Secretary for International Enforcement (or Drugs and Thugs, as it is known colloquially in

Washington), 'between extortionists and security companies . . . between licit and illicit business . . . and between criminals on the one side and political and bureaucratic elites on the other. Out of these seamless webs has emerged a triangle of crime, business and politics', which is 'extremely strong and resilient'.

But the final link between the oligarchs and the most powerful mafia groups was forged through a common interest – the need to launder money. The Solntsevo Brotherhood and the Chechens in Moscow, and other huge syndicates, like Tambovskaya in St Petersburg and Uralmash in Ekaterinburg, had reached the Second Phase on the path towards a global mafia status: they were all whole or partial monopoly controllers of specific goods and services. Across the world, the trade in narcotics was one of the most profitable criminal activities. All the major criminal groups in the former Soviet Union had built up extensive business interests in the manufacture of amphetamines and Ecstasy, in the importation of cocaine into Europe and, above all, in the distribution and sale of heroin from Central Asia into Eastern and Western Europe and the USA.

The oligarchs instinctively understood that Russia was a capricious and dangerous environment and that their billions of dollars were not safe there. They overestimated their ability to control President Putin, the man whom they chose to replace the weak and easily manipulated alcoholic President Yeltsin. Yet their instincts served many of them well – as an insurance policy, they needed not just to get their money out of the country; they needed it to be clean once it arrived. So did the organised-crime groups. Everybody needed to launder their cash. But before they could establish a worldwide launderette, they all – oligarchs and mobsters alike – needed to establish themselves abroad. The criminal groups now entered the most challenging stage of their development, the Third Phase: Transplantation Abroad.

4

SPREADING THE WORD

Immediately on arrival at Prague's Ruzyne prison in August 1999, Tomas Machacek put in a request to the Governor that he be placed in solitary confinement. 'I had no choice,' he explained. 'They would have killed me. No question. There were a lot of Russians there.'

It had been a hard fall for Machacek. Five years earlier, he had been recognised as one of the most promising young policemen in the Czech Republic when, at the age of just twenty-six, he was appointed leader of ALFA, the new Anti-Russian Organised Crime Unit. Now he was incarcerated in the isolation block where Czechoslovakia's erstwhile communist leaders had once locked up Vaclav Havel. An honest cop in a corrupt system, Machacek is a real-life Arkady Renko, the quietly intelligent detective in Martin Cruz Smith's novels, *Gorky Park* and *Stalin's Ghost*, engaged in a quixotic struggle with darker and much more powerful forces.

Machacek's downfall can be traced to the moment of his greatest success. In May 1995, ALFA got a tip-off that a mafia murder was being planned. Major Machacek, as he was then, coordinated fifty officers for a raid on the restaurant U Holubu (The Doves) in Prague's once-dowdy working-class district of Andel; 250 guests were dining on sushi when Machacek ordered his men to break up the fortieth birthday celebration for Viktor Averin, deputy boss of the Solntsevo Brotherhood.

As the raid got under way, Machacek noted disconcertedly that the Russians appeared neither surprised nor worried. 'None of them resisted – they all knew what was happening and lay on the ground obediently,' he said. 'None of them had guns, and we knew from our intelligence that their security guys were always armed.' Machacek went cold. 'We had decided to go ahead only a few hours beforehand. And yet somebody had tipped them off.' The implication was clear – a senior figure in the Czech police was working with the Russian mafia.

No charges were preferred against any of the guests, but ALFA did gather sufficient evidence to ban key Russian mafia figures, like Sergei Mikhailov of the Solntsevo Brotherhood, from the Czech Republic for ten years (most promptly moved to Hungary). 'At least we were able to send them a message that they could not use Prague as a spring-board from where they could travel the world and manage their various narcotics and arms businesses,' explained Machacek. 'Time, Gentle-men, please!'

This was both a blow and an insult to the Russians, as Prague and in particular the spa town of Karlovy Vary (Carlsbad) had become the top leisure destination for the New Russians in Central Europe (four-fifths of Carlsbad's splendidly pompous Habsburg properties are now Russian-owned).

Police forces around Europe hailed Machacek's achievement and, on a working trip to Washington, he was fêted by Louis Freeh, the head of the FBI. Freeh pointed out that the raid on U Holubu had provided the world's law-enforcement officers with the first detailed documentation and photographs of the Solntsevo Brotherhood and its associates. Still in his twenties, Machacek looked set for great things.

But although U Holubu was renowned as a meeting place for Russian and Ukrainian mafia and businessmen, they were not the only ones who enjoyed the facilities there. Adorning the restaurant were photographs of the owner, Antoly Katrich, 'with Czech politi-cians, Czech businessmen, actors and other celebrities', as Machacek recalls. 'For example, there was a photo of Katrich with . . . ministers. At our request, Jan Ruml, the Interior Minister, told the cabinet that they should desist from frequenting U Holubu and associating with these people. They ignored him.'

An anonymous letter had prompted Tomas Machacek to launch the raid on U Holubu in May 1995. Its author claimed that the Solntsevo leadership was planning to murder a certain Semyon Mogilevich during the birthday celebrations that night. Machacek knew that Mogilevich was a powerful man and a close associate of Solntsevo. But it was also rumoured that Mogilevich and Mikhailov had fallen out over a payment of $5 million.

Yet that evening Mr Mogilevich didn't turn up. Or at least he turned up only after Machacek had launched the raid. 'By the time I arrived at U Holubu everything was already in full swing,' said Mogilevich later, 'so I went to a neighbouring hotel and sat in the bar there until about five or six in the morning.' If Mogilevich is – as most police forces in Europe and America claim – the true *capo di tutti capi* of Russian organised crime, then he is always two steps ahead of everyone else in the game. Effortlessly.

Not long after Averin's birthday party, a few Czech politicians and newspapers began questioning the motive behind the raid. This developed into a campaign. Commentators and opposition politicians claimed that the storming of U Holubu was 'an outrageous assault on legitimate businessmen enjoying a night out'. A myth developed (still readily available on the Internet) that the police had carried out the raid Rambo-style, crashing through the ceiling and abseiling into the main hall. Rumours spread that Machacek and his close colleagues were unreliable and on the take.

'I used to just ignore the anonymous threats and telephone calls. And I dealt with the obscene letters sent to my wife,' he explained. But one August morning, when things seemed to have settled down, an officer of the police's internal investigation unit arrested Machacek out of the blue as he was arriving for work. He was disarmed and taken into custody, accused of malfeasance by a corrupt customs officer whom he had never met, in a location where he had never been.

The Habsburg Empire was the primary inspiration for Franz Kafka's two great fictional nightmares, *The Castle* and *The Trial*, in which an omnipotent and amoral bureaucracy, without mercy and without apparent reason, pursues a frightened individual known simply as K. Kafka's fictional world became real after Stalin installed the Communist Party as the 'leading force' in Czechoslovakia in 1948. Throughout much of the forty years that Prague endured communist control, people were kept in fear lest this administrative leviathan came knocking at their door with an arrest warrant. The Velvet Revolution in November 1989 was meant to put a stop to all this.

But while Kafka's bureaucracy may have moved into the shadows after the Revolution, it still lurked discreetly. Soviet structures had penetrated deep into the fabric of Eastern Europe – through the Party, the military, industry, the secret police, cultural associations. For the great majority who did not engage in political protest, life in this system was tedious but stable, and that stability enabled many personal and institutional links to bind together the elites of the Warsaw Pact members.

With his arrest, Machacek felt the full force of these opaque structures as he was publicly vilified. But the Czech state was compromised as well. Machacek's computers and files were stripped when he was put in jail, risking exposure of his entire network of informers and undercover agents. Disillusioned with his treatment, Machacek's close colleagues began leaving the Organised Crime Unit and other intelligence branches to seek work in the private sector. Regular policemen were also disillusioned. Trained under communism and hence used to obedient civilians, the police bemoaned the lack of respect they now encountered. 'We are underpaid and have no resources – the criminals have faster cars, much more money and contacts higher up, if things go wrong,' one said.

Eventually the courts recognised that Machacek had been stitched up and he was offered any job he wanted. 'I declined. I couldn't go back to an office where I would bump into people who I know had betrayed me, who were corrupt and about whom I could do nothing.'

Organised crime and corruption flourish in regions and countries where public trust in institutions is weak. Refashioning the institutions of Kafkaesque autocracy into ones that support democracy by promoting accountability and transparency is a troublesome, long-term process. The task is made doubly difficult if economic uncertainty accompanies that transition. Suddenly people who had been guaranteed security from the cradle to the grave are forced to negotiate an unfamiliar jungle of inflation, unemployment, loss of pension rights, and the like. At such junctures, those crucial personal networks from the communist period become very important. The Red Army evacuated its bases in Eastern Europe, but the equally effective, yet more seductive, force of favours-owed and promises-once-made stood its ground to exert a strong influence over the transition.

Poland, the Czech Republic and Hungary were the most sought-after destinations of Russian oligarchs and organised-crime syndicates like Solntsevo. They knew the terrain and, in the first two, language barriers were less formidable than in Western Europe. There was one thing that distinguished these three states from the rest of Eastern Europe – they were all fast-tracked to join the European Union, and that was the quickest route to the gold at the end of the rainbow. 'These countries were the gates to the West,' noted *Business Week*. 'Their growing economies and borders with the EU offered firms located in this region the most precious commodity – legitimacy.' Moreover, there was money to be made in these countries, and one commodity proved especially lucrative: oil.

Tamas Boros, known as the Giant or Big Tom, was walking in Budapest with his lawyer past a Polish Fiat 500 just before midday on July 2nd, 1998 when somebody detonated the eight pounds of TNT attached to the vehicle's underside. The blast sliced him literally in two. The explosion and consequent deaths shook Hungary badly. Until this point, the dozens of mafia murders committed in the Hungarian capital since the early 1990s had resulted in no collateral casualties – the assassins had proved strikingly accurate. The public response to mafia killings was even one of muted approval, along the lines of 'One fewer gangster in the world, so what?' But this was different. It took place in broad daylight just yards away from Vaci utca, Budapest's most fashionable shopping street, which was packed with people. Three innocent bystanders died with Big Tom, while twenty more, including foreign tourists, were injured as several vehicles were obliterated, causing carnage. The public was outraged and it wanted some answers.

Detectives at the Hungarian Organised Crime Squad had several leads to work on. If anything, their list of suspects was too long. For the past year, Boros had been dishing the dirt to them about his colleagues in the criminal fraternity. Now there were at least six Hungarian organised-crime groups making a bid for Boros's territory after his murder, and several became key suspects as the investigations dragged out over years.

It didn't take long for the Hungarian police to look east towards

Russia, working on leads that Boros himself had given them in his confession. 'It all started,' he told them, 'when this Russian guy called Uncle Seva turned up.' By the time of Boros's murder, 'Uncle Seva', aka Semyon Mogilevich, had already been declared *persona non grata* in Hungary and received a ten-year entry ban from the Czech Republic's Interior Ministry (slapped on him after the bust at U Holubu).

The police went on to discover that Boros had been involved in the biggest single criminal scam to hit Europe during the 1990s – the Heating Oil Scandal. Suppliers of heating oil from Ukraine and Romania to the Czech Republic, Slovakia and Hungary were exempted from paying duty on the product, so it was considerably cheaper than fuel for petrol engines. But once across the border, the gangs put the oil through a simple chemical treatment that rendered it compatible with motor vehicles. The petroleum was then sold to the gas stations, but the gangsters would pocket the tax revenue. 'The Heating Oil Scandal could have been solved with just two extra sentences in the law concerning the dyeing of oil products,' the Czech Republic's then Deputy Interior Minister, Martin Fendrych, explained. 'We pointed this out to the Finance Ministry and they sat on it for two years. Why? Go and ask them!'

The scam sucked billions of dollars from the exchequers of the three countries over a three-year period. The industry was so lucrative that it caused dozens of murders in all three countries as businessmen, customs officers, cops and politicians scrambled for a share of the profits. According to Hungarian police, Boros's claim that Mogilevich had moved in on the industry in Hungary was probably his death sentence.

Unfortunately, speculation is often what the police are left with when dealing with Semyon Mogilevich (or Papa, as Russian criminals call him). Law-enforcement agencies around the world have been seeking to prosecute Mogilevich for more than ten years now, but the man has a knack for never being in the wrong place at the wrong time. In a Tel Aviv café, Ze'ev Gordon, one of Mogilevich's key lawyers, told me, 'Mogilevich may be guilty and he may be innocent. I don't know,' he argued. 'But in order to establish the truth, you have to produce evidence that stands up in a court. And so far nobody has done that or even come close.'

There is a wealth of material about Mogilevich's supposed evil doings on the Internet, but the legal case against him is flimsy. He is no longer sought on charges of arms dealing and running prostitution rackets, as he once was. The FBI has him on its Most Wanted List, but has a warrant for his arrest only in connection with a large-scale fraud in which he is alleged to have fleeced Canadian investors of tens of millions of dollars, perpetrated through a variety of companies and known as the YBM Magnex scandal. The Feds do warn that Mogilevich is armed and dangerous, but they are not seeking him on counts of arms and drugs-running, for which in private they claim he is responsible.

Indeed, most Western law-enforcement officers engaged in anti-organised-crime work insist in private and in public that he is probably the most powerful Russian mobster alive. Describing him as 'one of the most dangerous men in the world', the British Government barred him from the United Kingdom following an extensive investigation into his business activities. 'I can tell you that Semyon Mogilevich is as serious an organised criminal as I have ever encountered,' insisted Clinton's Anti-Organised-Crime Tsar Jon Winer, 'and I am confident that he is responsible for contract killings.' 'Who did he kill?' I wanted to know. 'I cannot address the issue of who.'

This implies that Western governments rely on intelligence material that is not admissible in court. For all the periodic warnings about Mogilevich, Mikhailov and other big Russian mafia dons, Western police appear to have limited capacity to prosecute these men in courts of law. In 1996, the Swiss prosecutor, Carla Del Ponte (later made famous or notorious, depending on your viewpoint, at the Yugoslav War Crimes Tribunal in The Hague), oversaw a major case against Sergei Mikhailov for money-laundering. Despite having some first-class witnesses (including a Russian law-enforcement officer since compelled to go into witness protection in Switzerland), the prosecution made a dog's breakfast of the case. Not only was Mikhailov acquitted of all charges, but Switzerland paid him half a million dollars in compensation for wrongful imprisonment.

Neither Mikhailov nor Mogilevich travels to the West any more (although Mogilevich still retains his Israeli passport). But they potter happily around Moscow, seemingly unconcerned and apparently untouched by the Russian state.

Who knows how many thousands of punters tried their luck when Casino Capitalism opened up in Eastern Europe? Most left the game empty-handed. For every story of a dazzling entrepreneur creating a business empire in half a decade, there were dozens who gave it their best shot, but had to return in the end to the job market with not a penny to show for their endeavour.

Most business analysts would have placed Eural Trans Gas (ETG) in the no-hoper category when it set up shop in Hungary in December 2002. ETG had few resources, and the tiniest of premises in Csabdi, an anonymous village twenty miles west of Budapest. The nominal shareholders were hardly business-school material. Louise Lukacs was an unemployed actress from the Transylvanian city of Cluj. Her career had peaked almost twenty years earlier when she starred in *Tears of a Girl*, Romania's entry at Cannes, which was shortlisted for a prize. Louise explained that she had agreed to become an ETG shareholder because the company might pay her. 'At least to cover my phone bill,' she said. 'I have to pay more that $35 a month for the phone.'

Louise recruited two similarly unlikely pioneers to the venture in this emerging market: an IT worker and his partner, a nurse, who lived with her mother in a cramped flat. Like Louise, they were on the breadline.

A fourth shareholder, Ze'ev Gordon, Mogilevich's Tel Aviv lawyer, was clearly the odd one out. What was he doing there? What was anyone doing in this company, which had registered assets of $12,000 and an unmanned office in Csabdi? 'I was merely asked to act as a shareholder for a Ukrainian businessman, Dimitri Firtash. It was a service, that's all,' Gordon told me.

He certainly did Firtash a good turn. In its first year of business, ETG went from being a $12,000 business to recording a $2 billion turnover, posting pre-tax profits of $180 million. Not bad, eh?

But then there was the CEO, one Andras Knopp, a former Hungarian Minister of Education during communism, whose most recent job had been as the senior representative in Moscow of Reemtsma, the huge German tobacco concern. In an interview after the extent of ETG's success became clear, Knopp confessed that 'Strictly speaking, the shareholders remain three Romanian citizens and an Israeli, but the real parents are Gazprom and Naftohaz Ukrainy (NAK).' The Russian and Ukrainian gas conglomerates, he suggested, had not received the requisite paperwork to register the company in Hungary before December 31st, the cut-off point for new businesses in Hungary to qualify for offshore status (and greatly reduced tax liabilities). Instead, in order to secure the tax break, the unwitting Transylvanian trio and Ze'ev Gordon were parachuted in as intermediaries to form the company earlier.

This explanation was not implausible – instead of paying 18 per cent company tax, ETG would pay only 3 per cent company tax until 2005, coincidentally the date when its only two contracts would run out: one with Gazprom, and one with NAK to transport gas from Turkmenistan (the Caspian's most outrageous dictatorship) to Western Europe across Russia and Ukraine. A legal tax dodge – fair enough.

But why then did Gazprom and NAK flatly deny their parentage of ETG? NAK publicly stated that ETG was a 'Gazprom contractor'. Gazprom responded by saying that NAK selected ETG. And why did they sign a contract for a job that they could do themselves without difficulty? And why did they deny the fruits of this revenue to themselves and their shareholders, handing them instead to a shoebox operation from a Hungarian village?

Gazprom is a monster. With an annual turnover of just under $30 billion, it accounts for nearly one-third of global gas production, 8 per cent of Russia's GDP and almost a quarter of Russia's tax receipts. Gazprom aspires to be – and may well become – the single most influential energy company in the world (if it isn't already). As Minister for the Soviet Gas Industry just before the collapse of communism, Viktor Chernomyrdin, later to be appointed Prime Minister of Russia, channelled the USSR's immense natural-gas resources into a single state company in 1989. Four years later, the company was privatised. It has an effective monopoly control over the Russian gas-pipeline system. Any gas coming out of Turkmenistan, Uzbekistan or Kazakhstan that seeks a home on the Western European markets must travel through Gazprom's pipelines, giving the Russian giant considerable leverage over its direct competitors. In recent years it has become a brutal tool in Russian foreign policy, its clout used to exert pressure on former Soviet republics like Georgia and even on its largest client, Western Europe.

Why, then, would Gazprom pay another firm, with which it had no ostensible connection, to transport gas that Gazprom owns through Gazprom's pipelines? Gazprombank loaned ETG $70 million and guaranteed a $227 million commercial loan. It made no sense whatsoever – unless, perhaps, those strangers were friends in disguise.

By 2000, when Vladimir Putin succeeded Boris Yeltsin as Russian President, the patience of Gazprom's small but vocal private-investor shareholder group was running low. Their main irritation concerned the influence of a mysterious offshore company with offices in Jacksonville, Florida, called Itera International Energy Corporation.

The most tenacious private investor was William F. Browder, the grandson of America's wartime communist leader, Earl Browder. Browder's company, Hermitage Investment, had invested in Gazprom and he wanted to know why the energy giant was putting billions of dollars' worth of work Itera's way, which Gazprom itself could do perfectly well. Using public sources, he researched unusual payments between Gazprom and Itera. He discovered that senior company officials were organising huge transfers – and not just to players along the pipeline route. 'The arrogance was so extreme that there was no cover-up whatsoever,' Browder remarked. 'But that was helpful to us, because it enabled us to paint a very accurate picture.'

One of Itera's most lucrative contracts concerned the transport of gas from the fields of Turkmenistan to Ukraine, which landed them $120 million profit annually. But Gazprom's small shareholders, like Bill Browder, wanted to know why they should be deprived of these dividends. Furthermore, nobody could ascertain who was benefiting from those profits.

As soon as he assumed power, President Putin let it be known that he was not going to tolerate such arch theft, and he singled out Gazprom as a specific target for his attention. To the surprise of many, Putin was quick to make good on his promise, replacing the company's discredited CEO with a friend from his St Petersburg KGB milieu.

Itera's days as a Gazprom protégé were numbered. At the beginning of 2003, Gazprom announced it would not renew the contract, specifically for the transit of Turkmen gas to Ukraine. 'Why should

Itera make super profits using the facilities of Gazprom,' thundered the Deputy Chairman of Gazprom. The company, he continued, would henceforth run the transit operations itself.

Except that it wouldn't.

Two months prior to Gazprom's renewed public commitment to transparency and propriety, its bosses had signed a secret deal with the tiny ETG, the day after it was registered in Hungary. Similarly, Gazprom's Ukrainian equivalent, Naftohaz Ukrainy, had also signed up with the new company, giving the latter exclusive rights for the transport of Turkmen gas across Ukrainian territory to Western Europe.

Over the next year and a half, ETG's curious relations with shadowy companies in Cyprus, Turkmenistan, Moldova, the Seychelles, France, Britain and elsewhere emerged. And an internal memo from the Paris-based Organisation for Economic Cooperation and Development raised the possibility of connections between several of these companies and associates of Semyon Mogilevich.

Ever since news about ETG became public, Western journalists and police forces have been furiously seeking a smoking gun that might link Mogilevich to the scam. Roman Kupchinsky, a tenacious journalist who writes on organised crime for Radio Free Europe, came close when he published a letter by the Deputy Head of Russia's Organised Crime Unit, which explicitly linked Andras Knopp with Mogilevich in an alleged cigarette-smuggling racket. Within weeks, however, ETG had produced a sworn affidavit from the Russian lawman, which stated that the letter was a fake. The case collapsed.

Whether or not proof emerges of Mogilevich's involvement is immaterial in two respects. First, huge sums of money went into a company whose ownership structure is entirely opaque and which should not have been offered the contract in the first place. Second, this company ETG had a turnover of $2 billion per annum – with no proper oversight of these accounts, all manner of funds could be channelled through the company that were not necessarily the product of the Ukrainian gas trade. If ETG had been a huge money-laundering vehicle, no one would have known. Although the company has since lost the Turkmen–Ukrainian contract, its role has been replaced by another unnecessary intermediary, RosUkrEnergo, which is also part-owned by Dimitri Firtash, the man who Ze'ev Gordon explains was behind ETG.

For this perverse business operation to succeed, ETG (whoever it represented) required the absolute support of the Gazprom and NAK leaderships. But it also required protection from both the Russian and Ukrainian states (and indirectly from the notoriously vain, now-deceased dictator of Turkmenistan, Saparmurat Niyazov, whose insatiable appetite for cash was one of the main motors behind the scam) as these two gas giants are at the very heart of the energy policy.

The ETG scam remains a mysterious, inscrutable affair. Whoever conceived the idea was determined to remain anonymous. It is hard to ascertain whether it was gross corruption or simply criminal or, indeed, where the boundary between the two lies. But what it does demonstrate beyond doubt is that if a syndicate persuades a powerful state to acquiesce or cooperate in its schemes, then it has found the magic password to Aladdin's cave. For no organised criminal is as successful as the one who enjoys the backing of the state.

Conversely, a criminal master who loses the backing of the state becomes vulnerable. Mogilevich himself discovered this in January 2008 when bundled unceremoniously into a police van in the centre of Moscow. He was detained for several months on charges of tax evasion. However, there was an avalanche of speculation in both Russia and the US that Mogilevich's sudden fall was related to power politics in the Kremlin. Most commentators argued that Mogilevich, the gas broker, was a supporter of the Kremlin hawks, the *siloviki*. They elaborated that once Vladimir Putin had anointed the liberal former boss of Gazprom, Dimitry Medvedev, as his successor Mogilevich and his less than transparent business practices were a primary target. Other significant players with track records similar to Mogilevich were also picked up before and after his arrest.

The impact of this event, symbolic and practical, should not be underestimated. In the 1990s, the oligarchs and gangsters quite clearly controlled the Kremlin. Under Vladimir Putin, who systematically used popular hostility to the oligarchs to strengthen his political position as President, the situation was reversed: criminal and oligarch interests were subordinated to state interests. It does not follow that Putin and friends persecuted criminals or dispensed with corrupt practices. On the contrary, they flourished as before but they are now much more carefully controlled. Of course, it is often difficult to tell who is truly running the show – the chicken or the egg!

Winter came late to central Ukraine in 2000. Had snow covered the fertile fields and forests near the town of Tarashcha, as it usually did in early November, the hand sticking out of a pile of fresh earth on the edge of a beech wood would have remained undiscovered. As it was, two locals noticed it as they were returning to their village, and reported it to the police.

A local coroner established that the victim had first suffered a severe beating. It was hard to know, however, whether the flaying of his legs was the result of torture or of animals scavenging once the body was buried. Nonetheless, the coroner noted how 'the skinning revealed the leg muscles like in an anatomical illustration, and suggested that sadists had been at work'.

The corpse bore the marks of a gangland killing. Identification was difficult as it was headless, but matters were complicated still further when the coroner received an order from Kiev not to transfer the body to the capital, ninety miles away. He protested that he had no refrigeration facilities in Tarashcha, but Ukraine's Interior Ministry insisted that the corpse remain in the provinces. This was followed by a visit from Ukraine's Chief Coroner, who removed some organs and then ordered the local coroner to dispose of the corpse.

By now, Tarashcha's coroner knew that he was in the middle of a very sensitive case. This was not a conventional gangland killing: higher powers were involved. In this instance, the mafia organisation was the Ukrainian state itself. The MP who headed the Investigative Committee into Organised Crime and Corruption, Hryhory Omelchenko, has stated in Ukraine's parliament that the country's chief *capo* was none other than the President himself, Leonid Danilovych Kuchma. A former boss of the Yuzhmash missile factory in the industrial city of Dnipropetrovsk, Kuchma was known as a leading 'red director' – that is, a communist who actually worked for a living, as opposed to those who just made their way up the Party's greasy pole. Western embassies in Kiev hoped that Kuchma's relative youth and energy would drag Ukraine out of the torpor characterised by its first post-communist leader, Leonid Kravchuk, who was, in fact, a Communist Party boss from central casting. Like many others, the Western embassies were very wrong.

'It was a period in which the state was converted into a criminal political mafia,' said Omelchenko, the combative and impressively moustached MP in a pithy summary of his statements in parliament. 'The political system and the state institutions were under Kuchma's control in order to secure absolute power, an authoritarian regime that could exploit its power for the boundless enrichment of Kuchma's family and those oligarchs closest to him. To achieve these goals, he and his closest circles didn't shy from using any method, including the dirtiest ones, even physical assault of the most violent kind.'

Like most other Ukrainians, Tarashcha's local coroner was fully aware of the lawless nature of the state in which he lived. So it took considerable courage to defy the orders he received from Kiev. But he did: he kept the body even though, without refrigeration, it had begun to decompose rapidly. He was relieved when some days later a team of journalists pitched up from Kiev. They told him that the body belonged to Georgi Gongadze, a 31-year-old investigative journalist who had disappeared two months earlier.

Half-Ukrainian and half-Georgian, Georgi Gongadze had begun to prise open the lid of Kuchma's maggot-infested administration with his probing articles. Slowly it was becoming apparent that the Ukrainian Government had commandeered the judiciary, the police, the military, the Security Services and industry – in short, the central mechanisms of state – as vital assistants in the amassing of wealth and power by a federation of regionally based cliques. Of course, just like any other cabal of 'families', there were frequent fallings out, and indeed the system eventually came crashing down in December 2004 when former allies of Kuchma, Viktor Yushchenko and Yulia Tymoshenko, led the Orange Revolution that sought to replace venality with popular legit- imacy as the guiding philosophy of the state.

But until then, the Ukrainian experience was unprecedented. Even in Russia under Yeltsin, when the influence of the oligarchs over the Kremlin was at its highest, a certain distance existed between political and economic processes, not to mention personal ambition. But at the turn of the millennium in Ukraine, the oligarchs and government became one, fused together by the super-glue of the SBU, the post-independence intelligence service. But occasionally the SBU's bonding properties were not as adamantine as its masters would have liked.

Mykola Melnychenko was most fortunate that the SBU was having a rare off day on October 30th, 2002 when he applied for a passport to travel abroad. Perhaps its officers were too busy wondering where they should dispose of Gongadze's body. Whatever the reason, the day the journalist's body was discovered, Ukraine's Interior Ministry issued Melnychenko with a passport, which before long contained a visa for the Czech Republic, whither he left with his family three weeks later.

The SBU should have been more interested in Melnychenko's intentions. Just a week before receiving his passport he had left the SBU's employ, where he had worked as a Presidential Guard who spent most of the day close to or in Kuchma's presence. And for the previous twelve months Major Melnychenko had been illicitly recording conversations that took place in the Presidential office between Kuchma and his most senior colleagues. They had discussed all manner of subjects (including the troublesome Georgi Gongadze). When Melnychenko left for the Czech Republic via Warsaw, he packed 1,000 hours of digital recordings in his luggage. They were to prove very uncomfortable for Kuchma and his friends.

Surprisingly, when Melnychenko teasingly released just a few hours of the tapes, the former President conceded that the voice recorded was his own. But Kuchma argued that somebody or some organisation had doctored the conversations or taken them out of context. Kuchma refused to allow a parliamentary inquiry into the tapes affair, but did commission Kroll Inc. to conduct an independent investigation into Gongadze's death.

The Kroll Report claimed that it could prove the tapes had been doctored. But journalists and Melnychenko issued counterclaims refuting its key scientific assertions about the recordings. The FBI agreed with Melnychenko – the tapes were for real.

The contents of these tapes are so explosive that they were bound to provoke a furious debate about authenticity, in which both sides mobilised powerful allies. But Kuchma's admission that the voice was his is, in one respect, all one needs to know. More instructive than the contents (which, like most ordinary conversations, assume prior knowledge and therefore sound disjointed) is the language that Kuchma and his colleagues use. A simple cultural transfer and we could be listening to a clip from *Goodfellas* or an episode of *The Sopranos*. Kuchma is not the first president to use expletives on tape, but he makes Richard Nixon sound like the principal of a Swiss finishing school:

> **Kuchma (on the phone):** Listen, now they just showed me the newspapers. Crap – all these bollocks that is published. Well, Hrysha Omelchenko is continuing to publish a paper. (Pause) Well, what are you bullshitting? Eh no, right now the 15th of September he put out a paper. (Pause) . . . *Svoboda* [a news-paper] and shit is being published . . . There are such carica-tures there, and also insults, crapping totally on the President. (Pause) So invite Yulia [Tymoshenko – later co-leader of the Orange Revolution]! Fuck your mother! You invite Yulia, and ask her: 'Dearest, what the crap are you doing, bitch? Do you want us to screw the crap out of you completely or what?' And you can add: 'Why are you financing Omelchenko, why are you doing this and that?' You don't know the basics of your job or what? How things are done the rest of the world over? So if they aren't one fucking bit afraid of you, then fuck your mother. Well, why are you this way? Why should you be feared? It is our service that they are afraid of . . . It was I who appointed you . . .

And on Gongadze – Kuchma may not have ordered his murder, but one cannot but detect a certain appeal to the unknown interlocutor on the other end of the line to rid him of this troublesome reporter:

> **Kuchma:** . . . *Ukrainska Pravda*, well, this is completely already crap, insolence. Bastard, shit. The Georgian, Georgian, whore.
> **Unidentified individual:** Gongadze?
> **Kuchma:** Gongadze. Well, who could be financing him? . . .
> **Unidentified individual:** Well, he actively works with this, with [Member of Parliament] Moroz, with the newspaper *Hrani*.
> **Kuchma:** To court, maybe. Here, people's deputies. Let the lawyers take him to court. This goes to the prosecutor, right? It's just, crap . . . there is some kind of limit, son-of-a-bitch,

shit . . . Deport him, whore, to Georgia and throw him the
fuck out there.

Unidentified individual: Drive him out to Georgia and throw
him there.

Kuchma: The Chechens need to steal him and throw him away.

The language reveals utter contempt for state institutions and the
need for institutional control over individual ambition. Kuchma and
his cronies had seized the state and now wielded power and money
beyond the comprehension of most of Ukraine's fifty million inhabitants. For Kuchma and his pals, the state was nothing more than a
mechanism to facilitate their personal aggrandisement. But not surprisingly, it created a serious long-term problem for the country as a whole.
To compete on the world market, Ukraine needs to foster good relations with Russia (above all), but also with the European Union, the
United States and China (where it sells huge quantities of steel and
other raw materials). And yet a primitive clan system of government
is inherently unstable. It actively discourages the emergence of a strong
class of small and medium entrepreneurs, who are the key to the
diverse and flexible economy of a country in transition. In Ukraine's
case, greed, incompetence and oligarchic feuding eventually triggered
if not a breakdown, then a changing of the guard.

The Gongadze murder and the Melnychenko tapes accelerated the
demise of the Kuchma regime. But it is far too early to conclude that
the new rulers of Ukraine will succeed in persuading more democratic
practices and institutions to take root. Less than a year after the Orange
Revolution, which was supposed to do away with the mafia state, the
new government had collapsed in a flood of mutual recriminations
between the Revolution's leaders. The oligarchs, meanwhile, recovered
to fight against encroachments on their wealth and influence. Indeed,
some Western intelligence officers claim the evidence is mounting
that the decision to investigate the Eural Trans Gas scandal led to the
fall of Yulia Tymoshenko's government.

Organised crime is deeply entrenched in Ukraine and, away from
Kiev, where the spotlight of domestic and international scrutiny shines
brightly, powerful criminal interests continue to dominate. Henry Hill,
the main character in *Goodfellas*, remembered that his mob's wealth

grew from the moment when one of the biggest ports of entry on America's Eastern Seaboard came into operation in New York. 'The real money started coming in when they opened up the airport at Idlewild,' as JFK was originally known. Well, when communism fell, the ancient Ukrainian port of Odessa suddenly opened up.

As I stroll along Primorsky Boulevard from Sergei Eisenstein's famous steps towards the Opera House, Odessa looks magnificent. Indeed, the recent reconstruction of the city centre is so evocative of a glamorous past that I can imagine Anton Chekhov, Isadora Duncan and their fashionable friends sweeping in and out of the Londonskaya Hotel where they used to stay. A century ago a visit to Odessa, on the northern coast of the Black Sea, was de rigueur for the moneyed classes of Russia and Europe alike.

This elegant illusion is maintained as I walk up Derebasovskaya Street, where peddlers are wooing tourists by performing with live snakes and crocodiles (less harmful than some of the other reptiles that creep around here). The high street takes you past the house, now sadly under scaffolding, where the painter Vassily Kandinsky grew up. Just visible underneath the crumbling plaster is a golden key painted above the door. This puts most Ukrainians and Russians in mind of Karabas Barabas and the story of Buratino and the Golden Key. Alexei Tolstoy, a distant cousin of the great novelist, adapted the Pinocchio story in the 1930s to create a Russian version. Buratino, the little puppet boy in possession of the Key, is hounded by Karabas, an evil puppet master, who will do anything to possess it, as it opens the door to the Kingdom of Happiness.

Myths and fairy tales are popular in Odessa and, by a strange coincidence, decades after Kandinsky left, a man called Karabas actually moved into the House of the Golden Key. A puppet master maybe, but a living one whose trail would take me to a place where fairy tales cease and happy endings disappear in short wisps of gunsmoke.

To the north of Derebasovskaya Street, the ornate late-eighteenth-century façades are still ubiquitous, but the elegance fades: these French-designed buildings have clearly fallen on Soviet times, even before sinking into the mire of gangster capitalism. On Astashkina, a small quiet street, I wander into Steam Baths No. 4. The exterior is modest, but the inhabitants have spruced up the courtyard with hanging baskets. The stairs at the back, painted a rich green, lead to the Russian Sauna on the first floor. But before I reach the baths themselves, I come across several bunches of fresh flowers on the ground. Two plaques are attached to the wall above – the first engraved with the image of a man in his mid-forties, sporting cropped hair and looking sleek in a suit over a T-shirt; the second has on it a poem written by his closest friends after he, Viktor Kulivar 'Karabas', was felled on this spot by nineteen bullets from an unknown assassin's semi-automatic:

Kulivar

Viktor Pavlovich

To Your Eternal and Sacred Memory

Karabas!

April 21, 1997

Naveshchayut kladbishche starushki	Old women, friends and family
I druzya, rodnye v skorbnyi chas,	Visit the cemetery at this sad hour,
Predan zdes' zemle vozle tserkvushki	The sacred clay holds the remains
Viktor Pavlovich, nash dobryi Karabas.	Of Viktor Pavlovich, our dear Karabas.

Banknotes are nestled inside the flowers. Money lying untouched in a public place suggests profound respect for their late recipient, because in Odessa poverty and begging are readily visible.

The people of Odessa have a history of romanticising their city and its people. Known for its self-deprecating, almost Schweykian humour, the city's British equivalent would be Liverpool. Founded just over two centuries ago, the Pearl of the Black Sea has a rumbustious history in which crime, politics and a joyous licentiousness have always been further fuelled by large itinerant populations: seafarers, political refugees and commercial adventurers. Furthermore, it was until recently the most ethnically diverse of all Russophone cities. Until Odessa's Jews fled in the face of Axis Romania's military advance of 1941, they amounted to 30 per cent of the population. Most of those who remained were massacred. But like the Jews in a sister port, Thessaloniki in northern Greece, they did not conform to the stereotype of Eastern European Jews as poor rural dwellers or prosperous businessmen. Instead, they comprised much of Odessa's tough working class, from whom the city's legendary criminal community emerged, as chronicled during the early twentieth century in the stories of the great Isaac Babel.

Although not Jewish, Karabas fitted perfectly into the role of local criminal idol – and the more I spoke to Odessites of any nationality, the more convinced I became that he really was a heroic gangster who prevented social collapse and lawlessness.

No mobsters controlled a post-Soviet city with as much popular support and quite as effectively as Karabas did. But his primary instrument was not violence, but trust. 'He was a local boy and he was fiercely proud of Odessa,' argued Leo Zverev, a charity and social worker, 'and he maintained order. The bulk of our narcotics problem, for example, used to be based in the part of the city that we call Palermo, because there is so much criminal activity there. Karabas allowed the dealers to operate inside Palermo, but he blocked them from plying their trade anywhere else in the city. He was determined to hold down drugs consumption in this city.'

As economic breakdown and chaos spread across Ukraine following its independence from the Soviet Union in 1991, Odessa suffered a dramatic social seizure, with funds from Kiev largely drying up. With predators stalking the city and in particular the port and oil terminal at the foot of the Potemkin Steps, Karabas stepped in to assert his authority. Relying on a brigade system similar to the one operated by the Solntsevo Brotherhood in Moscow, Karabas established some ground rules that it was dangerous to break. It took me some time to persuade members of Odessa's underworld to speak – at times they seemed more obstructive than Soviet bureaucrats. But eventually they opened up to me – under the strictest condition of anonymity. Their opinion of Karabas differed little from that of civilians. 'He was a man of principle,' one leading mobster told me, 'rarely carried a gun and often went out without bodyguards. As far as he was concerned, violence was a last resort for a racketeer. And as he was recognised by all of us as the *avtoritet*, a Don, even by people like me who didn't work with him, this meant that levels of violence in Odessa were much lower than in other Ukrainian and Russian cities.'

'Any firm, and there were a lot of them, considered it an honour to be under Karabas's protection,' one local businessman explained. 'This was a guarantee not only of total security from outside attacks by rogue rackets, but also not infrequently from encroachment by the authorities. Besides this, he was in his own way a city arbitrator, acting as judge in commercial disputes between various "structures". The value of his services cost firms a tenth part of their net profits. The payout took place every month – even if there had been no need to seek out his services. And it would never have entered anyone's head to deceive him or attempt to conceal anything. Unthinkable. If someone was having problems, say, with tax auditing, not only might he reduce or postpone payments, he would even write off the debt altogether. "What is our gain in killing the goose laying the golden eggs?" he used to say.'

But Odessa, even in the calmest times, is an irresistible magnet for criminality and corruption. Despite Karabas's benign rule, every imaginable contraband passed through the city. As a port, it was a hub of human-trafficking. 'We'd open up containers and find hundreds of people packed into them,' described one former customs officer in the city. 'The stench was indescribable as they had sometimes been sealed in for weeks with no toilet facilities, and rotting bodies were also common.' As the migrant labourers from Asia who survived the trip continued the journey towards Poland in the hope of entering the European Union illegally, their place in the containers was taken by women from Ukraine, Belarus and Moldova en route from Odessa to brothels around the Middle East and Europe.

It was perhaps oil that caused Karabas's downfall. Odessa and Ilichevsk, ten miles from Odessa, are the most important export terminals for Russian oil. During communism, the bulk of the Soviet Union's refinery capacity was concentrated here. Russia was never likely to allow such a trifling inconvenience as Ukraine's independence to hinder its continued access to these facilities. Overall economic and political control of the city translates into billions of dollars, especially since President Putin's foreign policy is based on Russia's immense influence in the global energy industry. Moscow had no intention of allowing Ukraine to develop its port and refinery system independent of its own policy goals.

The Russians found a pliant partner in Leonid Kuchma. Less accommodating, however, was the Mayor of Odessa, Eduard Gurvitz. An energetic entrepreneur with great plans for the rejuvenation of the port, Gurvitz backed a scheme to transform the Odessa region from a mere exporter of Russian oil to an importer of Caspian and Middle Eastern oil, which it could then send by pipeline to Poland and the European Union. This involved the construction of a giant new terminal to the south of Odessa, which (unlike Odessa) could import oil as well as export it, thereby freeing Ukraine from over-dependency on Russian oil.

Although there was occasional friction between Mayor Gurvitz and Karabas, their goals for Odessa generally coincided. 'When the Chechens first tried to muscle in on the oil industry, Odessite business consulted Karabas,' said a local mobster, 'and Karabas had a clear strategy: "Leave Moscow to the Muscovites and Chechnya to the Chechens. Odessa belongs to the Odessites." And he blocked their entry into the market.'

Heroic though Karabas's strategy might have been, he was naive, according to Leonid Kapelyushny, a civic activist who knew both Gurvitz and Karabas well. 'Karabas had to go because he had one dumb idea,' he said. 'He believed in a national organised crime and rejected the idea of trans-national organised crime. And that's what did for him – every imaginable force in this country and from outside wanted control of the oil, and so Karabas and his Odessa patriotrism had to go.'

The gunning down of Viktor Kulivar 'Karabas' in April 1997 triggered a series of bloody political murders over the next year, and a sustained period of gang warfare as various mafia outfits fought over the huge territory that Karabas had controlled. When he heard the news of Karabas death, Mayor Gurvitz turned to Kapelyushny and said, 'Odessa doesn't yet understand what sort of man has been killed. Nor what consequences will now follow.' His death deprived Odessa of the one man capable of policing the city – which was precisely the point. 'After Karabas's death, the third force came into play,' explained a retired investigative detective who declined to be identified. By the third force, he meant a fearful alliance of gangsters, ex-communists, oligarchs, military intelligence and KGB, which even Darth Vadar would think twice about confronting. Gurvitz himself survived two assassination attempts in this period, but, despite widespread intimidation, he was re-elected in February 1998, only to be stripped of the post soon afterwards in a bizarre intervention by a court in Kirovgrad, a city hundreds of miles away, which had no jurisdiction over the Odessa municipality. Leonid Kuchma, however, welcomed the court's decision.

In the next few years, Kuchma's preferred strategy for the terminals and ports of the Odessa region sailed through unopposed, to the satisfaction of both Ukraine's oligarchs and Russia's industrial and political elite.

During his ten years in power, Leonid Kuchma presided over the total criminalisation of the Ukrainian Government and civil service. Most people understandably associate organised crime with drugs, prostitution, people-trafficking and similar activities. But the biggest bosses of Russia and Ukraine understood that if you wish to strike the really big money, you should invest in two 'legitimate' businesses – energy and arms. The trade in weapons to Yugoslavia saw a successful collusion between state and criminal elements; in Odessa a battle over oil exports broke the city in two. Karabas's death showed that not even the mafia can compete when the full weight of the state becomes involved in trans-national corruption and criminality.

The trade in illegal weapons, however, began under a different president. At the end of 1991 Ukraine's then President, Leonid Kravchuk, decreed the establishment of a commercial department at the Defence Ministry, whose main aim was to turn the vast store of Soviet weapons inherited by Ukraine into cash. It was not long before an Odessa company, Global Technology Inc. (GTI), was despatching the *Jadran Express* (despite its Croatian name, a Nigerian-registered ship) to the former Yugoslavia packed full of arms, in defiance of the UN weapons embargo. Given the oft-proclaimed solidarity between Russians, Ukrainians and their Orthodox Slav brethren, the Serbs, it is astonishing how many Russian and Ukrainian citizens and companies were involved in supplying the Croats, Bosnians and Albanians with guns. But as we shall see, it was states and groups from Africa who sent the greatest number of envoys to Ukraine to broker arms shipments from Odessa.

Like all key murders in the former Soviet Union, Karabas's remains entirely unsolved. Some clues as to who the assassins might have been were offered by the subsequent attempted murder in February 1998 of Leonid Kapelyushny, then the head of the city's Electoral Commission.

Three men emerged from a car and gunned him down, leaving Kapelyushny for dead. 'Before losing consciousness,' the sombre Kapelyushny told me, 'I at least noted that the car was registered in Transnistria.'

Odessa is only sixty miles from the border with the Republic of Moldovan Transnistria, which looks and sounds like the perfect setting for a Tintin adventure. This thin sliver of territory is the quintessential gangster state whither many criminals would scuttle having carried out their missions in Odessa. It has been a problem ever since the Transnistrian authorities proclaimed independence from Moldova in 1990, triggering a bloody, dirty little war that lasted for two years.

During the conflict with Moldova, Transnistria held its own in large part because it happened to host both Russia's 14th Army and its mighty arsenal of 42,000 pieces of stockpiled weaponry, ranging from pistols to tanks and a handy supply of surface-to-air missiles. After the collapse of the Soviet Union, the 14th Army in Transnistria was separated from the Russian motherland by the proclamation of an independent Ukraine. The 14th Army could have organised its return, but preferred instead to remain in Transnistria as a 'peacekeeping force'. But although this mighty fighting force offered *de facto* support to the breakaway republic, Russia (like the rest of the world) refused to recognise Transnistria – it is a pariah state. Since then, Transnistria's President, Igor Smirnov, a former 'red director' of a factory in the capital Tiraspol, has relied for support on a coterie of KGB officers, oligarchs and an uncharacteristically forgiving attitude of Gazprom to the huge debt that Transnistria has run up with the energy giant.

As Pavel Ciobanu ushers me into his Audi, I notice that he shares Karabas's dress sense, sporting the black jacket over the black T-shirt. The sky darkens as we speed in late autumn from Chisinau, the Moldovan capital, towards Tiraspol, capital of Transnistria. Instinctively, I clutch my wallet. Three days previously, travelling through Transnistria, I had been relieved of $50 by the border guards, who were happy to keep me in illegal custody until I coughed up. 'Par for the course,' diplomats in Chisinau assure me cheerfully.

But as head of the Moldovan Football Association, Mr Ciobanu is a welcome guest in Tiraspol and so the self-same border guards who had previously extorted me now waved us through, accompanied by obsequious salutes and nary a glance at our passports. Ciobanu speeds us towards the most unlikely top-of-the-table clash in European football, FC Sheriff Tiraspol v. Zimbru Chisinau.

As well as a criminal revenue-raising post, the Transnistrian border acts as a time machine. As you enter Tiraspol, Lenin rises on a pillar in front of the parliament building, while slogans remind people that 'Our Strength Lies in Unity'. We are indeed back in the Soviet Union and people have that unforgettable Soviet combination of boredom and exhaustion etched on their faces as they trudge along the bare streets. The vision of this social anachronism doubles the shock on arrival at the astonishing home of FC Sheriff Tiraspol.

The Sheriff complex has two full-sized soccer stadia, an arena licensed for international meetings of any indoor sport, a five-pitch training ground, a sports academy and a hotel, restaurant and bar, and is regularly rented out by the most powerful teams from Kiev and Moscow. I learn from UEFA, the governing body of European football, that it includes the only stadium in Europe that 'conforms to every single safety and security measure that we stipulate'. As a life-long fan of soccer, I can testify that I have never seen so sophisticated a training and playing complex in Eastern Europe. And for those Transnistrians with time on their hands and money to burn (a rare breed), there is even a Mercedes car showroom in the grounds.

In 1997, Victor Gusan decided to use his wealth to found a football club that could aspire to the final stages of the Champions League, the zenith of European sporting achievement. Having led a rich and varied life as the former Deputy Chief of Tiraspol Militia, Gusan turned his hand successfully to business in the early 1990s. While clearly a man with razor-sharp acumen, Gusan was probably aided in his rise by his friendship with a certain Vladimir Smirnov. Reputed to be Sheriff Football Club's biggest fan, Smirnov must have expended much effort in persuading the Government of the self-styled Republic of Transnistria to go ahead with the construction both of the stadium complex and the team. After all, Transnistria's annual budget amounts to just under $250 million. The stadium, in contrast, cost around $180 million. But then Mr Smirnov is both the Head of the Customs Service of Transnistria and son of the President, Igor Smirnov.

But not even the might of the President and his Communist Party could overcome the second hurdle facing FC Sheriff. In order to participate in any football competition, Sheriff must belong to a country that was a recognised member of UEFA. And ever since the Transnistrian authorities declared independence from Moldova, Tiraspol, the capital of Transnistria, has been excluded from UEFA.

So what could Transnistria do to put FC Sheriff on show? They'd spent all that money on the stadium complex and bought in some first-class players from Africa, the Balkans and Russia to cobble together a decent team, by regional standards.

The Football Federation of Moldova was, or course, recognised by UEFA. A deal was struck. Although Transnistria refuses to have anything to do with Moldova on any other official level, in matters football it recognises the sovereignty of Chisinau. The government in Chisinau thus maintains a rather feeble lever over the government in Tiraspol. FC Sheriff wins the Moldovan league at a canter every season. As the Moldovan/Transnistrian equivalent of Chelsea, it can buy better players than all the other teams put together. It is then able to play in the qualifying rounds of the European Champions League.

Of course, all this begs a large question: from where does FC Sheriff get its money? Apart from the stadium, the other striking thing about Tiraspol is the number of Western Union signs hanging outside shops. In transitional countries and the developing world, such high visibility of Western Union means one thing – a significant level of emigration to better economic climes. But I wonder if the world has ever seen anything like this. Grigory Volovoy speaks in a wry monotone. As editor of *Novaya gazeta*, he is one of the very few who dare raise their voices in Transnistria's living gulag. 'In the early 1990s, the population stood at 750,000. Now it is about 450,000. We have about 150,000 able-bodied people of working age left here.'

So notwithstanding the lure of the stadium, in the last decade almost half of all Transnistrians left to seek their fortune abroad. A stroll around the streets of Tiraspol makes it crystal clear that there is not much trickle-down from Sheriff.

There is, however, the phenomenon of trickle-up. In addition to the football club, Sheriff owns the biggest supermarket chain in Transnistria, as well as every single land and mobile-phone line in the country (a snip at $2 million in 2002). Although Russia is too coy to recognise Transnistria, Gazprom has been subsidising gas supplies to the territory to the tune of $50 million a year for more than a decade. And Itera, the Florida-based company with alleged links to the Solntsevo Brotherhood, is the majority shareholder of the metallurgical plant in Ribnitsa, the highest export earner in Transnistria.

But still you can't help wondering whether all this could conceivably finance FC Sheriff and the stadium. Remember that stockpile of Russian weapons? And indeed the estimated two to three factories that produce weapons unmonitored? These spew out of Transnistria via Odessa and into the worlds of war: the Caucasus, Central Asia, the Middle East, West and Central Africa.

Occasionally, President Putin suffers a crisis of conscience regarding Transnistria. 'Maybe it is time to close down this black hole,' he told Georgi Purvanov when the Bulgarian President pleaded with Putin to dam the lava of criminality that flows down from Transnistria and spreads throughout the neighbourhood. Bulgaria is used by various groups as an important staging point in the smuggling of weapons from Ukraine and Transnistria, and Purvanov understandably considers this most damaging for his country's image.

Putin mulled it over, but, in the end, decided to keep the black hole open. A few years back, the Russians agreed to allow an international agency to supervise the transfer of the 14th Army's weapons to Russia. At the time of writing half of these have been returned. 'Of course,' said one Western intelligence officer, 'we don't know how many of those made it to Russia and how many found their way elsewhere.' Western governments are particularly concerned by the leakage of the Russian surface-to-air missile, the Igla. In December 2003, 320 of these weapons were withdrawn, but the original inventory showed that there were 394 pieces. Somewhere around the world in unknown hands are seventy-four highly accurate missiles that can bring down a 747. Each one is worth about $50,000. 'There is enough kit in Transnistria to supply an entire army,' the officer said. 'It is worth millions and it is deadly.'

Transnistria is tiny – the size of Rhode Island. But it affects and debilitates countries across large parts of the globe. Its rogue border regime has a deleterious impact on both Ukraine and Moldova. This is why soon after the Orange Revolution in Ukraine, the new admin-istration turned its attention to the problem. 'If the border is securely sealed, the illegitimate authority in Transnistria will soon lose the economic foundation of its existence,' said the Foreign Minister, Boris Tarasyuk, in June 2005. Accusing former President Kuchma of complicity, Tarasyuk continued, 'The previous government used Transnistria as a springboard for contraband because the money chiefly flowed to Kiev. The situation has changed now. Ukraine is not inter-ested in the existence of a "black hole" on its frontier, neither is Ukraine interested in capitalising on the conflict in this neighbouring state.'

Boris Tarasyuk was Foreign Minister for only a few months before the first Orange Government collapsed in a welter of mutual accusa-tions and a deteriorating economic situation, encouraged in no small part by energy 'sanctions' imposed by Moscow. One perceptive analyst of Transnistria has suggested that the capacity of Moscow to dictate the politics of its 'near abroad' (and thereby sustain rogue regimes like Tiraspol) has been shored up since President Putin consolidated his control over the Russian energy sector as a means to project Russian foreign-policy power. 'As the EU is 60% energy dependent on the Russian Federation and has higher priorities in its agenda than conflict settlement,' the analyst wrote, 'the prospects of somehow strong-arming Russia are unrealistic.'

As head of the Moldovan Football Association, Pavel Ciobanu is, strictly speaking, neutral when it comes to the big game between Sheriff and Zimbru. But he is smiling as we head back to Chisinau after Sheriff's convincing 3–0 victory (ten wins out of ten for the season so far). 'Gusan's aim is to get Sheriff into the final rounds of the European Cup,' he explains to me. 'I think we'll do it in a couple of years.' This is bold ambition indeed, especially given the paltry atten-dance of just 4,000 spectators at the grandiose stadium, which can seat five times as many for what is supposed to be the biggest game of the season. 'Mr Gusan is very happy today. It is his birthday; he went hunting and killed a wild boar. And now he wins 3–0. He is doing great things for Moldovan football.'

PART TWO

GOLD, MONEY, DIAMONDS AND BANKS

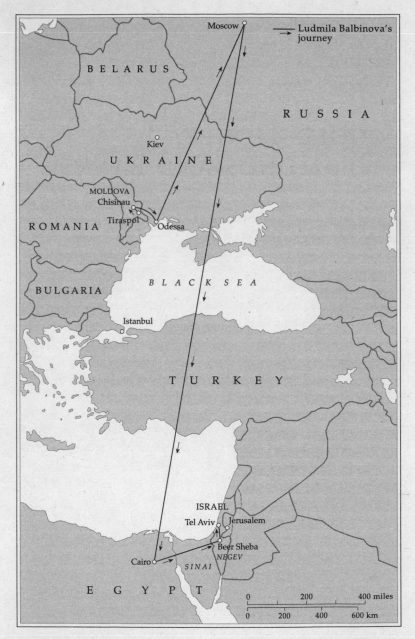

Sex trafficking from the former Soviet Union to the Middle East (Transnistria, capital Tiraspol, is a thin sliver of land stretching down the Eastern border between Moldova and Ukraine)

5

ALIYAH

The border that separates Israel and Egypt is barely noticeable. Staring down at the flimsy wire fence separating the Negev Desert from northern Sinai, I am surprised at how a country as concerned with its security as Israel permits such open access onto its territory from an Arab land. The police assure me that they patrol the border regularly, but I don't see a soul when driving up the northern half towards the southern tip of Gaza.

Until, that is, two camel heads rear up imperiously some two hundred yards in front of me. They are heading from Egypt into Israel, piloted by a group of four young teenagers: two jockeys and two guides. The camels are packed to the humps with smuggled goods, most probably cigarettes or narcotics, the bread-and-butter cargo for these cross-border traders. Seized by fear at the sight of my car, the boys urgently whip the great beasts, which bolt in the direction of an unlicensed pick-up truck before the undulating Negev swallows all three – riders, vehicle and camels.

Criminals in the eyes of the Israeli state, these smugglers nonetheless bear the torch of nomadic tradition, which has been all but extinguished among the Bedouins of the Negev. To be sure, theirs is a distorted inheritance. At the founding of Israel in 1948, 90 per cent of these Bedouins were involved in nomadic or semi-nomadic economic activity – almost entirely pastoral. But in fits and starts since then, Israel has tried to corral the roughly 100,000 Bedouins from across the Negev into seven urban settlements in the desert's north-western quarter. As a consequence, that statistic has been inverted – 90 per cent now work in low-wage industrial branches like construction or in the settlements' growing, if impoverished, public sector. A significant number of the 10 per cent who don't, now work as smugglers (there is no contest between this cash-rich trade and subsistence farming).

By regional standards, Israel can call upon immense security resources, but these are not limitless. And so the Bedouin farmers use their unparalleled knowledge of the desert terrain to refashion themselves as a critical cog in the industry purveying illicit goods and services to the Israeli consumer.

Most tribally organised communities coming into contact with the modern state over the past half-century have witnessed their traditional lifestyle come crashing down around them. The Bedouins are an excellent example. Like the Bushmen of southern Africa, the indigenous peoples of Irian Jaya or the Inuit of the Arctic, the Bedouins of the Negev retain a powerful cultural memory that no longer bears any proper relationship to their social and economic circumstances. How can you be a nomad in a desert that is home to huge private farms like the one that belonged to Ariel Sharon? The results are uniform across the world – indigenous communities suffer relatively high rates of birth, infant mortality and illiteracy.

And so it is the young Bedouin smuggler jockeys who nurture the flickering flame of their people's collective memory. The job is certainly more interesting and varied than any of the limited opportunities available in the settlements, and it means continued contact with their cousins across the border in Sinai. This profession is also growing, as the increasing incidence of drug abuse among the Bedouins testifies. Communities from whom land-based narcotics smugglers are drawn – Albanians, Bedouins or Tajiks, for example – usually suffer chronic rates of drug abuse. But the reasons behind the development of the illicit sector in the Negev do not lie primarily with the Bedouins, but among a group of immigrants to Israel who only started arriving fifteen years ago – the Russians.

When the Soviet Union collapsed and the economies in the successor states went haywire, the future looked both frightening and uncertain for the great majority of citizens. If the gangster capitalism in Moscow seemed scary, spare a thought for ordinary folk who lived on the periphery, especially in the Caucasus where war, civil conflict and sheer thuggery made even such mundane tasks as grocery shopping a hazardous activity.

Alexander Gentelev, a documentary film-maker, hurried home from work one freezing winter's evening in 1991. Makhachkala, the capital of Dagestan, where he lived, was as wild as it gets. He was still shaken up following the assassination twenty-four hours earlier of a good friend, who had left his job as a doctor to become involved in local politics. 'He was getting into his car and they opened fire from both sides. They shot him sixty times,' Gentelev remembers. 'But I had no reason to expect they would come after me. I was wrong.'

They came for him two days later. But Gentelev was lucky. 'I was most fortunate that evening for two reasons,' he told me in a café in Tel Aviv. 'First, I had a bad flu and was wrapped up very warmly. And secondly I had just been paid for a job. At the time, inflation was going mad and so this was a huge, thick wad of notes.' Out of the shadows stepped a couple of gunmen who opened fire. 'I was knocked to the ground and lost consciousness, but the bullet aimed at my heart was cushioned by the cash and so didn't penetrate my body!'

He was still very seriously wounded. 'As I lay in hospital in Makhachkala, I was warned that they would return,' he said. 'I didn't even know who "they" were and so I asked my brother to evacuate first my family and then me to Moscow. And at this stage, my wife said, "Right! Enough is enough! We are not going back!"' Fortunately, Alexander was Jewish.

Apart from when Stalin had a vicious anti-Semitic spasm just before his death, being Jewish in the post-war Soviet Union was not usually much worse than being anything else. As a Jew, one's professional ambition was often circumscribed in a way that did not affect Slavs and some other minorities, but in many respects all peoples in the Soviet Union were shat upon in equal measure.

From 1989 onwards, the Jews of the former Soviet Union enjoyed one valuable and exclusive privilege – they were eligible for Israeli citizenship and could get the hell out of Belarus, the Caucasus, Siberia or wherever else, with no questions asked. And many didn't wait to be the victim of an assassination attempt like Gentelev. They took the passport and ran. Soon hundreds turned into thousands, thousands into tens and hundreds of thousands, until within a decade one million Russian Jews had pitched up in Israel, amounting to more than 15 per cent of the total population.

'Most came because the gates were open and they knew that they could be closed again at any moment,' said Marina Solodkin who, after her arrival in Israel in 1991, went on to become the Deputy Minister for Immigration in the Sharon Government. 'For Jews like me, who were active in the underground in the 1970s, this was the Return Home, *aliyah* as it is called. But it was also very important for the mixed and secular families as well. Nobody knew how things would develop in the former Soviet Union – would there be pogroms or no pogroms? None of us wanted to play Russian roulette, as it were.'

It was not just the latent aggression of Russian anti-Semitism that triggered the exodus. There were positive reasons to come as well. The prospect of an Israeli passport and hence visa-free travel to most Western countries was a big bonus, as was escape from the appalling Russian weather and the allure of the Mediterranean and Red Sea coasts.

Israel, of course, is a country that has been built on immigration since its inception in 1947. The country boasts an impressive record in the absorption of large groups long before the former Soviet Jews came – the Moroccan and Iraqi immigration of the 1950s and, more recently, the immigration from Ethiopia. But it had never dealt with anything on this scale from such a well-defined and powerful culture. The Moroccan, Iraqi and Ethiopian Jews had no choice but to learn Hebrew and submit to Israeli culture in order to survive. But the Jews from Russia and Ukraine were very different – they came in huge numbers in a short space of time and they had a strong *Russian* cultural identity, which was often more ingrained than their Jewishness. In the profoundly secular Soviet Union, Judaism and Zionism remained a minority interest at best among Russian Jews. 'The former Soviet immigrants perceive themselves as the bearers of European culture in Israel, and 87% of them would like cultural life in Israel to be similar to that of Europe,' noted one study on the sociology of the immigration based on extensive surveys. 'However, only 9% believe that this is indeed the situation in Israel.'

Israel, it seems, was a foreign country for these Russians. 'The immigrants perceive Russian culture and language as superior to Hebrew. 88% of immigrants evaluate the impact of immigration on cultural life in Israel as positive or very positive, while only 28% evaluate the impact of cultural life in Israel on the immigrants as positive or very positive,' the report says. Israeli culture is frequently zealous (unappealing for those who were once compelled to weather Soviet zealotry) and defined by a conflict with an enemy, the Palestinians, who did not excite Russian Jewish sensibilities. But it was also Mediterranean, which in the eyes of Russified Jews meant indolent and hence inferior. And then there were economic issues. 'In addition to its size, another unique aspect of the Russian immigration was that many of the Russian immigrants were highly educated,' the economists Sarit Cohen and Chang-Tai Hsieh have written. 'About 60 per cent of the Russian immigrants were college-educated, compared with only 30 to 40 per cent of native Israelis.' This led to social tension and real resentment between the indigenous population and the incomers – Russian professionals wanted to muscle in on the labour market in large numbers. Not in the dirty, poorly paid jobs traditionally reserved for immigrants, but in the well-paid posts for highly trained men and women.

Russian immigrants very quickly established a complex society in Israel, which developed in parallel to the existing community. The state showed little inclination to become involved with the Russians, nor did it really have the capacity to do so. So as the Russians poured in during this first phase of integration, the two communities barely interacted at all – language and culture led to a period of mutual exclusion.*

It was the police who first noticed something odd happening. 'At the time, I was head of the intelligence in Jerusalem,' said retired

* Although the two communities are now becoming closer and more intertwined, I spent a pleasant evening in Putin, a bar in the centre of Jerusalem with a low-slung ceiling where second-generation Russian teenagers conversed only in Russian; where there is no Hebrew script, only Cyrillic; and where the DJ plays only the latest songs from Moscow. Without doubt the most bizarre manifestation of this cultural stubbornness is the emergence in 2005 of a political grouping in Jerusalem, Tel Aviv and Haifa called the Russian National Centre. Its members are Russian *Jewish* teenagers whose avowed goal is to seek the 'cleansing from mother Russia of all Yids, Chechens and other minorities'.

police commander Hezi Leder, 'and we started getting reports from my colleagues in Haifa and the north of Israel of a dramatic rise in the amount of criminality among young people. These were kids who were thirteen and fourteen, maybe fifteen years old, but they seemed to be outside the education system. And they were almost all Russian.'

By the mid-1990s there were more than 700,000 Russians in Israel. Most were entirely honest, like Alexander Gentelev from Makhachkala. His was the familiar immigrant impulse from around the world – the search for sanctuary from a troubled environment and a better life for his children. 'But if you have a million Russians here and just one per cent is a criminal element,' explained former cop Gil Kleiman, 'that's still a hell of a lot of bad boys!' Soon after Leder alerted his colleagues to the phenomenon of the youth gangs, police started to observe an increase in murders and assaults involving unprecedented brutality. The crime wave centred on Tel Aviv – or Sin City, as the tabloids refer to it – but was almost always contained within the Russian-speaking community.

After receiving an anonymous tip-off in September 1996, Kleiman and his squad were shocked to discover the fresh corpse of a pimp called Oleg 'Karpits' Karpachov. It was lying in a pool of blood in a high-rise apartment building. The autopsy report stated that he had been stabbed both in the forehead and the neck. 'The knife went through the skin, the veins, and the windpipe all the way to the spine which was severed,' wrote the report's author. Karpits was also hit by a blunt object and stabbed in the shoulder and back. 'The bulbs on his floor alone had been deliberately unscrewed so there would be no light,' continued Kleiman, 'so we knew that this was a seriously planned job. And later we discovered that when the murderers were coordinating the murder, they never used their cellphones for longer than a minute in case they were being tracked.'

More shocking than the circumstances of Karpits's death was what Kleiman and the special investigative team discovered about the deceased's world. They began to unravel a network of pimps, brothels, protection rackets, counterfeit documents and kidnapping. Apart from the sleaziness of this underground community, its most surprising aspect was its invisibility. This was an internal Russian affair that never impinged on the rest of Israeli society. Except, that is, in one respect

– the single largest business these street-level Russian syndicates were running was prostitution, and the clients were by no means exclusively Russian.

Embracing globalisation, Israel was becoming more permissive. Or, rather, parts of Israel were. Jerusalem may have registered a growth in the number of devout Jews moving there and crowding out the secular inhabitants, but the inverse was occurring in Tel Aviv, the centre of foreign investment and the boom in 1990s' Israel. The success of Israel's high-tech industry in particular accelerated the emergence of a yuppie class bent on conspicuous consumption, including extensive use of designer drugs, notably cocaine and Ecstasy. The contrast between the endless glitter and thudding beat of Tel Aviv's nightclubs and, just forty miles away, the austere garb and sombre mumbling of the Hasidim in Jerusalem is almost as eye-popping as the contrast between life in Israel and the bedraggled Gaza Strip. Moreover, a temporary reduction in tension with the Palestinians in the 1990s saw a return of mass tourism to Israel and these factors combined to turn Tel Aviv into one of the two major centres of prostitution in the Middle East (the other being Dubai). Brothels catering for every male pocket also began to flourish in tourist centres like Netanya and Eilat. Like most other advanced developing economies, Israel came under American pressure to liberalise its markets and investment policies. And along with increased inflows and outflows of capital and goods came the personal acquisitiveness that underpins globalisation, and which presumes that money can fulfil any whim or desire. Combined with the ubiquitous images of male and female sexuality, this consumerism encourages the sense (certainly among men and increasingly, it would seem, among women too) that sex is less an expression of intimate relations and more a marketed commodity subject to the same rules governing the sale of hamburgers or trainers, as one academic study argued:

> The concept of prostitution as a consumer activity is clearly evident on the Internet. One brothel Website boasts that it offers Israeli consumers the latest technology for 'online orders for call girls right to your home, and all in Hebrew!' The site even offers potential clients a service agreement stating that

they, like any client, will have the right to complain about the 'services' rendered, since, after all, 'The customer is always right.' 'Blazer,' an Israeli magazine for men, was duly impressed: 'What can I tell you? You've got to hand it to organised crime for really being organised. They learned from Domino's Pizza how to take orders. They asked me ... with mushrooms? Without? I asked them ... if it's not too hard, a natural blonde, tall, with basic command of Hebrew.'

Demand was rising rapidly and the Russian underground in Israel knew how to supply it.

In early summer 2002 as the Transnistrian soccer team Sheriff Tiraspol celebrated winning its fourth Moldovan championship in a row, across the city *Ludmilla Balbinova* was packing her suitcase. She was excited about her first trip abroad. Ludmilla knew that Israel was sunny and by the sea, but not much else. She was going to meet an old friend who was working as a waitress in Israel. 'You'll love it here,' *Victoria* told Ludmilla. 'I've got you a job – the work's easy, the pay's good and it is real fun.' What Ludmilla did not know was that, at the other end of the phone, Victoria had a gun pointed at her head.

Ludmilla was not unhappy in Tiraspol but, like many young people, she yearned for some adventure and fun. She thought herself fortunate that an acquaintance of a close friend had been so helpful in arranging both her documentation and travel – not easy in Transnistria, given that the republic is not recognised internationally.

In fact, this accommodating woman was a 'recruiter'. A majority of women trafficked out of Moldova and Transnistria are groomed and recruited by other women. The recruiters are motivated above all by money, but there are often other forces at work. Some are former prostitutes who have succeeded in buying themselves out of the trade by agreeing to work as recruiters back home. 'Sometimes the mothers of trafficked women act as recruiters,' explained Alina Budeci of La Strada, an NGO based in Moldova that assists trafficked women. 'We had a case where a mother was contacted by traffickers who said that if she ever wanted to see her daughter again, she would have to recruit three new women to replace her.'

The use of women is critical in order to reassure the victim. Trust is essential to the smooth functioning of any organised criminal activity. Except, that is, when the commodity being traded is a human being. In this instance, deceit must masquerade as trust. To reinforce the deception, the recruiter often accompanies the young woman (aged usually between fifteen and thirty) on the first leg of her journey. After her recruiter had secured Ludmilla a passport, she was put on a train to Odessa and then to Moscow in the company of ten other women. Once in the Russian capital, she was taken to an apartment near the Moscow River. 'This is when I first became very suspicious because they confiscated our passports and locked the apartment,' she said. 'We were imprisoned.'

From now on, whenever Ludmilla was taken outside, she was always accompanied by at least two thugs. After a week she and three other women were driven to Domodedovo airport. At passport control, she had a final chance. In a compassionate outburst rare in Russian state officials, the officer at passport control pleaded with her to reconsider. 'Do you really know where you are going?' he asked. 'Do you really know what you are doing? Are you sure you want to do this?' With one of the heavies literally breathing down her neck, Ludmilla had little choice but to dismiss the officer's kind appeal. It was like the sound of the prison door slamming shut and the key being turned.

On arrival in Cairo, she was met by some Egyptian men who took her to a hotel, where she and ten other girls waited for three days. In the early hours one morning, Ludmilla was bundled into a jeep and driven for several hours. 'The Bedouins took charge of us and immediately put us into a cave.' Although there are frequent reports of Bedouin smugglers raping the women they traffic (and indeed withholding them if they do not receive payment for their smuggling services), in Ludmilla's case the girls were given a choice. If they offered sexual services to their temporary captors, 'then the girls were allowed out, to eat properly and to have a break. About three of the girls did this, but I didn't,' said Ludmilla.

Just before they were due to leave for the next leg of their journey, one of these terrified women made a break for it. 'The Bedouins captured her and then, in front of us, they shot her in the knees.' As victims of knee-capping in Northern Ireland well know, being shot in the knees is one of the most painful punishments that can be inflicted. But this young Moldovan woman's fate was even worse. 'They just left her there in the desert to die.'

By now Ludmilla and her companions were terrified when the Bedouins again threw them in a pick-up truck in the dead of night. 'We drove for some time and then we were forced to crawl under a fence one by one. There were some other Bedouins meeting us on the other side, but then we were spotted by an Israeli border patrol, which came racing towards us. I was desperate for the border guards to reach us, but the Bedouins started shooting at our feet so we had to run as fast as we could to the next pick-up truck. We were hurled into the back and a tarpaulin was thrown on top of us. It was simply terrifying.' Having cut their teeth bringing contraband across the Egyptian–Israeli borders, like their younger brothers I saw on the camels, these more experienced Bedouin men have now adapted their skills to traffic women. They frequently rape and brutalise the women – it is a depressing degeneration of their traditions.

In a hotel in the Negev capital, Beersheba, Ludmilla was paraded in front of potential purchasers. 'The men spoke Hebrew most of the time so we couldn't understand, but then they would order us about in fluent Russian.' At first Ludmilla refused to get undressed. One of the Russians looked at her grimly. 'The word "refuse" doesn't exist here. Understand?'

By the time she arrived in Tel Aviv, she had been passed through the hands of Moldovan, Ukrainian, Russian, Egyptian, Bedouin, Russian Jewish and indigenous Israeli hands, half of whom had threatened her with violence. Her nightmare was only just beginning.

On a Friday evening in October as the Shabbat approaches, I set out with two male friends to visit the brothels of Tel Aviv. Under the fraying awning of the Banana VIP club, a sickly yellow light illuminates a thick Russian neck against the dark street. Unlike the guards at almost every public establishment I've entered in Israel, he does not check for bombs or weapons, but insists, in a touchingly Soviet fashion, on seeing our passports. He finally makes do with our driving licences and we walk three floors up a thin stairwell past several apartments. We enter the reception lounge where a couple of tense young men sit smoking and tapping their fingers against the armrests of cheap red sofas (along with red, the favoured colour of Tel Aviv brothels seems to be dark nicotine-yellow). Opposite the sofas on a slightly raised platform sit two women, occasionally exchanging some quiet words in Russian. One is dressed in a small pink top and taut bikini bottoms from which her buttocks stick out when she totters around on the four-inch heels that seem to be a de rigueur accessory here.

Behind the desk an exceptionally good-looking woman in her early twenties shares the look of infinite boredom which I note is as essential to whorehouses as the high heels. On either side of the lounge are corridors leading off to small rooms, which I can just make out are large enough to accommodate a single bed and are decorated in red with dim red lighting. Conventional wisdom suggests this to be the colour of romance, but this being my fourth brothel of the evening, I've already worked out that it effectively hides the filth on the carpets and beds. I have also discovered that it is regarded as normal for men to sit in the lounge, saying nothing, but waiting till the mood strikes (or not). They then approach one of the women quietly and the two disappear (the woman effortlessly snatching a towel on the way). Dead face. No emotion.

Three brash American teenagers stroll in and break the silence. The one Hebrew speaker among them asks the girl behind the desk the price: '230 shekels for half an hour; 250 for forty minutes.' 'Hey,' replies his friend, 'chill out a bit. Wait and see if they have any girls who are hotter than these,' he says, gesturing towards the two women.

Although barely eighteen (if that), this guy was not a novice in this house. Raised on McDonald's and with an apparently sluggish metabolism, he was pug-ugly to boot and I couldn't help thinking that he would have found it difficult getting laid through more conventional methods. But I was still unable to account for such an inhuman attitude to these women in one so young. My friend Gideon leaned over to me and spoke softly. 'You see them all the time,' he said. 'Their parents pack 'em off from the Upper West Side to Israel with a book filled with the phone numbers of synagogues, rabbis, *shuls* and a wad of cash. And then the minute they get here, they head for the whorehouses.'

Earlier that evening, we had seen much worse. We had started our tour near the Old Bus Station, which is where some of the tens of thousands of foreign workers hang out in Israel. Since the last *intifada*, the Palestinians no longer carry out the dirty and dangerous jobs, which are the preserve of immigrants elsewhere in the industrialised world. Their places have been taken by Romanians, Uzbeks, Thais, Filipinos, Turks – you name it. The importation of labour into Israel is a corrupt business in which organised crime also engages: globally, the International Migration Organisation has identified the trafficking of indentured or slave labour as the fastest-growing sector in the industry.

The men who hang out at the Old Bus Station are not trafficked – although dirt-poor, they are still probably the elite amongst this lumpen class. By any standards, though, this place is the pits. The buildings and streets are in disrepair, brightened up only by the odd flickering neon sign of a heart or a naked woman pointing to a hovel behind the shop fronts. The brothels themselves are the bottom of this mucky heap. I can barely describe the pathetic ageing women, listlessly chain-smoking in rooms seven feet by three, ready to service any passer-by for ten bucks (yes, ten bucks).

It is impossible to ascertain which of these women are compelled by traffickers and which by economic circumstance, as everybody in the trade, including the women, is wary of careless talk. It may be that high-class call girls enjoy the economic freedom their work affords them. But my short tour around Tel Aviv's brothels made it clear that for most women in the industry, the happy hooker is a preposterous myth. Similarly, it brought home how relentless the male sex drive is. Streams of men of different race, age and class trotted in and out of the brothels as I was visiting them. The Jews are both secular and orthodox; there are Palestinians from inside Israel and from the West Bank; there are a large number of Americans, Western Europeans and Japanese. Their faces indicate that they have overcome any qualms they may once have felt (if ever) about their purchase of these services. I wonder if they were told the real stories behind the women they are abusing – women like Ludmilla – how many would think again.

Instead of the holiday experience of a lifetime, Ludmilla was kept locked in an apartment from 6.30 in the morning. At 5.30 in the afternoon, she was driven to a brothel above a pizza parlour on Bugashov Street, where she was forced to work for twelve hours from 6 p.m. in the high-volume second shift. 'I worked seven days a week and had to service up to twenty clients per session,' she explained. That is a euphemism. Ludmilla was raped twenty times a night.

In Israel, as in most Western countries, it is the trafficked woman and not the client who is the object of law-enforcement procedures. When Ludmilla first succeeded in escaping, she was handed back to her pimp by the duty sergeant, who happened to be a client of the brothel. In response, she was beaten senseless by her 'owner'. The second time she got away, she handed herself in to a police station in another part of town. As is habitual, she was charged with being an illegal immigrant and thrown in a detention centre for several months as her deportation order was processed.

When she finally arrived back in Chisinau, destitute and trauma-tised for life, Ludmilla could not return to her home, partly for reasons of shame, but above all for fear of being found by her traffickers. Hers is an everyday story of life in Moldova, Ukraine, Russia, Egypt and Israel.

The day after I had spoken to Ludmilla, her case worker called. 'I forgot to mention,' she said, 'Ludmilla is now HIV-positive.' Unsur-prisingly, combination therapy is not readily available in a country like Moldova.

A few months after Brigadier General Hezi Leder had identified the growth in Haifa street gangs, he received a tip-off that a Russian oligarch was due to celebrate his birthday in Eilat. 'We didn't know who these people were,' explained one of Israel's most senior intelligence offi-cers tasked with mapping Russian organised crime, 'and we had to start from scratch. There were the low-level criminals – and we learned all about them; about the *vory-v-zakonye*, the *thieves-in-law*; about their tattoos; we had people who learned how to speak their slang. And then there were the big guys. They were hard, but we went for them all.'

The guests at the party in Eilat and at subsequent summit meet-ings in Tel Aviv read like a *Who's Who* of Russian business. The problem was that nobody in Israeli intelligence knew Who exactly was Who. And Who was Not. Maybe.

Testifying to the House Committee on Banking in 1999, the former Director of the CIA, James Woolsey, illuminated this conundrum when he asked the Congressmen to consider the following hypothetical situation.

> If you should chance to strike up a conversation with an articulate, English-speaking Russian in, say, the restaurant of one of the luxury hotels along Lake Geneva, and he is wearing a $3,000 suit and a pair of Gucci loafers, and he tells you that he is an executive of a Russian trading company and wants to talk to you about a joint venture, then there are four possibilities. He may be what he says he is. He may be a Russian intelligence officer working under commercial cover. He may be part of a Russian organised-crime group. But the really interesting possibility is that he may be all three – and that none of those three institutions have any problem with the arrangement.

A staggering number of Russians took out Israeli citizenship in the first half of the 1990s, among them prominent members of Yeltsin's inner circle, known as the Seven Stars, like Boris Berezovsky and Vladimir Gusinsky. Then there were budding industrial magnates like the Ukrainian Vladimir Rabinovich and the Russian Mikhail Chorny, who were under scrutiny by Western intelligence agencies. And then there were others who had been barred from entering Britain and the US, like Semyon Mogilevich.

There was even a scattering of gentiles, like Sergei Mikhailov, the boss of Solntsevo, who managed to wangle himself citizenship. 'Mikhailov has as much to do with Judaism as I have with ballet!' guffawed the ursine documentary-maker Alexander Gentelev, 'but he got his citizenship – no problem.' It has since been revoked and the corrupt Israeli officials responsible for granting it have been prosecuted.

None of these Russians had criminal records, except for misdemeanours during the Soviet period. All had the outward appearance of successful businessmen with track records which, on paper, bespoke dynamism and guts. Why would Israel want to turn them away?

For their part, the oligarchs and organised-crime bosses started colonising Israel for a number of reasons. It was an ideal place to invest or launder money. Israel's banking system was designed to encourage *aliyah*, the immigration of Jews from around the world, and that meant encouraging their money to boot. Furthermore, Israel had embraced the zeitgeist of international financial deregulation and considerably eased controls on the import and export of capital. And, like most other economies around the world in the 1990s, it had no anti-money-laundering legislation. Laundering money derived from criminal activities anywhere else in the world was an entirely legitimate business.

Israeli police have estimated that these Russians laundered between $5 and $10 billion through Israeli banks in the fifteen years following the collapse of communism. This is a significant sum for a small country like Israel. But it is less than 5 per cent of the huge capital flight from Russia during the 1990s and it pales beside comparable countries such as Switzerland ($40 billion) or the perennial champion of the Mediterranean league, the Republic of Cyprus, which as early as the end of 1994 was processing $1 billion of Russian capital *a month*.

The main reason for Israel's popularity was the simplest – many of these iffy businessmen were Jews, and in Israel they were not treated like dirt, but welcomed as valuable and respected additions to the family.

A disproportionate number of the most influential Russian oligarchs and gangsters were Jewish. Before the massive wave of immigration to Israel, Jews made up only about 2.5 per cent of the population of Russia and Ukraine. But they were hugely influential in the vanguard of gangster capitalism during the 1990s. A cursory search of the Internet will reveal countless racist sites fuelling the theory that the pillage of Russian assets during the decade was born of the World Jewish Conspiracy, once so beloved of the Nazis and (when it suited him) of Stalin. By contrast, many liberal commentators simply overlook the issue of Jewish involvement in Russia's and Ukraine's chaotic transition, presumably to dodge accusations of anti-Semitism. In fact, by avoiding any mention of the elephant in the living room, they facilitate its portrayal by anti-Semites as a jackal.

Although the Soviet Union was renowned for its antipathy towards most national identities that threatened its idealised image of *Homo sovieticus*, it did construct one specific barrier for Jews: the glass ceiling.

In virtually all the central Party and state offices, in almost all industrial branches and in most places of learning, Jews were systematically prevented from reaching the top. There were exceptions to this
rule – Lazar Kaganovich was one of Stalin's unloved Politburo
colleagues, and, in the 1980s, Evgeni Primakov emerged as an extremely
influential political figure, having prophylactically discarded his name
given at birth, Yonah Finkelshtein. But on the whole, if you were
Jewish, the key promotion would elude you.

In consequence, there were a lot of smart Jews who felt frustrated
in their pursuit of intellectual challenges and entrepreneurial opportunities. Where better, then, to exercise those skills than in the world's
toughest market (which officially didn't even exist!): the Soviet planned
economy. Over seventy years, they honed their business skills in this
grim totalitarian world where huge industrial behemoths would seek
to produce goods without regard to the laws of supply and demand.
Instead, enterprises would follow the targets (or norms, as they were
known) set down every five years by the State Planning Commission.
These rarely bore any relation to the available materials, raw or
processed, and so each factory would be engaged in a relentless and
exhausting struggle against shortages. Factories were often reliant on
suppliers based thousands of miles and several different time zones
away, with which there were no functioning communications. The
only way to meet those targets was to employ wheelers and dealers
who could hustle the right materials from any source anywhere. These
people were known as *tolkachi*, or fixers, and without the ingenuity of
the *tolkachi* in sustaining the wobbly edifice, the Soviet Union might
have buckled earlier than it did. And just as there were a disproportionate number of Jews among the oligarchs, so there were among
the *tolkachi*.

'Being Jewish, I couldn't study medicine as a matter of course,'
Vladimir Rabinovich, one of Ukraine's most notorious oligarchs,
explained. Rabinovich was then subjected to another burst of casual
anti-Semitism and was expelled from Technical College. He was then
compelled to begin his three-year military service. 'I had been with
my unit for just twenty days. The commander addressed us by asking,
"Who can get hold of five tons of steel tubing with a three-quarter-
inch diameter?" I had absolutely no idea what he was talking about,

but I volunteered nonetheless. "And how long do you need to get hold of them?" he asked me. "A minimum of one week," I replied. And that got me the job!' By ducking, diving, sweet-talking and pilfering, Rabinovich found the tubing and began his career as a *tolkach*. Most of his fellow Jewish entrepreneurs or mafia bosses boasted similar histories. Not only had they developed their entrepreneurial skills in the most trying circumstances, but they were not weighed down, as were their Slav peers, by the torpid traditions of the Tsarist and Soviet bureaucracies, which crushed any hint of personal initiative.

This ability was not restricted to the Jews. It is no coincidence that among organised-crime bosses, the other two chronically over-represented nationalities in Russia were the Chechens and the Georgians, whose talent for overcoming the daily consumer misery of the Soviet Union was similarly the stuff of legend. The criminals and oligarchs emerged from communities that inhabited the twilight periphery of the Soviet Union – although usually denied access to the central institutions, they were not pariahs. Instead they were compelled to seek out the possibilities of social and economic activity that existed in the nooks and cracks of the state. This experience was invaluable for many when negotiating the roller-coaster of post communist Russia.

For the Jewish oligarchs and gang bosses, Israel was both a retreat and, by dint of its passport, a door to the outside world. They did not wish to draw attention to themselves, nor did they wish to become an embarrassment for the state. This was no mere sentiment – it was a policy, hammered out between the most influential Godfathers at a meeting in Tel Aviv's Dan Panorama Hotel in 1995. The biggest names were there, including gentiles like Sergei Mikhailov, to ensure that they did not alienate the Israeli Government. 'They decided that Israel is no place for assassinations or settling their difficulties by killing one another,' explained Gentelev. 'These people did not want to engage in much business here. It was a place where you could launder a bit of money; where you could rest; and where you could find shelter. And receive a passport with which you could travel the whole world.'

The New Russians were already well settled in Israel by October 1995 when Bill Clinton's advisers convinced him to sound a warning about the 'dark side of globalisation'. Addressing the 50th Commemorative Assembly of the UN, the President called for a worldwide 'assault on terrorism, organised crime, drug trafficking and nuclear smuggling'. Clinton said that 'no one is immune', as he listed crimes like the Aun Shinrikyo 'poison-gas attacks on the Japanese subway, suitcase bombings in Israel and France, mafia gangs in Russia and the Oklahoma City bombing' that had shaken America in April of that year.

Because of the concentrated Russian presence, Washington turned its gaze onto Israel and by the mid-1990s the long if arthritic arm of American law enforcement was knocking on Jerusalem's door for information on a number of oligarchs and alleged criminals, like Mogilevich and Mikhailov. Encouraged by the State Department under Jon Winer, the Israeli police placed many of the most prominent Russians under surveillance in 1996. 'There was suddenly a huge interest in the oligarchs,' explained Irit Bouton, now Chief of Intelligence in the Israeli police Special Operations. 'It was like a baby boom in the world of crime.'

But huge problems matched the huge interest as the police tried to assess and contain the burgeoning criminality of the new world order. There was the familiar issue of definition: what constituted criminal activity among the oligarchs and what did not? Moreover, the oligarchs and gangsters could draw on effectively limitless financial resources to defend themselves and their image. And they did so assiduously. 'Don't worry about these guys shooting you,' an Israeli intelligence officer told me when I explained what I was writing about. 'They aren't that crude. They'll just sue you to death.'

Then there was the strong political pressure exercised on the Israeli police, both by their own politicians and foreign governments. Iosif Kobzon is renowned as the Frank Sinatra of the New Russia. A tremendously popular performer of schmaltzy songs in Russia, he also enjoys a rich political life: as an MP of the Russian Duma, and a backer or friend of many pro-Putin politicians and businessmen. In the early 1990s he was refused entry into the United States, but received an Israeli passport, despite a great deal of opposition. Moshe Shahal, a successful Tel Aviv lawyer, was then the Israeli Minister for National Security who established the Anti-Russian Organised Crime intelligence unit. He sighs when remembering the period. 'Both in the Knesset and in Government, we came across difficulties in trying to implement the

Simeon – the boy with everything:
the phone, the Merc, the grave.

Bulgaria's nascent capitalist class gathers for its Annual General Meeting.

The Late Ilya Pavlov – boss of Multigroup.

Stanko 'Cane' Subotic – one of the richest businessmen in the Balkans.

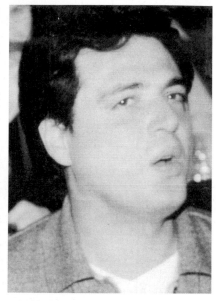

The late Vladimir 'Vanja' Bokan – inventor of the Balkan cigarette smuggling trade.

Arkan, Milica the cub and Arkan's Tigers.

Supporters of Milo Djukanovic, the man who brought Montenegro independence and the cigarette transit tax.

FBI poster seeking the arrest of Semion Mogilevich, from April 2003. At the time of writing he remains a wanted man.

Memorial to the late Viktor Kulivar 'Karabas'– gangster beloved of all Odessa.

'Mr. President,' say the Mafia, 'You are toothless. We are everywhere. Hand over power to us and we will introduce order into Russia and the CIS!'

Sergei Mikhailov, the boss of Solntsevo.

Ze'ev Rosenstein miraculously survived this assassination attempt
on Yehuda Halevy street in Tel Aviv.

Bedouin youngsters with their contraband having just crossed the
Egypt–Israeli border in the Negev desert.

Deepak Nachnani makes his feelings felt outside the Arthur Road jail as Sanjay Dutt is convicted of weapons offences in the court.

The ever-debonair Commander Rakesh Maria in Mumbai.

Dawood Ibrahim – King of the Mumbai Underworld.

Inspector Pradeep Sharma – Scourge of the Mumbai Underworld.

The murderous Bombay blasts of March 1993.

Merging Drugs and Guns –
the Cape Town Gangs.

new security policy.' On his instructions, for example, Kobzon was detained at Ben Gurion airport in January 1996 and refused entry into the country. But Shahal's directive was overridden, the former Minister says, by Shimon Peres, then Foreign Minister. Shahal explains that the then Russian Ambassador had called Peres and warned of severe consequences for Israeli–Russian relations if Kobzon were denied entry into Israel. The authorities, seldom susceptible to influence from countries except the United States, allowed him in.

It was inevitable that the arrival of one million Russians would have a substantial impact on the Israeli electorate: they represented votes that every established politician wanted to win. The central political figure in the Russian community was Natan Sharansky, the former Soviet dissident who was released from prison into exile in the mid-1980s. In the early 1990s he became the conduit between the oligarchs and the Israeli political establishment, accepting donations from some of the new arrivals from Russia and then establishing his avowedly Zionist political party, Yisra'el Ba'aliyah, in 1995.

Sharansky's was a powerful lobby as it controlled potentially several hundred thousand votes in a democracy in which small political parties are crucial in forming governments. One should not underestimate how strongly Israel's Russian-speaking community felt about its prominent members being branded criminals, as the ex-Russian media magnate and now owner of the Israeli paper *Ma'ariv*, Vladimir Gusinsky, pointed out. 'When we Russian businessmen, Jewish or otherwise, are called mafiosi by American newspapers, it's insulting,' he said. 'But when Jewish entrepreneurs from Russia are called that in Israel, it's not just insulting, it makes me howl with pain. It's wrong!'

The police had to negotiate all these conundrums and dilemmas in trying to formulate a coherent strategy in dealing with organised crime and in trying to understand its relationship to Russian immigration. But all this took place in the shadow of a very different issue, which absorbed not just most of Israel's security budget, but much of its political energy as well. 'The whole question of Palestinian terror,' said Commander Bouton, 'puts a strain on our resources working in the organised-crime area – we are always playing catch-up.' Marvellous opportunity for criminals, though.

The Palestinian issue is simply overwhelming in Israel. At times,

it almost seems that Israelis have willingly diverted all their intellectual faculties into consideration of this one matter. Everything appears
illuminated by the torch of the Arab–Israeli conflict, obscuring in the
process the fascinating and dynamic nature of Israel's own society,
especially since the collapse of the Soviet Union and the advent of
globalisation.

The existence of an external Arab enemy and, after the Six Day War
in 1967, a Palestinian enemy in the Occupied Territories has afforded
Israel a powerful domestic legitimacy. But the sacrifices imposed on
Israelis by security concerns were only ever one side of the coin: until
fifteen years ago, Zionism was underpinned by a remarkably strong
sense of collectivism, expressed most obviously in the *kibbutzim* movement, but also in the influence of the trade-union movement, the
Histadrut. A bitter opponent of the Soviet Union, Natan Sharansky
expressed the sentiments of many right-wing Jews when he railed
against his new home: 'The predominance of the government in Israel's
economy makes it the most socialist country outside the Eastern Bloc
... It is Israel's fate to suffer the worst from the centrally controlled
east and the democratic west.'

But for most Israelis the powerful state sector was an important
expression of solidarity among Jews, conferring a social and philan-
thropic substance to the national project. Globalisation is chipping
away at that relentlessly and in some places is driving a wedge between
the various parts of a highly differentiated society. 'Prime Ministers
like Menachem Begin and Ben Gurion were public servants, living in
small two-bedroom apartments,' said Uri Cohen-Aharonov, Israel's
leading TV crime commentator. 'They got up at 6 a.m. working for
Israel and were still doing so when they went to bed at midnight. Now
you say the word *kibbutz* and people laugh. Ariel Sharon has a huge
farm a few kilometres from Sderot where the poorest people in the
country live. The difference between the rich and ordinary people
reminds me more and more of the gap between rich and poor in South
America.'

After years of modest inflows, direct foreign investment suddenly
swamped the country, encouraged by the political stability accompanying the peace process following the Oslo Accords. Exchange controls
were relaxed, and suddenly billions were moving in and out of Israel

every year. In just eight years, foreign investment rose from $0.2 billion in 1992 to more than $8 billion in 2000. Within that context the Russian money-flows were seen by Israel's elite as an indicator of economic success, not of criminality. Even more spectacular was the increase in *per capita* GDP from $11,000 in 1990 to $18,620 in 2006. Visible wealth was increasing in striking contrast to the stagnation of the surrounding Arab countries. Less visible, however, was the steady rise in unemployment as investors directed their capital into industries with low labour requirements.

The collapse of the dot-com boom resulted in dramatic stories of suicides on Wall Street, but its impact was considerably harsher on the periphery of the globalising world. This was especially true in Israel, not just because of the concentration of wealth in the high-tech industries, but also because it coincided with the beginning of the Second Palestinian *intifada* in 2000. Austerity measures replaced the expanding budgets of the mid-1990s. Spending on the IDF (the Israeli Defence Force) increased to meet the challenge of the Palestinians, but spending on the police at first remained stagnant and was then cut in real terms. Above all, social programmes were trimmed and, in a very short time, the discrepancy between rich and poor that had begun to grow during the 1990s became very obvious. The change in Israeli society at the turn of the century was rapid and remarkable. As the hangover set in, Israel found itself with high unemployment, a growing budget deficit, a spiralling security budget and collapsing foreign direct investment. It also had a new sub-class of foreign labour (many of them trafficked) to replace the Palestinians now penned into the West Bank and the Gaza Strip; and a culture of avid consumerism that placed individualism firmly above the collectivism of the *kibbutzim*. Hostility to the Russians started to grow again, especially with regard to perceptions about criminality. When asked about crime in a country-wide survey about attitudes to immigration from the former Soviet Union in 1999, 24 per cent of Israelis had a 'very negative view' of the Russian-speaking community. When asked the same question in January 2003, that figure had risen to 38 per cent. A month later, however, something happened that led Israelis to reassess who the criminal culprits might be. The Russians had agreed at the 1995 El Dan meeting in Tel Aviv to avoid acting in an ostentatious criminal manner within Israel. Now Israelis were about to discover that the years of champagne and excess in the 1990s had spawned a new phenomenon – indigenous Israeli organised crime. And, unlike the Russians, these people cared very little about their public image.

Ze'ev Rosenstein's Mercedes pulled over in front of a small currency-exchange shop on Yehuda Halevy Street. It was midday in December with the eastern Mediterranean's short winter still at bay. 'A couple of policemen were arguing with a guy sitting in a red car,' Eli, a man in his forties, told the *Jerusalem Post*, 'then came the boom . . . And they all disappeared.'

'It was a big, big bang,' said Alon, who still works at the Tabul bakery opposite, 'and then I see a body flying up into the air. A lot of people came – the police, just like a terror attack. For the first twenty minutes, everyone thought it was a terror attack. We didn't think it had anything to do with Rosenstein, we thought it was Palestinians.'

In fact, this was the seventh attempt on the life of Ze'ev Rosenstein, who had for several years been at daggers drawn with the Abergil family. But in contrast to earlier ones, this failed assassination took place in a busy, slightly run-down street in south Tel Aviv. Rosenstein, 'the wolf with seven lives' as he is known, drove away with a few bruises and scratches, but three innocent bystanders were dead.

The media outcry was fuelled by popular indignation. 'It's not like we don't have enough bombs in this country as it is!' said Bilha, who worked at the corner supermarket a few yards from where the bomb went off. 'Are they completely insane? What have we come to? Jews blowing up Jews?'

The police blamed the Interior Minister for starving them of resources. 'We don't have the resources to fight a two-front war,' said Gil Kleiman after the bomb. Kleiman, who had cut his teeth uncovering criminality in the Russian underground, was now spokesman for the Israeli police and clearly frustrated. 'It's a very big bed, and a very small security blanket, and we have to move that blanket around. So if your blanket is covering anti-terror work, those are police officers who can't be doing anti-crime work, which is checking and stopping vehicles, and doing what proper police criminal procedures are. You can't do both at the same time.'

Ariel Sharon called an emergency cabinet meeting and the Government promised an extra 500 million shekels ($100 million) in the fight against crime. Newspaper commentators began to compare Rosenstein, the Abergils and four other families with the Palestinians in terms of threats to the Israeli state. Interestingly one of those families was a Bedouin clan.

'The indigenous Israeli crime syndicates are different from the Russians,' explained Menachem Amir, the country's leading criminologist. 'The Russians were very careful. And were able to impose discipline because they were based on an organisation. The Israeli crime groups were families.' This meant that in structure they were much more like the Sicilian mafia than the Russians were. 'When you have crime based on families, then issues such as honour and vendettas come into play,' Professor Amir continued. The existence of family feuds may result in the occasional innocent victim, as in the Rosenstein case, but in another respect they assist the police. The blood-letting enables intelligence officers to monitor what is going on in the crime community, 'which means that the Russians and similar organisations are more effective and more dangerous'.

Gambling had been the traditional industry around which the Israeli crime syndicates gathered and thrived. After the Oslo peace accords, the Israelis permitted the Palestinians to open a casino in Jericho to complement the floating casinos in the Red Sea, which hovered just outside Israel's territorial waters. The Rosensteins and Abergils were alleged to have controlled much of the pay-offs from these, as well as the profits from organised gambling trips for Israelis to Turkey.

But in the 1990s the Israeli syndicates branched out and moved into an even more lucrative area. The families, 'perhaps thanks to their long-standing ties in Antwerp', the DEA reported, 'continue to be the major elements in the transfer of large shipments of Ecstasy from Belgium [to the United States]'. Those ties referred to one of the four key commodities from which organised-crime groups around the world make their largest profits: diamonds. The other three are arms, narcotics and energy products.

Ecstasy was one of the few drugs where the American market was not yet supersaturated. Europe is the top manufacturing base for this synthetic drug, which stimulates a feeling of well-being and in particular a sense of goodwill to one's fellow humans. The main Western European centre is Amsterdam, although industrial-scale busts have been made since the turn of the millennium in Serbia and Bulgaria as well.

In 2003, the US State Department issued a report which claimed that Israel is the hub of global Ecstasy trafficking, having branched out from Europe to the US. 'Israeli drug-trafficking organisations are the main source of distribution of the drug to groups in the US, using express mail services, commercial airlines, and recently also using air cargo services,' the report states. For a country as dependent on American financial, political and military support, this was acutely embarrassing to Israel.

The DEA implied in one report that the turf war in New York, Las Vegas and Los Angeles over the Ecstasy trade may be directly linked to the open warfare between families in Israel. It is perhaps appropriate that Israeli gangsters have such influence in Las Vegas, as this was the old stamping ground of America's most notorious Jewish criminal, the late Meyer Lansky, and his protégé, Bugsy Siegel. Lansky was one of the very few indictees ever to be extradited from Israel to the United States. He sought Israeli citizenship in the early 1970s when on the run from American law enforcement. Golda Meir was only convinced to allow the extradition when her aides explained that Lansky was involved with the mafia. 'No. No mafia! Not here!' she exclaimed.

Ze'ev Rosenstein posed a much greater threat to Israel than Lansky ever could. Both he and his wife were members of Prime Minister Ariel Sharon's then political party, the Likud. The Abergils were also members of Likud and, in one famous incident, a Labour member of the Knesset accused a cabinet minister (later assassinated by the Palestinians) of links with Israeli organised crime. Jon Winer had offered Bill Clinton serious evidence of the criminal penetration of Likud, a further suggestion of how crime since 1989 was beginning to undermine the country's social fabric.

But in 2004, under pressure from the US, Israel acted by arresting and extraditing Rosenstein, who was wanted by America for the sale there of more than 700,000 Ecstasy tablets (although Washington agreed that, if found guilty, Rosenstein would be able to serve his sentence back in Israel).

Because of specific political issues, Israel was one of several countries around the globe that was vulnerable to swift penetration by organised crime in the wake of two epoch-changing events. The first was the collapse of communism in Eastern Europe and the former Soviet Union, which as we have seen had a unique impact in Israel. But the extent of the internationalisation of organised crime and the role that Israelis played in it would not have been possible without globalisation – and one aspect in particular, the deregulation of international financial markets. The new freedom for capital to travel around the world was not restricted to money from those huge corporations that had slipped the moorings of individual countries and their regulatory systems to assume a global presence. The laundering of profits from illicit activities was also about to enter its Golden Age. And lest we fall into the error of thinking that Israelis or Jews had a particular penchant and ability for engaging in organised crime, it is worth remembering that the centre for the global money-laundering industry was a few hundred miles away in a very different country: the United Arab Emirates.

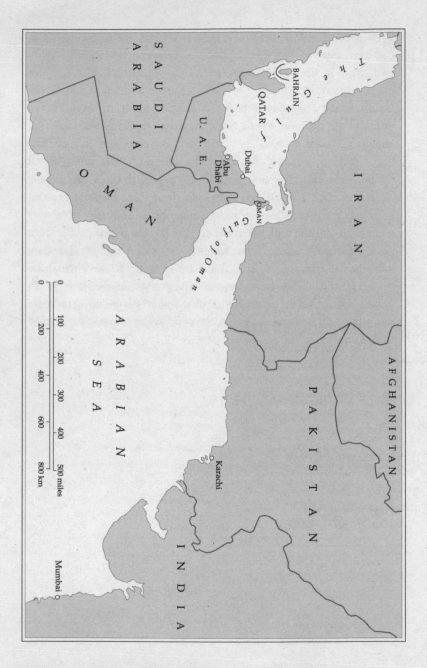

Dawood Ibrahim's turf: Dubai–Karachi–Mumbai

6

XANADU I

> And 'mid this tumult Kubla heard from far
> Ancestral voices prophesying war!
> Samuel Taylor Coleridge, 'Kubla Khan'

On the morning of Friday March 12th, 1993, they emerged after dawn in their millions. From cracked and crumbling Victorian mansions, from spiffing Art Deco bungalows, from new high-rises, from tin shacks, from under fraying tarpaulin covers, from gutters and from city sidewalks: the working people of Bombay* launched their chaotic charge on the most besieged, battered, but resilient transportation system in the world.

Like deranged wasps, the auto-rickshaws darted around the streets, stinging any fool in their way. Yet more numerous were the angular black-and-yellow taxis. Modelled on little Fiat 1100s that even the Italians have forgotten, these beasties scurried and squeaked like motorised rodents, squeezing through gaps in the traffic where none were apparent. By 1993, India's steady liberalisation had allowed imperious European, American and Japanese cars onto the market to compete with the domestic Ambassador (né Morris Oxford III Series) and Marutti (né Suzuki Alto).

And, of course, on the dilapidated stations of the Western and Central Railway lines, fists were thrown, shirts torn and saris pulled as the commuters from the northern suburbs engaged in their daily Darwinian scramble to get on the inexplicably reliable urban trains to reach the south of the city.

'I have never quite understood how traffic in Bombay moves and I understand more about this subject than most,' mused Rakesh Maria,

* The city's name was changed to Mumbai in 1997. References to Bombay denote events before that date.

the charming former Deputy Commissioner of Police (Traffic), 'but mysteriously it does progress.'

Once the frenzied movement of people begins in the morning, it doesn't stop until many hours after sundown. It is accompanied by sticky heat and an incessant din of horns, shouting, begging, squealing and ranting – on and on until one thinks only of seeking sanctuary from the assault on the senses.

But at 1.28 p.m. on that March 12th, a new and most sinister element joined the merry pandemonium: the roar of half a ton of the world's most powerful military explosive, RDX, ripping up from the underground garage of the Bombay Stock Exchange (BSE) and into the pit where traders were just preparing for the lunch bell.

This is always the busiest time of day at the BSE. Traders, hawkers and food sellers, with their cornucopia of fruit, samosas, curries, lassies, dosas, sweetbreads and more, descend on the area to assuage the hunger of the businessmen and women who stream out of the Exchange and its surrounding buildings for their brief half-hour lunch period. But on this day they didn't scamper out. They were thrown out, dismembered and dead, while the mass of concrete, glass and metal decapitated and disembowelled the street vendors, their friends, their customers and their families.

'Four brothers of a migrant family from northern India ran a sugar-cane-juice stall near the BSE,' recalled Hussain Zaidi, author of *Black Friday*, the most detailed history of the bombings, which was later made into a riveting documentary movie. 'The fifth brother returned shortly after the blast to find his siblings lying dead in a pool of blood. Then there was Gokulchand Gupta, who had run a panipuri stall there for thirteen years. Gupta's head was blown off. His only son, Premchand, who was seventeen, was charred beyond recognition.'

Twenty-two-year-old Mukesh Khatri had gone to the Baroda Bank, which had a branch at the BSE. He was queuing outside the building when the bomb went off. 'There were pieces of glass flying all around, many were embedded in my body and my face,' he remembered. Drenched in his own and others' blood, he somehow managed to drag himself on foot to a hospital almost one mile away.

The effect of this calamity on the traffic in downtown Bombay was, of course, dramatic. Panic mutated into hysteria to ensure the onset of localised gridlock. Ambulances and police cars were as immobile as the rest, leaving those victims still alive writhing in agony. Eighty-four died and 217 were injured in the BSE blast. This was the beginning.

Over the next two hours, a further seven bombs went off at crowded locations throughout the city, while grenades were thrown in another two places by men on motorcycles. The deadliest explosion occurred outside the Regional Passport Office in Worli at 2.50 p.m., when a bomb placed on a double-decker bus lifted the five-ton vehicle off the ground. Not a single body on the bus could be identified, while a merciless shower of burning metal and glass pierced the organs and limbs of hundreds of passers-by and residents: 113 dead, 227 injured.

Around the same time, Deputy Commander Rakesh Maria was investigating a further explosion at the headquarters of Shiv Sena, a young Hindu nationalist party that had its power base in Bombay, the capital of Maharashtra. Hindus were clustering around the Shiv Sena building, chanting anti-Muslim slogans and demanding retribution. 'I addressed the leader of the mob and told him that the bombs had nothing to do with religion,' Maria said, 'but were part of a much bigger conspiracy.' This, he added, seemed to disperse the tension. At around the same time, however, he received news over his walkie-talkie that a mob had started attacking Muslims indiscriminately in the district of Mahim.

The unstoppable city had ground to a bloody halt.

Thirteen years later, as the sun sets across Mumbai's police headquarters, an elegant Victorian mansion in khaki and cream, Maria leans back behind his chunky wooden desk. A distinguished-looking Punjabi with an assured military bearing, he recalled: 'I had been away from it all on a course in advanced urban traffic management in Tokyo, but returned here to some turbulent times. As soon as I got back on January 5th, 1993, the Chief Commissioner put me in charge of the Mahim Chicken's Neck to ensure that the VIPs were able to travel from the airport to the centre.' Just east of Mahim fort, the Chicken's Neck is a narrow chicane where Bombay's two main north–south arterial roads merge to form the ninth circle of vehicular hell. Rakesh Maria was charged with securing the passage of VIPs to the city centre because Bombay was in crisis: anti-Muslim riots had erupted here in December 1992 and again in January 1993. Many of these riots, indeed, broke out in and around Mahim.

The turbulent times that had greeted Maria on his arrival back in India's commercial capital had commenced even before the riots. Over the previous five years, the BJP, a new political party that espoused an aggressive form of Hindu nationalism, had fostered an obscure religious dispute in another part of India – Ayodhya in the northern province of Uttar Pradesh. Following an ominous pattern, the events around the destruction of the Babri Mosque in Ayodhya, far away from Bombay, had unsettled relations between the majority Hindus and minority Muslims in several parts of India. In Bombay itself, the Hindu mob followed the exhortations of nationalists to attack Muslims indiscriminately. 'The day I took over responsibility for the Chicken's Neck was the day the riots broke out again,' said Maria. 'I was at the junction in Mahim opposite St Michael's Church, where Muslim workers stored wood, when the Hindus attacked them,' he continued. Although he is not a Christian, Commissioner Maria's surname suggests that he is, and he never disabuses people of this assumption as it affords him a certain neutrality when dealing with tensions between Muslims and Hindus. As the Hindus surrounded the Muslim workers, Maria rushed to the scene and started firing in the air. 'I warned them all to disperse and, from that day forth, there was no confrontation in this part of Mahim.'

Unfortunately Maria's courage was not mirrored elsewhere among Bombay's police. Altogether 900 people, more than two-thirds of them Muslims, the rest Hindus, were slaughtered in those riots as law-enforcement officers stood and watched. 'We failed the Muslims of Bombay and we failed the people of Bombay during that time,' one senior police officer told me. This dereliction of duty was to have the most severe consequences, most notably the March bombings. 'Until 1993,' argued Maria, 'Bombay's underworld was the most secular part of this city. In other spheres, we saw communal issues having an impact, but we never for a moment imagined that this could affect organised crime.'

During the riots, the Hindu mob in Mahim had sought out and destroyed the offices of one Tiger Memon, a mid-level gangster and renowned smuggler who owed allegiance to the most powerful crime organisation in Bombay. According to his friends, Tiger Memon was livid when he learned about the attack on his HQ and he immediately set about planning his revenge. To do so, however, meant conferring with his boss. But although his boss was a Bombay lad, he no longer lived there. Wanted both by the police and rival gangsters in connection with a string of serious homicide charges, Dawood Ibrahim Kaskar had skipped bail in 1984 and left the city he loved. He moved westward to a place that had long enjoyed a warm, tangled relationship with Bombay, but which could hardly be more different.

A few miles east of Heathrow Airport, my cab drives past an advertising hoarding the size and shape of a skyscraper. The image of hypermodern buildings stretching towards the heavens beckons drivers on the M4 to leave the light-grey chill of London and fall instead into the embrace of a new earthly paradise – Dubai.

Stepping into my air-conditioned cab eight hours later, a peculiar oblong video greets me with an exhortation to visit the Mercato Mall, a deliciously ill-conceived re-imagining of Venice; then to buy Gold, Gold, Gold; and finally to invest in an apartment at the Burj Dubai.

Burj Dubai is one of several pinnacles in the novel architectural movement that I call Emirate futurism, and which expats call The Master Plan of Sheikh Mo (a cheeky, if endearing, reference to Sheikh Mohammed bin Rashid Al Maktoum, Dubai's enlightened despot). The *burj* or tower comprises several clustering metallic sheaves that soar into the air. The bottom thirty-seven floors will become the world's first Armani Hotel, designed by the fashion guru himself. The final height of the core sheaf is being kept a secret. When the developers first announced the Burj in 2003, it was due to reach 500 metres into the sky. Each year, they have enhanced this vertiginous vision – 600, 700 and now over 900 metres. This is partly to keep competitors in Taiwan and Kuwait guessing, lest they trump Burj Dubai's goal to become the tallest building in the world, and partly, I suspect, the result of a keen urge on the part of The Master Planners to clothe any news about the city's development in excited hyperbole. This urge occasionally surfaces as an Orwellian spasm, such as the slogan that proclaims the birth of the Burj on huge billboards down the main drag of new Dubai: HISTORY RISING.

This new Dubai hosts glitzy visitors from all over the world – David Beckham, Michael Schumacher and Tiger Woods are regular visitors.

Celebrities and the world's most powerful businessmen and women are lining up to purchase some of the eye-popping construction projects that are multiplying like a rampant virus down the coast and into the desert. Rod Stewart was quick to purchase Great Britain, an integral part of The World, islands of luxurious real estate all fashioned to resemble a physical image of the globe when seen from above. Then there is the fabulous complex of Palm Jumeira, Palm Deira and Palm Jebel Ali, huge tracts of land reclaimed from the sea in the shape of three giant palm trees. Visible from space, this is set to become one of the most sought-after addresses on the planet.

Come one, come all . . . if you have the money. And if you do, then few (if any) questions are asked about how you came upon it or what you want to do with it. Dubai's discreet attitude to cash has enabled the city to attract leading figures from industries beyond sports and showbiz over the past decade. Russian arms dealer Viktor Bout, renowned as the Merchant of Death, used to park his planes in Sharjah, Dubai's neighbouring emirate ten miles away, while he received his cheques for services rendered to warring factions through Western banks there. The largest cigarette smuggler in the Balkans established his offices in the Burj al-Arab, the sail-shaped Arab Tower, the world's first ever seven-star hotel (with seven-star prices starting at $1,500 a night).

And for a decade from 1984, Dawood Ibrahim watched as the new Xanadu rose up out of the desert. From his sumptuous residence, The White House (so called because it was in fact about the only building in Dubai to be painted entirely in black), Dawood controlled his empire, with offices in London, Nepal, Pakistan and Sudan. And although Dawood was unable to travel to Bombay, he succeeded from his base in the Gulf in consolidating and expanding the biggest criminal network Bombay had ever seen.

Dawood was bought up in Dongri, a dirt-poor area of central Bombay with a large but not exclusively Muslim population. His father was a lowly police inspector, but this did not deter young Dawood from becoming involved in petty street crime. With his friends and brothers, he would go down to the bustling Crawford Market where he started scamming gullible traders and bargain-hunters. 'His first trick was to offer a customer an expensive foreign watch,' recalled a member of his youthful gang. 'After taking the money he would vanish, while the customer would be discovering that Dawood had switched the watch for a stone or some such worthless object during the wrapping.'

A natural leader, in his mid-teens Dawood and his elder brother, Sabir, joined – and before long took charge of – a Muslim political movement known as the Young Party. Under its previous leadership, the Young Party had a reputation as a militant Islamic outfit, but once the two Kaskar brothers had wrested control of the organisation, they remoulded it into an efficient criminal gang. To fund the Party activities, Dawood and his pals robbed a bank, resulting in a first conviction, which was later overturned by the High Court. As a criminal, having a policeman as a father did have a few advantages. D-Company was born.

Since independence in 1947, organised crime had troubled India little and the four dons who ran Bombay's mafia world were an unobtrusive presence with no great reputation for excessive violence. The economic system that Jawaharlal Nehru had championed after independence saw India erect mighty protectionist barriers to discourage the import of luxury and consumer goods, thereby boosting India's industrial capacity and maximising the exchequer's income from tariffs. The first illicit trade to emerge was the smuggling and production of liquor, but it was not long before the cash generated from booze was equalled by money earned from another commodity – gold. Gold has always been central to the local culture and Indians spend a small fortune on the metal at weddings, both in the form of dowries and as jewellery. To circumvent paying the massive tariffs, a substantial smuggling racket evolved in the 1950s and 1960s, which saw tons of gold shipped annually between Dubai and Bombay. This was a stable industry and the authority of the four dons who controlled it went unchallenged in the underworld for three decades.

By the late 1970s, Dawood and Sabir's gang of Konkani Muslims had made a name for itself as the leading incubator of street toughs in Dongri. Emboldened by this reputation, they hired themselves and their subordinates out as muscle to the smuggling operations of the big dons. Sabir had real ambition and began to establish the group's own smuggling network. The Dongri boys began to ruffle a few feathers, notably among the Pathan gang run by the legendary don, Karim Lala.

Then in the early 1980s, two things happened – the first would change Dawood, the second would change Dawood, Bombay and India.

The last two or three weeks of February 1984 saw the gentle warmth of Bombay's winter yield to the suffocating humid heat of summer. Although Sabir Ibrahim's wife was carrying the couple's second child, he could not resist the sweet aroma of Bombay jasmine, which lured him night after night to the heady atmosphere of Congress House. It was not political idealism that drew Sabir to the place where the founders of the Congress Party had plotted and planned India's future free from colonialism. In the intervening years, this historic building had degenerated into a brothel, and in this brothel lived Chitra, a pretty prostitute in her late twenties for whom Sabir nurtured a powerful infatuation. It was one o'clock in the morning when Sabir picked up his mistress for a romantic ride in his white Fiat Padmini.

'At some point, Sabir noticed that an Ambassador was following him,' said Ishaq Bagwan, a senior police inspector at the Malabar Hill Station. 'But it was covered in flowers and so he must have assumed that it was a couple of newly-weds.' Inspector Bagwan cuts a sympathetic figure, sitting taut in his khaki uniform, but he has tired of the world of gangsters, which he first became acquainted with that night. 'It was when he stopped at the Prabdhevi petrol station that it happened,' the Inspector continued. Five men armed to the teeth leaped out of the Ambassador. They were led by Amirzada Pathan, a leading gangster and favourite of Karim Lala. In a chivalrous gesture, the gunmen pulled Chitra out of the car so that she might be spared the almighty barrage of bullets they then fired at the driver's seat. As Sabir slumped forward onto the steering wheel of the Padmini, one of the assailants came forward and triumphantly slit his wrist.

A couple of bloody incidents had preceded Sabir's murder, but Bombay had never seen a slaying as gruesome as this, nor one that would unleash such fury. From the late 1980s, the city was to become much more violent. Inspector Bagwan was not surprised that Dawood would attempt to avenge the death of his brother. 'When Amirzada was put on trial the following year,' he recalled, 'I was in court as a junior officer when another man walked in and, without hesitating, shot Amirzada dead on the spot. As the killer tried to escape out of

the window, I fired my pistol at him and wounded him in the leg –
that is how we were able to arrest him. He had been hired by Dawood.'
There was pandemonium – this was not a country accustomed to
exchanges of gunfire inside its courtrooms. Before long, a warrant was
issued for Dawood's arrest in connection with the revenge killing.

At the time of Amirzada's trial and murder, trouble of another sort
was brewing elsewhere in the city. A charismatic, tough independent
trade-union leader and former physician, Dr Dutta Samant, persuaded
Bombay's 250,000 textile workers to lay down their tools for an indef-
inite strike. The Prime Minister, Indira Gandhi, was adamant that the
mill owners should not yield to the workers' demands for higher wages
and better conditions. Dr Samant's militancy represented a huge threat
to India's post-war tradition of quasi-state socialism where the
Government dictated to both management and unions what they could
and could not do. The workers stayed away for a year, during which
time clothing joined alcohol and gold as the smugglers' stock-in-trade.

The strike ended not with an agreement, but with the virtual collapse
of Bombay's textile industry. 'It rendered nearly 1.5 million workers
jobless, causing untold hardships to families,' according to a confidential report of the CBI (India's FBI equivalent, the Central Bureau
of Investigation) on the growth of organised crime in the city. 'The
strike forced the mill hands and their children to join the ranks of the
goondas [mobsters] to make ends meet . . . Today the vast areas under
the textile mills and the *chawls* (tenements) around them in Central
Bombay have become ideal hide-outs of gangsters.'

Few policemen know the world of the gangs as well as Inspector
Pradeep Sharma. The founder of the Special Operations team in 1995
to curb gangster violence, he began his career as a modest sub-inspector
in the Bombay police in 1984 and was posted to the station at Mahim.
'There was already a complex and complicated gang equation in Mahim
with several different groups. But by then job racketeering had become
very important.' The gangs were exploiting the high level of unemployment, Inspector Sharma explained, by seizing control of the labour
market. 'This was very important for their rise at that time.'

The collapse of the textile mills was an economic trauma from which
India's manufacturing powerhouse never fully recovered – the strikes
marked the beginning of the end of Nehru's social capitalism and

prepared the ground for the liberalisation of the early 1990s. And with a sudden huge increase in the number of unemployed in central Bombay, especially in areas close to Dongri, the social conditions were perfect for the rise of a new, more violent generation of organised crime – the time of Dawood had come.

When Dawood skipped India for Dubai in 1984, few Westerners could have located the city state on a map, let alone talk authoritatively about the place and its people. Arabs, Iranians, Baluchis, East Africans, Pakistanis and west-coast Indians, by contrast, had a deep historical acquaintance with Dubai. At the end of the Second World War it was barely more than a coastal village that had survived largely on its wits since its only indigenous industry, pearl fishing, had been wiped out by the war and by the Japanese development of cultured pearls.

In the barren years between pearls and petrodollars, Dubai quietly resurrected its trading links across the Straits of Hormuz with Iran and across the Arabian Sea to Bombay. Because both Iran and India pursued policies of severe protectionism to build up their domestic industries, Dubai's traders found they could exploit their own light taxation regime by importing all manner of material into Dubai and then exporting it to Iran and the subcontinent. 'The bottomless pit that is Indian demand for gold funded many, many people here in those years,' explained Francis Matthew, an expat for decades who is now an editor at Dubai's largest publishing company. 'Almost every Indian woman needs it for her trousseau and her dowry; different kinds of gold, different kinds of plate for the various areas of India.' This goes back to Rashid, the legendary founder of modern Dubai, who reinvigorated Dubai's role as a trading hub, including its dormant tradition of 'independent trading', as it is known in the Emirates, or 'smuggling', as the rest of us call it. Sheikh Rashid, the early visionary of Dubai, was on Indira Gandhi's personal list of wanted smugglers for many years. But although he could not step foot in India, he took a cut from the profits of every trinket or gold bar sold into India. So this is when the big trading families in Dubai made friends with the big trading families in Bombay and in Karachi. Those friendships lasted.

In terms of influence, Dubai's ruling Al Maktoum family ranked second only to the Al Nahyans of Abu Dhabi. The discovery of huge oil reserves on Abu Dhabi territory proved a godsend to Dubai and the other five emirates that formed the new state of the United Arab Emirates (UAE) in 1973 after the British decided to withdraw all its forces east of Suez. At present rates of extraction, Abu Dhabi's oil will last for another 200 years. The Al Nahyans' cash makes the fortunes of Roman Abramovich and the other Russian oligarchs look paltry. After less than half a century, the Al Nahyan fortune (which is interchangeable with Abu Dhabi's capital reserves) is estimated to stand at around $500 billion – half a trillion.

Abu Dhabi has been generous in its subsidies to the six other emirates of the UAE, which have no comparable oil fields. But it is a measure of the perceptiveness of the Al Maktoum leadership in Dubai that as early as the 1970s it began preparing for a future when Abu Dhabi would no longer be content to underwrite the federal budget. Dubai itself has modest oil reserves, which even so account for 15 per cent of the city state's income, but these will dry up within the next decade. In the 1980s, the Al Maktoums decided to diversify – probably spurred on by the traditionally competitive relationship with the Al Nahyans. Thus did they conceive the plan to build Jebel Ali port, its sixty-six berths the largest marine facility in the Middle East.

While critics scoffed at the grandiose project, the decision to create the new port and trading zone was quickly vindicated. In 1979, Dubai had learned a valuable lesson from the Iranian Revolution and the Soviet invasion of Afghanistan: trouble has its bright side. Frightened by the instability in their own countries, Iranian and Afghan traders moved to Dubai, bringing with them their businesses, thereby bolstering the local economy. With neither income nor sales tax, Dubai steadily developed a reputation for being a safe place in the Middle East to stash your money. Since then Dubai has always boomed during a regional crisis.

For Dawood Ibrahim, Dubai was the perfect retreat. The city welcomed the wealthy; it welcomed Muslims; and it was not the least bit interested in how people had acquired their money or what they intended to do with it. Dubai also had long-standing contacts with Bombay, and a large part of its elite was involved in the trade that Dawood wanted to make his core business activity – gold-smuggling. Furthermore, thanks to their strategic vision, the Al Maktoums were making the city state a very comfortable place to live. Before long, Dawood's house had become a place of pilgrimage for Bollywood celebrities and the stars of Indian and Pakistani cricket, two of Dawood's abiding passions. Still, he had to be circumspect. Dubai has proven to be a civil host to many gangsters in the past two decades, provided they behave with discretion. 'The UAE is essentially a state where if they don't like you, they can just simply throw you out,' noted *Firoz*, a Bombay lawyer who has occasionally acted as a messenger between the Ibrahim family and the Indian Government. 'And the fact that Dawood and his people thrived and prospered in Dubai, well, it could not have happened without the knowledge and – in a sense – the complicity of the ruling family.'

As Bombay's economy began collapsing in the 1980s, dozens of mini-mafia operations started up across the city. They were small gang-based operations engaged in extortion, gambling and territorial disputes between and within districts. The traditionally passive city experienced a grim upsurge in violence and murder as the gangs fought for supremacy among themselves and applied ever more ruthless sanctions against those from the business community who refused to pay up for the rackets.

From his distant outpost in Dubai, Dawood set about uniting the various gangs under his leadership. As a gangster, this was a formidable achievement. Chief among his lieutenants responsible for recruiting the emerging groups into the D-Company was a young Hindu mobster from Chembur in eastern Bombay called Chhota Rajan (Little Rajan).

While still a teenager, Chhota Rajan started running a racket in cinema tickets and was swiftly recruited by the local gang leader, Bada Rajan (Big Rajan). Together they extended their gang's influence northwards, gaining a reputation for violence on the way. When a rival gangster murdered Bada Rajan, Chhota Rajan exacted a daring and swift revenge. Dawood was impressed and recruited him into the D-Company. Before long, Chhota Rajan, the Little Man, had become the key figure inside Bombay, bringing together ten or more disparate gangs and creating one of the world's great mafias. The limbs of this operation stretched north to Gujarat, further to Uttar Pradesh and even into Kathmandu, where Dawood's people successfully cultivated members of Nepal's autocratic royal family. Like the new organisations that were emerging elsewhere in the world, the D-Company was made up of cells that paid tribute to Dawood, but which enjoyed considerable autonomy on their own patch. In the early 1990s, the CBI produced a detailed analysis of how it worked:

> His brother Anis Ibrahim controls all the violent characters in the gang who are utilised for running the protection and extortion rackets and for maintaining the gang's supremacy in the terror market. Dawood Ibrahim patronises many small gangs and gets the violent crimes committed through them. While allowing a certain degree of operational freedom to these gangs, he sees to it that they remain totally dependent upon him. If any gangster starts showing the sign of becoming independent, he is ruthlessly eliminated . . . The smaller gangs are given the contract of eliminating a rival or an intransigent businessman.

In return for their loyalty, the gangs were able to boast the Dawood brand name, which not only afforded them considerable protection from other gangs, but might also ensure an easier ride from the police. Dawood and his brothers were major crime figures with an India-wide reputation. They became the target of India's key intelligence and crime agencies, like the CBI and, later, India's spy service, the Intelligence Bureau (IB). But in Bombay itself, the police had not sufficient resources to maintain order in their districts without the help of the local gangs.

Chhota Rajan was responsible for supervising the D-Company affiliates, earning him the epithet among police circles of 'Dawood's Home Secretary'. He was also in charge of the countless murders perpetrated by the D-Company. Tiger Memon, meanwhile, coordinated the landing of gold, silver and other consumer goods in and around Bombay. As India's economy ground to a halt in the final years of the 1980s, the Bombay mafia experienced a huge growth and, with it, competition and inter-gang violence. Towards the end of the 1980s, the D-Company started to splinter and serious rivals to Dawood's criminal hegemony made themselves felt. The killings escalated and eventually Chhota

Rajan felt compelled to flee the city for Dubai. Another Little Man, Chhota Shakeel, started to assert himself within the D-Company's Bombay operation, to the chagrin of Chhota Rajan – the two Little Men did not like each other.

The Bombay textile strike signalled a comprehensive decline in the Indian economy, which reached its nadir in 1991. Globalisation saw investment capital sniff out new liberalising or 'emerging' markets while avoiding those like India's, which were resisting the new codex of deregulation. With imports rising and exports declining, India hit a huge balance-of-payments crisis – dues on its external debt were now devouring 40 per cent of GDP and the country was swaying drunkenly in the throes of an economic infarct. From within the Congress Party a group of influential reformers, led by the Finance Minister and later Prime Minister, Manmohan Singh, argued that the time had come to break with the sacred tenets of Nehruism.

In effect, Singh and his colleagues announced the consequent, if staggered, dismantling of India's protectionist traditions. A year later, in 1992, Minister Singh looked back on the dramatic changes he had introduced with considerable pride. 'When the new Government assumed office in June 1991, we inherited an economy on the verge of collapse. Inflation was accelerating rapidly. The balance of payments was in serious trouble. The foreign-exchange reserves were barely enough for two weeks of imports. Foreign commercial banks had stopped lending to India. Non-resident Indians were withdrawing their deposits. Shortages of foreign exchange had forced a massive import squeeze, which had halted the rapid industrial growth of earlier years and had produced negative growth rates from May 1991 onwards.' Singh had indeed stabilised the Indian economy and set it on a radically different path of liberalisation, including embracing globalisation (newly triumphant over communism). The end of the Soviet Union, one of India's most important strategic and economic allies, had not gone unnoticed in New Delhi. Amongst the raft of measures introduced by Singh was the freeing up of foreign-currency exchange rules and a plan gradually to lift controls on the import of gold.

By the early 1990s, police estimated that Dawood Ibrahim's annual turnover stood at around a quarter of a billion dollars from his Indian operations alone. By now he had a thriving legitimate construction and property business in Dubai, not to mention business interests in Karachi, Kathmandu and London. Most of the Indian profits derived from the huge expansion in the gold-smuggling trade over which the D-Company had presided. This represented a significant contribution both to India's economic woes and to the gathering strength and accompanying political influence of the shadow economy.

The impact of economic reform on Dawood and other shadow business moguls was dramatic. Before long the staggered relaxation of the gold regime started to inflict real pain on Dawood and the D-Company. By allowing the market to determine the price of gold instead of its bureaucrats, the Indian Government was steadily draining Dawood's primary source of income. Inevitably people began to ask why they should buy from Dawood when it was possible to purchase gold for virtually the same price on the legal market. Dawood still controlled the perfect infrastructure – he could land any amount of goods in the ports and bays in and around Bombay; he could bribe any number of customs officials and landing agents to ensure a trouble-free passage of his goods to their markets in Bombay and beyond. But the market in smuggled gold was no longer there.

It did not take Dawood long to choose a new product. New markets in other illicit commodities were booming around the world and many traders from these markets were setting up shop in Dubai, attracted – like Dawood – by the sun, the gold and the unobtrusive regulatory framework of the place. Russians were arriving in large numbers for the first time to the Gulf paradise; South Africans and South Americans also began showing up; Dubai was beloved of the Balkan mob; while representatives of consumer countries like Great Britain had a historically strong presence there. Dawood took the obvious plunge and started trafficking in drugs, chiefly in heroin bound for the European market and mandrax for South Africa. And in Dawood's part of the world, if you want to guarantee the success of a narcotics business, there is only one organisation you need to cosy up to – the Inter-Services Intelligence (ISI), Pakistan's secret service.

At the end of December 1992, Dawood celebrated his birthday with the usual A-list movie and sports stars from the subcontinent. By this time, however, circumstances back in India were beginning to sow discord among the group. The activities of the two Hindu nationalist parties, Shiv Sena (Shiva's Army) in Bombay and the BJP (Indian People's Party) across India, were stirring up frightening memories of the violence that accompanied partition in 1947, when several hundred thousand Muslims and Hindus were slaughtered as millions rushed to the perceived safety of their co-confessionals in Pakistan and India. The BJP and Shiv Sena campaigns, with their demands to fashion India into a Hindu state, were an immense challenge to the secular traditions of the Congress Party, which had dominated the post-war period. I was a reporter in the Balkans at the time, and it was clear that, more than any other colleagues, it was the correspondents of the Indian media – all highly educated and secular – who most fervently supported the integrity of the Yugoslav federation in the face of competing nationalist movements. It is not hard to understand why: on one level, they were writing as much about India as they were about Yugoslavia.

In Dubai, Chhota Rajan, hitherto Dawood's most trusted subordinate, grew suspicious of the emergence of a Muslim-only caucus among the D-Company's leadership.

At this point, the history of that leadership assumes aspects of an Elizabethan or Jacobean Revenge Tragedy. It is a sign of profound failure and dysfunction when the politics of revenge begins to consume mafia bosses. In September 1992, Chhota Rajan's rivals in what was effectively the D-Company's Supreme Council in Dubai ordered a spectacular murder to be carried out in a ward at the JJ Hospital, Bombay's central infirmary – the victim was a close Rajan associate. Rajan realised that Dawood must have approved the murder. Two policemen as well as the intended victim were killed during this operation, which attracted huge publicity around India. A senior officer of the Bombay police takes up the story. Chhota Rajan 'burst out in anger against the caucus and Dawood decided he should be killed and buried in Dubai itself. Bhai Thakur brokered for peace and Chhota Rajan was asked to either go on his knees and beg for forgiveness of the caucus or face death. He was given twelve hours to decide.'

The next day, Chhota literally genuflected in front of Dawood as the boss demanded, and begged to be pardoned. This Dawood duly granted. Chhota Rajan's enemies had whispered into Dawood's ear that Chhota Rajan had designs on the organisation. Now he was on the defensive and, to rub salt in the wound, Chhota Shakeel ordered the murder of three Rajan loyalists based in Nepal. Dawood would later have great cause to regret his humiliation of Chhota Rajan, as his erstwhile lieutenant was set to become a bitter enemy.

The communal tensions in Bombay itself were beginning to take their toll on the D-Company. According to his friends, the Hindu Chhota Rajan suspected that his nemesis, the Muslim Chhota Shakeel, was encouraging this communal mistrust in order to sideline him.

Dawood was an observant Muslim who regularly undertook the *hajj* to Mecca and he was visibly unsettled by the attacks on Muslims in Uttar Pradesh, Gujarat and Bombay. There is no doubt that Dawood was deeply disturbed by the resurgence of Hindu nationalism and the violence inflicted on the Muslim minority. From his informants in Dubai, Hussain Zaidi, whose knowledge of the Bombay underworld is unparalleled, has pieced together what happened next at Dawood's office:

> The other phone, whose number was known to barely half a dozen people, rang. Shakeel answered it and, handing the receiver to Dawood, tactfully move away to the other end of the room.
>
> There was a long muttered conversation.
>
> When Dawood hung up, his demeanour had changed visibly, the earlier dejection replaced by resolution.
>
> Shakeel remained seated quietly.
>
> Dawood walked towards him. 'They called,' Dawood said. Shakeel had never asked and Dawood had never explained who 'they' were. It is believed that the term referred to top officials in Pakistan.
>
> 'They say that they want to land some important cargo in Bombay through our landing routes at spots near Shekhadi and Dighi. Tiger and Taufiq will handle the entire operation of landing, paying the doctors and other such things. In exchange, they will arrange total security for our business.' He paused and then continued meditatively, 'I think that this cargo will not be ordinary stuff . . . It could be something meant as a retribution for the demolition of the Babri Masjid and the

massacre of Muslims. I told them that if it only means using my infrastructure and nothing beyond that then I have no problem. I can seek solace in the fact that the blood of my brothers will be avenged.'

Dawood took out a cigar from his pocket and tucked it between his lips, a sign that he was feeling relieved. Shakeel lit the cigar for him. Although the don had not said it in so many words, it was clear that the cargo would be death.

Twenty-seven-year-old Badshah Khan admitted to nerves when his Pakistan International Airlines plane touched down in Islamabad, the Pakistani capital, in February 1993. One of his fellow passengers had suffered a suspected heart attack during the flight from Dubai, compelling the pilots to make an emergency stop in Lahore. This was a bad omen. But Badshah Khan was more worried by the knowledge that he had no visa in his passport – it was, after all, an Indian passport and so was bound to attract the careful scrutiny of the Pakistani authorities. Still, at least he was there with several of the lads, and after all Tiger Memon himself had organised the trip. Even so, he was greatly surprised when he and his friends were escorted off the aircraft and taken to their accommodation without having to prove their identity in any fashion. Clearly, Pakistan was expecting them.

The next day they were driven a couple of hours outside Islamabad to a deserted forested location. Here they were greeted by an Operations team from Pakistan's secret service, the ISI. 'I had seen such characters in Hindi movies,' Badshah explained, 'men who were assigned the task of beating up our thin and short heroes, but end up getting beaten themselves. But these two guys, the Babajis, looked really dangerous. They could have taken on all our screen heroes together in the blink of an eye!' The raw recruits were streetwise – they had grown up ducking, diving and thieving on the streets of Bombay – but the most they had ever threatened anyone with was a knife or their bare fists, and they lacked training. Their new mentors were trained to perfection.

'The location of the camp was perfect for our requirements. There were six men to look after the camp: the two Babajis, two servants who served food and cleaned up, and two armed guards. Our meals were delivered by jeep every day at the same time. I marvelled at the excellent organisation,' recalled Badshah. 'One of the Babajis announced that he would now begin training us in the handling of instruments of death. He was carrying an AK-56 rifle. When we came into the field again, we were shown automatic pistols, handguns, light machine guns and Kalashnikovs . . . For the next two days, we did nothing but target practice . . . I realised why we had to travel all the way to Pakistan for the camp. There was no other place where we could have received such training; anywhere else the booming shots and loud reports would have attracted too much attention.'

I look at the warm and likeable face opposite me in a café at the top end of the indefatigably busy district of Bandra. Often referred to as fashionable, Bandra's allure is usually only obvious when you enter smart modern buildings. On my way from the station to the restaurant to meet Badshah Khan, a rabbit-sized rat ran over a couple of rake-thin heroin addicts lying prone and semi-conscious on the sidewalk. Poverty and squalor are ubiquitous in Mumbai, casting a permanent shadow on the attempts by New India – revelling as it does in the unevenly distributed wealth of globalisation – to project a shining image of slick success. The gangs of Mumbai have grown out of the slums, acting almost as an organic, if malevolent, response to the hip bars and conspicuous consumption of the growing, confident middle class. Badshah Khan and his family were evicted from their home when he was just fourteen by a fraudulent land speculator, and the once-promising student had fallen in with a bad crowd around the giant slum of Dharavi.

Away from the crowd in a modest family restaurant that served exquisite spicy prawns, Badshah Khan is dressed in a long white Indian shirt, baggy white cotton trousers and a small white cotton hat. He is cultured and thoughtful. As he talks about his former life, it is hard to imagine that he played a crucial role in the Bombay bombings of 1993. But then he also voluntarily played a crucial role as state witness in exposing how parts of the operation were planned and executed.

'After lunch that day at the camp,' he continued the tale of his training in Pakistan, 'we were shown some black soap-like lumps. Babaji said, "This is RDX – Research Developed Explosive" . . . We began chatting after he set it up. Suddenly an explosion rocked the jungles and mountains. The noise seemed to shatter my eardrums. The sky was raining stones and mud, and the earth beneath my feet was shaking . . . I think more than ten minutes went by after the explosion before the curtain of smoke gave way and I could see and hear properly. We moved towards the spot where the bomb had been placed. The pit was many feet deep.' This was the material that they would be planting across Bombay in one of the most densely populated places on Earth less than a month later.

On the evening of March 14th, the day after the bombings, the Commissioner of Bombay police called in Deputy Commissioner (Traffic) Rakesh Maria. 'Have you rested?' he enquired politely, but well aware that few – if any – officers had slept the night before (and certainly not DC Maria). The Commissioner explained that the prestige of the Bombay police was at stake in the investigation of the attack and that he had selected DC Maria to uphold it by taking over the detection of the case.

'I felt numbed by this, of course,' Maria said. 'This had been thrust on me so that I would have to shoulder responsibility were we to fail. And if I were to fail, what then?'

7

XANADU II

The shadow of the dome of pleasure
Floated midway on the waves;
Where was heard the mingled measure
From the fountain and the caves.
It was a miracle of rare device,
A sunny pleasure dome with caves of ice!
Samuel Taylor Coleridge, 'Kubla Khan'

'We received a report of one vehicle, a Marutti, abandoned in Worli.'
Rakesh Maria leaned back in his chair as he remembered the events. 'I
took my team of sixteen officers out there and it was obvious that the
vehicle had been left in a hurry. There were a lot of roadblocks in that
area designed to hinder the work of the underworld. Being part of Dawood's
D-Company, the bombers would have known that, so they left the vehicle
rather than risk being caught.' The car was registered in the name of
Rabiner Memon, Tiger Memon's sister-in-law. DC Maria led his team to
the Al-Hussein building where most of the Memon family lived. The
police broke down the door to the empty apartment and started looking
around for any possible clues. 'I noticed a scooter key on the fridge,'
Maria continued, 'and I thought we'd better check it and see.' Maria had
received another report of an abandoned motor scooter elsewhere in the
city – the traffic police had already taken it in for examination. 'I took the
key along and tried it in the scooter – Bingo! It fits! And so I turned
round to my men and said, "We've hit the jackpot!"' There was something else about that scooter – it still had its cargo of RDX on board.

Maria had uncovered the identity of the chief domestic conspirator,
Tiger Memon, within a matter of hours. It was an astonishing piece
of detective work, even if he and his team were assisted by the lax
discipline of the bombers and a healthy dose of luck. Despite the early

breakthrough, there were still many years of investigation facing the Indian authorities: the bombings were not the work of a small lean terrorist cell, the type that would proliferate in Europe, Asia and the Middle East after September 11th 2001. The atrocity in Bombay was ambitious in its scope, and it required a sprawling organisation like Dawood's to make it work, because at its heart lay the import of eight tons of RDX from Pakistan and only Dawood's operation could guarantee this. But because the plan was executed by a criminal syndicate based in Bombay, it meant that dozens of people were involved, wittingly or unwittingly. Most of the landing agents, corrupt customs officials, bent policemen, drivers, fishermen, storage facility owners, vehicle owners and other accessories to the crime had no idea that they were part of this particular conspiracy: they assumed that, as usual, they were bringing in gold, drugs, consumer goods, or weapons for onward sale. But the D-Company did not lead an exclusively underground existence. On the contrary, its influence extended to Mumbai's most famous industry, Bollywood.

Around midnight one mid-April eve in 1993, Rakesh Maria was interviewing yet another suspect in the bombing case. 'Your police always goes after small fry like me and lets off influential people,' the man noted bitterly. 'I mean if you are really serious, then why don't you arrest Sanjay?' 'Sanjay, Sanjay who?' the policeman demanded to know. 'Sanjay Dutt! The film star, son of the MP, Sunil Dutt.'

Dutt senior and his wife Nargis were one of the grandest couples in India. He, a Hindu, was a powerful force inside the Congress Party, who as a young actor had married his glamorous Muslim paramour. In 1993, the then 34-year-old Sanjay had just broken through into Bollywood superstar status. Like many Bollywood stars and directors, he was cultivated by the Bombay gangsters, who indeed continue to finance movie production in the city to this day. Sanjay was on friendly terms with Anis Ibrahim, Dawood's brother, and although his father was a Hindu, the entire Dutt family was sensitive to the fear that had spread among Bombay's Muslims during the riots of December 1992 and January 1993, and had sought to help the community. The nationalists at Shiv Sena had issued veiled threats against the Dutts, which persuaded Sanjay to ask Anis Ibrahim to send weapons so that he might protect himself and his family.

What Dutt did not know was that the AK-47s and grenades he received were part of a much larger series of deliveries from Dubai in preparation for the bombings in March. Over the next thirteen years, Dutt served a total of eighteen months in police custody as he awaited his trial and sentencing. Finally, on a sweltering Tuesday in November 2006, I watched as the bemused Bollywood actor made his way into the old British colonial jail on Arthur Road to hear the verdict in his case, Accused 117. Dutt was found guilty of illegal possession of a weapon, but not of conspiracy in the bombings case. Jostling for attention in the scrum stands Deepak Nachnani, a journalist and NGO leader with straggly hair that is tangled and grey. He is holding up a board demanding the extradition of Dawood Ibrahim for his role in the bombings and offering a reward for anybody who assassinates him. 'Sanjay Dutt's father was a minister and MP; his sister is an MP; but Sanjay Dutt should face the maximum punishment under Indian law,' he explodes with indignation.

But interestingly, Mr Nachnani appears to be in the minority. Most Mumbaikers still regard Dutt as a hero and a star. Since his arrest in 1993, he has starred in several hit movies, often playing the role of mafia don. There is an affection for Bollywood stars and the Mumbai mob that persists, despite the turbulent events of the 1990s. Dutt continues to enjoy cordial relations with Chhota Shakeel, Dawood's right-hand man. But his suspected involvement in the Bombay bombings did mean that over the course of the 1990s some of the links between Bollywood and the mafia were exposed, although there is still much to be uncovered.

Dutt's involvement was one of many surprises that Rakesh Maria's team unearthed during the investigation. Over many months, India's various law-enforcement agencies were able to construct a fairly comprehensive picture of Dawood's extraordinary network across Bombay and the planning and execution of the whole operation. Given the hopeless inefficiencies and rivalries that characterise Indian law enforcement, this was a very creditable performance.

Dawood himself remained calm in Dubai, although one person who fled the city state as soon as news of the bombings filtered through was Chhota Rajan. Convinced quite rightly that Chhota Shakeel now intended to kill him, Chhota Rajan broke with Dawood and disappeared, surfacing occasionally in Kuala Lumpur, Bangkok and other Asian cities.

Chhota Rajan still commanded a considerable gaggle of gangs in Bombay. He sent messages to the other major Hindu dons in the city, like Arun Gawli, suggesting that they form a tacit alliance against the D-Company. 'It was at this point that the IB got in touch with Chhota Rajan,' a Bombay deep throat told me. The Intelligence Bureau and its sister agency, the Research and Analysis Wing (RAW), are India's intelligence and counter-intelligence services. Normally they are not charged with investigating the activities of organised crime, but if a syndicate has become involved with a major security issue, then the IB and the RAW will assume control of any investigation. 'The IB's thinking was that if Dawood was being run by the ISI, Pakistan's secret service, then they should perhaps employ Dawood's enemies to undermine his influence,' said the source.

During the Yugoslav wars, organised criminal syndicates throughout the Balkans effectively hijacked most state institutions and subordinated them to their interests. In Pakistan and India at exactly the same time, the opposite was happening: the gang wars of Bombay that exploded with renewed violence in the 1990s were in part a proxy conflict between the intelligence agencies of India and Pakistan, ensuring that they were even more dangerous and unpredictable than hitherto. This ratcheting up of the gang wars, conferring a communal and an intelligence dimension on them, had unhappy consequences for local law enforcement.

By the mid-1990s, the Bombay police were registering a rise in the murder rate that was comparable with those of Moscow or Johannesburg, confirming the apparent link between drastic economic and political reform, on the one hand, and gangsterism on the other. The collated police reports detail hundreds upon hundreds of murders of shocking brutality during this period. The majority were committed in the merciless tit-for-tat war that Chhota Rajan and Dawood had launched against each other. Chhota Rajan's capability was based on his comprehensive knowledge of the structures and networks of his former boss's empire. He himself had, after all, spent almost a decade building it on behalf of Dawood. The IB's strategy was working – Chhota Rajan was depleting Dawood's ability to function – and, in the eyes of the IB, that meant that they were limiting the ability of the ISI to carry out its covert activities through the D-Company. It also had the side-effect of weakening Chhota Rajan's operations, which were themselves under attack from Dawood's operatives.

But for Bombay law enforcement, it was an uncomfortable mess that reinforced its nationwide image as a corrupt and incompetent police force. To combat the violence, the police established three special anti-crime squads in 1995.

Inspector Pradeep Sharma was sitting in his Bandra office one afternoon in late 1996 when there was a knock on his door. 'An informant came in and told me that Babloo Srivastava had sent a four-man team into the city from Uttar Pradesh in order to kidnap one of Bombay's wealthiest businessmen.' Srivastava was a notorious gangster with links to both Dawood and Chhota Rajan. He had been extradited from Singapore to India on suspicion of having committed about eighty major kidnappings and murders. He was, in fact, organising the kidnapping of the Bombay businessman from the confines of Delhi jail. 'This was about two in the afternoon,' continued Inspector Sharma, 'and so I ordered a couple more on my team to come with me to Santa Cruz, just close to Bandra where the informant had said the gangsters were hiding out.' When they arrived at the apartment, one of the policemen knocked on the door. 'Hello!' he called out, 'it's the milkman. I have your delivery.' Inspector Sharma pauses for dramatic effect. 'As soon as he'd said he was the milkman, the gang just started shooting wildly from inside the apartment. But within a couple of minutes, we'd killed them both. Only then did we discover that the other two gang members were out and had escaped.'

The two deceased had fallen victim to what are known throughout India as 'encounters' – in effect shoot-outs between gangsters and police. Inspector Sharma is the encounter king, having killed more than 120 Bombay gangsters in shoot-outs, a bigger tally than any other policeman in the city. I cannot recall anyone I met during my journey through the global underworld who displays such a controlled and focused machismo as this scrupulously polite and deeply serious man. Gangsters and some civil-liberty groups claim that these 'encounters' have in fact transformed the police into extra-judicial execution units, or death squads. The 'encounter' teams forced Arun Gawli, an early ally of Dawood who later became one of his principal Hindu enemies, to construct an elaborate security mechanism around his head-quarters in central Bombay. Numerous armed guards were placed behind four heavily locked gates, all studded with CCTV and state-of-the-art communications. More recently, Gawli has given up his status as don in favour of a seat in the Maharashtra Provincial Assembly, but he still calls encounters 'police contract killings', having lost, he claims, sixty friends in the shoot-outs. 'Okay,' Gawli admits, 'there were days a while back when I went astray. But this sort of murder campaign is unacceptable.'

Since the formation of the anti-crime squads, the number of deaths attributed to encounters has been more than 100 a year. 'I sometimes take out between six to eight of them in a week,' confirms the Inspector with evident pride.

But he failed to take out *Mahmoud*, one of Bombay's most successful contract killers, whom I arranged to meet in what turned out to involve an elaborate game of musical cafés. Every time I thought I had arrived at the right teashop, I received a message to finish my drink and move to another one. At the third one, the sharp, good-looking, if slightly weather-beaten features of *Mahmoud* smiled benignly at me. 'I have to take serious security precautions when I come to Bombay,' he explained. 'I don't want to come across any police encounters, and I certainly don't want to encounter any of my former colleagues.' In stark contrast to the other people from this milieu whom I met, Mahmoud spoke refined and sophisticated English. 'I studied electronics at college in Pune,' he beams proudly.

In 1989, armed with his degree, Mahmoud made the short 75-mile hop west from Pune to Bombay, India's naked city. Before long he had secured a job fixing photocopying machines. 'I was paid about $50 a month for this work and I was living in a room with ten other men,' he continued. 'It was really hard.' One day Mahmoud intervened when he saw a gang of boys bullying a kid on the streets. A man approached him and congratulated him on his bravery and asked him out for a drink. 'For the next eighteen months, this guy showed me a good time – we went to bars, we met women, he gave me money and I didn't have to do anything. It was great – I was young, fit, good-looking and this was what I had come to Bombay for!' Mahmoud's benefactor was, in fact, an associate of Chhota Shakeel, the rising star and future *chef du cabinet* in Dawood's D-Company.

Once the friendship was firmly established, his mentor explained who he was, what he did and for whom he worked. He offered Mahmoud the chance to join full-time. 'The thought of returning to a $50 job in that hovel meant there was no real choice – I was in.'

Mahmoud was taught to use a *kutta* – a pistol manufactured in Uttar Pradesh whose barrel has a tendency to blow up. 'The first shot is usually safe; after that it's pretty useless. That means that when you're doing a job, you only have one crack at it.

'Most of the hitmen were picked up or killed in encounters. But not me. There are two reasons: one is planning. We would monitor a target's route for two to three months. We knew all his habits, so there would be no surprises. The second is secrecy – if you or your colleagues blab, you're dead.

> 'My first successful hit took place in Andheri in early 1991. As was often the case, we planned to carry it out at a busy cross-roads in the afternoon when the rush hour was in full swing. We would get a car to block the road by the traffic lights – the target was driving a Marutti Esteem, it was a very prestigious car at the time. But he couldn't go forward because we'd blocked the lights and he couldn't go back because of the traffic. There were two teams. The first team approached the car and broke the window glass. Then I went in and boom – straight at the head. It was always straight at the head because you only got one shot at it. I always delivered the goods, which is the message we would send after a job. Once it was done, I disappeared. I never went home after a job and nobody knew where I was.'

This warm, urbane man laughed and spoke animatedly in the café, later offering perceptive comments on contemporary social and economic issues facing India, then dropping in to a mosque to say prayers, before talking lyrically about Mumbai and its traditions. It was almost impossible to reconcile this with the knowledge that he was a calculating, cold-blooded killer. I felt deeply perplexed – how can

I warm to a murderer, I wondered? My experience in the Balkans led me to conclude that most murderers are not congenital psychopaths, but people (usually men) whom circumstances and authority encourage, persuade and enable – in short, 'permit' – to violate the ultimate commandment: thou shalt not kill. But this man still made a choice. And his choice is all the more shocking precisely because he seemed both normal and intelligent.

In 2002, Mahmoud had negotiated an honourable discharge from the Company – a very tricky thing to do.

'I was married with kids by then and my wife had no idea what my real job was.'

'Has she still no idea?'

'I told you – secrecy is critical. I was never caught because nobody knew who I was or how I operated. I never made the mistake of relying on anyone else.'

I had one final question of Mahmoud. 'How did you feel at the moment that you executed a hit?' Like so many Indians, he chose a cricketing metaphor to answer, referring to the West Indies' magnificent batsman and captain: 'Like Brian Lara when he hits the ball for six!'

By the late 1990s Dubai was still not fully entangled in the deepening mess of Mumbai gangs and international politics, even though many had relocated to the Emirate. But then Dubai thrives on conflict, provided none of the drama takes place on its territory. Desert Storm, the Palestinian Intifada, 9/11, the American attack on Afghanistan and the second Iraq war all led to people funnelling large sums into Dubai. 9/11 provoked a spectacular flight of Arab money from the United States into Dubai. The estimates range from between several hundred billion to two or three trillion dollars. By the mid-1990s, 63 per cent of the UAE's income was derived from non-petroleum sources. Dubai itself had become the largest free-trade zone in a region stretching from southern Europe to Singapore. It had traditionally attracted large amounts of capital from the subcontinent, Central Asia, East Africa and the Middle East – now Dubai sought to invite Western money to invest. With no tax, a beautiful coastline, sunshine all year round, no bombs or assassinations (everyone benefits from Dubai and nobody, including al-Qaeda, wants to disrupt it), and enough shopping malls to satisfy a small planet, it did not take long before money was pouring in from every part of Europe.

Not only was Dubai the entrepôt for commodities from throughout a vast region that stretched from Russia down to South Africa and across to India, but it naturally developed the largest money market as well. And there was no control over this *whatsoever* – you could take as much money out and bring as much in as you liked, whether in suitcases full of cash, converted into gold bars or diamonds, through one of the many banks founded to take advantage of this ever-growing flow, or through the *hawaldars* and *hundis*, the unlicensed money-changers who are the mainstay of the informal financial economy on which the migrant labourers depend.

The pursuit of dirty money is a complicated business. Capital springs from human labour to give life to the global economic environment. It emerges from the source before broadening into a fast-flowing river rushing down from the peaks and distributing itself unevenly across the fertile lowlands through channels both organic and man-made. As it cuts unpredictable paths, some drains off unnoticed, perhaps wending through a toxin-infected swamp before seeping back into the main network. Here and there, one may encounter apparently pristine pools that are in fact contaminated with colourless, odourless chemicals. Only the most expert biochemist can tell the good capital from the filthy lucre as it mixes and mingles. Capital itself is neither dirty nor clean – it is human activity and human values that determine the colour of money.

The fall of communism and the deregulation of the international financial markets in the late 1980s triggered a huge injection of cash into the global economy. Traders scanned the globe for the most profit-able opportunities. The clients they represented sought out their services for a number of reasons: some were looking for the maximum rates of return; others were seeking to avoid paying tax; companies were also demonstrating their commitment to new markets; and then some investors wanted to launder their money and remove the stain of its criminal origins. The sums involved were vast. By the mid-1990s, the foreign exchange markets alone reached a volume of trading that exceeded $1 trillion *every day*. This was more than forty times the value of daily global trade. In the world of licensed financial trading, malfeasance only came to light when related losses either destroyed an institution, as when Nick Leeson's derivatives trading on the Japanese stock market brought down Barings Bank; or when outside regulators were tipped off about malpractice, as happened in the staggering case of the Bank of Credit and Commerce International (BCCI). Several scandals, from BCCI to Enron, have demonstrated that the world's most famous private audit companies cannot be relied upon to alert governments to large-scale malpractice in the banking or corporate sectors. Indeed, the auditors appear to have been extremely lax in flagging up the mounting problems in both BCCI and Enron.

The United States was the only country in the world that had passed extensive legislation outlawing money-laundering prior to the 1990s. Building on the landmark RICO (Racketeer Influenced and Corrupt Organisations) Act, passed in 1970 to deal with organised crime, Congress then introduced two further bills in the 1980s, which were aimed at dealing specifically with the laundering of drugs money. This led to the Drug Enforcement Administration setting up sophisticated sting operations that were designed to hit the pocketbooks of Colombian drug cartels and their accomplices, like Panama's President, Manuel Noriega.

Money-laundering is that most peculiar of things – a predicate crime. It is one step removed from the criminal deed: the act of transferring a large sum of money is not intrinsically illegal; the illegality lies instead in the association with the criminal act that generated the cash in the first place. Law enforcement has to prove not that money was transferred, but that it was ill-gotten.

That is difficult enough. But once international currency controls were relaxed in the late 1980s in the name of capital's freedom of movement, it became still more complicated. If it had the evidence, US law enforcement could make a money-laundering charge stick when the offence took place in the United States. If it occurred in a foreign country, then the only way Washington could go after the alleged criminals was by invading said country. In some cases – Panama, for example – that's exactly what it did. But although Washington has traditionally felt less constrained than most governments about invading other countries, it does not have the wherewithal to do so every time it hears of something fishy going on in the banking sector. America's own banks were required to assume an ever greater regulatory burden, summed up by three guidelines – CDD: Customer Due Diligence; KYC: Know Your Customer; and SAR: Suspicious Activity Report. In addition to being an arcane discipline, the fight against money-laundering is overburdened with acronyms.

The struggle against organised crime had thus created an awkward conundrum for the United States, which went to the heart of the still-larger issue of the relationship between the liberalisation of inter-national capital markets and global governance. The European Union was already grappling with this over a very concrete issue and not getting very far. Within the EU, there was absolute freedom of move-ment for capital, goods, services and people. But member states had different traditions and laws in banking and tax. Luxembourg and Austria (as well as the non-EU countries, Switzerland and Liechtenstein) had banking secrecy laws that allowed citizens to hold nameless accounts, which no state official was permitted to scrutinise. The exist-ence of those accounts drove a coach and horses through any attempt to monitor money-laundering inside the EU. Luxembourg, Austria, Switzerland and Liechtenstein fought tooth and nail to retain their banking secrecy code as it encouraged huge inflows of capital into their countries.

America faced the same problem on a global scale. 'If our banks are required to adhere to a standard, including offshore, and other banks do not and rush for deposits in those US banks,' said Senator John Kerry in 1988, 'we will have once again taken a step that will have disadvantaged our economic structure and institutions relative to those against whom we must compete in the marketplace.'

The implication was that a globally level playing field in the banking sector would anyway require a worldwide regulatory regime. 'If, after a reasonable period of time, these countries do not enter into agree-ments and implement laws against money-laundering,' warned Robert Gelbard, Assistant Secretary of State in 1995, 'then the Secretaries of Treasury and State and the Attorney General will recommend to the President whether sanctions should be applied. And these sanctions could include the prohibition of electronic fund transfers and dollar clearing to financial institutions in the subject country. In other words, these would be very dramatic measures, which would eliminate their ability to do business through the US financial system.' Given that the United States accounts for a quarter of the world's trade, such sanctions are as punitive as you can get without actually declaring war.

The Clinton administration elevated its AML (anti-money-laundering) strategy to its list of most solemn commandments (even if its moral case was badly punctured by the presidential pardon to the fugitive financier, Marc Rich, in 2000). But progress was patchy. The G7's new vehicle to enforce compliance, the Financial Action Task Force (FATF), had a tiny staff, which rendered it largely ineffective. Liechtenstein and Switzerland snubbed the whole idea, while the United Arab Emirates (Dubai included) resisted compliance with FATF regulations most vigorously. 'In the 1990s, it was a free-for-all in Dubai,' explained a European diplomat who worked on Dubai's money-laundering issues. 'There were no controls here and the authorities were tenacious in resisting the FATF.' And as Firoz, the lawyer from Mumbai with links to Dawood, explains, Dubai posed America with a serious dilemma. 'American policy in the Middle East is held hostage to the fear that if you push someone too much, then you might end up with someone a lot worse. The US is not happy with the Emirates because it has attracted a lot of shady companies, but at the same time it is seen as a safe haven for the US in the region. American troops can land there and enjoy R&R – its advantages outweigh its disadvantages. It's one of the few places where Americans feel safe and they are not keen on seeing change.'

Although the 1990s were the heyday for high-profile characters like Dawood Ibrahim and Viktor Bout in Dubai, the city also witnessed a huge growth in investment by Western companies seeking to get a slice of the market. Dubai could not countenance the imposition of rigorous controls on the import and export of money, as the United States was demanding at the time, as this would have confounded the city's unique selling point (Bring Your Money to Dubai: No Questions Asked!) and undermined the entire strategy of turning the place into the trading and financial pivot between Africa, Europe and Asia. It was all looking rather grim until Dubai heard the distant drumming of the cavalry galloping to the rescue: George W. Bush had arrived at the White House!

The new Bush team had a very different approach to money-laundering from its predecessor. Clinton's global AML strategy was ridiculed by the neo-cons as a dastardly anti-competitive European plot. 'Before 9/11 the fundamental concern is to fight what the White House perceives as a European tendency to try to make everybody's regime as business-unfriendly as possible,' explained a senior economist, who worked at the Treasury under both Clinton and Bush, before moving over to a key position in one of the top international financial institutions.

In the vanguard of the Bush campaign was Larry Lindsey, Director of the National Economic Council and Deputy Secretary of State to the Treasury:

> Between 1987 and 1995, the government collected 77 million currency-transaction reports, something on the order of 62 tons of paper. Out of that, it was able to prosecute 3,000 money-laundering cases. That is roughly one case for every 25,000 forms filed. In other words, entire forests had to be felled in order to prosecute one case. But it gets worse: of the 3,000 money-laundering cases prosecuted, the government managed to produce only 580 guilty verdicts. In other words, in excess of 100,000 reports were filed by innocent citizens in order to get one conviction. That ratio of 99,999 to one is something we normally would not tolerate as a reasonable balance between privacy and the collection of guilty verdicts.
>
> There is another angle: since banks are used as enforcement agents, the Treasury Department engages in sting operations to monitor compliance. Officials go to a bank and tempt it to commit a crime. Between 1990 and 1995, 290 defendants were charged as a result of sting operations, with 29 convictions. That's one in 10. And that's out of thousands of sting operations. By any standard of cost-benefit analysis, we are asking for a lot of compliance to catch a few people.

For Bush and his team, the only good AML strategy was no AML strategy. Then came 9/11.

'There was a 180-degree flip,' remembers the senior Treasury economist. 'After 9/11 no AML regime is too strong for the US. Any kind of concerns about secondary effects go out the window. The brief is everybody has to have this regime and the stronger, the more onerous, the better – no cost is too high.'

The Patriot Act was designed to put paid to any outlandish notion that President Bush was soft on terrorists and money-launderers. But there was a problem: money-laundering and terrorist-financing are two very different things, as the Treasury man explains, 'In money-laundering, you are looking for dirty money trying to become clean. In the case of terrorist-financing, you are looking at clean money that becomes criminal. The crime is no longer a predicate crime, but a subsequent crime, and your whole optic changes as a consequence.'

Ironically, Larry Lindsey's pre-9/11 nightmares were about to come true. A part of the war on terror was the war on worldwide financial transactions – a very blunt and ill-fashioned instrument. 'The whole notion that somehow the model for AML can just be translated into terrorist finances is fanciful,' the economist continued.

'But if all you have in your tool kit is a hammer, then the whole world looks like a bunch of nails. You get the Office of Foreign Assets Control (OFAC) and stretch still further their original brief, which was to block stuff from Cuba. Take the Balkans: it was hard enough when they had to block Slobodan Milosevic's cash – you know how many Slobodan Milosevices there are in the Paris phone book alone? There are thirteen of them. To shut down an organisation like al-Qaeda where the possibilities for false positives on Islamic or Arabic names are staggering, you quickly realise you've got a lousy tool for the job. But seeing that OFAC and FATF are the *only* tools that you have, they become the frontline in the battle against terrorist-financing after 9/11, despite being hopelessly ill-fashioned.'

Suddenly you are confronted with a mountain of complex and pernickety work – most of it in unregulated overseas banking networks – with barely a clue where to start.

Fortunately for the Feds, only a rank no-hoper would have missed the fact that eleven out of sixteen 9/11 hijackers had received their cash from Dubai. And it wasn't long before a multi-agency posse from Washington had saddled up and ridden into the desert kingdom. To judge by the 9/11 Commission report, they received every assistance from the UAE, even if this still meant working through hundreds of boxes of financial documentation, literally in tents in the desert, with temperatures soaring to well over 100 degrees in the shade.

Now the US and Britain (a faithful adjutant in the newly formed AML division) stepped up their pressure for everyone to comply, and four months after 9/11 the UAE passed a law that satisfied most of FATF's hallowed forty recommendations. 'They have done everything asked of them in terms of legislation,' a European diplomat concurred, 'but, as we know, implementation is the critical issue.'

In 2002 Sheikh Mohammed went on the offensive by announcing the establishment of the Dubai International Financial Centre (DIFC), a bold bid that would transform the city into the largest financial market between Frankfurt and Singapore. Some of the world's biggest banks and financial institutions proclaimed that they would set up their offices in the DIFC. Sheikh Mohammed encouraged everybody by announcing that the accompanying regulatory authority would not be bound by the laws of the UAE, but by a new code of governance based on the most progressive and transparent Western principles.

There was no doubt that Dubai was doing everything it could to appear the embodiment of rectitude. But while there was no reason to doubt the city's commitment to an onshore financial centre that would stand up to the toughest scrutiny, there was a little catch. In order to accommodate the DIFC and all the new business it would attract, the authorities announced a multi-billion-dollar construction plan, which envisaged an immense westward expansion of the city along the coast, including such grandiose projects as the Palms and the Burj Dubai.

And here a small inconvenience was encountered. Since its foundation, the United Arab Emirates had been subject to a self-imposed brake on its development – only Emirati citizens could own property within the territory. The expats who came to enjoy the weather and the tax-free lifestyle had to rent, denied the possibility of exploiting one of the most solid and lucrative investments anywhere in the world. So, hard on the heels of the unveiling of the DIFC came the news that, in many of the new building zones, foreigners would be permitted to purchase property and hold the freehold. The frenzy began. Dubai became quite literally the biggest building site in the world. During the expansion of the country's airport, when the residential and office construction had already begun, *one-third* of the world's cranes were working in Dubai.

Driving down Sheikh Zayeed Road is an unnerving experience. Beyond the indoor ski run, skeletons of wire and metal tower menacingly. Vast breezeblocks swing capriciously from the cranes as any sense of human scale is lost and the otherwise ubiquitous sun is here obliterated. You are able to watch a process akin to the whole of downtown Manhattan being built in three years. For the moment, it still looks like an experimental set for the Fritz Lang movie *Metropolis*, as though these dwellings were being prepared to house the subjects of a totalitarian nightmare. The overpowering sense of science fiction is further enhanced by the armies of robotic workers, crawling all over the construction sites. They wear standard dungaree uniforms, but differentiated by colour – there is a green, a blue, a red and a yellow army, each tasked with erecting a different building.

Four years after Sheikh Mo's announcement, Dubai and the UAE had yet to pass the legislation permitting foreigners to hold the freehold in designated areas, let alone define what freehold means Dubaistyle. But that did not stop a ferocious rush as foreigners signed up and handed over a 10 per cent deposit for The Meadows, South Ridge, The Glades and all the other suburban names culled from America, South Africa and Australia. The concession for the creation of New Dubai was given to five companies, all owned and run by sheikhs who are close to Sheikh Mohammed. These concessions are worth billions and billions of dollars. Before the first foundations of this project were laid, investors were doubling their money by speculating. With just 10 per cent of the price required to reserve a property, once you secured a contract, it was possible to wait a matter of months and then sell on the building for double its original price. Investors began to pay just to get onto the waiting list for the most fashionable properties.

The bubble was beginning to form. 'Let us fast forward to 2007–2008,' proposed Matein Khalid, a business columnist for the *Khaleej Times* in Abu Dhabi. 'Published figures suggest the Big Five developers will deliver 150,000 units. Since every loaded Joe Schmoe from Bombay to Lahore to Meena Bazaar fancies himself a developer, another 30,000 units can be added. There are about eighty private developers desperate to sell their projects in Dubai. This means the supply overhang is at least 180,000 new units, even assuming no projects are announced in the next two years. Let us look at Dubai Municipality figures on demographics and rentals. The city's population is 1.3 million . . . Because of an influx of expats, a small supply–demand squeeze caused rents to spiral up by 70 to 100 per cent in two years. But in 2007–2008, a phenomenal 200,000 new units will hit the market. This means that we need about 800,000 new expats who are not labourers, housemaids, tailors, minimum wage bachelors or the Sharjah/Ajman commuters to fill this unit. In essence, a doubling of the professional high-income salaried population of Dubai in the next two years. Realistic? Not at all . . . Lo and behold, the brutal economics of oversupply, the kiss of death for property bubbles all over the world, now begin to hit the market.'

Every time a bubble forms, supporters of the project insist that this one will not burst with the violence that so many earlier ones did. Dubai, they claim, is different – because the city is so uniquely attractive to global wealth (a rather bleak reflection on the cultural standards of the moneyed classes). They will never allow the pyramid to collapse because they are so committed to Dubai's growth as one of the major international engines of capitalism. Just like the Florida property-market bubble that prefaced the Wall Street Crash of 1929 and all other subsequent real-estate pyramid schemes, the property market in Dubai has attracted a lot of criminal money. Despite the protestations of the authorities that the city has cleaned up its act, little (if any) of the money pouring into this venture is scrutinised.

As is so often the case, I turn to my old friends from the Balkans to find out how things really work, in this case Ranko Lukic (one of the very few people in Dubai happy to talk on the record), at one of the hyper-posh hotels in new Dubai. A youthful entrepreneur who was educated both in Serbia and the United States, Lukic hovers in the grey economy like most successful businessmen from Eastern Europe. Having cut their teeth under communism, they have developed an acute nose for sniffing out how you strike deals with a minimum of fuss. But when he first arrived here, he received a shock when he transferred $3,000 to his local lawyer from Citibank Dubai.

'I get a call back and this aggressive guy says, "What is the purpose of this transfer?" So I tell him it's none of his business, it's between me and my lawyer. But I was absolutely astonished and I had to fill out some form before they would transfer this lousy three grand! But of course, Citibank is an American firm.

'When I had two lots of two million euros transferred to the Emirates bank here so I could purchase property along Sheikh Zayeed Road, the bank called me and said, "Tell us, please, the origin of this money." So I tell them that it comes from my tobacco farms in Zimbabwe! And they say "okay" and no more questions asked. Job done! Why would they want to know where my money comes from? If they ask too many questions, they won't get sales!'

Once the house or apartment is registered as belonging to an individual, he or she has successfully washed the money and it can be reintroduced into the legitimate financial system anywhere in the world.

Dubai may be soulless, but a certain honesty underpins the fantasy of a stately pleasure dome for the world's super-rich. Only two things rule here: the dollar and Sheikh Mo. Dubai may be a huge undemocratic money-laundering centre in the Middle East, but the country embraces free trade and globalisation; it is stable in a region renowned for violence; it has not relied on oil for its wealth, but invented itself as a novel force in the Arab world. Furthermore, as long as the United States and Europe permit the existence of offshore banking centres, they remain guilty of hypocrisy. For organised crime, these are equally important instruments, offering a variety of additional services such as flags of convenience, shell companies to disguise illegal activities, and freedom from prying tax authorities. The only credible reason for their growth and success is the fact that many corporations in the licit economy use them for exactly the same reasons (especially tax evasion). The Government of the United States could force them to lift their banking secrecy codes overnight, if they threatened to apply the same sanctions on offshore centres that they do on the onshore banks.

'You could do it quite easily,' said a senior National Security Council official involved in the hunt for drugs and thugs during both the Clinton and Bush administrations. 'You go to Liechtenstein, which is one of these places, and you just put a gun to its head and say, "If you don't put an end to these practices, we're going pull the trigger."

I suggested this under Clinton, but unfortunately the idea was turned down.' Without offshore banks, it is not only the mobsters who would find it onerous to shuffle their money and companies around. Enron would have found it a lot harder too.

The issue of money-laundering will continue to haunt Dubai as it strives to represent itself as a model of transparency. But there is an even higher cost that the city has had to pay for its success – a human cost. For beyond the permanent traffic jam between Dubai and Sharjah lies Ajman, the tiniest of the UAE's seven emirates. Celebrated among the expats as hosting the only liquor store in the country where you can purchase booze without a licence, Ajman is also a popular location for the labour camps where the vast army of cheap migrant labourers, who are building the new Dubai, are compelled to live.

Ajman itself is a featureless city, but as you travel towards it east from Dubai, the ubiquitous traffic jams suddenly disappear. Soon almost all vehicles except the one I'm travelling in have evaporated. This is eerie. In the distance, the huge lonely dunes of the desert form an oscillating, yet monotonous, panorama. It is already dark, and set back ten yards from the road are high, crumbling grey walls surrounded by dust, sand and scrub. I walk into a yard next to a barracks to find a few plastic chairs occupied by a group of fourteen men. Most look undernourished and ageing, but the eldest is thirty-five. They welcome me with bows, smiles and quiet chatter. For four months their wages have been unpaid by the Saudi-owned business that contracts these men out to do maintenance work on buildings under construction. Until the wages were stopped, they had been receiving $160 per month. For this they were obliged to leave Ajman in a bus at 5.30 a.m. to start work in Jebel Ali forty miles away at 7.30. There followed twelve hours of back-breaking work under a sun that drives most people off the street after half an hour's exposure. They are then packed back to their barracks in Ajman, where they are expected to provide and cook their own food.

The conditions are subhuman. About sixty men are required to share one stinking toilet, which forces an involuntary retch when one stands within five yards of it. Eight to fifteen men live in one room – the Nepalis in one, the Bengalis in the next, the Pakistanis in the next and the Indians in the next. They sleep on thin mattresses spread across the concrete floor or on rickety metal bunkbeds. The only other facility is a single gas ring on which they all have to cook.

In a cacophonous Babylonian chorus, they tell how two months ago they downed tools and actually took their grievance to Dubai's new Employment Police. The existence of this new office reflects how hundreds of thousands of foreign labourers in the city are showing signs of restlessness, including strikes and protests such as blocking highways. Dubai cannot afford to become synonymous with labour militancy and a strong union presence. But this army of migrant labourers is starting to grow very restive as they contrast the unfathomable opulence of the Dubai they are building with the aching squalor of the world they inhabit. Their female compatriots, who work as domestic servants, observe the discrepancy close up. In the Emirates these women have no rights as they are not classed as 'workers', but as 'family members' of their employers, which leaves them vulnerable to appalling abuse as trans-national skivvies. At least the UAE has finally abandoned the import of tiny boys to work as camel 'jockeys' in one of the country's favourite sports. Before the practice was ended, there were countless reports of victims being abused as well as sustaining the most severe injuries as they entertained the sheikhs and their guests. At the very bottom of the pile are the women who are trafficked to the Emirates by force. There are no NGOs permitted here to defend these women. In Moldova, La Strada, the NGO that assists trafficked women, despairs of the UAE: 'We have one girl who managed to call her mother once,' said Alina Budeci. 'She is imprisoned in an apartment in Dubai. She is constantly watched and never allowed out. All she does is service clients day in, day out. We get no response from the police in the UAE. If they are trafficked there, the situation is usually hopeless.'

Slowly it is dawning on the visionaries of Dubai that they must work more diligently to ward off any eruption of trouble in paradise. And so a few concessions are now being made to these people without rights.

Commendably, the police ordered the Saudi company to pay the back-wages (though, in the event, they only paid half what they owed). The police also ruled that the men's barracks be supplied with water. 'After about two weeks, they turned up with this tanker,' Ibrahim explained to me as he poured some water from it. 'Taste this!' he said, handing me the cup. 'Uggh! It's salt!' I said as I spat it out. 'Yes,' he said, 'that is our new drinking-water supply.'

Hom Bahadur Thapa looks on sadly as I gag from the salt water. He has the gentle good looks common to Nepalis, whose features act as a bridge between India and China. He is one of the 175 million people in the world who have left their homes since the late 1980s, usually to escape poverty, by offering their labour to more dynamic economies. He was also the victim of a duplicitous 'snakehead' – a trafficker of migrant labour. 'I paid 100,000 rupees [$2,500] to come here from Kathmandu – it was all our money from the family and I had to borrow some more. My wife and child are back home, relying on me. My wife is now sick and they are receiving nothing from me. I just want the money owed to me so I can get back to Kathmandu.'

That's not so easy because when foreigners go to work in the UAE, their employers take their passport and keep it. These men are indentured to their employers, who may keep them on slave wages for years before letting them go on a whim. But they are also indentured to the snakeheads. The man to whom Hom paid 100,000 rupees to secure a job and passage to Dubai had assured him that he would be earning $550 a month once he arrived there. But when it transpired that he was lying about the wage, Hom was still obliged to pay the remainder of the 100,000 rupees with interest (the collusion between employer and snakehead is transparent). So Hom, like the other men in the barracks, were brought here under false pretences.

The free movement across borders of capital, goods and services lies at the heart of globalisation as it has emerged in the last twenty years. Until now this has largely been one-way traffic, with developing countries facing demands to open their markets and leave behind the common post-war policies of protectionism. This was a difficult transition for most countries, especially those which – unlike India, Korea and China – do not enjoy economies of scale. Thus the West began to export its manufactured goods to the developing world, and the West established factories and repatriated the profits, while refusing to reciprocate by opening its agricultural market. Equally damaging, however, are the fierce restrictions that the West places on labour migration, or the 'missing global flow' as it is sometimes called.

Globalisation will only work if the free movement of capital, goods and services is complemented by the free movement of labour, or at the very least a more generous movement than exists now. We have designed an uneven playing field with at least one major consequence that undermines the progress of globalisation and even brings the process into question.

Incalculable numbers cross borders illegally in search of work every year. But while many are willingly smuggled by arrangement, millions are trafficked. This means that force, blackmail or deception are used in getting them to their destination (if, indeed, they make it that far – the journey is often extremely hazardous). It is a paradox that as the demand in Western economies for migrant labour has increased during the 1990s, so controls on the borders have been tightened almost everywhere. This has created a huge market for the transfer of people, driven by the demand of Western business for cheap, untaxed labour.

Despite Southern Illinois University's large student population, Carbondale was not a happening place in the mid-1970s. But I had ended up there as a visitor because my father had foolishly accepted a guest professorship to translate the works of the great Russian film director, Sergei Eisenstein. Fresh out of secondary school, I needed to earn money, but as a non-US citizen the licit economy was out of bounds (sort of). In the evening, I was a highly lauded pizza deliverer at Mama Gina's (this was a time when an English accent could still add a quarter to the tip). But during the day I worked at the packing plant of Nutrition Headquarters, where I first came across America's profound obsession with vitamins and supplements. For ten hours a day, I had to stand at a desk and pack customers' orders before they were shipped out (the majority, I seem to recall, bound for Florida).

I dare say that these days Nutrition Headquarters is an upstanding employer of legally registered labour – after all, I notice that its headquarters now stands on Nutritional Plaza Drive, doubtless in honour of all the jobs it has created for American labourers! Unfortunately, back in the Victorian days of my youth, Nutrition Headquarters was clearly prepared to employ illegals. Not only was I the only Caucasian among the workforce, but I was the only English speaker. The great majority were Vietnamese and, like me, too cowed and frightened to protest against our conditions and pay. The supervisors were uneducated white

American females who prowled around the shop floor like wolves, almost salivating at the prospect of a worker found slacking. I was eventually canned when a stomach bug forced me to visit the restroom every hour. I still remember the face of the short, curly-haired brunette in her thirties as she proudly announced in nasal tones how my employment was being terminated for unauthorised visits to the washroom. I could scarcely contain my joy, but the other wretches who lost their jobs during my time there trembled and wept before shuffling off to an uncertain and perhaps destitute future.

Since my revealing experience among the migrant labourers of Carbondale, our consumer culture has become yet more bloated with choice and hypermarkets. The need for unskilled labour (especially in the agriculture sector) has reached unprecedented levels, while the indigenous populations in the West now entirely eschew low-paid work in unsafe conditions. The trade in labour is huge and because it is largely illegal, only criminal entrepreneurs can operate it.

To satisfy the demand, employers approach 'gangmasters' in their area with requests to provide cheap labour. The illegals are then required to pick cockles in Morecambe Bay, England, for $1.60 an hour, or to slaughter cattle in Pennsylvania on an industrial scale for $2.50, or to pick olives in Italy, Greece and Spain. Even Japan, which traditionally sought to avoid the import of foreign labour, witnessed a doubling of its resident foreign population from 1975 to 2001 as the country's ageing population proved ever less willing to undertake the 3D jobs: dirty, dangerous and difficult.

The gangmasters are in touch with the snakeheads, who recruit and arrange the transport of the migrant workers. The snakeheads and their accomplices will prise open any crack they see in a border regime. They bribe immigration and consular officials regularly to secure visas (several of the big Russian gangsters like Sergei Mikhailov secured their Israeli passports by dint of bribes paid to a low-level official). They pack trafficked labourers in false compartments in trucks, or squeeze them like sardines into the holds of floating rust-buckets, which may or may not make the trip across the Indian Ocean or Mediterranean.

Of course, the workers continue to leave their impoverished villages; their families still club together to pay for the passage abroad; and dozens of countries depend on the migrants' remittances. But it is a hugely lucrative and exploitative market that is managed by criminal syndicates. Moreover, once the workers have arrived, they of course have no recourse to health or welfare services in the event of trouble.

In recent years, there has been a steady downward pressure on the illegal global labour market and the wages that itinerant labourers can command in many parts of the world. This is just the very beginning of a phenomenon that will grow ever more influential in the decades to come in all aspects of the global economy. This is China. The sea of cheap surplus labour that waits patiently in the Chinese country-side is seeping out into the wider world. Nobody boasts economies of scale like the Chinese.

Lieutenant General Dahi Khalfan Tamim, head of Dubai's police, was adamant. 'We will fight anything that will impact negatively on society,' he declared as he set out a new crackdown on prostitution in the city. He certainly had his work cut out. That evening I visited a club called Cyclone in Bur Dubai, across the creek from Deira. It is a vast, square-set two-storey complex with uniformed and plain-clothes security guards checking everyone entering. Or rather every man entering – there are no women seeking admission. Dubai is still mourning the death of Sheikh Mohammed bin Rashid Al Maktoum, the man who ruled the city for three decades, reinventing it in the process. His death has led to the cancellation of the Dubai Shopping Festival, the annual consumerist mega-binge that witnesses the world's wealthy swooping down on Dubai for even more spectacular tax-free bargains than usual. The lost Shopping Month has cost Dubai an estimated $3 billion in earnings and the pressure is now mounting on his son Sheikh Mo to exempt this youthful annual spree from older and inconvenient local traditions.

At Cyclone, the management pays its respects by placing a ban on live DJs for forty days. The club's other core activity, however, continues unimpeded. As I enter the main area, there are two oval bars on either side of the entrance. Between the two is an invisible line. The dozens of girls crowded around the left bar never cross over to the right bar, and vice versa. I step into the left-bar zone to order a drink. Within seconds of stopping at the bar, a hand grabs my wrist and a Chinese woman of about nineteen starts talking. 'You like me? No? You want to sleep with me? I am very good at sex. Only 400 dirham [$100]. I am *very* good.' I smile and decline politely, provoking a sore look of disappointment – not, of course, because she had been so drawn to my middle-aged jowls, but because the longer it takes to find a punter at Cyclone, the less the woman can charge. 'By three o'clock in the morning,' explains Ted, a twenty-something New Zealander who is, he tells me, broadening his horizons through global travel, 'you can pick 'em up for fifty dirham. That's why you see the Africans hanging outside at three, four o'clock because by then the girls will sleep with anyone for any price.' He grinned.

The right oval bar is populated by Russian and Ukrainian women. A large blonde in her twenties approaches me and wonders if I would like to sleep with her.

'I am Professor of Sex,' she growls, 'I teach you all good things.'

I talk to her in pidgin Russian and she to me in pidgin English. We both find the encounter amusing. I turn down the offer, but buy her a drink instead, which surprises her. 'Why are the Chinese women over there, and you over here?'

'We have an agreement,' she says. 'Nobody breaks it yet. But the Chinese want so much. They want all the business, and these girls are younger and they ask for less money. We hate them.'

The Russian and Ukrainian prostitutes are being steadily edged out of the market because of the bottomless supply of young Chinese women who are prepared to sleep with men for fewer dollars than the Eastern Europeans.

For those not well versed in this market, the Chinese zone of Cyclone is an intimidating experience. By the time I scurried back to my hotel, I was beginning to wonder who was the predator, so bitter is the competition for the sex dollar among Dubai's foreign prostitutes.

Dubai's crackdown on the trade is, of course, pure hot air. The primary class of people that the city wants to attract to live and work in the city comprises young single males. Relationships between non-Arabs and Emirati women are very rare and discouraged. Instead, the testosterone-filled newcomers are encouraged to seek other distractions.

There is virtually no petty crime in Dubai. It is one of the safest places to live in the world. So when violence comes calling, it sends shockwaves through the place. Late on Sunday, January 19th, 2003, Sharad Shetty, a successful hotelier, entered the India Club in Dubai, a grand club for Indian expats built on land donated by Sheikh Rashid himself in 1964. Mr Shetty had come for dinner with friends, but as he strode through the main door and into the hall, two men in their twenties approached him and pumped five bullets into him before rushing to their getaway car. Dubai police were quick to link the killers with Chhota Rajan as Mr Shetty was one of Dawood Ibrahim's closest advisers. Three years earlier, Dawood's men had attempted but failed to assassinate Chhota Rajan when he was lying in hospital in Thailand. This was Rajan's reply.

Mumbai's gang warfare was now being played out in the exclusive areas of Dubai and the authorities decided upon drastic measures. They swooped against both Chhota Rajan's and Dawood Ibrahim's associates. Two of Dawood's brothers were quickly arrested and eventually deported to India. Dawood himself had started to scale down his Dubai operations as early as 1998 when he sold the fabled White House and spent less time in the city. Instead, he became ever more reliant on Pakistan, eventually moving to Karachi where he now lives in the opulent hill district of Clifton under the protection of the Pakistani state. He remains an influential figure in the Mumbai mafia, but he is dependent on the goodwill of the ISI. India demands his return to face trial, but the Government in Islamabad denies his presence on Pakistani soil – an untruth that was well documented even before the glorious society wedding took place between Dawood's daughter and the much-revered former captain of the Pakistan cricket team, Javed Miandad.

The investigation into the Bombay bombings, which lasted for fourteen years before dozens of suspects came to trial, revealed how deeply gangsterism in Bombay had subverted the city's economic and social life. Above all, the organised-crime syndicates that rose from the swamps of chronic unemployment and poverty had absorbed the film industry, Bollywood, one of the world's great cultural icons. Who made films; how much for; who became stars; who distributed the movies – all this was decided by financial patrons like Chhota Shakeel.

Sharad Shetty's spilt blood at the India Club was reason enough for Dubai to close in and neutralise the more prominent members of

Mumbai's mafia. But the constant diplomatic pressure that India had applied upon the city state also played a significant role. India's economic importance to Dubai far outstrips that of Pakistan, even if the latter country is a Muslim state.

Violent crime is very rare in Dubai and, when it reveals itself, swift retribution usually follows. But it does not follow that crime and the shadow economy simply bypass the place. The licit market in goods, services and capital is as unbridled here as it is anywhere in the world. The shadow economy is similarly unrestricted, and it is Dubai where the money from the two economic systems converges and where one can begin to perceive just how symbiotic relations are between the black and the white economies.

THE THEATRE OF CRIME

Jaime Queiroz Lopez had reached the end of his tether. For several days, Nelson Sakaguchi, a fellow director at the Banco Noroeste, a leading Brazilian private bank, had been stalling on an urgent request. The board had ordered Sakaguchi to hand over to Lopez all the documentation relating to the previous three years' business of its overseas operation based in the Cayman Islands. Now, on this February morning in 1998, Mr Sakaguchi started to formulate yet another excuse. This time Lopez lost it. Grabbing hold of his terrified colleague's lapels, he screamed, 'Look – no more stories! I want to see the figures and I want to see them now!'

It must have been a disorienting moment for Sakaguchi – a supremely successful international banker who had previously run one of Brazil's most influential banks in New York, and who felt comfortable at ministerial-level meetings of the World Bank and the International Monetary Fund; a man regarded by all as hyper-efficient, with no trace of personal vanity, but equally lacking in human warmth; and a man who for fourteen years had enjoyed absolute control of Banco Noroeste's overseas accounts. Now he cowered at the fury of Lopez and muttered quietly, 'You know, I have always had gambling in my blood.' Then he broke down and was finally compelled to show the figures.

For the first time in anyone's memory, Mr Sakaguchi was no longer in control.

In reality, matters had slipped out of Sakaguchi's hands three years earlier, on the day his department received a fax from a certain Mr

Tafida Williams, the Director for Budget and Planning at Nigeria's
Ministry of Aviation. In the fax, Mr Williams explained that a Nigerian
customer of Banco Noroeste had suggested that the bank might be
interested in an investment possiblity with the Ministry of Aviation.
The customer was indeed well known to Mr Sakaguchi and so he read
the Nigerians' offer with interest. A unique and very lucrative opportunity had arisen, Mr Williams explained. In 1991, the Nigerian
Government had moved the country's capital from Lagos to Abuja and
the time had come to create a major new airport to service the needs
of the fastest-growing city in Africa's most populous country. The
Aviation Ministry and the Central Bank of Nigeria were now looking
for external investors in the airport project. The rates of return, Mr
Williams intimated, would be highly attractive. Shrewd banker that he
was, Nelson Sakaguchi replied to the fax saying that his company
would like to explore the possibility of cooperation.

Before long, a limousine was whisking Sakaguchi from Heathrow
Airport to a swish hotel in central London to discuss the proposal with
a heavyweight delegation from Nigeria. As he entered the hotel suite,
an elegant, slightly thickset man handed him his card, 'Paul Ogwuma,
Director – Central Bank of Nigeria'. Although Sakaguchi had never
met Nigeria's most senior banker, Ogwuma's reputation in the world
of international finance was solid. And he was there with his deputy,
his deputy's wife and a senior representative of Nigeria's Aviation
Ministry. The atmosphere at the meeting was both cordial and
businesslike.

Sakaguchi may have seen himself as a risk-taker, but he had never
played for such high stakes. The Nigerians were seeking about $50
million for the airport and Banco Noroeste's capital only totalled $500
million. But the potential profits from the deal were enormous. Before
long, he had authorised the first transfer of $4 million and there was
more to come.

Mr Tafida Williams from the Ministry's Budget and Planning Dept
was not among the delegation to London. Just as well, really, because
Williams (or Bless Okereke, to give him his real name) would never
have passed muster as a Departmental Head. In his early twenties and
uneducated, Bless was struggling to fit into his recently acquired role
of sophisticated civil servant. It was late 1995 and as Sakaguchi started

signing the cheques, young Bless began receiving a commission for his role in securing the deal with the Banco Noroeste. Fatally starstruck, he couldn't resist playing the big man and flaunting his new-found wealth. He left his tiny room, known in Nigeria as Boy Scout lodgings, and rented a spacious apartment in his home town of Enugu, the dusty capital of the eponymous Nigerian province. He also acquired a brand-new Jeep, which he loved to show off around town. His sudden promotion into the moneyed classes must have astonished his friends and relatives, inviting speculation, jealousy and admiration in equal measure. 'He was just a young boy out of his depth,' explained Umar Mamman Sanda, a sober investigator from the Economic and Financial Crimes Commission (EFCC) in the Nigerian capital, Abuja. But his spending spree was not merely due to the *joie de vivre* that unexpected windfalls engender. Like many young Nigerian men, Bless was proving himself. These days a young man's rite of passage in Nigeria is a peculiar hybrid. To enter manhood, earlier generations had confronted the dangers of the forest and jungle as they engaged in a physical and spiritual battle with the high representatives of the animal kingdom. But the twentieth century had wrought huge changes on Nigeria and now the smell of Bless and his lucre attracted less noble creatures, wearing Ray-Bans and gold bracelets.

Poor Bless turned out to be cursed. His money had transformed him from hunter into prey. By drawing too much attention to himself, he threatened to jeopardise the safety of his colleagues and the whole operation that had generated such wealth in the first place. That at least is what Inspector Sanda from the EFCC surmises, and he has a deeper understanding of this case than anyone. That evening in Enugu, Bless noticed that a car following his Jeep was a little too close for comfort. As it gained on him, he leaped out of the Jeep and ran into the courtyard of a hotel, with the pack in hot pursuit. He jumped over a fence and into the neighbouring courtyard only to find himself cornered. He was dispatched with a few bullets. Many Nigerians will tell you that although their country is riddled with crime, it nonetheless boasts low levels of violence. And they are correct. But there are exceptions. And because Bless Okereke was involved in what became the biggest single Advance Fee Fraud (or 419 scam, as it is also known) in history, he was one of those exceptions – a bit-part player in a drama which, according to the exuberant description of the EFCC website, 'has all the characteristics of a successful movie: thrill, drama, sex, power, greed, suspense, tragedy and you name it'. (*Sic*) Oh, and at least two murders as well. Bless had been chosen for his role by Chief Emmanuel Nwude, Nigeria's most accomplished scammer.

As he awaited trial on charges of criminal conspiracy in his modest, neat home in Coita, just outside São Paulo, Nelson Sakaguchi denied that he had noticed anything fishy about the Nigerian deal. To this day, he swears he had no idea that his main business partner in the Abuja airport scheme was in fact Chief Nwude. Although uneducated and described by one lawyer as 'a thug', Nwude demonstrated confidence and ability in wriggling around the sewers of Nigeria's corruptocracy. He was a successful businessman, but he was not, as he claimed at that London meeting, Paul Ogwuma, the Director of the Central Bank of Nigeria.

Everyone agrees that Sakaguchi was the victim of the most monumental fraud, but nobody understands why such an experienced banker would fall for the scam, nor why he would have filched his employer's money in the process. In charge of Noroeste's overseas accounts in the Cayman Islands, Sakaguchi is accused by the bank's lawyers of having skimmed hundreds of millions of dollars from them between 1995 and 1997 in order to pass it on to Nigeria. Sakaguchi insists he was the victim of a fraudulent scam pure and simple, and he was not stealing from his employers. Each transfer was made in parcels of less than $6 million. Had he gone over that figure, he would have required a higher authorisation. Sakaguchi dispatched the money through dizzyingly circuitous routes in the United Kingdom, Switzerland, Hong Kong and the United States. In Nigeria alone, seventeen different banks were used to shuffle and disguise the money. But despite the huge sums and their unusual passage around the world, nobody thought fit to raise the much-hailed red flags of the Western banking system. 'Without any doubt,' said Noroeste's asset-recovery lawyer in São Paulo, Domingos Refinetti, 'the banks just waved it through and shut their eyes.'

From the banks, the tens of millions of dollars went into the pockets of Nwude and his main associates, the husband-and-wife team, Christian Ikechukwu Anajemba and Amaka Anajemba. They embarked on a game of global Monopoly, building palaces in Nigeria, buying real estate in Redondo and Huntingdon Beaches, California, and investing in an impressive array of properties in north London. They were good investors. 'It made our job easier when it came to getting the money back,' noted Keith Oliver, the London assets-recovery lawyer. 'The houses had increased in value so much that we were able to cover a good deal more than we had at first anticipated.'

While the motives of the Nigerian scammers were never in doubt, Sakaguchi's gullibility beggars belief. There is no evidence to suggest that he was in league with the scammers – he was a genuine victim. But he was funding this wild gamble with somebody else's money. Thousands, if not millions of man hours have gone into the Noroeste investigation, which stands as the third-biggest bank theft in history. (Nick Leeson's destruction of Barings Bank and the looting of the Iraqi National Bank after the US invasion of March 2003 take the top two places.) And yet not a single lawyer, judge, policeman, fraudster, friend or spiritual adviser of Nelson Sakaguchi can answer the two central questions: Why did he do it? And how was he taken in?

'It's hard to see how he was fooled by this,' remarked Keith Oliver, holding up a letter from the fraudsters boasting the distinct letterhead: The Federal Reserve Clearing House, Chadwell Heath, Romford, Essex. There are no residential suburbs in north-east London that are more anonymous and bland than Chadwell Heath. Nonetheless, just to double-check that overnight the district had not developed into a major centre of international finance, Oliver spent a few hours motoring around the Heath, 'just so I could swear in my affidavit that there was definitely no Federal Reserve Clearing House there!'

But by this time Sakaguchi was in regular correspondence with Chadwell Heath's Federal Clearing Bank and similar institutions as though they were genuine. In all likelihood, he had lost any grasp of the difference between reality and illusion. He was seemingly completely trapped by the addictive fear common to victims of the 419 scam (named after the relevant clause in Nigeria's criminal code).

The 419 scam comes in many shapes and sizes – it sometimes arrives as an appeal to rich Westerners to come to the aid of an impoverished African child; letters, faxes and emails beseeching Americans in particular for funds to erect a new church or to bolster a congregation are frequent – in these cases, the motivation of the victims is well intentioned and charitable. Other lucrative prey of the 419 scammers are the lovelorn, in particular middle-aged widows and divorcees who develop virtual relationships with West African toy boys, who slowly leach them of their savings as an advance on a sexual congress that never happens.

But most of all, the 419ers appeal to the basic instinct of greed. Annie McGuire, a Californian victim of the fraudsters, explained that she had a decent education, 'a good IQ, and simultaneously I owned and ran three businesses before retiring in my late forties. My husband and I *had* a very comfortable, growth-oriented retirement fund.' And yet, as she confessed, 'We wanted more – we wanted to send our grand-children to private schools; we wanted to set up trust funds for them and hire experts to teach them how to manage their money. We wanted to travel, and have summer and winter homes to save our aching joints from inclement weather. My husband wanted horses, I wanted a drop-dead audio system. I figured I'd been around enough to make a lot of quick money if the opportunity presented itself.'

Unfortunately for Annie, she unwittingly hooked up with a high-end Nigerian scammer who allegedly traded in commodities. Before long she discovered that he had channelled close to one million dollars of her own and other investors' money into a fake holding account in the Bahamas. Although she was in deep trouble, Annie was unusual in that she went to the FBI. A majority of scam victims develop a peculiar psychological dependency on the perpetrator – the more money they lose, the more desperate they are to believe the promise of tanta-lising riches, and the more prepared they are to throw good money after bad.

Every year countless Europeans and Americans are fleeced of thousands, tens and hundreds of thousands of dollars each. They all believe that they are going to make millions of dollars by hiding and transiting money that purports to originate in the dormant accounts of dodgy Western businessmen, or of the widows of former African dictators like Nigeria's late President Sani Abacha or President Mobutu of Zaire, now the Democratic Republic of Congo.

The scam is simple: in order for the victims (or *mugus* as they are known in Nigeria) to get their excited paws on the fabled millions, the scammer will at some point request that they transfer a facilitating fee of several thousand dollars to the bank's 'lawyer'. This is why the 419 scam is also dubbed the 'advance fee fraud'. Once hooked, the *mugu* is asked for ever greater sums, lured on by the fictive promise of millions just around the corner. 'The fraudsters exploit a simple failing in human psychology,' said Alhaji Ibrahim Lamorde, Head of Operations for the EFCC in Lagos. 'If you have already invested, say, $1 million in a project and your partner says you need to put in another $200,000 for the return to be realised, people think "Well, compared to the $1 million, $200k is not such a big amount." And so in it goes, before the partner comes back two weeks later with a request for a further $150k.' It is the same motive that drives an addicted gambler. 'They wriggle like a fish on the end of a line,' concludes Mr Lamorde.

Ultrascan Advanced Global Investigations in the Netherlands, which specialises in uncovering 419 frauds, has reported that citizens in thirty-eight developed countries admitted to losses of more than $3 billion in 2005 alone. These estimates are necessarily low because they exclude all those victims who did not confess their gullibility to law-enforcement agencies. Most victims report feeling an intense mixture of shame and guilt when suckered by 419ers, and in March 2003 a 419 victim turned to murder for the first time to express his frustration. Jiri Pasovsky, a 72-year-old Czech pensioner, stormed into the Nigerian Embassy in Prague and shot dead a secretary after the Consul General explained that he could not return the $600,000 that Pasovsky had lost to a Nigerian scammer.

Every time Nelson Sakaguchi transferred another $3–4 million, he expected the returns to start rolling in. Instead, Chief Nwude and his accomplices requested a further payment in order to pay for fabricated legal fees or bribes. And as Sakaguchi's losses mounted, so did the compulsion to pay out more millions in the hope of retrieving the ever greater sum invested. At some point in any 419 scam, the anxiety must mingle with a thickening despair that leads straight to a living hell. Sakaguchi's response to this descent was to seek advice from *macumbe*, Brazil's syncretic religion that melds West African animism with Christianity. Maria Rodriguez was a *macumba* priestess whom Sakaguchi was wont to consult.

During the lengthy investigations into the Banco Noroeste affair,

Maria Rodriguez introduced some welcome levity for the participants. At one point, the Brazilian Government gave exceptional permission for a Swiss judge to hold hearings in Brazil to establish whether Sakaguchi and some of the Nigerian conspirators should face trial for money-laundering in Switzerland. (Sakaguchi was eventually convicted and sentenced to thirty months in a Swiss jail.) The judge heard testimony from Maria Rodriguez. Domingos Refinetti, representing Banco Noroeste, was present and recalled the scene.

'I wanted money from Sakaguchi,' Rodriguez said, 'because I needed to buy 120,000 white doves for a particular ritual. By having the pigeons,' she said, 'Sakaguchi would be relieved of his problems. Sakaguchi delivered the pigeons.'

'And how might one keep the pigeons?' enquired the judge. 'Surely they were flying all over the place?'

At this point, the judge could contain himself no longer and began laughing. Curiously enough, Maria Rodriguez said that she then asked for money for 120,000 black pigeons. The judge, barely able to control his mirth, said, 'I suppose if you've bought up 120,000 white doves, you will have driven up the price and you need to buy the black pigeons in order to restore the equilibrium in the pigeon futures' market!'

The cost of the pigeons and the advice were no laughing matter, however. Altogether Sakaguchi siphoned a breathtaking $20 million from the Caymans into Brazil and into the coffers of the late Maria Rodriguez.

Across the Atlantic in Lagos and Enugu, Chief Nwude and his main accomplice, Christian Ikechukwu Anajemba, were exploiting the social and business clout that big money brings. Nwude was appointed a director of Union Bank, one of Nigeria's biggest. He put about the story that he was a canny oil trader who had recently joined the big league: he began to collect cars, both classic and modern, including Mayburys and Rolls-Royces. Anajemba imported millions of dollars' worth of marble for his new mansions while purchasing fabulous jewellery for his wife, Amaka, who would later be dubbed Queen of the 419s by an admiring Nigerian press. And while accounts were haemorrhaging, while huge sums of obscure origin were chugging from bank to bank, and while audits were being merrily signed, nobody noticed a thing – not in Brazil, the Caymans or the US; not in the UK, Switzerland or Nigeria. *Nada.*

There are important reasons why Nigeria has become the Broadway of Crime – it is home to the most successful culture of financial fraud in history. As in any good theatre, the audience (or victims in this case) must be willing to suspend disbelief for the illusion to work. Nigeria offers the perfect facilities for budding impresarios because it is the world's greatest example of a remarkable hybrid: the Potemkin state, in which an elaborate façade of institutions conceals their complete lack of substance.

Dressed in a brightly coloured African shirt and tight trousers that hug a sinewy body, Dede Mabiaku forcefully expresses the popular belief that 'Europeans' are responsible for Nigeria's ubiquitous corruption and specifically for 419 scams. 'They invented the computer!' he explains. Dede is on his way to a party thrown by Hakim Belo Osagie, one of Nigeria's most successful bankers. Dede himself is a popular singer. The nephew and protégé of Fela Kuti, the great musician admired the world over, Dede is adamant that the roots of Nigeria's kleptocracy lie in Western culture. He talks of the tradition of companies exploiting the natural resources of Africa and giving nothing in return, and of how corruption was an essential tool in these companies' business practices. '419 and the scams are merely the redressing of the global balance,' he says. 'If Europeans get ripped off, they deserve it. They are greedy and trying to make money out of African people.'

There is a large element of truth in what Mabiaku says and the legacy of colonisation has been decisive in the fashioning of modern Nigeria. Europe has been cherry-picking Africa's riches for more than two centuries (more recently America and now even China have been feeding at the trough). The European colonists extracted Africa's commodities (whether slaves, palm oil or diamonds), and in exchange they left borders and bureaucracy, countries and central banks, tariffs and taxes. In short, they left behind the modern state, that intricate web of institutions which over many centuries bound Europe's rulers with her ruled.

The Africans had not requested these institutions, nor was there much evidence that they wanted or needed them. But to succeed in their commercial endeavours, the Europeans could not do without them – in the late nineteenth and early twentieth centuries, they felt the urge to build railways, cultivate palms and dig mines across Africa. And in doing so they demanded protection for their contracts, which the word of a chief (the local way of doing business) could no longer guarantee. Such significant investments as the Europeans made required security that would survive the chief's death and override any subsequent dispute about rights to the land or to the commodity in question. And for that they needed borders, banks, taxes, lawyers and courts. The Europeans erected the façades of their states, but behind them traditional societies remained very different.

But although Dede Mabiaku's indignation is well founded, it disguises a great chunk of hypocrisy. This is in fearful evidence at the party being held by Mr Osagie at his villa on Ikoyi Island. Among the wealthiest areas in all Nigeria, Ikoyi is tucked away from the permanent traffic jam on the mainland (residents avoid the hellish drive to the airport by taking the helicopter shuttle). Armed with a Harvard MBA and a reputation of genius in banking, Osagie lives in a vast mansion where he personally greets each of his 300 guests. Dressed tastefully in well-cut black slacks and shirt, he smiles as the raucous assembly helps itself to champagne on tap. In the garden, the stage is set for stand-up comedians and the cream of Lagos musicians, like Dedi, to perform. Blake and Crystal Carrington would be hard pressed to mount a display of such gaudy opulence.

Nigeria's passage into the global market, floating atop the world's sixth-largest oil reserves, has created one of history's most divided societies in terms of income distribution. The razor wire and searchlights protecting the rich in this part of Lagos are sadly reminiscent of the walls behind which most whites in South Africa live. These Nigerian walls have done immense damage to one of the most important African institutions – the responsibility of the *oga* or 'big man' in the community to the less well off. Instead of distributing money, food, clothes and housing to the village, the big men who have grown fat on oil corruption now hoard their millions in mansions behind elaborate security arrangements.

The Nigerian elite has become rich even beyond many Westerners' imagination. Since the 1970s, they have been sucking the profits from the country's oil resources almost directly from the wells and into their pockets. Yet this voluminous revenue stream did not dissuade Nigeria from accepting massive Western loans during the 1970s. With Robert McNamara at the helm, the World Bank was working as indefatigably as an insurance salesman on commission, cajoling the developing world into taking out huge sums on tick. During McNamara's tenure from 1968 to 1981, lending rose from just under $1 billion to almost $12.5 billion and Nigeria was an important client. This was the beginning of the massive global debt scandal in which we are all still embroiled.

Of course, Nigerian oil revenue was not used as repayment for the loans. Instead, the burden was shifted onto Nigeria's poor, for whom the country's rulers made no welfare or development provisions. Nigeria was about to take the Potemkin state to a new level. Its refurbishment lovingly creates all the external attributes of a bureaucratic state – flags, UN speeches, forms to fill, grand buildings with big golden plaques saying Central Bank or Ministry of Labour – but they are mere scenery on a stage. The Central Bank has no money, the Ministry of Labour no jobs. But a small group used the illusion to divert national income into their pockets and those of their families and friends. The state was effectively privatised (which in the 1980s was, of course, in keeping with the zeitgeist of late Reaganite and Thatcherite economics), but the recipients of the money were under no obligation to provide the services that the state might otherwise be expected to deliver.

With the petrodollar rush came huge contracts for public works, which were handed out to Western companies that were colluding in the bribery process. 'A government of the contractors, by the contractors, for the contractors' is how Ishola Williams of Transparency International described the notorious rule of General Ibrahim Babangida, known in Nigeria as IBB, from the mid-1980s to the early 1990s. A former general in the Nigerian Army who resigned his commission, Williams knows whereof he speaks. 'The scumbag companies made common cause with Nigerian politicians to rip off the Treasury,' explained Stephen Ellis, a leading scholar on West Africa, whose indignation provokes his lapse into the vernacular, 'and for banks like BCCI this was perfect. Because they could facilitate these deals between Western companies and the Nigerian elite, and they don't cry foul because they were corrupt themselves. So BCCI was skimming off everybody and aiding such phenomena as capital flight.'

In 1983, the gifted Nigerian writer, Chinua Achebe, wrote, 'Nigerians are corrupt because the system under which they live today makes corruption easy and profitable; they will cease to be corrupt when corruption is difficult and inconvenient . . . The trouble with Nigeria is simply and squarely a failure of leadership. There is nothing basically wrong with the Nigerian character. I am saying that Nigeria can change today if she discovers leaders who have the will, the ability and the vision.'

Ironically, Achebe penned this on the eve of the worst excesses of poor leadership, when a series of military coups allowed the consolidation of corruption as an ideology. It was during the rule of IBB that the US Drug Enforcement Administration (DEA) noticed how Nigeria was becoming the major trans-shipment centre for cocaine destined for Europe and for heroin en route to the United States. Furthermore, it appeared that the organisers of this business enjoyed access to the very highest offices of state.

The Nigerian military effectively announced the start of an unending party of grand theft. And to this day, anybody who visits the country can see it in full swing, from the minute they attempt (and surely fail) to pass customs without paying a bribe at Lagos's chaotic Murtala Mohammed airport, to the day they leave when they will have to dispense largesse to a wide variety of airport staff if they are to stand a chance of securing a seat on their flight home. 'You go to market, somebody will try to cheat you,' says Nuhu Ribadu, head of the EFCC and the country's senior anti-corruption policeman. 'You take a taxi, somebody will take something – you must have your eyes open all the time.' If you want to fill your car with petrol (in a land awash with gasoline there are permanent shortages), you must bribe; get into a decent restaurant, you must bribe; pass through the ubiquitous police checkpoints, you must bribe. Every single economic or social transaction must be refracted through the prism of graft. And all this is decreed by the example set by the oil thieves at the very top.

'Every day the Nigerian economy loses between 150,000 and 320,000 barrels of oil,' explained Gary K. Busch, an adventurous American businessman who has worked with mafia-style entrepreneurs in many parts of the developing world including Nigeria. 'These are stolen by 'bunkerers', who have small tanker vessels, which load the oil in the Delta and trans-ship this stolen oil to offshore tankers, which deliver it to other West African states. Further inland illegal tanker trucks load the oil and refined products and drive these into neighbouring countries for black-market sale. At the current price of around $50 per barrel this amounts to a "leakage" of around US$7.5 to US$16 million a day. On a monthly basis this amounts to around US$365 million or US$4.4 billion a year.'

There is of course no intrinsic moral problem in Nigeria profiting from its natural resources. But the unwillingness of its small band of hyper-rich to distribute its billions in any equitable manner has very serious implications and unpleasant consequences. While maintaining one of the most venal military establishments in the world, Nigeria does nothing to succour its second army of tens of millions of unemployed and destitute; 60 per cent of the population lives below the poverty line. Equally distressing is the collapse in life expectancy, which, according to the UN, dropped from fifty-four years old for Nigerian males in 1995 to forty-three in 2006. The corruption at the very highest levels sets an example that is mimicked throughout Nigerian society. If you want to prosper, you have to cheat.

In the mid-1980s, the giant investment house, Merrill Lynch, contracted two different firms to clean and guard overnight their headquarters in New York's financial district. And every night over several months, the cleaners and the night watchmen would make their way to the files storing the details of customers to whom Merrill Lynch had granted 'preferential' status. They held credit cards with which they could enter any financial institution and withdraw $52,000 on any one occasion, no questions asked. The Nigerian cleaners and night watchmen busied themselves for several months photocopying all these details on the company Xerox, before transferring the information onto blank credit cards in preparation for one mighty spending spree.

One night the Nigerians let down their guard and left one of the photocopied pages by the machine. Before long, Merrill Lynch had called in the US Secret Service which, through a quirk of agency history, has responsibility for financial and counterfeiting crimes as well as its more familiar role of presidential guard duty. 'That was the first time that we caught on to the Nigerians as scammers,' remembers the ex-USSS agent Mark Sidbury. 'And they were good.'

Over the next few years, the Secret Service registered major financial crimes perpetrated by Nigerian gangs in several major US cities, from Atlanta through Chicago to Los Angeles. They involved anything to do with money: insurance scams; current account scams; credit-card fraud; counterfeiting of money and passports; as well as the creation of networks offering US citizenship through marriages of convenience. Above all, the Secret Service observed the speed with which Nigerian fraudsters would adapt technological innovation in the financial sector to their own purposes. A distaste for violence worked in their favour as they drew far less public attention to their crimes than those working with drug cartels or the more traditional protection rackets of the *Cosa Nostra*. The amount of money involved, however, was staggering.

The Merrill Lynch case occurred when banking systems were at the very beginning of computerisation. What the Nigerian fraudsters demonstrated was a capacity to blend an advanced understanding of mechanical and electronic technology with a convincing theatricality. When surveying the undulating landscape of Nigerian crime, it is hard not to develop a sense of admiration for the loving care and creativity with which it is fashioned.

Most Nigerians involved in crime simply mimic the behaviour of their thieving elite. This tiny band of billionaires is drawn mainly from the west and north of the country. But those who commit crimes overseas are disproportionately drawn from Nigeria's east, as was the case in the New York scam. There are more than 300 ethnic groups in Nigeria, but broadly speaking the country is divided into three main language groups – the Yoruba in the west, including Lagos; the Hausa in the north; and the Igbo in the east. It is too crude to identify these as three separate peoples as the differentiation within each language group is vast, rather like calling Russians and Poles part of the same tribe – which would raise eyebrows in Moscow and hackles in Warsaw.

After almost a century of colonial rule, the three groups embraced independence in 1960 with very different roles in the new state. By 1966, the Muslim Hausa had come to dominate the army; the Christian

Yoruba provided much of the civil service and the intellectual elite of the country; while the Igbo in the east continued their role as some of the most effective traders in the world. When oil was discovered, it was mostly in the Niger delta to the east. Igbo leaders felt disinclined to share their wealth either with the north and its unproductive, almost feudal system, or with the Yoruba in the west, whom the Igbo perceived as insufferably arrogant. In 1967, the Igbo announced their secession from the country and the declaration of a new state, Biafra. Not surprisingly, the Hausa and the Yoruba were in no mood to let this precious part of the country slip through their hands. Civil war devastated the east until 1970, when Biafra – broken, battered and famished – surrendered.

Ever since then, the Igbo have complained that they have been excluded from the riches of Nigeria by the Yoruba and Hausa. The rich of the west and the north became even richer, while the Igbo returned to their old ways. For hundreds of years, the Igbo had forged trading routes along the coast of West Africa as far as South Africa. In collaboration with the emirs of the Hausa and their trading counterparts from Lebanon, they also pioneered a trans-Saharan route that stretched as far as Mecca, Medina and Jeddah in what is now Saudi Arabia.

Thanks to wars and apartheid, these traditional routes were less easily negotiated in the 1970s than was once the case (although some of the many Nigerians studying in the Soviet Union and its Warsaw Pact allies assisted in the delivery of supplies to the ANC in southern Africa). And so they started looking further afield – London was a popular destination, as were New York and Washington, DC, while other Igbo found their way to Thailand, where a proportion soon became involved in the dispatch of heroin to Africa and the West. By 1990 Nigerian nationals (the majority of them Igbo) made up 30 per cent of all people imprisoned at British ports of entry for heroin-smuggling, according to the Howard League for Penal Reform. This may be explained in part because Nigerian passport holders are frequent targets of customs officers around the world.

The Igbo entrepreneurs were driven abroad both by the perceived prejudice and greed of the northerners and southerners, but also by the consequences of the most appalling mismanagement of the

Nigerian economy. By the end of Babangida's rule, the country had ratcheted up almost £30 billion of debt. Large-scale criminal fraud had been a persistent problem since independence, but with rising unemployment, rampant inflation and a collapse in the value of Nigeria's currency, the naira, defrauding indigenous Nigerians was becoming ever less profitable.

There are two basic types of criminal syndicate: the commodity traders and the protection racketeers. The former kind is divided into three principal groups: producers, wholesale traders and retailers. Each sector is usually, but not always, associated with a specific ethnic group, and the three sectors will establish cooperation across international borders as production or extraction of a commodity invariably takes place a long way from its most lucrative retail markets.

Protection racketeers, such as America's *Cosa Nostra*, very occasionally develop a trans-national operation, but are usually contained within a single state's borders; yet, like Tony Soprano and his pals, successful racketeers will also cross over into commodity trading by establishing control over the local retail outlets for whatever the market may demand – drugs, women, etc.

In the world of illicit commodities, on rare occasions the producer will play an important role as a wholesale trader and even as the final retailer. The most visible example is the Colombian cartels. They are able to use their monopoly position as refiners and wholesalers in order to outsource the cultivation of the coca to the poverty-stricken growers of Peru and Bolivia. And in the case of Amsterdam, the pivot of distribution of coke in Europe, they use traders in the local Colombian community as the primary importers into Holland.

Turkish syndicates control large parts of the heroin trade's wholesale distribution and, in countries like Germany and Great Britain, much of the retail end as well. But they play no role in production, which is highly decentralised over large parts of Central and South-East Asia (Afghanistan and Burma in particular).

Throughout the world, it is the most adventurous wholesale traders and risk-takers in the licit economy who are also most closely associated with criminality in popular perception. Being at the heart of the global economy, trade is a key component in the world of organised

crime. On the whole, Western and Northern Europeans are not associated with large-scale criminal activities except in their crucial role as
consumers.

This goes back to when Europeans sought to gain a competitive
advantage during the mercantilist period of the sixteenth to eigh-
teenth centuries by encouraging the state to back an expansion in
foreign trade. Had there been any laws to break, these adventurers
would have been the first global organised criminal syndicates. Instead
they merely offended moral values by appropriating whatever they
came across in exchange for alcohol and the clap. But the early days
of high-risk freebooting and pillage became bogged down by colonialist paraphernalia – this was not needed, on the whole, to calm
the natives, but to secure the advantages of imperial expansion over
other European competitors. So European trade was bound intimately
with the goals of the state: in the form of the colonialist army, it
would protect merchants and, as the state defined what goods were
licit and what illicit, its merchants tended to accept that definition in
exchange for armed protection that gave them a competitive edge.
When Britain decided in the nineteenth century that it was accept-
able to sell opium to the Chinese in large quantities, there was no
indignant uproar on the part of British merchants. Instead, there was
a rush for profits – the state said it was okay, and merchants didn't
need to be told twice.

Other trading nations did not enjoy such high levels of protection,
nor did they have an interest in accepting European state definitions
of which goods were permitted and which not. They built their success
as traders on other foundations – proximity to the sea; access to valued
commodities; exclusion from ruling structures and low economic
development; proximity to major geographical and political borders.
An inherent aspect of their trading is risk-taking and the scavenging
of new markets – places that lie on the edge of organised trading
networks, of states and of systems of moral values. And on the whole,
these traders do not judge a commodity by its social function in its
place of origin or consumption. They judge it by its profit margin.

As trade liberalisation was hailed in the late 1980s and early 1990s
as a cornerstone of the new world order, traders started travelling
further and in greater numbers than ever before in search of new

opportunities to buy and sell. In the forefront were those peoples, often minority communities, who had centuries of tradition in trading and living on their wits along the furthest frontiers of global commerce: the Lebanese, the Chinese of Canton and Fujian provinces, the Balkan peoples, the Jews, the Muslims of India, the Sicilians, the Vietnamese. And it was from a minority of these traders that the pioneers of the new global shadow economy were also drawn.

Of course, crime also relied on producers, such as the Russians and the Colombians. But it is the conveyor of illicit goods and services that plays the most visible part in this global drama. Among the most phlegmatic and inventive of all are the Igbo.

Infected by the corruption of the Nigerian state (itself a cankered product of British colonialism), the Igbo traders of the 1980s and 1990s dealt in those products without regard to any moral considerations, save a clear and admirable aversion to violence. But then along came an invention that enabled them to steer financial fraud operations without even crossing the threshold of their front door – the fax machine. And soon the Yoruba, the Hausa and dozens more of Nigeria's ethnic groups took up the example of the Igbo and began indulging in one of the most exuberantly mischievous examples of crime in history. The possibilities would multiply with the proliferation of the personal computer around the world; cyber crime is a new type of criminal threat that assumes several different forms. But the Igbo can stake a strong claim as trailblazers.

For many Nigerians the degree to which their country has become associated with, and even defined by, the 419 culture is both a scandal and a disaster. But according to the musician Dede Mabiaku, the 419 scams were merely the diseased chickens of colonialism coming home to roost in Europe and the US like some moral avian flu in the era of globalisation. The huge popularity of the 419 anthem, 'I Go Chop Your Dollar', suggested that these sentiments are widely held in Nigeria:

> 419 no be thief, it's just a game
> Everybody dey play em
> if anybody fall mugu,
> ha! my brother I go chop em

Refrain:
National Airport na me get em
National Stadium na me build em
President na my sister brother
You be the mugu, I be the master

Oyinbo man [White man] I go chop your dollar,
I go take your money and disappear
419 is just a game, you are the loser I am the winner

The fax machine triggered the advent of global scamming from
Nigeria, but it was the proliferation of the Internet that transformed
the practice into a goldmine. The scammers put an immense amount
of work into their ploys, and again it is hard not to admire their commitment to theatricality and detail. But ultimately they depend on the
victim's greed or gullibility. Police across the Western world have been
overwhelmed with pleas for help from victims, but there is very little
they can do because the crimes are conceived and executed in areas
outside their jurisdiction. 'Frustrating and sad' is how EFCC boss Nuhu
Ribadu described the ability of criminals to stall trial proceedings literally over decades. 'We are yet to record one successful conviction for
Advance Fee Fraud (419) in Nigeria. Yet, we have over 200 Nigerians
serving jail terms in more than fifteen countries abroad.' The remarkable Ribadu has rectified the situation since he made that observation
in 2004.

The fraudsters' ability to evade prosecution is not simply bad luck
for the poor suckers who have been fleeced by 419 scammers. Nigeria
and its culture of corruption pose two immense challenges: one
concerns the stability of Nigeria itself. An increasingly critical energy
supplier outside the Middle East and the former Soviet Union, Nigeria's
future is of interest to countries across the world. But kleptocracies
are notoriously unstable. This is especially true if such states embrace
a large number of ethnic groups with competing elites. In Nigeria's
case, the problem is further exacerbated by the economic tensions
dividing the Muslim north and the Christian south.

Nigeria's second problem is possibly the largest single difficulty for
the successful globalisation of commerce – the absence of the rule of

law. The country's emergence out of venal military dictatorship has been very difficult. Unfortunately, although a *sine qua non*, the regular holding of elections does not guarantee a successful democracy. Most obviously in the Balkans, but elsewhere as well, political parties are a vehicle for economic interests to gain access to the state and an unfair or criminal advantage. But equally important in undermining the consolidation of democratic roots is the absence of an impartial judiciary and a disinterested legal system. Business needs to enjoy confidence in the institutions of democracy, known as the rule of law, if it is to risk investing in those markets. For globalisation to work, the world needs to be a level playing field: the West has to stop its protectionist practices and it has to reassess its resistance to the free, or at least a freer, movement of labour. The developing world in turn needs to address the issue of corruption and the strengthening of the rule of law. This raises the awkward question of global governance and standards that might be compatible across the world. Nigeria – plagued by the colonialist legacy, the curse of oil and modern confessional tensions – demonstrates how problematic is the application of universal policies in a world that boasts such diverse local cultures and painful historical experiences. The mixed messages that emanate from America and Europe further exacerbate this: on the one hand, they encourage transparency and good governance in the developing world by applying a system of conditionality that includes both punishment and incentives; on the other hand, they are desperate to secure energy supplies from countries like Nigeria and are prepared to bend the rules, especially when confronted by the competitive pressure of Chinese and Indian oil requirements. To be blunt, if the Americans and Europeans demand that oil-producing countries adopt higher standards of transparency and anti-corruption measures, these countries are increasingly in a position to respond by saying, 'Fine – if you don't want our oil, we'll sell it to someone else!' And they have plenty of eager buyers.

It does not follow that the issue of transparent government is doomed. Although not decisive, the external and internal pressures on Nigeria to clean up its act have not proven totally feeble. In the first five years of the millennium, Nihu Ribadu and his team at the EFCC have emerged as the vanguard in the struggle against corruption and organised crime. And their prosecution of the Banco Noroeste case, the largest recorded fraud in history, with the assistance of lawyers and policemen in Brazil, the United States, Britain and Switzerland, has become a touchstone.

It was not until August 1997, when the Spanish Banco Santander made a bid to take over Banco Noroeste, that the directors of the Brazilian bank realised that the world's largest 419 scam had been perpetrated under their noses. In December 1997 at a joint board meeting, an official from Santander questioned why half of Noroeste's capital was sitting in the Cayman Islands largely unmonitored. He wanted to examine it to see if returns on this capital gave value for money. The Caymans account amounted in theory to $190 million, almost two-fifths of Noroeste's total value. Nelson Sakaguchi was on vacation at the time and so it was not until two months later that Jaime Queiroz Lopez finally put him up against a wall and extracted the relevant documentation.

The fraud was discovered instantly, but it took some weeks before the auditors were able to ascertain that $242 million had gone missing – $191 million in cash and the remainder as outstanding interest. Sakaguchi was not the only person with a lot of explaining to do. Two subordinates in his department also appear to have colluded in the theft. It was perhaps most embarrassing for the reputation of Price Waterhouse Coopers who, as external auditors, had given Banco Noroeste six clean bills of health during the period of the fraud. This was unlikely to inspire confidence in a company that was still recovering from its inglorious performance in the BCCI scandal.

The Simonsen and Cochrane families, who owned Banco Noroeste, decided to foot the bill of $242 million themselves to ensure that the sale to Banco Santander went through. Then for six years very little happened. The two families learned the grim fact that while the border-less flows of cash through the banking system are hard to stem, it is equally difficult to facilitate cooperation between the criminal-justice systems of two states, let alone four or five. Chief Nwude and Mrs Anajemba (her husband had been assassinated by now) were free to spend, spend, spend.

'The problem is that nobody was looking for it who knew how to look for the money,' explained Bill Richey, a former Florida State DA who was asked by the Simonsens and Cochranes to search for the money across the globe. And so Richey made a smart move – he called a buddy who used to work for the Internal Revenue Service as a criminal investigator. 'You know the IRS are tax people, the American Gestapo!' he said. 'My guy is a very nice man, but he's a very efficient and effective forensic accountant investigator.'

Tracing the money to Switzerland, England and the US, Richey assembled the A-Team of asset-recovery lawyers in London, Kentucky, LA, New York, Geneva, Hong Kong, Singapore and Lagos. Slowly but surely, the A-Team started to claw back the assets located outside Nigeria. But to get the job done properly, they would need convictions of the criminal group in Nigeria. 'And until 2003,' one of the lawyers pointed out, 'that was a non-starter.'

Chief Nwude and Mrs Anajemba had already been busy bribing the police, bribing journalists and bribing the courts. They were untouchable. Until, that is, Nigeria's very own Elliot Ness appeared on the scene.

Nigeria's parliament established the Economic and Financial Crimes Commission at the request of President Olesegun Obasanjo in 2002. The United States, the IMF and the EU were all pressing Nigeria to tackle the notorious levels of corruption throughout government and society. This had become an urgent issue for the West, as Nigeria's importance as an oil supplier was growing in the wake of turbulence in the Middle East, Central Asia and Venezuela.

What few expected when the EFCC started work properly a few months later was that its director, Nuhu Ribadu, would develop such an unbending devotion to rooting out corruption and crime wherever it might be found. Through a reedy, almost effeminate voice, this thin, bespectacled and earnest-looking man in his mid-forties expresses his immutable determination to tackle Nigeria's great enemy: 'It is corruption that gives Nigeria this terrible image, that drives people from our country; it is corruption that gives rise to these crimes like 419; and because of corruption nobody wants to do business with us. We must bring to justice the powerful, rich, corrupt people who have turned this into a country of fraudsters and cheats.'

Ribadu doesn't just talk the talk. In the first three years of its existence, the EFCC recovered more than $1 billion in stolen assets.

He put away Nigeria's ex-chief of police and his own mentor, Tafa Balogun, when he suspected him of misappropriating $30 million (it turned out to be $150 million). The EFCC led a successful prosecution against a sitting Provincial State President and, in countering accusations that he is a cat's paw of President Obasanjo, Ribadu pointed out that – before Obasanjo left office in 2007 – he had taken down the Senate President, a key Obasanjo ally. 'I am investigating everybody', he said at the time, 'former heads of state, the present leadership, almost everybody from the President downwards.'

It would be optimistic to believe that Ribadu and his 500 staff members are going to dig out all the weeds whose roots go deep down into the country's social and political fabric. But the EFCC's record of incorruptibility has made a significant difference. Policing global crime is becoming increasingly difficult, but if it is to make headway, then anti-corruption strategies in emerging markets such as Brazil and Nigeria are absolutely critical. Corruption is the swamp in which breeds a particularly efficient and heartless species of parasitical criminal.

In 2005, Chief Emmanuel Nwude visited Ribadu at his home and insisted that he accept the gift of two brown paper bags that the Chief had brought with him. In them were $75,000 in cash. The wealth of the criminals and corrupt officials has been sufficient until now to mould and bend the criminal-justice system in their favour. Not only did Ribadu pursue Nwude on charges of attempted bribery, but he pursued him for his attempted kidnap of a key prosecution witness during the Chief's first trial.

But the decisive witness in the trial against Nwude in November 2005 was Nelson Sakaguchi. Domingos Refinetti, Banco Noroeste's São Paulo lawyer, finally persuaded Sakaguchi to visit Nigeria and meet his nemesis, the Chief. Amaka Anajemba had already started her prison sentence after agreeing a plea bargain. When Nwude's trial opened, he pleaded not guilty. After Sakaguchi's testimony, the Chief changed his plea and is now behind bars with all his money confiscated, in addition to a hefty fine of $10 million.

Nelson Sakaguchi and his motives remain an enigma. After pleading guilty to money-laundering in Switzerland and serving time there, he now sits quietly at home in Coita waiting to hear when the charges of criminal conspiracy will come to trial. He insists on his innocence by arguing that he did not have the authority to transfer the money and that the entire operation was sanctioned by the board.

Whatever Sakaguchi's fate, at least the money is no longer at the disposal of Nwude and his team. Tens of thousands of other victims have been less fortunate than the Cochrane and Simonsen families. 'I will not accept a case if it's less than $5 million, it's not worth the chase,' is the candid admission of Bill Richey, the US lawyer. 'I'm not going to tell you what the clients have spent here, but they have spent significantly less than half of what we have frozen all around the world. When we finish dealing with the parties in Nigeria and . . . we find the final recovery and the case is finally over, I think the clients will probably receive a return of about five to one on their investment.' But then Richey adds, 'It's a sad day that in order to recover, if you are a victim of a crime, you have to be able to afford it.'

But that is one of the disheartening lessons of the Banco Noroeste scam. The tens of thousands of other victims of 419 scams have no such recourse to their funds. Global justice does not come cheap.

BLACK AND WHITE

Lucy Tshabalala found she could not move. 'I couldn't control my body and I was shaking,' she said. The customs officer at Los Angeles Airport, LAX, had told her she could go, but she didn't. 'I wanted to move *sooo* badly, but it was like there was a magnet holding me down.' Instead, in a near-cataleptic panic, she haltingly asked the officer where she could get a bus to Santa Monica. He paused. 'Wait here one moment, ma'am.'

May 1st, 1994 was a joyous day for most South Africans. The country's first free elections three days earlier had given the African National Congress a thumping majority and Nelson Mandela, the most admired politician in the world, had just become President-elect of his country. 'I received my passport on April 18th, my birthday,' Lucy recalled, 'and a week later I went to vote. I told myself I was a lucky person and that this vote was the chance of a lifetime.

'I wanted to see pictures of Nelson Mandela celebrating our victory, but then the customs man came back – with big, big shiny dogs! Big black shiny dogs.' Lucy's voice deepens and her hand gestures expand as she draws an imaginary pair of shiny sniffer dogs. They were still sniffing with gusto as customs officers led Tshabalala away for a strip-search. But the officers had no need of the shiny dogs to find the 1.5 kilograms of heroin strapped tightly around her stomach. 'They were so excited! Bingo!' Lucy recalled. 'They told me that this was the biggest haul at LAX for some years. They were thrilled. And all I could think was that I would never see Mandela on television. Instead I imagined headlines on CNN – *Sowetan Woman Arrested at LAX!*'

And so, at the very moment South Africa took its first steps on the arduous road to recovery from apartheid, one of its young daughters began her own progress through the valley of despair. After being sentenced in Los Angeles to six years' imprisonment for narcotics offences, Tshabalala was transferred to the Danbury Federal Correctional Institution in Connecticut. Located next to Candlewood Lake, it is a low-security prison whose alumnae now include Martha Stewart.

At first, it was a relief for Lucy. 'In some ways, life was better than in South Africa because I was fed regularly,' she said. But a year after her arrival she was raped by one of the warders. 'He had befriended me and I thought he cared about my situation,' she said. 'Instead, he just manipulated me to get sex.' It was her word against his and if she reported it, she said, 'he would have killed me'. Instead, she bottled it up and suffered a nervous breakdown. This led her to the Federal Medical Center Carswell at Fort Worth in Texas, known locally as the Hospital of Horrors. Carswell has an appalling record of mistreatment of prisoners, testified to by the high incidence of warders convicted of sexually abusing the inmates. Lucy's condition deteriorated, but she was sustained by two fellow prisoners. 'They looked after me. Perhaps they wanted to make up for what their menfolk had done – you see, they were Nigerians.'

Four months before her arrest in LA, a tall, educated man, Kingsley Noble, introduced himself to Lucy as she trawled the dingy restaurants of Mooi Street at the edge of Johannesburg's business district in search of work. She was desperate to earn money to finance her degree course in economics at the University of South Africa. She was the first girl from her village school in the north-eastern province of Mpumalanga to be admitted to college. Her family circumstances were typical. The father had left her mother with small children to seek work in Jo'burg. He settled in Soweto, the satellite township where black labourers were forced to live, and which became a symbol of popular resistance to apartheid. Lucy's father found himself a string of new 'wives' there, the last of whom wanted to have nothing to do with Lucy and his other children.

Lucy was young and pretty, but itinerant, unemployed and home-less when Mr Noble appeared to take pity on her. 'I had never met a *kwere kwere** who could speak English like a white person. He said he came from Ghana – he was so educated and you know we think all those *kwere kwere* from places like Ethiopia or Zimbabwe, we think that they suffer more than us and that they are all shooting guns,' she said, 'but he had money and he was smart, and then he bought me a meal in the restaurant where I had just failed to get a job! I was so confused.'

Lucy followed Kingsley's invitation to live with him at his hotel in Hillbrow, which, although close to a lot of rich white suburbs, was rapidly gaining a reputation in the new South Africa for being a centre of drugs and prostitution. And Nigerians.

Within two years of South Africa's borders liberalising in 1993, some 60,000 Nigerians had moved there. At first, they received a warm welcome, in part because Nigeria could claim an important place in the anti-apartheid solidarity movement. Nigeria was the other large power on the continent and many in Mandela's ANC believed that Africa's salvation lay in strategic cooperation between the two countries.

But before long this welcome had fermented into resentment. Xenophobia accompanied the sharp pain caused by a sudden rise in unemployment levels as the new government struggled to manage the transition from apartheid to black majority rule. Demands for an end to immigration were heard across the political spectrum from all three communities, black, white and coloured, while the term 'Nigerian' became a generic term of abuse for foreigners in general. This is why Kingsley Noble insisted to Lucy Tshabalala that he originated from Ghana when they first met – even before the elections of 1994, the term 'Nigerian' had acquired pejorative overtones.

Above all, the Nigerians were branded as criminals in South Africa where crime had, in a few short months, become the decisive political, social and economic issue. And Hillbrow, or Little Lagos, in Johannesburg was the centre of Nigerian life. Hillbrow became the most feared no-go area in one of the world's most crime-ridden countries.

As we have seen, Nigerian criminal gangs generally operate on principles of non-violence. Nigerians in South Africa (or more accurately

---

* A derogatory Zulu term for black Africans from outside South Africa.

the Igbo who make up 80–90 per cent of them) are no exception. Into Hillbrow and other parts of South Africa they have imported an egalitarian system of tribal councils, which stipulates that territories should not be fought over, but agreed upon and discussed. 'Arbitration not Aggravation' could be their slogan.

Nonetheless, South Africans came to perceive Nigerians as the worst criminals because they were highly visible, working tirelessly to expand the consumption of drugs and the use of prostitutes across *all* communities in South Africa, and offering further evidence of their unparalleled ability in devising financial scams and fraud.

Under apartheid the culture of the underworld was affected by separate development as much as everything else – young blacks, coloureds and whites did not mix and so there was little or no cultural cross-fertilisation. The consumption of narcotics was very clearly defined – blacks smoked *dagga* or *zol*, as the country's home-grown cannabis is known; coloureds smoked 'buttons', crushed mandrax tablets, manufactured locally, and then mixed with low-grade *zol*; and some young whites used heroin or, very rarely, cocaine (because the apartheid regime controlled its borders very tightly, these drugs were rare and so usage among whites was also very low).

The Nigerian drug dealers identified early on that the market was ready for diversification and so they started introducing different communities to new drugs. That meant making *dagga* more easily available to the coloureds and whites, while pushing the 'buttons' beyond their traditional home of the coloured districts and townships. Black, white and coloured youth often came into contact with one another via the good offices of Nigerian suppliers.

By 1994, Nigeria had developed into a new and very significant hub for the distribution of cocaine from West to East, and of heroin in the opposite direction. And while heroin consumption remains low in South Africa, coke and crack have become very popular in all three communities. And for the Nigerian traffickers to succeed in prising open the South African market, they needed to recruit mules. Mules are people, usually very poor, who wittingly or unwittingly carry the drugs to their retail destination. The Nigerians needed them to bring cocaine into the country, and heroin from South Africa to the United States. Heroin from Afghanistan and the Golden Triangle was transported to neighbouring

Tanzania and Mozambique by separate networks, usually Pakistanis and East Africans, although some Nigerian teams have been picked up and prosecuted in Thailand.

Lucy Tshabalala had no idea that Kingsley Noble, her 'Ghanaian' Igbo sugar daddy, was a coke and heroin dealer until one day there was a knock on their hotel-room door. It was a Nigerian signal (one knock followed by a gentle arpeggio of fingers on the door). 'Not the loud Bang! Bang! Bang! Bang! that is unmistakably South African,' as Lucy confided while rapping the table demonstratively. And because the knock in the hotel was Nigerian, Kingsley Noble opened the door.

'Two cops, one black and one white, crashed into the room screaming, "Where's the coke? Where's the fucking coke?"' And, naive as she was, Lucy wondered why the police had launched an armed raid in search of a soft drink. They locked her in the hotel cupboard. 'I was so scared – I thought they were just going to shoot me there in the cupboard.' But instead she heard the screams of Noble as they pistol-whipped and kicked him in an attempt to force him to reveal the whereabouts of his stash. They left empty-handed, but when Lucy managed to get out of the cupboard, Kingsley was quivering in a pool of blood on the floor. To help him out of a mess, Lucy finally agreed that she would accompany a shipment of gold to the United States, but the day her flight left, Kingsley and his boss demanded that she take heroin instead, ensuring that she would greet South Africa's new dawn from the darkness of America's penal system.

And she was not alone. All manner of innocents were ensnared by the engineers of the new illicit economy. Crime sucked the lifeblood from the new South Africa like a deadly leech, leaving it debilitated and wracked by fear and insecurity. Stories of murder, car-jacking, extortion, rape, mugging, gang warfare and more drugs littered the pages of the local and international press.

Most ordinary people lived in fear of random acts of violence or of becoming involved in some nightmare through ignorance or despair, as Lucy Tshabalala did. In the 1990s, Colombia was South Africa's only rival in the stakes for the highest murder rate in the world. The fact that Jamaica suffered 30 per cent fewer homicides at the time is another indication of how serious this problem was. In hard figures that meant that around 20,000 South Africans lost their lives at the hands of their compatriots every single year (in 2005 almost 52,000 rapes were reported in South Africa and, given the usual ratio of reported to actual rapes, the real figure seems astronomical).

Not even the most embittered South Africans can blame Nigerians for this level of violent crime. In fact, as we know, the turmoil and terror were generated from within South African society, a profound legacy of apartheid that paved the way for unprecedented domestic violence and criminality that mingled dangerously with mutual suspicion between communities. This neuralgic nexus that has such visible consequences in the area of street crime masked the work of more significant trans-national criminal enterprises that were merrily nesting elsewhere in Africa, but regarded South Africa as their grandest prize.

There were two separate criminal industries that had designs on South Africa. The first was narcotics, whose main players hailed from Nigeria, Italy and South America; the second was the trading of weapons for sub-Saharan Africa's valuable minerals – diamonds, copper, zinc and a little-known substance called coltan. Primarily involved in this second business were Russians, Belgians, Americans, French, Brits and Israelis.

South Africa was in a unique position in the 1990s. The fall of apartheid was different from the fall of communism because the racist state was already a developed market economy. This meant that it bequeathed a rich and advanced infrastructure to a new administration, but one whose policing capacity was exceptionally weak. Until 1994, the Government had no interest in spending any money on the majority of its population – that is, the blacks and coloureds. The primary concern of the new democratic government was naturally to address that appalling imbalance. But this sudden shift placed a huge strain on South Africa's budget. The new police force faced immense challenges and so, despite South Africa's reputation worldwide as a producer of crime and criminals, the country was in fact one of the most desirable *targets* for trans-national criminal syndicates. The fragile new government had to devote the bulk of its resources to domestic policing. Its borders were porous and its transport links open to the highest bidder – drug runners and arms dealers.

Under apartheid, the notorious Group Areas Act, which defined which races could live where, combined with the older practice of using black males as a labour reservoir for work in the mines and heavy industry. This led to an extraordinary concentration of males living in squalid urban conditions, the townships. Many women were left to fend for themselves and their children in the rural areas, ensuring not just that poverty would be handed down to the next generation, but that it would worsen.

Replicated over a century, these circumstances engendered two distinct but related gang cultures – one, known as 'The Number', was found throughout the coloured and black inmates of South Africa's prisons. The other lay in the coloured and black townships.

The legend of the Number Gangs demonstrates a prodigious collective imagination, fusing Zulu lore with the imagery of the colonial British army and the romanticised heroism of the banditry that arose in the wake of South Africa's gold rush of the late nineteenth century. The three gangs (the 26, the 27 and the 28) trace their heritage back to the 1890s and the memory of Nongoloza, a Zulu who preyed on itinerant workers in Johannesburg at the head of a gang called the Ninevites. From this thin skein successive generations of prisoners wove an elaborate history that contains most elements of religious mythology, including a prophet, arcane rituals, a sacred text (written half on a bull's hide, half on a stone), their own language *sabela* (a mixture of slang Afrikaans and Zulu with regional dialects) and a priestly hierarchy of incomprehensible complexity.

Number members have claimed, often with good reason, that their association was the rawest form of resistance to apartheid, and certainly the predominantly white prison guards feared its influence (an important initiation of The Number involved stabbing a prison guard). But adherents also launched bloody intra-Number wars (particularly between the traditionally hostile 26s and 28s), which sometimes revolved around the central doctrinal dispute over the admissibility of homosexuality within The Number.

This system belonged inside prison. When members emerged, they were granted respect, but hierarchy in the townships belonged to a different type of organisation – the gangs. And nowhere were the gangs more powerful than in the coloured townships of Cape Town.

The motorway from Cape Town International airport into town crosses through a number of townships, like Mitchell's Plain and

Guguletu. Men, women and children zigzag through the motorway traffic to get from one township to the next. At night, these pedestrians often stagger drunkenly, one reason why South Africa boasts one of the worst road-death rates in the world. Either side of the highway, the sun bounces off the tiny corrugated tin shacks in which whole families live. Above them stands a dense web of wires, which are draining electricity illegally from the main grid. In the luckier districts, European aid programmes have erected lines of toilets, offering the inhabitants a minimum of personal dignity. Crammed in like battery chickens, originally by the apartheid regime, they survive to this day on pitiful wages, should they be fortunate enough to find work. The squalor is all the more distressing for being only a few miles from some of the most opulent residential districts in the world – where swimming pools and tennis courts are regarded more as necessities than luxuries.

'Force people to live on top of one another like that,' says Al Lovejoy as he describes the townships that he knows intimately, 'and you are bound to pick up social stress that expresses itself in violence. What I could never understand is why there wasn't *more* violence.' His muscle-bound arms covered in tattoos, Al sits opposite me drinking South African plonk and rolling a spliff in a student bar in Stellenbosch, the centre of the country's wine industry and erstwhile intellectual hub of white racism.

Al was brought up by parents who inflicted unspeakable brutality on him as a child. Packed off to criminal reform school, he was soon using drugs and quickly found his way to prison. As a teen, he swung between prison and the streets. He was accepted as a gang member in Cape Town's District Six, which sits half a mile to the west of the city centre. In the late 1960s, the Government announced its intention to evict all the residents from District Six and to rehouse them in new townships up to twenty-five miles away. The move sparked outrage among the black and coloured communities, while some of Cape Town's liberal whites also expressed their disgust at the prospect of wealthy whites taking possession of Zonnenbloem (Sunflower), as the area was to be renamed. The various campaigns led to the postponement of the bulldozing and reconstruction of District Six. And it was here that some of the most famous gangs of the 1970s and 1980s emerged to define Cape Town's violent street culture. Although white, Al Lovejoy was accepted by the local coloured population and before long he joined one of the gangs.

'I became a Mongrel after the most terrible fight I have ever been in . . . All of a sudden this [knife-wielding man is] looming up in front of me. A huge black square thing rises up, blocking out the starlight behind him, and crashes towards my head. I hurtle sideways and it hits the side of my face, clipping my shoulder and nearly dislocating it . . . My adrenalin's pumped up to the max and I go for his hair with both hands, ripping his head downwards and kneeing him in the face with everything I've got. I hit dead square and he flies back, hitting the wall behind him with one almighty wet crack. I'm not in the mood to stop, so as his legs buckle and he starts sliding down, I grab his hair again, plant his head on the ground, kick the everlasting shit out of him . . . The fucking fucker's tried to brain me with something made of wood, corrugated iron and fucking cement.'

This was a common experience of adolescence for young blacks and coloureds in the Western Cape and elsewhere. The police under apartheid did little to discourage such aggression – the core of their philosophy celebrated violence against coloured or black people, regardless of who perpetrated it. If young blacks and coloureds were beating the shit out of one another, it means they weren't demonstrating against apartheid or taking to the bush with the MK, the ANC's military wing.

Drugs were, of course, woven into the fabric of gang life (another type of social control). And the culture surrounding their sale and distribution magnified the brutal socialisation that the township youth went through. Al explained, 'Dealers are the first step up from the slime in the food chain and they almost always work for somebody . . . Runners are the middle-management of the narcotics industry . . . It is their job to pick up cash and drop off stock and also to report what is happening down on the street to their masters . . . They need to be clever too. They provide the buffer between the *boere* [cops] and the bosses.'

Al talks as we drive into the Stellenbosch township late at night – this is the ultimate nightmare for South African whites and not something I would recommend that anyone try at home. But as we get out of the car, Al is relaxed. 'You don't need to lock it. You can even leave

your laptop on the front seat. Nobody will touch it if you're with me.'
And indeed, when we enter the warren of shacks, we receive a warm,
relaxed welcome from all and sundry.

As apartheid began to crumble in the late 1980s and early 1990s,
the opportunities for the bosses started to grow rapidly. Two super-
gangs emerged in the Cape Flats: The Americans led by Jackie Lonti,
and later in opposition to them came The Firm (a carefully planned
amalgam of several gangs excluded by The Americans).

According to one of his lieutenants, Lonti was responsible for introducing crack into the Cape Flats.

'He was one of the first guys that went to Brazil – he went over to
Latin America to go and negotiate deals and from then onwards these
mules were coming to SA. These were the kids of rich Muslim Indian
families. Many occasions they would get phone calls from Jackie Lonti
or his men to demand money from the parents of these kids, whom
he held captive at one of his venues, and if they didn't pay . . . then
he would threaten the families.'

The Americans had ambitions that went well beyond Cape Town –
South Africa was a huge market. And as another of his collaborators
has testified, Jackie had the great idea of appropriating the mystique
of The Number in order to spread his operation. 'I'm not good with
dates, but sometime back then, in the 1980s, Jackie spent a while in
jail. When he came out, he brought The Number out onto the street.
To deal now, you had to know prison gangs.' Lonti proclaimed that
The Americans were the external representatives of the 26.

The Number was a countrywide phenomenon. By claiming 26 for
The Americans, Lonti was able to expand his dealership among gangs
simply by using brand recognition. By dint of its arcane, rigid structure, The Number had no power to prevent the theft of its identity,
and before long The Firm had proclaimed itself the 28, which, of
course, also accentuated the bloody hostility between the two mega-
gangs. As South Africa's borders effectively dissolved and all manner
of new narcotics came into the country, the gangs were able to distribute
the new goods faster and more efficiently than in any other country
that was opening up to the outside world (like Russia).

If The Americans created a loose association of gangs across South
Africa, The Firm took the idea a step further by establishing a regular

cartel with a coherent business strategy. Like the Nigerians, The Firm's leader, Colin Stanfield, understood that there were large gaps in South Africa's shadow economy. So he used The Firm's financial muscle to set up an informal bank. Enterprising members were given start-up capital to set up bases along the Cape Atlantic and Indian Ocean coasts, with the specific aim of encouraging rich young whites to emulate their peers in Europe and the United States in acquiring a taste for cocaine.

For two hundred yards, wasteland separates a huge police station from Valhalla Park, the coloured district with the dark Wagnerian name and a fearsome reputation for its gang and drug culture. The home of Colin Stanfield, it looks too small to be troublesome – just like the Bogside in Derry, Northern Ireland, which looks far too quaint and neat to be the centre of such rage and confusion. But it remains to this day one of the most violent and dangerous places in all South Africa, where anger and crime mix in a powerful cocktail.

Just as the police stations of the Royal Ulster Constabulary used to be protected by watchtowers and barbed wire, so this police station looks like a fortress under siege. The police, though, must be emboldened by the knowledge that they can call on ADT, an American-owned security company, to dispatch an Armed Response Unit (ARU) should a band of tooled-up Valkyries decide to swoop down from Valhalla.

Where would South Africa be without its ARUs? For every member of the South Africa Police Service, there are four and a half private security personnel in the country. Licensed to use firearms, these men's primary task is to protect the white middle classes from burglary and assault. The latter live in stupendously affluent districts characterised by high walls, high-voltage electronic fences and high levels of anxiety.

In part thanks to the ARUs and in part because life was ever thus, whites are in fact far less likely to be victims of crime than blacks and coloureds, as the townships are the main locus of violent crime. Nonetheless, the ARUs have played a critical, if rather oblique, role in maintaining peace in post-apartheid South Africa. Although the security forces in the Soviet Union and Eastern European countries kept a close eye on their citizens' activities before the collapse of the Berlin Wall, they could all boast a normal police force, which was involved in parochial crime-busting, traffic control and helping old ladies across the road (regardless of nationality or creed).

South Africa's apartheid police force was different – more explicitly political. Their main job was to ensure the functioning of the Group Areas Act and to keep the blacks and coloureds in their allotted districts. You can only enter or exit many of the large townships over road bridges – points that can be easily closed by a few men with guns and vehicles. The South African police had no role to play inside the townships – drunkenness, theft, rape, murder and their consequences were all problems that the townships had to deal with themselves (unless, of course, the perpetrators had strayed into white areas).

The police were the iron fist of apartheid. The Security Services (especially those who worked fighting communists across borders in countries like Angola and Mozambique) were even worse. Along with their main job of obliterating Angolan or Mozambican villages, they moonlighted by smuggling diamonds and other valuable commodities from neighbouring countries into South Africa. Less policemen and more proto-organised crime syndicates, these were not nice people. Often trained killers, they were indoctrinated in the belief that black and coloured people were lesser human beings. And they demonstrated only the most rudimentary skills of parochial crime-busting, traffic control and helping old ladies across the road.

When Peter Gastrow was asked by the ANC's First Security Minister to act as his chief adviser on the issue of police transition, he knew the extent of the problem. 'A lot of the police force had been concentrated on white urban areas and then all of a sudden there were no pass laws, and people could go anywhere,' he remembered. 'These cops could no longer just give a fellow a few whacks to get a confession out of him. They couldn't understand all this new bullshit about serving the people. They had always *told* people what to do, and now they had to *serve* them! This created great confusion – you can't imagine . . . you had Swedes and Dutch coming over here and telling them about how policemen had to respect human rights! South African cops! Ha, ha, ha!' Gastrow bursts out laughing at the thought of a shock troop of Scandinavians in woolly jumpers teaching battle-scarred Boer hard nuts how to relate to someone else's pain.

In the first half of the 1990s, Nelson Mandela and the ANC's liberal allies knew that the apartheid police represented a real threat to a peaceful transition. As Gastrow argues, some disgruntled whites were encouraging the incipient civil war among Zulus between ANC supporters and those of the more conservative Inkhata Freedom Party. They were doing so because if this conflict among the Zulus were to escalate, it could fatally undermine the move to black majority rule. If the whites had begun to mobilise in response to this war, claiming the need to defend themselves, the South African Police looked ominously like a militia-in-waiting.

'So we had to develop a deliberate strategy,' explained Gastrow. 'You had a powerful security police that was feared by the new government. The first task was to identify the chain or network of the key people who run the security figures – well-known senior officers; then remove some of them to break up the chain.'

It was too risky, however, to throw them out – the last thing you needed was a group of embittered officers with a similarly unhappy loyal following kicking around the streets. Unlike the Russians and Eastern Europeans, or the United States following the 2003 invasion of Iraq, South Africa's new rulers understood that you cannot throw policemen and military personnel onto the streets and expect to maintain a stable society. 'So we sat them down and said, "You and I know that you were involved in some horrible things. And I am not saying as an ANC person that we were all angels – but what about taking a big pension, eh? No big fuss, no big announcements. I don't want to force you – let's negotiate." And they took it. People took it. But where the leaders were offered these packages, the rank and file were not and there is still a lot of bitterness among those guys now – they felt abandoned by their leaders, abandoned by the former President de Klerk, and abandoned by the National Party.'

The emergence of the Armed Response Units proved to be a blessing in disguise, as white police who were unhappy about serving in the new South Africa Police Services flocked to make up the numbers. Furthermore, the costs for the ARUs were borne not by the state, but by the white middle-classes who were only too willing to pay a little extra to maintain a comparable standard of protection to that enjoyed under apartheid.

By 1998 the state was spending 22 billion rand ($4 billion) on the

entire criminal-justice system (including the courts and prisons as well
as the police). But the turnover of the private security firms had reached
a staggering 50 per cent of this sum – 11 billion rand. All these funds
were channelled into domestic policing as the new government had
to ward off the twin evils of social collapse and conflict along racial
lines. This left the state exhausted, always playing catch-up with the
new democratic reality.

The crime that best represented South Africa's perceived lawlessness during the 1990s was armed car-jacking. Stories of tired
commuters being hauled out of the driver's seat at traffic lights and
being shot before the car-jackers sped off laughing were common-
place. To the outside world, it looked like brutal opportunistic theft
committed by cynical joyriders taking advantage of the post-apartheid
turmoil. In the country itself, it provided a forceful reminder of how
the issue of race affected every act. The victims were usually white
and the perpetrators black. For many whites, car-jacking confirmed
their suspicions about blacks. In an atmosphere of fear, accentuated
by gruesome media reports, some whites believed that every young
black male was a gun-toting joyrider waiting to pounce. For their part,
blacks would watch well-to-do whites parade imperiously along the
highways in their ever-grander luxury cars and 4x4s while they
remained mired in poverty. Wasn't this material gulf, they wondered,
the very essence of apartheid – the system that was supposed to have
been dismantled?

To this day when street crime is visible in South Africa, it is invariably refracted through the prism of racial politics. This is certainly the
case in private conversations, while in public it appears in coded form
to prevent accusations of racism. This intense yet covert debate about
crime within the framework of racial politics is predictable and usually
sterile. It certainly did not shed much light on the car-jacking industry.
In a revealing survey of convicted car-jackers, a researcher at South
Africa's Crime Institute discovered that 70 per cent of incidents were
pre-ordered. Car-jackers would look out for specific makes and models
of vehicles and would only move when one came into view. And
although in more than 90 per cent of cases the hijackers threatened
victims with a firearm, in more than 90 per cent of those cases no
shots were fired. These were not crimes motivated by racial revenge

or violence in the first instance, they were the coal face of a huge and dynamic criminal industry that covered all of southern Africa.

In the late 1990s, some 15,000 cars and 5,000 vans and trucks were hijacked annually in South Africa, while another 100,000 were stolen while unattended. About two-thirds of these crimes took place in a single province – Gauteng – at whose heart lies Johannesburg, South Africa's pulsating economic engine. Most vehicles were at the high end of the market: Mercedes, BMW, Lexus and any make of 4x4. Together the total annual value of this theft amounted to *billions* of dollars. As the years went on, the number of temporary kidnappings increased dramatically because the hijackers had to prevent the victim's security firm from switching on the automatic vehicle trackers that became a common accessory on South African vehicles before they did anywhere else in the world. Delivery to the buyers took place usually within an hour of the car-jacking and the perpetrator would be rewarded with about $300, which exceeds the monthly income of most blacks. One of the convicted explained that, on a good day, he and his accomplices could seize five vehicles. The recipients of the stolen vehicles were syndicates that could immediately respray the vehicle and re-engineer the chassis and engine numbers in accordance with the registration documents purchased from corrupt officials at the vehicle licensing centre for around $3,000. From here, often with the connivance of corrupt police officials (including many white officers), the cars would be driven to neighbouring states – Namibia, Botswana, Zimbabwe, Mozambique, Swaziland and, further north, Angola, Zambia, Malawi and Tanzania. Once they reach their destination, the cars are either sold for cash or, as Jenni Irish, a specialist in South African organised crime, explained, 'They become an important form of currency and are regularly used to pay for other goods such as gold and diamonds.'

In order to prosper, most criminal syndicates are obliged to attempt to 'capture' or 'semi-capture' the state at some level. This embraces a broad range of corrupt activities, from paying off the official in the vehicle licensing office to installing your allies in senior cabinet or civil-service positions. But much of the tragedy of sub-Saharan Africa in the late twentieth century lay in the ability of opportunists, dodgy businessmen, mercenaries and gangsters to wrest control of key parts of the communications infrastructure. Cars played an important role as an ersatz currency, but, in order to move goods about, you needed a better form of transport. This was where aeroplanes came into play – from the light propeller-driven to cavernous Ilyushin and Antonov transporters. And in that realm, there were many princes, but only one king.

Even Chubb and ADT, the top two private security firms in South Africa, would have been impressed by the $3 million mansion in the fashionable Sandhurst district of Johannesburg. The multimillionaire owner from Russia never thought he would need to call an Armed Response Unit to protect it. He had his own paramilitary team patrolling the perimeter and interior 24/7 with machine guns and dogs. But one afternoon in March 1998, he could have used some back-up. Masked gunmen with superior firepower and a boxful of grenades stormed the main gate and the kitchen, where an old Russian woman was chopping vegetables. 'She grabbed a large watermelon and smashed it on the head of one of the gunmen before she was knocked unconscious by a rifle butt,' as the investigative reporter, Andre Verloy, described the enterprising *babushka*'s response. 'The masked men fled with six million dollars in cash, but left paintings and expensive artefacts untouched. A message had been sent to Viktor Bout.'

Born in Dushanbe, the capital of the Soviet Republic of Tajikistan, in 1967, Viktor Bout developed into a gifted linguist with a ferocious intelligence. Graduating from the Military School of Foreign Languages in Moscow, he ended up working in Mozambique and Angola at the time of the collapse of the Soviet Union. Both countries had been the focus of violent proxy conflicts during the Cold War.

Although still in his early twenties, Bout – slightly rotund with a clipped moustache – succeeded in establishing a number of air cargo services, using old Soviet equipment. His planes were parked in the Emirate of Sharjah, his companies registered in another emirate, Ajman, while he used the Standard Charter throughout the UAE for his financial transactions. Bout's experienced pilots from the former Soviet Union developed a reputation for flying into those conflict regions that were so dangerous that nobody else would risk it.

By his own admission, Bout supplied the leader of the anti-Taliban

Northern Alliance with weaponry during the mid-1990s before one of his planes was grounded in territory under Taliban control. After negotiating the release of his pilots, Bout then started supplying the Taliban with weapons as well. According to a senior official who served under both Clinton and Bush and was responsible for monitoring Bout's activities, 'The UAE was the only country which recognised the Taliban, along with Saudi Arabia and Pakistan. This was how Bout established the links with them through his aviation companies. There was a lot of cooperation between Afghanistan's airline, Ariana, and Bout's aircraft.'

At this time, Bout relocated to South Africa, doubtless attracted by the climate and lifestyle, but also to keep an eye on his burgeoning operation, supplying war materials to factions in four major wars, one in Angola, the others in Liberia and Sierra Leone, and then finally in the Democratic Republic of Congo.

With his considerable financial clout, Bout bought up Mafeking airport just south of the Botswana border, lock, stock and barrel, installing his mechanics and administrators there and even paying the salaries of immigration officers. This was a key hub in the dispatch of weapons to other southern African countries, from where the planes would return with a payload of minerals and even commodities like rare fish and gladioli (for sale in the United Arab Emirates).

But Bout obviously made enemies in South Africa. A few days after his house was broken into, more gunmen opened fire at his car in broad daylight as Bout and two assistants were driving through Johannesburg. 'Either they were reiterating the warning,' a senior operative with The Scorpions, South Africa's elite anti-corruption unit, told me. 'Or whoever wanted to kill him put our guys onto the job,' he added laughing, 'because South Africans invariably bugger these things up!'

Whatever the truth, the redoubtable Mr Bout decided the time had come to end his sojourn under South African skies (never underestimate the significance of a good climate in illicit operations). He fled with his family back to Moscow virtually on the first available flight. In Russia, he has since been able to avoid the attentions not only of South African gunmen, but of Interpol, whose writ shrivels feebly when it reaches Russia's borders.

But from Moscow, he did at least acquire some new customers. The unparalleled success of his pilots and navigators in delivering weapons to war zones had begun to turn some powerful heads. Nobody else could boast that they had supplied arms to both sides in the Angolan conflict; to the Taliban; to Charles Taylor, the butcher of Liberia; to the limb-severing warriors of Sierra Leone; and to God knows who in the Democratic Republic of Congo.

But the mystery gunmen in Johannesburg were not his only detractors. In 2000, the United Nations published a damning report into Bout's activities, which led Peter Hain, veteran anti-apartheid campaigner who was by now a British Foreign Office minister, to label him 'the leading merchant of death'. Hain explained that Western intelligence services had established Bout's companies as 'the principal conduit for planes and supply routes that take arms, including heavy military equipment, from East Europe, principally Bulgaria, Moldova, and Ukraine, to Liberia and Angola. The UN has exposed Bout as the centre of a spider's web of shady arms dealers, diamond brokers, and other operatives, sustaining the wars. Without someone like him we would be much, much closer to ending the conflicts.'

From his ministerial seat, Hain explained to me how he decided to go after Bout. 'When I was Africa Minister,' he said, recalling a speech he gave in the Commons, 'I was getting all this intelligence from MI6 and other intelligence services, which showed there was a systematic traffic of arms going into Sierra Leone via Liberia and into Angola in return for alluvial diamonds. I was getting these reports saying that it was Viktor Bout's planes taking this stuff in. And I said, "Well, what are we going to do about this? We know the schedule of the flights. Why don't we just shoot them out of the air?" "Oh," said my civil servants, "you can't do this, Minister, because it's against international law." I said that we must disrupt him because, in the case of Sierra Leone, these very guns and ammo and other military equipment were actually being aimed at our soldiers. On the one hand, we had sent in British soldiers to save Sierra Leone from the insurgents, and on the other hand we knew the very arms supplier who was providing the means to attack our soldiers, and not doing anything about it! In the end, we put some of the arms dealers out of business and severely disrupted Viktor Bout. As a result of lobbying I did there with the

Emir of Dubai, Sheikh Mohammed, we closed him down there as well
and he then retreated back to Russia.'

Three years later, Viktor Bout was back in the thick of things. Only
this time, he was providing his services to the American war effort in
Iraq. Dismissed as an oversight by the UK and US governments, Bout's
name had mysteriously slipped off the United Nations' Most Wanted
List at around the same time. Privately, the French Government
expressed its fury, suggesting that this was Bout's *quid pro quo*. And
although the French had an axe to grind about the war in Iraq, not to
mention its own shameful record on the supply of weaponry in
exchange for minerals in Africa, it would appear that Bout had pulled
off an impressive stunt. In fact, the subsequent outcry gave Treasury
officials enough evidence to persuade President Bush to sign an executive order targeting Bout's US assets. Nonetheless, the Iraqi interlude
is instructive as it demonstrates how major criminal figures like Bout
can continue to function by existing in that peculiarly opaque nether-
world where money, criminals, crises and security services mix so thoroughly that only the most trained analyst can separate the individual
parts.

Viktor Bout is one of the few contemporary criminals who enjoy
the distinction of having inspired not one, but two Hollywood movies
(with a third under consideration), the most recent being the under-
rated *Blood Diamond*, starring Leonardo DiCaprio as an especially
convincing South African mercenary. Andrew Niccol, the New Zealand-
born director and writer of the movie *Lord of War*, has said that his
lead character, Yuri Orlov, played with real style by Nicolas Cage, was
based on about five people, but he admits that one of them was Viktor
Bout. The movie captures the ease with which the shadow economy
functions on a global scale, and perhaps its biggest flaw is to suggest
that Ethan Hawke's American Interpol agent, Jack Valentine, has the
resources and the authority to pose a real threat to Orlov. The arms
dealer provides a variety of clients with weapons from Ukraine and
the former Soviet Union. His main client, André Baptiste, bears an
eerie resemblance to the deposed Liberian dictator and mass murderer,
Charles Taylor, who in one scene offers Orlov a dazzling choice of
diamonds in payment for the guns and ammo.

This one episode represents the essence of a remarkable criminal enterprise – the sustained and hideously violent rape of the animal, vegetable and above all mineral resources of Sierra Leone, Liberia, Angola and the Democratic Republic of Congo during the 1990s and the early 2000s. The multi-billion-dollar enterprise includes politicians, gangsters, businessmen and large corporations, who all work relentlessly to sate both their unquenchable avarice and the global consumer's equally rapacious demand for mobile phones and things that sparkle.

Nature has endowed Angola with abundant resources. Unfortunately, its leaders have been busy fighting for so long that they neglected to spread the country's natural largesse among the people. Not that Angolans bear exclusive responsibility for the carnage. Even before it declared its independence from Portugal in November 1975, the country had sunk into a fractious civil war that overnight became a four-way proxy war between Soviet military intelligence and Cuba on the side of the governing MPLA, and the CIA and the South African Defence Force (SADF) in similarly inglorious coalition with Jonas Savimbi's anti-communist UNITA.

That brutal struggle, which saw Cuban and SADF forces assume an ever-greater fighting role, continued until the end of the Cold War. It finally petered out in 1991 and, after much cajoling, the two sides agreed a truce, then a peace agreement and finally elections. Savimbi was a defeated man. Some of his fighters had given up. Ordinary people were desperate that the tyranny of war be overthrown. And UNITA had no friends anywhere in the world (except for grand mobsters like President Mobutu Sese Seko of Zaire). Surely the game was up? Only lemmings would have been attracted to another *casus belli*. And so, instead, Savimbi played on the greed of a handful of rich Angolans and a long chain of foreigners by seizing a majority of the country's most productive diamond mines and alluvial pits.

The *gampieros*, the men who risk their lives digging on the river bed for diamonds, are cousins of the Ural River fishermen who catch sturgeon – both are involved in dirty, dangerous work to extract a commodity for which they are paid a pittance, but which is making others very rich. By 1999, conservative estimates put UNITA's revenue from its diamond operations at $4 billion in under a decade. The value of the stones when they reach the market is roughly ten times that figure. And during that same period, there was nobody in the diamond industry through whose hands, wittingly or unwittingly, conflict or 'blood' diamonds (so called because of the deaths which their passage to market caused) did not pass: from De Beers, the immensely powerful South African conglomerate, through to the workshops of India, where 80 per cent of the world's diamonds are polished, and on to the many dealers in Antwerp, Tel Aviv, London and New York. At least this was so until the so-called 'Kimberley Process' certifying the stones' origins was inaugurated in 1999.

It was the perfect trade circle. Weapons manufactured mainly in Eastern Europe and the former Soviet Union (but some from Western Europe, Israel and the United States) would be flown into the conflict areas of Africa. Russian pilots were especially welcome as they often knew the terrain well from the Cold War period. The weapons were traded for diamonds, which were dispatched to South Africa, Israel and northern Europe and, once sold, went through the normal polishing process before arriving at the retail jewellers in perfect shape. The only people who lost out were the dead and maimed Angolans, but everyone else (including the exchequers of Russia, Europe and America) was making good money.

During the Cold War, armed conflict in the developing world was driven by the clash of ideologies – there was no great competition for oil, diamonds or timber between the US and the USSR because both superpowers had sufficient access to both. Rebels did not need to fund their operations because they received support from a sponsoring superpower. While millions of Vietnamese, Koreans, Ethiopians, Guatemalans, Afghanis and, indeed, Angolans might understandably take issue, this bipolar struggle acted as a partial restraining influence on the practice of extracting and selling resources in order to prosecute civil war.

Once those constraints are lifted, the parties to a civil war seek out the nearest money-making opportunity. It is especially easy for African militias in mineral areas where the extraction process is cheap. Almost all the diamond wars have taken place in countries where the diamonds are alluvial, sitting on river beds – militias do not have the time or money to invest in deep mines. But Africa is at an especial disadvantage because its commodities are legal on Western markets. Diamond sellers and jewellers may not enjoy enormous social status, but they are certainly a few notches above drug dealers, and few people would argue that their trade is immoral.

And it's not just diamonds. In the mid-1990s, the overthrow of President Mobutu in Zaire (since renamed the Democratic Republic of Congo or DRC) fused with the aftermath of Rwanda's genocide and the existence of exiled Hutu militiamen in the eastern DRC. The country is two-thirds the size of India but with one-twentieth of the subcontinent's population. By 1998, a conflict had broken out that, in terms of participating armies and numbers killed, is comparable with the Great War in Europe – up to four million deaths in a five-year period. It has been an immensely complex conflict and one that has not only drained the blood of far too many Congolese, but of Africa itself, impacting far beyond the borders of the DRC.

A map of the main zones of conflict between the various armies and militias coincides with a map of the main concentration of the country's natural resources. They pillaged anything they encountered, be it timber, gorillas (8,000 out of a population of 11,000 were slaughtered, mostly sold as bushmeat), copper, diamonds and a little-known compound called coltan; 80 per cent of coltan's global production is mined in the DRC and so the deposits became bitter battlegrounds in a four-way struggle (and sometimes more) between the armies of Rwanda and Uganda as well as the Hutu Interahamwe and the Mai-Mai militias, where peasants were forced to mine the material, which at one point reached the staggering price of $300 per kilo.

Coltan's desirability resides in its properties as an efficient conductor that can resist very high temperatures, and it is an essential component in laptops, mobile phones and PlayStations. This begs serious questions about organised crime and its relationship to the 'legitimate' economy. Ordinary people around the world may think that they have no relationship with trans-national criminal syndicates, but anyone who has used a cellphone or computer notebook in the past decade has unwittingly depended on organised crime for his or her convenience.

Until the year 2000 it was possible, if one listened very hard, to hear an occasional 'tut-tut' from Western governments about the entanglement of commodities that were sold on Western markets and war in Africa. At the same time, the Western Europeans and the United

States singled out organised crime as one of the most treacherous craters in globalisation's 'dark side', as President Clinton dubbed it. And yet Western access to commodities like coltan depended on the offices of organised-crime groups working throughout southern and western Africa, as well as between Africa on the one hand and the former Soviet Union and Europe on the other.

It was certainly possible to identify some of the more prominent players in the chain – like Viktor Bout. It is another matter trying to gather sufficient evidence to arrest a Bout, let alone find a court with the appropriate jurisdiction. James Bond's nemesis, SPECTRE (Special Executive for Counter-intelligence, Terrorism, Revenge and Extortion), would have welcomed a character like Bout because he fits the stereo-type of a trans-national organised criminal – fingers in every pie, prepared to deal with anyone who wants to buy weapons, and an ambi-tion that sometimes smacks of a desire for world domination. But Bout is the exception; most major organised syndicates are made up of clusters of dozens of minor conspiracies, which move a product or service a little further down the chain of distribution.

In the end, Bout appeared to overplay his hand by allegedly selling weapons to the FARC in Colombia in what was in fact a DEA sting operation. On a visit to Thailand in March 2008, he was arrested and at the time of writing is waiting to see whether he will be extradited for trial on terrorist and gun-running charges to the United States.

Cocaine and heroin are widely defined as illicit and so they remain clandestine from harvest to final sale – but the further coltan or diamonds are from their place of origin, the quicker the bloodstain fades. Combating organised crime is very difficult, in part because in areas such as banking or licit commodity trading, the actors, motives, processes and objects of commercial exchange move back and forth between the light and the shadow so fast that it renders moral or legal definition impossible.

Until the turn of the century, there was little evidence that the volu-minous trade in African blood minerals would be noticed, still less interrupted, notwithstanding the public concern about organised crime in the Western world. But then something rather unlikely happened.

A merrily shabby office in a respectable west London suburb seems an unlikely venue for the throbbing hub of resistance to the trade in blood diamonds. Charmian Gooch was not yet thirty when, in 1995, she and two friends formed an NGO called Global Witness. 'We were monitoring the work of a lot of organisations dealing with the environment, and another lot dealing with human rights. And we just kept seeing the bits in between, which connected the two areas, but which nobody was investigating. We try to look at issues that are being neglected, but which urgently need addressing, and then come up with practical ideas for tackling these problems.'

With the minimum of resources and at considerable personal risk, Global Witness decided to map every twist and turn in the road that brought diamonds from Angola to London and New York. On field trips to countries, they were shot at and threatened and at times they felt they were tilting at windmills. 'We were very, very small. We had no money, as ever, but it meant we were incredibly focused on achieving change,' Charmian continued. 'I went to Angola posing as a documentary film researcher. All the diplomats, journalists and NGOs I spoke to said this was a bad time to work on the role of conflict, or "blood diamonds" in funding conflict, because they were trying to cut a big deal with UNITA by turning them into a big diamond company and giving them a stake in the peace process. We were sceptical that this could work, but out of respect we pulled back for a while. As we predicted, it didn't work and so we started researching.'

And in late 1998 they published their report, *A Rough Trade: The Role of Companies and Governments in the Angolan Conflict*. Apart from illustrating who all the bad guys on the ground were, they pointed the finger at the Western corporate world. De Beers was the central target, as it enjoyed a near-monopoly on the sale of rough diamonds through its London subsidiary.

The impact of the report was immense and within two years, with the backing of Congress, several European governments and – conspicuously – De Beers, the diamond trade moved towards establishing the Kimberley Protocol. Named after the historic centre of the diamond industry in South Africa, Kimberley signatories obliged themselves to engage only in the purchase and sale of diamonds that had a Country of Origin certificate.

Global Witness followed up its first report with others dealing with West Africa. Before long, the UN published its own report under the chairmanship of Canadian diplomat Robert Fowler. This document went further than any other in naming Western companies complicit both in the arms trade to, and diamond trade from, Africa. Douglas Farah, an exceptionally talented *Washington Post* reporter, then uncovered an al-Qaeda network involved in the West African diamond trade.

These developments confirmed that in order to address a problem of organised crime at its point of origin in Africa, it was necessary to introduce regulation further down the line on the demand side, at a point where criminal influence was no longer felt. Slowly the manufacturers of mobile telephones are adhering to a protocol, which tracks the origin of coltan from Africa, similar to the Kimberley Process for diamonds.

There is still a long way to go, but Global Witness has successfully highlighted that organised crime is not about sinister corporations planning on taking over the world. It is about a complex interplay between the regulated and unregulated global economy, which defies simple solutions, but need not be left to fester as it was until Global Witness finally forced Western governments to acknowledge their co-responsibility for the problem. The team also raised the issue of how ordinary citizens in the West are much more closely connected to major criminal industries than they might otherwise realise. If Western governments want to do something about organised crime, they need to give full support to mechanisms like the Kimberley Process, as well as curbing the behaviour of corporations and the consumer.

President Thabo Mbeki came under considerable pressure to broker a peace deal for the DRC. At the same time, Western governments criticised him for being too indulgent towards Robert Mugabe as Zimbabwe's President started his steady descent into violent senility. 'The whole time Mbeki had to be mindful of his need to persuade Zimbabwe's army to get out of the DRC,' explained a senior security aide to the South African leader. 'But the generals were making huge sums of money from the mineral exploitation in the DRC. Mbeki had to tread with utmost care around Zimbabwe and its President, while at the same time trying to come up with some material incentives to persuade the generals to dismantle their operations in the DRC. That's not easy – not easy at all.' And he was right.

South Africa finds itself unhappily trapped between the light and the shadow. It is the only country in the world in which the first and the developing worlds exist side by side from one end of the land to the other. The first world provides good roads, 728 airports (according to the CIA's 2004 estimate), the largest cargo port in Africa and an efficient banking system. By Western standards, property prices are strikingly low and the lifestyle for wealthy immigrants whose conscience can live with the country's huge social divisions is enviable – great food, great wine, holidays of a lifetime every year, and you still get change out of a twenty-dollar bill.

The developing world accounts for the low tax revenue, overstretched social services, high levels of corruption throughout the administration, and 4,700 miles of land and sea borders, which contain more holes than a second-hand dartboard. 'When the transition took place, you could buy your very own airport if you wanted,' said Mbeki's security adviser in a resigned tone, 'and in fact that's exactly what some people did!'

The combination of first-world discount luxury plus the business opportunities that the developing-world infrastructure offers has proved irresistible to organised crime, and to major players both in the game for sub-Saharan resources and in the international traffic of narcotics.

Exports of cannabis from southern Africa (chiefly to Europe) are growing faster than from any other producer region in the world, now accounting for about 10 per cent of global production. A great deal of dope has traditionally been grown in KwaZulu-Natal and Eastern Cape, but exports were negligible because of the apartheid regime. Within the last five years, however, marijuana from all over southern Africa (notably from Swaziland and Tanzania) is now sent to South Africa for trafficking into Europe. According to the British High Commission in Pretoria, South Africa has become the largest single supplier of cannabis to the United Kingdom, now outstripping Jamaica by a ratio of 2:1.

Al Lovejoy described how you smuggled Swazi grass across the border into South Africa down to Jo'burg and then on to the Cape for export. He and his accomplices found a squat close to the Swazi border where they set up 'a generator, scales, presses and vacuum machine to begin packing'. Across the border, 'Led by the Swazi smuggler, they hefted the bulky bags of zol and began walking in the dead of night. The Swazi was carrying the handset and counter-night-vision goggles

– looking out for sloppy Interpol and DEA task agents.' Although he has shifted a lot of drugs, Al knew that the key to success was vigilance. 'Don't fuck around, China, Interpol and the DEA are active in all the agricultural and manufacturing narcotics hotspots, worldwide.' Anyway, 'The zol was taken to base camp and eventually packed into the usual twenty-five by twenty-five-centimetre, kilo and half-kilo blocks and then vacuum sealed to 98 per cent. The rock-solid bricks were then washed, packed into boxes, taped, labelled and put on the truck. They totalled about 300 kilograms.'

On the way to the Cape, the cars drove about nine miles apart as a precaution against being tracked together by police helicopters. At one point, the second vehicle in search of petrol 'drove into town and managed to blow out the right-rear tyre against a pavement. Guess who came to his assistance? The gattas [cops], of course! The zol was in boxes labelled as if he were moving house . . . The boere [cops] helped him change the tyre, unpacking the boxes of zol to get at the spare wheel, while up on the hill outside of town, Brother E and I sat in cold silence sweating the possible loss of over a million bucks' worth of zol.'

Al got away with it on this occasion, and had also undertaken successful runs of South African dope via Brussels and Paris to Amsterdam. On his return he would bring many hundreds of Ecstasy tablets to satisfy the demand of South Africa's growing clubbing culture. His story confirms the thesis advanced by Ted Leggett, an American who has become South Africa's most experienced drugs analyst and now works for the UN Office on Drugs and Crime in Vienna (UNODC). 'All this suggests,' he writes 'that some sort of international barter is going on, with our dagga [cannabis] being traded for more potent drugs overseas . . . We don't have to trade dagga directly with Afghanistan or Burma in order to get heroin back, because international brokers service a complex network of supplies and demands at once. These syndicates may even service demand for non-drug products, such as cellphones and automobiles. Cash is taken from countries with hard currency, and commodities are shuffled between the rest.'

Although he insists that in South Africa the drug is not associated with violence and has a benign social impact, he believes its economic function has changed dramatically so that 'Cannabis is more than a harmless local herb that feeds rural schoolchildren. It may be the linchpin on which the whole local drug economy is based. Without *dagga*, we would have to be paying for our hard drugs with the weak rand, which might price them beyond the reach of any but the most fanatical and criminally inclined addicts.'

South Africa has become the new pivot for the international drugs trade. Heroin comes in through East Africa and is then shipped to the US; cocaine comes here from South America before being transported to Spain and Amsterdam. But the heart of this problem lies elsewhere – in Washington, DC.

PART THREE

DRUGS AND CYBERCRIME

BUDDIES

'Open the back for me, please, Dan.' Quiet yet firm – that's how they speak around Metaline Falls. *Dan Wheeler* walked around his pick-up truck and unbolted the tray. 'Let's clear away all that stuff, please, Dan.' Wheeler started hauling the grubby but neatly piled strips of chromium that were lying on the flat-bed. The customs officer at the border crossing into Washington State helped by shifting the snow chains, toolbox, rags, oil cans and the detritus common to an artisan's vehicle. 'I'd like a look at the propane tank, please, Dan.' Wheeler skipped under the car to unbolt the steel frame and thick weld mesh that shielded the tank – a mesh that another border official had recommended to Dan as a means of reducing the chance of an explosion if the truck were back-ended.

Stooping deliberately, the US customs officer positioned his nose just above the propane tank's outlet valve. A jet of noxious gas flew up and the guard straightened smartly. Then he tapped the fuel gauge, which shimmered gently – the normal reaction.

'Thank you, Dan. What fuel is the truck running on right now?'

'I'm not sure. Gasoline, I think.'

'Switch it over to the propane, please, Dan, and turn on the engine.'

Dan switched the fuel supply and started cranking the engine. Nothing. He tried again. Then again. Third time, the Liquid Petroleum Gas (LPG or propane) reached the carburettor and the motor burst into life. The officer bent down and breathed in the exhaust pipe – he could tell from the fumes that this was propane; it has a very different odour from gasoline exhaust. He had ascertained what he needed to know: Dan Wheeler was not smuggling BC Bud, one of the most popular and potent brands of cannabis in the world, from Canada into the United States. These elaborate tests were necessary – the only other way he could have established Dan's innocence would be by sawing open the LPG tank. And the resulting explosion would have blown apart him and everything else within a 500-yard radius.

'Okay, Dan. Just come on into the office to fill in the forms and you'll be on your way!'

Wheeler fumed, 'Hey, can you at least give me a hand with reloading the car?' The officer turned and grimaced before helping reluctantly.

As he headed away from eastern British Columbia through the spectacular evergreen forest of Colville National Park towards the slush and wooden shacks of Metaline Falls itself, Dan's mood darkened. How many times had he been through that damn border? And how many times did he have to take his whole truck apart? And he knew that they liked him. There weren't many of their regulars who could talk with such authority about the things those boys loved – guns, hunting and fishing. 'I guess that's why they're so good at their job,' Dan thought. He was sincerely impressed by their thoroughness, even though it inconvenienced him most times he travelled.

By the time he arrived at the storage compound in Spokane, Washington State, Dan's spirits had brightened, but he was on alert. After entering the pin code to the main gate, he started unloading the chrome strips into his rental lock-up under the arbitrary gaze of the CCTV cameras. Finally, he drove the truck into the space, closed the door and hooked up his lamp to the cigarette lighter. 'With my tool kit, I dove underneath the truck, careful to place a little blanket underneath so I didn't pick up too much dirt – it's those little touches which make the difference between professionals like me and the amateurs who will at some point get caught.' Removing the weld mesh as he had done at the border, Dan then unbolted the propane tank and swung it around ninety degrees so that he faced the semispherical end.

Telling me the story inside his voluminous garage and workshop, Dan demonstrated the routine with the propane tank. 'You can't tell by looking at it, but if you chisel away at the right place with a screwdriver and a hammer, you bust away this glass-fibre body filler, which

I use to cover up a socket,' Dan explained. He then started to unscrew a small square nut. Pang! 'There we go!' he exclaimed with a broad smile. And the end of the tank comes off.

There was no mighty explosion. Instead, I saw small-bore copper tubes inside, which ran from the external sniffer valve, gauges and fuel pipe to a small cylinder of propane used to fire camping stoves. 'The truck actually runs for fifteen klicks on the camping propane, and of course if anyone checks the sniffer valves or the fuel gauge, everything appears to be normal,' said Dan proudly.

When he followed this procedure in the Spokane lock-up, the remainder of the tank was stuffed with fifty pounds of Bud from Beautiful British Columbia or God's Country, as the locals like to honour its wealth of natural beauty and resources. 'That compound was my hot zone,' Dan recalled earnestly, 'Even when you've taken every precaution imaginable, you can still hear the squeal of the Feds' tyres in your mind. There was no retreat from the lock-up and no possibility of talking your way out of fifty pounds and $200k in cash.'

In BC fifty pounds of Bud is worth US$55,000 at wholesale prices. In Spokane, two and a half hours from the border, its value had almost doubled to $100k. If Dan could be bothered (which he often could), the trip to California added another $50k to his haul. If he drove it to Kentucky, he could sell it there for $200,000, almost four times the value in BC. And if he took it as far as Miami . . . well, we'll hear about that later. The turnover of Dan's business was $100,000 a week with minimal capital outlay. As Stephen Easton of the venerable Simon Fraser Institute in Vancouver has noted, the profits from this trade are seductive even for its most junior participants. 'For a modest marijuana growing operation of 100 plants, harvest revenue is from thirteen kilograms of marijuana sold in pound blocks out the back door valued at $2,600 per pound. This amounts to slightly less than $20,000 per harvest. With four harvests per year, gross revenue is nearly $80,000. A conservatively high estimate of production cost is about $25,000. The return on invested money is potentially high: around 55 per cent.'

For the ordinary folk of western Canada, nothing competes financially. For the pros, like Dan and his buddies, it comes close to being a licence to print money. 'I was part of a three-man team,' Dan continued. '*Marty* coordinated all the grow ops to deliver the fifty pounds per week – that's no easy job. Much of it came from his own farms, but some smaller ops sold to him, and you have to maintain the quality, hey. This is a highly competitive market and the guys we sold to, they knew their shit real good.' *Michael*, the third partner, coordinated sales in the United States. 'Look,' said Michael, whose laid-back appearance conformed much more to the hippyish stereotype than Dan's just-back-from-felling-an-entire-forest look, 'there are a lot of problems – not just the question of your clients' reliability, but the security issues. God knows how many cellphones we use – we only use 'em for a week or so, then we chuck 'em away. There's a real damn problem remembering all the different phone numbers.'

Michael conceded that Dan was in many ways the linchpin of the operation. 'The bottleneck has always been in getting the stuff into the US. But that's the big market – there's thirty million Canadians, but everyone in Canada either grows it themselves or has a buddy who does, even in Vancouver or back east. There's close to 300 million Americans and that's a massive market. Taking it to market – that's the real pro work and that was Dan's niche.'

Marty, Michael and Dan are part of an industry that the BC Organised Crime Agency valued at $4 billion in 2001. At the time of writing, it is worth one-third more, according to most estimates, which means that it is responsible for more than 5 per cent of BC's GDP. Around 100,000 workers are engaged both full-time and part-time in the cultivation, distribution, smuggling and retail of marijuana, compared to 55,000 working in the traditional sectors of logging, mining, oil and gas combined. Only manufacturing employs more people – and this is all according to official statistics of Canadian law enforcement. Although BC remains the main producer, the farming of marijuana has been spreading steadily eastwards over the past ten years and most provinces now boast a flourishing industry.

The implication of these figures is stark: western Canada is home to the largest *per capita* concentration of organised criminal syndicates in the world. In turn, Canada has become one of the biggest law-enforcement headaches anywhere – organised crime has broken out of the ghetto of marginal communities and conquered the middle classes. 'In a town like Nelson,' says Dan, 'I would estimate that about

30 per cent of households are involved in grow-ops of some size or other, but in the Slocan valley, I reckon between half and 70 per cent of the households will be involved.'

From atop the reassuring slopes of Elephant Mountain (so called as it clearly resembles a dozing pachyderm) I gaze across the west arm of the Kootenay Lake at Nelson's rooftops. As they stack prettily up a steep green incline, they look ripe for transformation into the image on a cheesy jigsaw puzzle. In the background beyond looms the sharp peak of Silver King, the mountain whose precious metal deposits attracted large numbers of immigrants from southern and eastern Europe at the turn of the nineteenth century. To this day, this twee settlement resembles the idealised images of small-town America before it was blighted by unregulated advertising hoardings and fast-food joints. Almost every store in Nelson has a picture of its manager or owner with their arms around Steve Martin and Daryl Hannah, in commemoration of the time when the town was indeed transformed into America for the filming of *Roxanne*, a feeble update of *Cyrano de Bergerac*. Hollywood likes Nelson: for its unspoilt looks; for the Kootenay's stunning countryside; and because, of an evening, the crew gets to smoke Cuban cigars and fat joints packed with BC Bud.

But despite these attractions, Nelson and the surrounding area have been in steady economic decline for a couple of decades. Although its tourist and media industries are growing, these have not yet compensated for the slow demise of the traditional mining sector and the crises that have afflicted the logging industry. President George W. Bush dealt the most punishing blow to BC's economy in recent years by bending to pressure from the American lumber industry and imposing a 27 per cent tax on Canadian softwood sales into the United States. Regulators of the North American Free Trade Agreement (NAFTA) and the World Trade Organisation (WTO) subsequently ruled that this was an outright violation of America's free-trade responsibilities. The Canadian Government calculated that in three years after the imposition of the tariffs in May 2002, 7,000 jobs were 'permanently lost in logging, sawmilling and remanufacturing across BC . . . Including indirect impacts, job losses have risen to a reported 14,000. A common myth assumes that these impacts will disappear with a settlement in the softwood dispute and that jobs will come back to BC communities. This is not the case, as our communities continue to witness mill closures.' As indeed has been the case.

Many of those who once worked in the traditional industries have moved into marijuana. The trade in weed has attracted large numbers of highly skilled workers who, as I discovered on a trip into the BC interior, have been quick to redeploy their skills into producing vast quantities of marijuana. Three of the four annual harvests are produced exclusively indoors (products of the summer outdoor harvest are often sought-after by connoisseurs, but your average consumer can usually be counted on not to give a damn). But the word 'indoors' does not quite do justice to the extraordinary installations in which some of the plants are grown.

As our 4x4 embarks on the forest road, I am reminded of the train ride in Friedrich Dürrenmatt's dark surrealist novella, *The Tunnel*. As the train goes deeper into a tunnel, the dank bricks wrap themselves ever tighter around the carriages, forcing the travellers to confront their worst nightmares. At first BC's interior is not quite as threatening as Dürrenmatt's trip through a hellish Swiss tunnel – the leaves are not so dense as to block all the sun as we rush northwards for an hour, maybe two, through the towering evergreens. But eventually the sun is bound to set and there are no cellphone signals here. If the vehicle breaks down, then the living nightmares of British Colombia's infinite interior will appear. Trekking home is out of the question – the terrain is littered with a plant known as the devil's club. These tough stalks three to four feet tall are topped by a ball covered in vicious spikes. As you walk through them, the club swings back and rips deep into human flesh. But the great fear is the grizzly bear. The world's most powerful natural predator, the grizzly plays cat-and-mouse with its victim, breaking its bones and its will, then laying it in a shallow grave before returning three days later to munch on the body after it has softened up. Thank God I've come here with a group of three professionals.

The men look, smell and move like loggers, their senses finely attuned to the outback. As well as scanning for the telltale signs of grizzlies, they keep their ears open for the distant twittering of heli-copter rotors – 'Could be game wardens, could be RCMP [Royal Canadian Mounted Police], could be DEA,' one mutters. They talk like loggers, too, which is almost never.

I thought it was tough terrain for the 4x4, but when we finally arrive at the clearing that is our destination, I am rendered speechless by the vision of an idle mustard-coloured industrial digger with its bin resting triumphantly upwards. How do industrial diggers travel to the middle of nowhere? But even more impressive are the two seagoing containers, each forty feet long, which are sunk into an enormous hole in the forest. Accessible only through a door reached by some makeshift stairs cut into the ground, they are easily covered over by earth if necessary. The containers are humming. Cables lead away into the forest. 'Proximity to a power cable is an important factor in the location,' said Jim, who had rigged up the electric supply. An engineer with BC-Hydro, Jim formerly worked on constructing the dams that have helped turn Canada's most westerly province into one of the world's biggest power suppliers. 'Basically, in order to get the power from the main cables, I have to build a series of sub-stations capable of reducing the voltage until we reach the grow-op.'

Inside the two sea containers, hundreds upon hundreds of freshly planted cannabis saplings are starting to crane towards the equally numerous halogen lamps. This facility also has a system of CO_2 injections, as one of the horticulturalists explained to me. 'You are much more in control of the environment by introducing CO_2 at the right time of the day and night. The more CO_2 you give 'em to deal with, the more they like it and they grow into fatter, healthier plants. Increases their potency and you can double the yield and beyond.'

At the beginning of the 1990s, the best yield from indoor grow-ops was about three-quarters of a pound per one-kilowatt lamp. The most recent advance in cultivation techniques has more than doubled this to over two pounds per harvest cycle. Aeroponics is a still more efficient way of channelling nutrients to the plant than hydroponics. 'If you circulate the nutrients through liquid, which is what hydroponics is, you lose efficiency because not all the particles are small enough to enter the roots. But by misting the roots – and it's a very fine mist – the intake of nutrients is still higher. This cultivation method is without peer.'

Of the many things BC has in abundance, space and electricity have been decisive in transforming it into one of the world's great marijuana farms. Space, because the RCMP and the US's DEA just cannot find the great majority of the largest grow-ops (especially after they are hidden deep underground in sea containers). 'The DEA may have unlimited access to BC,' Senator Larry Campbell, former Mayor of Vancouver, told me, 'but do you know how many logging trails there are in the Kootenays? I mean you can bring in every Blackhawk heli-copter you want – forget the haystack, you're looking for a needle in a jungle!'

As for electricity, the lamps feeding the cannabis may need huge amounts of power by normal domestic standards, but by the standards of BC's vast hydroelectric capacity, the amount is negligible.

Back home in the Slocan valley at the end of another tough day, Dan places one of his favourite shows in the VCR. 'You're going to love this,' he says. 'This'll show you just how dumb Americans can be!' he adds in gleeful anticipation. Presented by Rick Mercer, the CBC TV show is called *Talking with Americans*. The host travels across the length and breadth of the United States and encourages Americans to give their reactions in the spirit of neighbourliness to fictitious events in contemporary Canada. 'Congratulations, Canada!' an attrac-tive New York woman gushes, 'On your first 100 miles of paved highway!' Or 'Congratulations, Canada! On opening your first univer-sity!' In one show, Mercer persuades an Ivy League English professor to denounce in all sincerity Canada's supposed annual ritual of setting its elderly citizens adrift on ice floes as a method of demographic control. And even the Governor of Arkansas (*not* Bill Clinton) is gullible enough to send his best wishes on camera to Canada's Prime Minister for having constructed the world's first parliament made from ice.

Popular resentment towards America and the intellectual insularity of Americans is part of everyday life in Canada. It is persistent, low-level, sometimes dumb and sometimes funny. It also reflects the infer-iority complex tinged with irritation that characterises many Canadians' relationship with their southern neighbours. Within a few days of my arrival in the country, I – like many foreigners before me – have been invited to play 'Name the famous Canadian', before the host reels off a legion of celebrities from Michael J. Fox through Shania Twain to Glenn Gould and J.K. Galbraith – luminaries whom a majority of Americans believe to be as authentic as Apple Pie, but who are in fact Canadian, at least by birth.

This social anti-Americanism assumes a more serious form when economic interests are at stake, as demonstrated by the very different attitudes towards the United States in two neighbouring provinces, BC and Alberta. The latter's economy is heavily dependent on investment from American companies, first and foremost because of Alberta's burgeoning oil industry. Already Canada is the largest single supplier of petroleum to the United States, ahead of Mexico, Saudi Arabia and Venezuela. The province's potential reserves are estimated at a gigantic 175 billion barrels of recoverable petroleum, but this is in the form of so-called oil sands, an intense mix of hydrocarbons, sand and clay from which it is expensive to extract oil. For this Alberta needs the cooperation of American oil companies, their most fervent customers. And the benefits are considerable – in 2004, the oil yielded US$10 billion in taxes and royalties to the provincial government, contributing to the transformation of Alberta into the fastest-growing economy in the country and the new centre of affluence.

Of course that wealth is the consequence of America's hunger for gasoline, and this has fused with Alberta's traditionally close ties with the US to confirm the province as the most pro-American in Canada by a long chalk. The quintessential representative of Alberta is Canada's Prime Minister, Stephen Harper, who built his political career in the provincial business capital, Calgary. In the 2006 general elections, he led the Conservative Party to a clean sweep in Alberta for the first time. A firm friend to President George W. Bush, he is the most vocal supporter of closer ties with the United States in Canadian politics.

Although right next door to Alberta, British Columbia presents a very different political profile. Here a majority of the seats in 2006 went either to the Liberal Party, the traditional centrist grouping, or the New Democratic Party, a left-leaning party. Most strikingly, in the key marijuana-growing areas, parties supporting the decriminalisation or legalisation of marijuana won huge majorities. In the Southern Interior of BC, a constituency that includes Nelson and the Slocan valley, the parties won 80 per cent of the vote as opposed to the Conservatives' 20 per cent, whereas in neighbouring Alberta constituencies, the Conservatives received an average vote of just under 60 per cent.

BC, and indeed Ottawa, have locked horns with the United States over the softwood dispute and, equally importantly, over marijuana. These two issues have contributed decisively to the emergence of a more virulent anti-Americanism in BC than in the rest of Canada. To be sure, British Columbians often appear confused about where their loyalties lie; after all, BC has always nurtured secessionist sentiments that rail against the perceived bureaucratic behemoth in the federal capital, Ottawa. Indeed, in the BC interior there is a strong gun culture that shows affinities with the militia mindset common in Washington, Montana and other neighbouring American states.

But the issue of cannabis is defining attitudes to the United States in BC and Canada with ever greater clarity. About 60 per cent of Canadians now favour decriminalisation or legalisation of marijuana possession. BC, however, is way out in front – more than 75 per cent of British Columbians want a relaxation in the law relating to cannabis possession. In doing so, BC has entered into a collision course with the United States.

Similarly, cannabis is also influencing attitudes in Washington towards Canada – Vancouver in particular. In 2003, the then Canadian Government announced its intention to introduce legislation decriminalising the possession of less than fifteen grams (about half an ounce) of weed. This would not make possession legal, but the offence would attract a small fine and the recipient would not be encumbered with a criminal record. The US reaction was swift. 'You can't wall this off, saying, "We're only talking about a little cannabis,"' exclaimed David Murray, special assistant to Washington's Drugs Tsar, John P. Walters. He then added an apocalyptic afterthought: 'Our experience is they [various narcotics] come together like the Four Horsemen!'

Since his appointment in December 2001, Drugs Tsar Walters has placed the issue of BC's cannabis trade close to the top of his agenda. 'Canada is at risk, I believe, at a very great risk,' Murray told me in his Washington office, 'more than they have been willing to acknowledge. The level of crime is in certain provinces really undermining the legitimacy of their own institutions. The issue seems to be a certain Canadian complacency, a sense of self that is disastrously innocent,

absolutely unwilling to acknowledge – they find themselves in opposition to us.'

As the tension between the US and Canada over marijuana has
surfaced, it has again highlighted one of the most controversial, difficult and dangerous aspects of global organised crime: the United States'
policy on, and policing of, the international trade in narcotics.

In 1987, US paratrooper Steve Tuck suffered a serious spinal injury
when doing a jump in Central America. Invalided out of the army, he
spent a year and a half at the renowned Walter Reed Army Hospital
in Washington, DC. Twenty years and another twelve operations later,
he remains in severe pain and on the same dose of morphine he was
given at the time of his accident. His body was remoulded into a sack
full of metal. On medical advice, he turned to marijuana for pain relief
and was soon growing the stuff for himself and friends in northern
California. In 2001, just as John P. Walters was acquainting himself
with his new role as Drugs Tsar in Washington, Tuck did a runner
from justice after the police came after his cannabis farm – his easiest
escape was a hop across the border to Vancouver. The Canadian
Government welcomed Tuck and even licensed him to sell marijuana
seeds to be used in research. At around the same time, the US began
extradition proceedings against Tuck.

In November 2002, the 36-year-old was relaxing by puffing on a
large spliff at the New Amsterdam Café in East Vancouver. It had been
a tough day – Tuck had been protesting outside the hotel where John
Walters himself had been staying during his first official visit to
Vancouver. Walters intended to acquaint himself with the severity of the
narcotics problem in BC's economic capital. The two men had been
sparring in the media. At a press conference Walters described Tuck
and his friends as 'darker angels of society' for advocating the use of
marijuana for medicinal purposes. Tuck had countered in an interview that was transmitted countrywide on the Canadian Broadcast
Company by denouncing Walters as a liar.

After the rigours of such a day, the New Amsterdam Café and its
gentle clientele provided welcome relief for Tuck. That night was music
night and so people had dressed up. 'It looked like any yuppie bar in
any major city,' recalls Steve. 'Then several men in black, all with the

same standard-issue trenchcoats, with the ear-pieces and the high-powered mikes marched into the café. I knew straight away they were Secret Service.' The visitors were bad karma enough for the café's laid-back customers. But worse was to transpire as the agents fanned out. 'I recognised him immediately – John P. Walters, the President's Drugs Tsar!' Walters strode up to Tuck as if he knew him. 'It was surreal. He obviously knew who I was and just started saying that this was a disgrace and then, pointing right at me, "Arrest this man!"' Walters stared at the joint and Tuck's stash. *Of all the gin joints in all the towns in all the world, she walks into mine* . . . 'But he was staring me down and shouting at me, and so I just took a toke of my joint and blew the smoke right in his face!'

For a split second, the atmosphere in the café turned nasty – the other customers were rising through the fog of smoke in anger at the presence of this unwanted guest. The bouncers were beginning to wrestle with the Secret Service men, while the chief of Vancouver's police was explaining to Walters that he would not be arresting Tuck as he was doing nothing illegal.

Tuck tried to calm things down. He announced to the other guests in the café that this was the famous John P. Walters. He advised everyone to sit down and talk. But that did not prevent the Drugs Tsar from continuing to berate his hosts, the guests at the café and above all Steve Tuck. Finally, the police persuaded Walters to leave.

Tuck felt vindicated, but two years later Walters's spirit returned in the form of Canadian police, who forcibly removed Tuck from a Vancouver hospital, with a catheter and IV tubes still attached, before bundling him into a car, hooded and manacled, and handing him over to US federal agents a couple of hours later. He was slung into jail and left there, suffering excruciating pain because of the embedded catheter.

Tuck's encounter with Walters was not the only surreal moment of the Drugs Tsar's visit. The voters of Vancouver, or Vansterdam as it had also become known by now, had unexpectedly just elected a mixed bag of environmentalists, leftists, vegetarians and dope smokers to run the municipality. Standing proud at the head of this woolly-jumper invasion was Larry Campbell, the city's coroner, best known for his consulting role on Canada's smash-hit cop show, *Da Vinci's Inquest,* whose plots often unfold in Vancouver's drug-addled quarter of Downtown Eastside.

But apart from serving as coroner, Campbell had for many years been a senior officer of the Royal Canadian Mounted Police's Drugs Squad. Like a minority of former RCMP officers and DEA agents, he ended up questioning his role in busting addicts come what may. 'It wasn't really until I became coroner that my position started to shift,' he told me in his parliamentary office in Ottawa, 'because in that position you start to worry less about enforcing the law on the users, and to worry more about how you keep these damn people alive. Vancouver was always a high drug-usage area, but in the 1990s there was a glut. Afghanistan was rocking. The Golden Triangle was rocking. In 1976, when I was on the Drugs Squad and we took down a pound or a key, it'd have a big effect on the street. They weren't even cutting the stuff then. You had to go hunt the addicts to find 'em. By '96, they were all over the city – outside the back door, in the parking lot, in the parks, on the streets. One day we just woke up in Vancouver and said: Holy Jesus, this place makes Needle Park look like a children's playground. We gotta do something!'

After his encounter with Tuck, John Walters was heading off to see an even more sordid den of iniquity – Insite, the clinic set up in Vancouver where they administered heroin to addicts under medical supervision. For while cannabis was the recreational drug of choice for most of British Columbia's users, heroin (which was strictly illegal) had gained a stranglehold over large parts of inner-city Vancouver and other urban areas in BC. This was not only a serious law-enforcement issue, it was first and foremost a public-health issue. And Larry Campbell and the new administration were determined to come up with effective solutions to the problem.

Campbell and his allies visited Europe and acquainted themselves with a system called harm reduction, developed particularly in Holland and Switzerland, which replaced traditional drugs programmes that sought in the first instance to punish drug users with ones that sought to assist and rehabilitate them. Vancouver went on to deploy their version, known as the Four Pillars. Essentially, this assumes the drug user to be a victim rather than a perpetrator, and seeks ways in which the health and social services can embrace the addict as a way of minimising risk to him or her and to the wider society. A critical element of the programme is needle exchange, whereby the state provides unused needles to addicts to reduce the infectious spread of HIV, hepatitis C and other communicable diseases. Similar programmes have been hugely successful in Europe, especially in high drug-usage cities like Zurich, Amsterdam and Edinburgh.

But Mayor Campbell went one further than this. In 2003, he sought and received the approval of the Federal Government to open an injection site at a BC medical facility in Downtown Eastside, where addicts could receive professional help in administering heroin. And if this were not enough, the Federal Canadian Government announced at the same time its intention to decriminalise possession of cannabis.

For Walters and his Office of National Drug Control in Washington, DC, Sodom was being built just miles from the US border. It was time to issue a warning, so David Murray was dispatched to explain to the Canadian Government that the US 'would have to respond' to decriminalisation, implying that border traffic between the two countries, which enjoy the most profitable commercial relationship anywhere in the world, might be disrupted. Murray warned that decriminalisation would result in 'the loss of the mutual cooperative partnership we've had with Canadians regarding our borders, regarding the integrity of the hemisphere, regarding our commerce, regarding the implications of trade and value to ourselves; the loss of that would be something truly to be regretted'.

Larry Campbell said he got a still clearer message from a higher authority. 'Walters told us that he could shut the border down,' he said. 'And so I made some offhand comment about it being a shame to see LA in the dark.' Campbell offers a mischievous smile as he alludes to California's partial dependence on electricity and natural gas from BC.

The debate between Washington and Ottawa and the future course of narcotics policy have enormous implications for the global shadow economy, for trans-national organised crime, for international policing, and for domestic policy across the world. They impact on governance, on international relations, on social and health issues, but most crucially on economics – especially if the UN is correct that 70 per cent of financial resources available to organised crime derives from the narcotics industry.*

But if economic globalisation has enabled this huge expansion, cultural globalisation has also played a part, advertising the pleasures offered by narcotics in regions that were opening up as markets. Rave culture, for example, and the accompanying use of drugs such as amphetamines and Ecstasy, swept across the world, reaching Japan, Thailand, South America, Israel, Russia and elsewhere. It was transported effectively by backpackers and the Internet alike. Very soon, chemists from Serbia, Bulgaria, Thailand and Israel were learning the tricks of the trade from their counterparts in Holland – production of the new generation of drugs was no longer confined to the slopes of the Andes or the remote fields of the Golden Triangle (not that the coke- and heroin-traffickers didn't benefit from the dozens of new and unmonitored commercial routes springing up around the globe).

The upshot of this was increased supply and increased competition in the market, which resulted in lower prices and thereby increased demand for virtually every mass-produced recreational drug. There was, however, no comparable increase in the capacity of the world's police forces to deal with this expanded activity in the drugs market. Indeed in some countries, like Russia, the police's ability to control illicit markets collapsed, especially since the military was frequently involved in the distribution of narcotics from Central Asia into Moscow and beyond. And when the drugs market expands, so does related criminal activity. In its first major assessment of the global narcotics industry, published in the mid-1990s, the UN pointed out 'that in Britain 75% of serious crimes are associated with drugs; that 70% of the income of the criminals who are drug addicts is generated by theft; that drug addicts need £43,000 a year to support the addiction. In surveys most addicts cite theft, fraud, begging, prostitution, and drug trade as their main sources of income or are prepared to tap such

---

* There exist endless academic and policy debates about the absolute and relative size of the markets in illicit commodities and services. But due to the obvious difficulties in gathering this data, this is not a debate I intend to engage in. Where I think it is important, I will refer to data published by generally credible sources (with health warnings attached, if necessary).

sources.' This, of course, puts a huge additional burden not just on the police, but on the entire criminal-justice system.

With support from the great majority of its members, the United Nations Office on Drugs and Crime advocates a policy of uncompromising prohibition on drugs – a policy that confers the right on the state to deploy its full police resources to intervene and destroy the narcotics market. With a commodity such as fissile material (where police forces have a fighting chance of tracking regions of production and constituencies of demand), prohibition has a real chance of achieving its stated goals. But with narcotics, where demand is immense and relentless, prohibition drives the market towards the only place capable of satisfying that demand and regulating the industry: organised crime.

Lev Timofeev, the former Soviet dissident mathematician turned analyst of Russia's shadow economy, has written one of the most comprehensive economic studies of the drugs market. His conclusions are stark:

> Prohibiting a market does not mean destroying it. Prohibiting a market means placing a prohibited but dynamically developing market under the total control of criminal corporations. Moreover, prohibiting a market means enriching the criminal world with hundreds of billions of dollars by giving criminals a wide access to public goods which will be routed by addicts into the drug traders' pockets. Prohibiting a market means giving the criminal corporations opportunities and resources for exerting a guiding and controlling influence over whole societies and nations. This is the worst of the negative external effects of the drug market. International public opinion has yet to grasp the challenge to the world civilisation posed by it.

From an economic point of view, a person's decision to enter into the drugs trade as a producer, distributor or retailer is entirely rational, because the profit margins are so high. This is all the more compelling in countries like Afghanistan and Colombia where chronic levels of poverty are endemic. Time and again, narcotics-traffickers have demonstrated that their financial clout is sufficient to buy off officials even in states with very low levels of corruption, as in Scandinavia. In most countries, traffickers can call on combined resources of billions of dollars, where national police forces have access to tens or hundreds of millions (and are further hamstrung by a complex set of regulations constraining their ability to act).

On the whole, governments do not argue that drug prohibition benefits the economy. They base their arguments instead on perceived social damage and on public morality. On the contrary, it distorts the economy because it denies the state revenue from taxes that might accrue from the purchase of a legal commodity (not to mention the immense costs of trying to police the trade and the incarceration of convicted criminals). This huge financial burden is one reason why so many economists, like Timofeev, and indeed one of the great organs of the British establishment, *The Economist* magazine, are adamant in their support of the legalisation of drugs. 'Ultimately,' argues Ted Galen Carpenter, Vice-President of the venerable American right-wing think tank, the Cato Institute, 'the prohibitionist approach is an attempt to repeal the economic law of supply and demand, and therefore it is doomed to fail.'

Timofeev has identified a further problem. With the manner of a boffin who seems permanently distracted by some knotty intellectual conundrum, he outlined his findings to me in his wooden dacha just outside Moscow. He is a man as far away from the world of drugs and its related social evil as one may imagine. 'The growth of funds available to the drug business,' he argues, 'along with its enhanced managerial capability make it possible to diversify their risk assets by transferring capital to other markets. This is precisely what the organised-crime groups do when they are shifting their assets from one illicit activity to another. For instance, the Sicilian mafia invested proceeds from smuggling cigarettes and emeralds into the drug business. In the "hot spots" across the world (such as Afghanistan or Chechnya) drug dealers invested a considerable proportion of their income into illegal arms shipments.'

Prohibition is also a godsend to terrorist networks. Organisations like the Taliban and Al-Qaeda fund their activities through the narcotics trade. In this respect, the inability of the NATO-led force in Afghanistan to pacify anything beyond the centre of Kabul since the invasion of 2001 has been a disaster. Cultivation of the opium poppy had sky-rocketed by more than 1,000 per cent within the first year of Afghanistan's occupation. It was not long before the Taliban was rearming itself by taxing this opium harvest. Attempts by Western governments and agencies to limit the poppy harvests have been an abysmal failure. The only way you can prevent the Taliban and others from sustaining their military capacity through drug sales is to legalise narcotics. When a punter buys some grass, crack or Ecstasy on the streets, only a tiny percentage of the money covers production costs. The great bulk goes towards paying off the distribution network for assuming the risk in bringing an illegal commodity to market. This was demonstrated irrefutably by the economics of alcohol prohibition in the 1920s and 1930s. Then, as now, Canada, which dumped Prohibition a few years before the US, became a key supplier of the illicit substance. By 1933, the world's largest producer of alcohol was Seagram, a Canadian company, and its success was not accounted for by Canadian drinkers.

Some argue that there is a cultural difference between today's illegal narcotics and alcohol. There may well be a *cultural* difference, but with regard to the relationship between drugs and organised crime, the economic argument is central – and here there is absolutely no difference between illicit alcohol and illicit drugs. The astronomical profits generated by drugs lie in these commodities' illegality. There is no institutional regulation that might influence the value of the commodity, and so the price comes down purely to what the consumer is prepared to pay. The only indirect involvement of the state lies in its deployment of policing methods to break up the smooth functioning of the market.

In Washington, I asked David Murray, John P. Walters's affable and amusing adviser, if he can counter the argument that prohibition leads to organised crime's violent control of the drugs market. 'What about OxyContin?' he asks rhetorically about a synthetic opiate, which, like its cousin Viocodin, you can risk buying over the Internet. (But I wouldn't if I were you.) 'Well, it's the single most-abused drug in America behind marijuana. And it's legal. It's medically produced; it's in a prescription regulatory system. But people are holding up pharmacies with guns to get it. I thought you were going to eliminate the violence and the crime and the profiteering by making it something that the state produces and regulates?' A fair stab by Murray, but by putting OxyContin into a prescription regulatory system, you are blocking the consumer's access to it, since to get hold of the painkiller you must first convince a doctor that you are ill enough to require it. That's why people are prepared to use guns, because the market is highly proscribed.

If a country supports prohibition, it is also *guaranteeing* that on the supply side all profits will accrue to underground networks; and on the demand side it is *guaranteeing* that any social or public-health problems associated with drug-taking will only come to light in the great majority of cases once they are out of control. If the UN is right and drugs account for 70 per cent of organised criminal activity, then the legalisation of drugs would administer by far the deadliest blow possible against trans-national organised criminal networks.

But don't take my word about the inefficacy of narcotics' prohibition. Have a look at a report based on access to confidential British intelligence reports. Tony Blair's government was on the whole a big supporter of the United States' War on Drugs. It is no surprise then that it tried to suppress its own report, so stark were its findings:

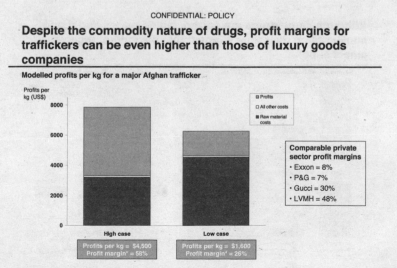

CONFIDENTIAL: POLICY

Despite the commodity nature of drugs, profit margins for traffickers can be even higher than those of luxury goods companies

Modelled profits per kg for a major Afghan trafficker

Profits per kg (US$)

☑ Profits
☐ All other costs
■ Raw material costs

Comparable private sector profit margins
· Exxon = 8%
· P&G = 7%
· Gucci = 30%
· LVMH = 48%

High case — Profits per kg = $4,500 / Profit margin* = 58%

Low case — Profits per kg = $1,600 / Profit margin* = 26%

* Profit margin = profit/revenues
Source: HMG data, team analysis. Data is for for each kg of heroin processed and successfully shipped to Turkey. Costs of seizure are reflected in lower revenues . 'High case' refers to low costs (including product costs), high sale price, and low seizure rates; vice versa for 'Low case'.

Western government interventions have tended to have a short-lived or negligible impact on retail prices downstream

Governmental interventions against the cocaine trade in Colombia

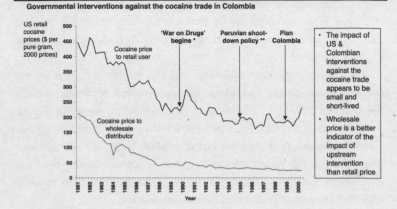

- The impact of US & Colombian interventions against the cocaine trade appears to be small and short-lived

- Wholesale price is a better indicator of the impact of upstream intervention than retail price

* US/Colombian campaign against the cartels
** Unidentified light planes flying between Peru & Colombia
Source: ONDCP, 2001, US Institute for Defence Studies

Although some drugs are seized, falling prices and rising consumption over time suggest that the market receives an ample supply

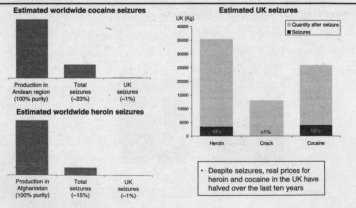

- Despite seizures, real prices for heroin and cocaine in the UK have halved over the last ten years

Note: HMG data, UN documents

Conclusions on the drugs supply market

- Over the past 10–15 years, despite interventions at every point in the supply chain, cocaine and heroin consumption has been rising, prices falling and drugs have continued to reach users
  - government interventions against the drug business are a cost of business, rather than a substantive threat to the industry's viability
  - however, by increasing risk, government interventions are likely to have slowed the decline in prices

Lev Timofeev argues that prohibition tends to distort the market, favouring cartels and monopoly tendencies. This is because, he continues, larger organisations are more efficient at enforcing their monopoly than smaller ones. Translated into the vernacular, this means that big criminal groups can beat the shit out of smaller ones.

In 2005, Dan Wheeler decided to break up his partnership with Michael and Marty. There was no falling out between the three of them, but Dan was unhappy about the direction of the trade. 'I was offered the opportunity of doing a trip to Miami,' he said. 'It was a new kind of deal – for every one kilo of Bud I delivered in Florida, I would be paid one kilo of pure cocaine, the idea being that I'd then bring it back here.' Dan was silent for thirty seconds. 'No way . . . No fucking way. What you have to understand about weed is that it attracts people who have a healthy attitude to life. It never promotes aggression, and most of the people I've come across involved in the trade on both sides of the border are thoroughly decent people. The people who handle coke are very different, and in the past few years I have seen coke and its entourage make ever deeper inroads into places like the Kootenays.' The purveyors of cocaine in BC are also becoming increasingly interested in expanding into rural areas and competing in the profitable BC Bud market. In BC and Vancouver, the most powerful and visible organised-crime syndicate is the Hell's Angels.

There are two reasons for the strength of Vancouver's Hell's Angels. The first is common to most chapters of the movement worldwide – organisational discipline. They have a strict hierarchy and place a premium on absolute loyalty. It takes many years before an aspiring Angel can get anywhere close to the centre of power. Trainees, or 'prospects', are expected to carry out any orders handed down from the full-patch members – instructions can range from clearing up after a meeting to engaging in extortion by the threat or use of physical violence. Because the aspirant must be prepared to accept years of drudgery and hanging around before he (I use the gender advisedly) might be considered a member, Hell's Angels are impossible to infiltrate, sharing a security system that is as effective as the Chinese triads. Infiltrating the mafia, the Colombian cartels, the Balkan or Russian mafias is, by contrast, like falling off a log.

The second source of the Vancouver Hell's Angels' power is the group's control over the city's port. 'The Hell's Angels are involved with bringing in whatever's profitable – marijuana, cocaine or precursors,' said Brian Brennan, chief investigator for the drug squad of the RCMP. 'They still have influence in the ports – their influence on cocaine is still strong and we are now seeing them in synthetic drugs.' The Hell's Angels exert that influence through friends, business associates and corrupt officials, and control of the port has meant control of cocaine. Vancouver is used to import cocaine both directly from Latin America and from the United States, but it is also used as a transit point for cocaine going into the US. 'What you've seen in recent times,' Brennan continues, 'is an increase in violence as the struggle for control of the grow-ops heats up.'

The Hell's Angels established themselves as a major criminal group decades ago, and in that time the RCMP can count the number of convictions on the fingers of two hands. 'Is the problem big?' asks Brennan rhetorically. 'Absolutely – it's huge. The number of grow-ops is beyond the capacity of law enforcement as a whole, not just the RCMP. And the money being made by the organised groups, like the Hell's Angels, means that they can walk away from properties that they own without batting an eyelid. We're talking about a house worth $500,000 on the lower mainland of British Columbia, and if the police go and seize a thousand plants in that house, they'll just walk away. Because they are making so much money that they don't care about losing that investment.'

The RCMP cooperates closely with the DEA in trying to stem the flow of marijuana to the US, but as I speak to Brennan, I detect for the first time a note of irritation creeping into his voice – not when talking about the DEA, but when talking about Washington politicians and their criticism of Canada's drugs policy. Because this rhetoric implies that the RCMP is doing a poor job in holding back that flow. 'The US,' continues Inspector Brennan, 'has a legitimate concern that the amount of marijuana from north to south is growing – there has been an increase in seizures, so maybe we're getting better at the border – it's hard to measure. But I must stress that only two per cent of what is domestically consumed in the United States comes from Canada. They make a lot of a fuss about it, but it's down to the fact that the relationship between the two countries is really good, the border is very long and so it is likely to be porous. It's big news if something like the tunnels are discovered in Canada, but in the last year, they found about twenty-seven tunnels between Mexico and the US.'

It took me a while to understand the implication of what Brennan was saying. BC Bud is a $6 billion industry. According to the RCMP, between 75 and 90 per cent of marijuana produced in BC makes its way onto the American market. But the US and Canada confirm in their official Drug Threat Assessment that this amounts to a mere 2 *per cent* of America's cannabis consumption. Even I can do the maths on that one. One might legitimately ask what in God's name are they smoking in the US? Frankly, there are no accurate figures as to what it is or where it comes from – the only thing we all do know is that there's a hell of a lot of it!

'You know what the figures tell you,' a DEA analyst told me in a discussion that we had about BC Bud, 'they tell you that we have a big problem of civil disobedience in the United States.' He wasn't kidding.

Americans who support the spirit of liberalisation in Canada are usually people like Steve Tuck who like to use the drug themselves. But in May 2006, Vancouver received an American guest whose visit set the cat among the pigeons back in Albany, NY, whence he came. David Soares was no drug user – indeed, he expends much time and energy trying to get people off drugs. But unlike most of his fellow Americans in law enforcement, he doesn't believe that slinging drug users in jail and throwing away the key (as happens in New York State) improves the common lot. 'My advice to Canada,' Soares said in a dramatic speech at a Vancouver conference, 'is stay as completely far away from US drug law policy as possible . . . You, Canada, are headed in the right direction!'

But the biggest surprise of all about David Soares is that not only is he black, but he is an elected official, the District Attorney no less, of Albany County in New York State, which means that he has legal jurisdiction not just over the city and county, but over the whole government of New York State.

David Soares proved an illuminating guide to inner-city Albany. 'This was the drive-in. People would come off Highway 9, pull in and shout. And a member of the Robinson family would just throw the drugs down – it was a sort of fast-food outlet for drugs,' he said, getting out of his official car and taking me to the end of a slightly run-down residential street. Pointing to a row of bollards, he said, 'We blocked the street off to prevent direct access from the highway.' In front of us, endless traffic zoomed along one of America's larger-than-life x-lane super-roads. 'The white folks from the suburbs would turn in here, buy their drugs from the African Americans and then shoot back out to the safety of the suburbs.

'About five years ago, there was an article in the paper,' Soares continued, 'where one of the Robinson family talked about dealing drugs and about there being no consequences, and the police took offence at that. So we got together a multi-agency task force to take down the Robinson family. Which we did. What we were not successful at doing was stabilising the community. And what we didn't know was just how powerful the Robinson family had been in the local market. They kept things more or less under control.'

Without the Robinson family, all sorts of new dealers came in to fill the void. The twin problems of drugs and violence got worse. 'This community was abandoned,' says Soares with a rare tinge of bitterness in his voice. 'Until you have a strategy which combines law enforcement with community development and economic development, we're always going to be dogs just chasing our tails. And that's the truth.'

At this moment, a battered car drives slowly by and a young man pops his head out of a window. 'Hey, man,' he calls to Soares, 'you like the job I've been doing?' Soares, whose diction has up to this point been precise and eloquent, glides easily into the vernacular.

'What job you been doin', brother?'

'I been cleaning up that mansion house.'

'Man, I *do* like the job you been doin'!'

Wherever David Soares walks, the people of West Hill come to greet him, to chat about their family and work, to tell him about their drug-rehab progress. But above all, the people of West Hill come to thank him. This spontaneous adoration and respect almost has the ring of a corny Hollywood movie from the 1950s. In my Walks through the Underworld, I rarely encountered anyone who appeared both so thoroughly good and so thoroughly determined to do good in the face of powerful forces ranged against him or her. This remarkable 36-year-old lawyer has offered the minority communities of inner-city Albany an alternative vision to an existence plagued by the twin cul-de-sacs of drug dependency and prison. But more importantly for the United States, he has proved that the country's democracy is not entirely hostage to the vested interests of money and established networks and to those who can afford to run for office – and that it is still possible to run for office on a programme easily denounced by those vested interests, but based nonetheless on unpleasant truths. But most important of all, he has proved it is possible to run on an awkward but courageous programme and win.

When he landed a job as Assistant Prosecutor in the DA's office in Albany County in the late 1990s, Soares was thrilled. 'I couldn't wait to start this job,' he told me, 'and for the first year of being a prosecutor, I would say it was one of the greatest of my life.' He wanted to contribute to the smooth and successful functioning of Albany's law enforcement, and busting drug users and drug dealers was part of that. 'But then something happens because you see the same people over and over again. You put people in jail, and then they come out and you put them back in. Then you put in their cousins, then you put in their mother and then you put in their father, and you start to see a mother/daughter combination. The mother was in jail and the daughter was being arraigned – the mother is released, the daughter goes in. And something clicks and you ask yourself, "What are you doing?"'

In 1973, inspired by President Nixon's War on Drugs, Nelson Rockefeller, Governor of New York, introduced a new set of Drug Laws that remain in force to this day, continuing to bear his name. For possessing a risible amount of any drugs, New Yorkers risk draconian sentences of between fifteen years and life in a state penitentiary. And New York State pays out more than $500 million every year to keep incarcerated those who have fallen foul of this regime.

Three years after Rockefeller had promulgated his New York Drug Laws, six-year-old David Soares arrived in Pawtucket, a small mill town in Rhode Island. He had come from Bravo, the most westerly of the Cape Verde islands, the Portuguese-Creole-speaking community off Africa's west coast, whose other most famous inhabitant is the singer Cesaria Evora. Growing up in a poor black neighbourhood, Soares developed an understanding of the mechanisms of deprivation and its consequences. But thanks to his exceptional intelligence, his experience as a second-generation immigrant unfolded as a fairy tale and he ended up winning a scholarship to study law at Cornell.

Soon after he joined the DA's office in Albany, one of President Clinton's initiatives made money available to set up a community prosecutor's office, whose job was to liaise with leaders in those areas of the city where there were high crime rates. Nobody wanted the job, but Soares was the obvious candidate. Although 30 per cent of the city's population is African American or Hispanic, he was the first and only Assistant Prosecutor from the minority communities. 'Naturally the melanin content of my skin made me an instant expert in the area of community prosecution,' he remarked with a wry smile.

And before long, his experience in working in the inner city challenged his assumptions about law enforcement and about the Rockefeller Laws in particular. 'I would go to court every morning, prosecuting an individual every day, believing that the job I was doing was going to make that corner a clean corner and a safer corner. But every single day I'm going into the court and I'm prosecuting this kid that I saw arrested on the block, and I'm coming back and there's a new kid, same age, same complexion, doing the same thing. And it was just incredible that here we were doing the same thing every day – locking up and destroying entire communities. Meanwhile on the other side, I'm watching law enforcement and they're coming in saying:

Here's a $20 street rip – what we call a twenty-buck control buy. We were shooting fish in a barrel. This was supposed to be good law-enforcement work? Resolving problems? Cleaning up communities? No – this was a factory! This was a money-making operation – a collars-for-dollars scheme that I was not going to be part of any more. I made my stand because I was tired of watching people on the corners getting pummelled. It's the same feeling, I imagine, as grabbing slaves and putting them on a ship.'

Perhaps the most terrifying statistic of all that Soares uncovered was that in Albany County (minority population 13 per cent) more than 95 *per cent* of imprisoned Drug Laws offenders were black or Hispanic. Whichever way you look at the figure, it can only mean one thing – something is rotten in the state.

Special Agent Matthew Fogg knew that he had to be careful, but found it difficult holding his tongue. Ever since he testified in Congress in 1989 that his boss, Ronald Hein, was a racist and should not be appointed to the prestigious position of US Marshal for the DC Superior Court, he had encountered difficulties in his career. Despite being outcast by his fellow police officers, Fogg's courage in speaking out as whistle-blower was eventually vindicated in 1998 when a jury awarded him $4 million plus full back-pay in his suit against Janet Reno, then US Attorney General, and the Department of Justice. Not only did the court conclude that Fogg had been the victim of racial discrimination at the hands of his bosses, but that the US Marshals Service was institutionally racist.

The landmark ruling was neither the beginning nor the end of Fogg's determination to highlight corruption and racial discrimination both within the ranks of America's law-enforcement agencies and in their application of the law in various communities. Fogg made a lot of enemies. On one occasion, he was set up by his own colleagues during an operation to arrest a fugitive in Baltimore and was almost killed. That was during the early 1990s when he had been seconded to the DEA from the US Marshals Service where he served as a Deputy. His job at the DEA was to supervise a Metropolitan Task Force that would carry out drugs sweeps in the largest cities across the country.

Fogg is a tall, tough-looking guy, but his speech is modest and gentle even when his anger quickens. Even now that he is in his fifties, and despite a life of hard knocks, he still seems bewildered at how unfair and unjust the world can be. 'Over the course of my career, I've been responsible for locking up somewhere in the region of 2,000 fugitives,' he told me at an office in Washington. 'Cos I was involved in dragnets – we swept everything moving in all the major cities around the country. At the Task Force, we'd fix the operation with the local Police Department and supply them with federal funds for it, give 'em overtime and everything. We'd give the dragnets fancy names like Operation Gunsmoke or Operation Sunrise and it was a ninety days' deal. In that ninety days you go hog-wild on locking up as many folk on anything you could get. But of course we would concentrate on the urban areas mainly, where African Americans and people of colour were; 85 per cent and more of the folk we arrested were black or Hispanic.'

Dispirited at hauling in hundreds of men and women from his own community, Fogg came up with a new proposal for his boss at the DEA. 'I suggested we go out to Potomac, Maryland, and to Springfield, to places where whites live, and out to Alexandria, because our job was to find the drugs and white folk do drugs too. The DEA ASAC, the Special Agent in Charge, got hold of me and said, "We gotta talk about this." He said, "Fogg, you're right. People do drugs everywhere. White folks do drugs too. But Buddy – we start going out into those areas with the Task Force, those people know judges, lawyers, politicians and, let me tell you something, they'll shut us down and there goes your overtime. We'll go after the weakest link, instead."'

The discussion degenerated into an argument. 'This is selective enforcement, I told him. Man, I said, we even got white guys in the force coming up to us saying we're doing too many black guys. Me and the other black guys on the force, we'd talk about this all the time, but we never did anything about it. And then I realised. Here we are, part of the plantation, doing the massa's bidding.'

Because of the system of financial incentives that is built into the war on drugs, and because of the protection from prosecution, as described by Fogg, that white communities enjoy, this war in the United States is waged against blacks and Hispanics. In the light of his experiences, Matthew Fogg is now convinced that the strategy is designed as an institutional tool that is used to control African American communities and limit their economic and social opportunities. This is taking conspiracy too far, but there should be no doubt that the war on drugs inflicts massively disproportionate damage on America's underprivileged minority communities. The ability of the criminal-justice system to levy crushing penalties of imprisonment, and for law-enforcement officers to be rewarded for the numbers charged and convicted, is an open invitation for corruption.

Fogg concluded that the harm done to African Americans by the policing of drugs far outweighed the harm caused by the drugs themselves. There is now a growing number of former law-enforcement officers from federal and state agencies, including the DEA, who, like Matthew Fogg, speak out in favour of the decriminalisation or legalisation of narcotics in the US. And like most of these men and women, Matthew Fogg does not use drugs. He discourages their use among his community. But although in the late 1990s he represented a growing constituency that has support among members of both Democratic and Republican parties, no single politician seeking office ever dared challenge the orthodoxy of the war on drugs in public. However compelling the arguments for a liberalisation of America's drugs laws might be, in the hothouse of Washington and state politics, it is a third-rail issue – touch it and you're dead.

That was until David Soares came along.

In the late 1990s, working as an assistant DA and using his office of community prosecutor, Soares embarked on projects to try to clean up the West Hill inner-city area, the focus of Albany's narcotics trade. His first focus was on the environment. 'There's a reason why people don't deal drugs in the suburbs in front of nice fresh-cut grass. It's because there's something about the environment that sends out a signal to the offender which says this type of behaviour is not accept-able here. But when you have boarded-up buildings, when you have overgrown bushes and cars abandoned in lots, it sends a message that says anything is tolerated here. We set about removing some of those obstacles – trimming the trees, cutting the grass – and we were using offenders in bringing that about, while also instilling in them the idea that this is their neighbourhood. They began to see that they were not cleaning the broken glass and syringes off a basketball court as punishment, but because their little brothers and little sisters would be playing here later on. In less than a year, we were able to drive down the emergency calls without increasing the number of arrests.'

Soares's success didn't just interfere with the drug-dealing network, it started to irritate a political network – a very powerful network indeed. 'This became an issue for my boss at the time, who would sit in his office and talk for hours about what I'm doing wrong. I was, for example, getting trashcans for people who wanted trashcans. What they were concerned about was that I was attempting to destroy a system. If you were a resident and you wanted a trashcan in front of your house, you would call the committee men, who would then contact the Deputy Ward Leader, who would then contact the Ward Leader, who would then let the Mayor know that there was a trashcan needed. They would inform you who got you the trashcan, and they would inform you about what you needed to do to repay this. That's been the political culture – it's called The Machine.'

The Machine reacts poorly to those who challenge its authority. Soares's bosses started withdrawing resources and support staff. Before long, he found he was no longer able to do his job. He was treading water with no prospect of advancement in Albany. Once you have disturbed The Machine, you can expect no mercy, especially not from his boss, the DA Paul Clyne, member of one of the most influential Democratic families in the city and an unbending supporter of the Rockefeller Drug Laws.

Soares decided to sell up and move to Atlanta, a magnet for thousands of middle-class blacks from the north-east. '"Do you really want to move?" my wife asked me. And I said, "Yes." She accused me of running away like some kid from school. "If these guys had been at school in Pawtucket, you would have punched 'em." She brought back my little Pawtucket spirit.'

The next day, Soares gave the train to Georgia a miss and walked into Paul Clyne's office to inform the DA that he intended to run against him in the forthcoming Democratic Primary. 'The meeting lasted seven minutes,' Soares recalls. 'He laughed the first five and he then fired me in the next two.'

The Machine, an old-style Democratic Party operation similar to the Daley dynasty's fiefdom in Chicago, has always governed Albany, and there was one community that had never been granted membership. 'The Party appoints the judges; the Party appoints the Chief of Police; the mayors; everyone here – the legislators all come out of the same institution. But there's only one African American judge and then there's me – only two in any policy-making positions in this county. But the issue of race has never been dealt with here – they live there and we live here. They'll tell you that they employ a lot of African Americans in the city. What they don't tell you is that they're all picking up trash!'

In the autumn of 2004, Soares stood against Clyne in the Democratic Primary and then again in the election to the DA's office, as Clyne stood against him as an independent. Soares had been out on the stump, holding rallies and knocking on doors throughout Albany county in all communities, although whites made up more than 80 per cent of the electorate. Soares placed reform of the Rockefeller Drug Laws at the centre of his campaign. 'The Rockefeller Drug Laws smack of everything that is offensive,' he said at the time. 'The image of the criminal-justice system is Themis, and she has a scale, a blindfold and a sword. It is supposed to be just. If we lose faith in the criminal-justice system, then what do we have? We have chaos. The Rockefeller Drug Laws are offensive to the image of Themis. We know that the drug law acts negatively on African Americans and Hispanics so disproportionately that the fact that it is still on the books today makes you wonder. I don't like to look at this in terms of race so much, but to say here is an issue that is important to everyone. Addiction is something that affects everyone, whether it is crack cocaine or alcohol. Most people, whether it be immediate family or a cousin, have that experience; they know what damage addiction does to families. So to have a system that treats addiction in the way that it does, so disproportionately, is wrong.'

In both the primary and the main election, Soares whipped Clyne and all other opponents. His election destroyed the political consensus in New York State. On the eve of his election victory in November 2004, Soares said, 'It is unquestionable that . . . the days of this antiquated statute are numbered. The fact that the most vociferous, inflexible member of the New York State DA's Association is in jeopardy of losing his position, and primarily on the issue of the Rockefeller

Drug Laws, is a moment for pause for every single elected official in the state of New York.'

It is also a message to Congress and the Presidency – slowly the American people may be reflecting that, after almost four decades of the War on Drugs, dependency levels and usage are higher than ever before; the price of all major recreational drugs has been declining resolutely over that period; and the state has wasted hundreds of billions of dollars in a criminal-justice system that delivers a lot of crime, but very little justice. The funds used to sustain bureaucracies like the DEA which prosecute the War on Drugs are a drop in the ocean when compared with the gazillions that organised-crime syndicates have earned because Washington is determined to drive the market underground. The social and criminal problems related to drug abuse will never go away until the state can exercise control over the industry as a whole.

And that is just in the United States. Pity those less affluent countries who fall victim to America's War on Drugs. Above all, pity Colombia.

MARCH OF FEAR

Soldiers

The road to Jamundí, fifteen miles south of Cali, is quite a tour. First I drive past the training ground of Cali America Soccer Club, owned by the Rodríguez-Orejuela clan aka the Cali Cartel. A few miles further on, I am astonished to see a full-size bullring belonging to the Ochoa brothers, erstwhile partners of the late Pablo Escobar in the Medellín Cartel. Jamundí is a favoured recreational destination for narco-traffickers (as they are universally known in Colombia), where they have built grand *fincas*, complete with lakes, full-size floodlit soccer pitches, indoor and outdoor pools – all on the same property. Right at the far end, the *fincas* stop abruptly and the modest dwellings of the impecunious Indians begin.

As the little town tails off, there is a welcoming sign at the beginning of a drive lined by tall green hedges. Underneath the words 'My Little Home: Psychiatric Hostel' there is a phone number and an arrow pointing down the drive; 200 yards further on around a couple of bends is the Little Home itself, set in delightful grounds – although the rusty green-and-red iron gates and the barbed-wire fencing are less welcoming.

At 5.30 on May 22nd, 2006, the commander of one of Colombia's crack Special Forces Units stopped his convoy of three cars at just this spot. Accompanied by nine men and a civilian informer, he emerged from his car and strolled towards the gates – the informant had assured him that there was more to My Little Home than meets the eye.

Without warning a group of uniformed men who had been lying in wait opened fire on the police unit, killing its commander instantly. Twenty-eight gunmen were hidden amongst the unkempt undergrowth adjacent to the drive. 'We were just preparing supper at the time,' said a member of staff at the hostel, 'when all of sudden there was this tremendous noise of gunfire from the gate.' A couple of the police officers had thrown themselves into the open drains for protection. 'We heard these men screaming, saying, "Stop, please don't shoot! We're police!" And then, "We have wives and children."'

But the shooting went on for a full twenty minutes until every last policeman was dead. When a regular police team came to clean up the mess, they found that one of the attackers had made a point of placing a bullet in the back of the head of the civilian – as a message, perhaps?

Unnatural deaths like those at Jamundí are always a shock in this country, but never a surprise. There is a bewildering number of potential perpetrators – a whole book's worth of murdering acronyms has been stalking this country for thirty years, each staking its claim to political and moral superiority by means of massacre, torture and bombings. And that's just the freelancers. The police and the military have frequently acted as unaccountably as the traffickers, the paramilitaries or the guerrillas.

Colombia's powerful Marxist guerrillas, the FARC, are often mentioned first as possible culprits in attacks on the military or the police like the one in Jamundí. They certainly operate quite close to the town; they derive a large part of their income from cocaine; and they have never shied away from mounting armed assaults on government agents. As if to emphasise this, while I was visiting Jamundí, a FARC unit was busy killing six policemen on the other side of Cali with pipe-bombs which they had been taught to build by members of the Provisional IRA. But these days their military units rarely penetrate this far into urban areas and the attack did not fit the profile of a FARC operation.

Then there were the local paramilitaries (known as the AUC), who often fight alongside the regular army against the FARC. Claiming to be upholders of the right to private property (especially to that property which they have seized by intimidation and murder), many members of the AUC had disarmed in a deal brokered with the Government earlier in the year, only to emerge as new organised criminal gangs in the lawless *barrios* that grow tumour-like from the nether regions of all major Colombian cities.

And finally, there was the Cartel del Norte, successors to the even more infamous Cali Cartel. Although the Cartel del Norte had lost its leader, Fernando Henao, a year earlier after a New York court had sentenced him to nineteen and a half years in jail, the business was still functioning smoothly under his partner, Diego Montoya. The cartel was sure to be a prime suspect.

Whoever pulled the trigger, it was not difficult to guess the motive – cocaine.

Indeed, it quickly emerged that cocaine was at the heart of this case, but the identity of the Jamundí killers still took everyone by surprise. It was not the FARC, the AUC, the ELN, the MAS, the PEPES or any other self-appointed law enforcers who perpetrated this crime. The Special Forces team was executed by none other than a 28-strong platoon from the 23rd Mountain Brigade of the regular army. The Colombian military has, of course, never been retiring in its use of force; and it boasts one of the worst human-rights records in the world. But it is highly unusual for the military to murder their colleagues from the Special Forces. This came as a real shock to everyone – to the Colombian people, to its President, Alvaro Uribe, and his government; and it came as a big and unpleasant shock to members of the US Congress and President George W. Bush.

The platoon commander, the square-jawed Colonel Bayron Carvajal, at first issued a statement describing the incident as a tragic case of 'friendly fire'. It had happened at night, he claimed, and the soldiers had mistaken the unit for FARC guerrillas. The eyewitnesses from My Little Home and the neighbouring Indian houses were baffled – they knew the attack took place in broad daylight and that the distinctive uniforms of the Special Forces would have been instantly recognised by the army.

Far from being friendly fire, this bore the hallmarks of a calculated execution. Furthermore, as the Attorney General Mario Iguarán investigated the matter a little closer, it seemed suspiciously as though the soldiers had been acting to protect whoever owned the drugs. 'This

was not a mistake, this was a crime,' he proclaimed after a prelimi-
nary investigation. 'They were doing the bidding of a drugs trafficker.'

There was good reason for the long faces in Washington when this
news hit DC. The United States had recently handed over the last
wedge of the $4 billion it had donated to Bogotá under the auspices
of Plan Colombia. This five-year plan, introduced by the Clinton administration and expanded by President Bush, had been designed to save
the world from the joint scourge of cocaine and the FARC; 80 per cent
of these funds was earmarked for upgrading the military. With the
exceptions of Egypt and Israel, Washington lavished more hardware
and cash on the Colombian armed forces in the first years of this
century than on any other in the world. The dual aim was to eradicate
coca plantations, the cocaine business and the left-wing guerrillas. But
in Jamundí, those self-same recipients of military aid were working
on behalf of narco-traffickers and murdering policemen! What had
gone wrong?

As well as a reputation as the most violent, Colombia is one of
the most richly endowed Latin American countries, with fertile
plains that produce the finest coffee in the world; gorgeous Atlantic
and Pacific coastlines; jungles stuffed with exotic wildlife; mineral
resources from emeralds to coal and oil; the majesty of the Andes;
part of the Amazon basin; and even a city, Medellín, whose climate
is rightly described as 'eternal spring'. On my first day in the capital,
Bogotá, a Colombian wit explained that when God made the Earth,
he decided to give this one country every form of munificence he
could muster. 'When all the other countries complained that this
amounted to discrimination against them,' my friend continued,
'the Lord turned to them and said, "Just wait till you see some of
the people I'm going to give Colombia. Then you'll be happy with
your lot!"'

This idea of a paradise stained by a satanic, venal minority is a
common theme in Colombia. Behind the seductive power of magical
realism in the Nobel Laureate Gabriel García Márquez's *One Hundred
Years of Solitude* lies an intense consideration of the role that violence
has played in Colombian history, where a sincere struggle in the name
of a cause or ideology is repeatedly eclipsed by, and subordinated to,
the violence it begets:

'Tell me something, old friend: why are you fighting?'

'What other reason could there be?' Colonel Gerineldo Márquez answered. 'For the great Liberal party.'

'You're lucky because you know why,' he answered. 'As far as I'm concerned, I've come to realise only just now that I'm fighting because of pride.'

'That's bad,' Colonel Gerineldo Márquez said.

Colonel Aureliano Buendia was amused at his alarm. 'Naturally,' he said. 'But in any case, it's better than not knowing why you're fighting.' He looked him in the eyes and added with a smile:

'Or fighting, like you, for something that doesn't have any meaning for anyone.'

As a BBC correspondent, I had seen a deal of butchery in the Balkans and in the Caucasus, but Colombia's reputation for violence unsettled me. When I left London for Bogotá, it was the only time during my investigations that I was distinctly worried that I was taking an unnecessary risk. My fear was, of course, an exaggeration and a deeply unfair criticism of many of this country's warm and outgoing people. An exaggeration – yes. A fantasy – no. Just over a week before my departure, I had enjoyed dinner in Washington with a friend, a most gentle man, who said as we parted, 'This is not a joke, you know. It really can be a very dangerous place.' He knew better than most. Six years earlier, his wife had stopped at traffic lights in Pereira, a town 100 miles west of Bogotá, when a motorcycle pulled up beside her car. The pillion rider then took out a gun and shot her dead in front of the nanny and her four-year-old daughter. My friend fled to Washington and is unable to return to his home country to this day. And while in Colombia I met an inordinate number of people forced to bear the murder of a family member or of close friends.

Even by Colombia's standards, the mayhem over the past twenty-five years takes the breath away. The violence of the nineteenth and twentieth centuries came in many shapes and sizes – full-scale rebellions or armed uprisings; arbitrary government incursions to intimidate or cleanse an area in preparation for its seizure; individual terror, or fearful massacres. The rivalry between the Conservative and Liberal

Parties fashioned the political framework; while the issue of land ownership provided the economic motivation. One of its many high-points, sparked by the assassination of presidential candidate Jorge Eliécer Gaitán, in April 1948, is known simply as *La Violencia*, a decade-long festival of blood-letting, which was eventually brought to an end by a reconciliation between the Liberals and the Conservatives, the two parties that had dominated both the country and the bloodshed for more than a century.

Until this point, violence in Colombia had been largely a domestic affair. And indeed during the 1960s, Colombia's people dared to imagine a future of greater civil harmony; of slow but steady prosperity; and of growing influence in the north of South America. Not only did an internal consensus appear to develop, but there was none of the overt political manipulation by American companies, by politicians or by mobsters that was so visible in Central America and the Caribbean.

Then three things happened in just over a decade that were to force this country down every circle of Dante's hell. And there it remains to this day – the greatest victim of the most relentless organised-crime networks in the Western Hemisphere: networks which in the process have become hideously intertwined with an entirely different form of politically motivated armed conflict.

First, in 1968 in an attempt to bolster its domestic economic perform-ance, Colombia proudly established The Institute for Advanced Chemical Research as part of the Universidad Nacional de Colombia in Bogotá, which started to train top-class chemists, who were later to find lucrative work in the employ of the Medellín and Cali cartels.

Second, at around the same time, American horticulturalists began to grow marijuana in sufficient quantities to meet most needs of the US's domestic weed market. This led to a depression in the healthy cannabis trade that had sprouted around Colombia's northern coast. Those traffickers who had made an impressive living in the north looked to diversify their agro-portfolios to reverse their declining fortunes in marijuana futures.

This search coincided with the third development: a dramatic return to fashion of cocaine among the thirty- and forty-somethings in Florida and the north-east. As America's baby-boomers turned from protest-ing to making money, they sought a champagne-style narcotic that

represented this shift in their lives from philosophical introspection
to brash acquisitiveness. Cocaine had none of the mess associated with
shooting up – just a quick snort and head out to Studio 54. It wasn't
long before everyone wanted a piece. 'No longer is it a sinful secret
of the moneyed elite,' reported *Time* in a July 1981 edition featuring a
cocktail glass full of coke on the cover:

> nor merely an elusive glitter of decadence in raffish society
> circles, as it seemed in decades past. No longer is it primarily
> an exotic and ballyhooed indulgence of high-gloss entrepre-
> neurs, Hollywood types and high rollers, as it was only three
> or four years ago – the most conspicuous of consumptions,
> to be sniffed from the most chic of coffee tables through crisp,
> rolled-up $100 bills. Today, in part precisely because it is such
> an emblem of wealth and status, coke is the drug of choice
> for perhaps millions of solid, conventional and often upwardly
> mobile citizens – lawyers, businessmen, students, government
> bureaucrats, politicians, policemen, secretaries, bankers,
> mechanics, real estate brokers, waitresses.

There had been little research into the drug since it had been
pilloried and then banned by the American Government during the
1920s. Most people thought erroneously that it was not very addictive
and that it had no serious side-effects. And if that wasn't enough – it
was rumoured to enhance sexual performance.

Demand was going through the roof and the plodding rural
economies of Peru and Bolivia could not keep pace. This conjuncture
persuaded a group of Colombians – the narco-traffickers – that there
was money in them there Andes.

Narco-traffickers

To discover how they got their hands on this source of cash, I visited
a downtown Bogotá nightclub to meet a man nicknamed The Demon,
but whom everybody addressed as 'Nixon', perhaps a playful reference
to the late US President.

After walking through a harmless bar area peopled by men in their mid-thirties to late forties and women in their early twenties, my friends and I walked into a hall containing a large indoor swimming pool in the shape of a figure of eight. Across the middle was a gaudy Rialto-style bridge, while around the walls there were little enclaves surrounded by the most tasteless red drapes. In each enclave was a group of four to six men drinking, while naked young women thrust their crotch into the face of one man at a time to the rhythm of the accompanying Latino Euro pop played at thunderous volume. Each to his own, I suppose, but not really my cup of tea.

Fortunately, Nixon took us to a floor overlooking this bacchanalian parody where we could at least hear ourselves talk. Nonetheless, he insisted on bringing two young prostitutes with him, one of whom sported the largest bosom I have ever seen (Colombia prides itself as the world leader in breast enhancement). By now Nixon was so coked up that he was talking like a machine gun. To kick off, he produced a handkerchief with the flourish of a stage magician for his audience to examine and then carefully drew it through the hole that years of cocaine usage had burned through his septum.

'I was a young teenager – completely normal – from Boyacá, about two hours from Bogotá. I had no idea about drugs when one of my cousins turned up from New York.' The 1960s and 1970s witnessed a significant exodus of Colombians seeking work in the States after the country's textile industry collapsed, and among the emigrants were the first cocaine traffickers, including Nixon's cousin. The two men would purchase coca paste from the growers in Bolivia and Peru, processing it into cocaine hydrochloride themselves and then sending it up to relatives who had nestled in the burgeoning Colombian communities of New York and Miami. 'My job was to transport the stuff within Colombia, usually by car or truck,' Nixon explained, 'then from the coast or the airfield it would go either directly to New York or to Mexico or the Caribbean.'

Nixon was swept up by drugs and the surreal experience of becoming very rich very suddenly while still young. He snorted, screwed and shot his way across Colombia. Until January 1994. 'My boss was driving down one of the main streets in Bogotá and I was in the passenger seat,' he recalled. 'And then it happened just like people have always described it. Two guys on a motorbike stop by us at the lights and the pillion rider pulls out a gun and starts shooting my boss. I ducked under the dashboard looking for my gun, but I couldn't reach it. But my boss managed to get the car out of the line of fire and he survived despite taking three bullets.' That was when Nixon got out of the high end of the business. 'We soon found out that the hit had been ordered by my boss's partner and I thought: this is too much. My girlfriend and I now had a little daughter and I didn't want her to end up fatherless.' Nixon managed to downgrade his status – instead of shifting kilos, he started dealing in grams to Bogotá's emerging yuppies.

In his heyday, Nixon belonged to a respectably sized wholesale operation. But this had been a mere tributary that trickled into the raging river of cocaine flowing to New York from its source in Cali, 200 miles south-west of Bogotá. The Cali Cartel was one of the top three cocaine clans to emerge in Colombia during the 1970s and 1980s. In an agreement with the other two clans, who were based in Medellín, the Cali Cartel had carved up the US export market with precision – New York belonged to Cali. Anyone exporting there would have to link up with their operation.

In 1981 and 1982, the Ochoa clan, partners in crime with Pablo Escobar in the Medellín Cartel, convened a series of meetings at their ranch, Las Margaritas, to which the major cartel bosses from around Colombia were invited. The most senior delegation to join Escobar and the Ochoas were the Rodríguez-Orejuela brothers, Gilberto and Miguel, who controlled the Cali Cartel.

These high-level summits were prompted initially by the abduction of the Ochoa brothers' sister, Martha, who was snatched for ransom by left-wing guerrillas. But the gatherings became much more – indeed, despite the mutual suspicion that later decayed into deadly hostility, this was the foundation not so much of empires, but of an industry that thrives to this day and continues to shrug off all attempts to sabotage it.

The individuals at Las Margaritas were all eventually killed or imprisoned. Nonetheless, for almost twenty years, the Escobar, Ochoa and Rodríguez-Orejuela groups were the most important figures in the global shadow economy that grew up alongside the licit economy, as the US and Europe pushed through the liberalisation of financial and commodity markets – the economic cornerstone of globalisation in the 1980s. In key respects, the Medellín and Cali cartels succeeded in anticipating the mechanisms of globalisation and for many years they were also able to merge their illicit operations with licit ones.

The three clans made strange bedfellows. The Ochoas were from a smart and wealthy middle-class family with a passion for horse-breeding, while Escobar grew up in the slums of Medellín, ducking and diving through the trigger-happy world of Colombia's petty crim-inals. In Cali, the Rodríguez-Orejuelas were more familiar with Escobar's lifestyle, but it was the Ochoa family that made the intro-ductions between Escobar and the Rodríguez-Orejuelas, and succeeded in maintaining the peace before the two groups' mutual loathing led to a bitter struggle between them.

During the discussions at Las Margaritas, they made two momen-tous decisions. First, they agreed to fund a clandestine organisation, MAS (*Muerte a los Secuestradores*, or Death to the Kidnappers), a private militia that would later blossom into the more powerful and organ-ised right-wing paramilitary, the AUC. Second, they agreed to carve up the North American cocaine market – Escobar was awarded the colour code Yellow for Miami, the Ochoas were Blue for Los Angeles, and the Cali Cartel were Red for New York.

Although he enjoyed a reputation as the most notorious narco-trafficker, Pablo Escobar was not in fact as successful as the Rodríguez-Orejuela brothers. These two had first come to the attention of the police for their role in a series of high-profile kidnappings in the late 1960s. By the mid-1970s, the elder brother, Gilberto, had gathered sufficient funds to buy a light aircraft, with which he ferried the semi-refined coca-paste from Peru to Cali. Here he would arrange the final stage of processing into cocaine hydrochloride before shipping it off to the States.

Within a few years, the Cali Cartel's fleet numbered more than 700 aircraft, which were dispensing drugs all over North America. In a country where geography usually makes transport a nightmare, Cali's location is perfect. To the east and south lie coca and opium-poppy cultivation areas, while to the west Buenaventura's deep harbour is only a short drive away. Upon this geographical serendipity the Cartel built a superbly efficient corporation. Even the Drugs Enforcement

Administration (DEA) could not entirely disguise its admiration for the Cartel's business acumen (admittedly after the gang leaders were arrested in 1995):

> The Cali mafia's annual profits were estimated at between $4 and $8 billion a year, and the organisation operated like a well-run multinational business with Cali mafia leaders micro-managing business decisions in Colombia and in the United States. They were able to run their global enterprise through a sophisticated system of telephones, faxes, pagers and computers, and employed an intelligence network that rivalled those of most developing nations. The Cali drug lords controlled the Cali airport, the taxi system and the phone company. They knew who came and went in Cali, who talked to the police, and who was cooperating with US law enforcement agencies.

The DEA was right to identify the Cartel's intelligence-gathering capacity as the key to its success. 'They knew who we all were and who our informants were – they had phone numbers, movements – completely ahead of the game,' remembered Jim Milford, who headed up the DEA's team responsible for hunting down the Orejuela clan. The DEA only understood the extent of the Cartel's surveillance capacity after it seized an IBM mainframe computer, comparable to systems used by major banks, from a building in Cali in 1996. Here they found telephone logs that had been leaked by insiders from the municipal Telephone Exchange detailing all calls from US agents in Colombia to their contacts in Cali.

This was typical of the operation, which was always looking to maximise its competitive advantages. Gilberto, who took pride in his *nom de plume*, The Chess Player, conceived three master-strokes.

At home in Colombia, he eschewed the flamboyant violence with which Escobar turned Medellín and Bogotá into abattoirs. Instead, he preferred to exploit the chronic weakness of the Colombian state by subverting virtually every public or private institution that might assist his business, up to and including the Presidency. Banks were an early investment target of the Cali team. Having created its own in 1974, El Banco de los Trabajadores, the Cartel bought into banks elsewhere in Central and South

America that had close ties to banks in Miami and New York.

Equally importantly, Gilberto developed the policy of 'state capture'. Less prosaically, he bought protection from the entire government by corrupting presidents. His influence reached its apogee after the election of President Ernesto Samper in 1994. 'He gave a bunch of money to Samper,' a former senior government official told me, 'and everyone in Samper's gang ended up jumping cartwheels to accommodate the Cali Cartel.'

Finally, to produce 100 tons of cocaine, you need millions of gallons of precursor chemicals. The great bulk of those chemicals are produced in the United States and the European Union. Some, like potassium permanganate, are easy to bring in because they are used for the manufacture of food like pizza bases. But for others you need a licence. The Cali Cartel's answer to this problem? Simple – establish Rebaja, the largest drugstore chain in the country, and you can import anything you want with no questions asked!

Money-laundering in those days was still a simple affair, with neither banks nor governments giving two hoots as to the origin of large amounts of cash. As the noose tightened a little on the financial system during the 1980s, the Medellín and Cali cartels perfected the black-market peso exchange system whereby dollars earned in the United States would purchase fridges, TVs, cars and other consumer durables, which were then smuggled into Colombia and resold for pesos. 'Since the early 1970s, Colombians have purchased contraband goods, knowing that they are part of the illicit drug money-laundering chain,' explained Francisco Thoumi, Bogotá's leading authority on organised crime. 'They have sold real estate, art objects, fancy cars and jewellery at inflated prices to mysterious individuals, who paid in cash without questioning the origin of the funds involved. From their point of view, the responsibility to control those actions was the state's, not personal or social.' Just as the state is indifferent or unable to police large tracts of Colombia, Thoumi argues, so people feel no reciprocal responsibility to the state and are instead happy to ignore its judicial and policing systems. 'Why are those constraints weaker in Colombia than in other societies?' he asks rhetorically. 'In Colombia everything is allowed, there are no personal or social sanctions. Every illicit act is tolerated and even approved as something brilliant, heroic, clever and cunning, but if the responsible person gets caught, he is left to hang out by himself. In other words, there is great social tolerance to anyone who obtains results, independent of the means used, but at the same time there is no trust or solidarity.'

Overseas, Gilberto pioneered the strategic commercial alliance with counterparts in Mexico, Spain, Italy, Brazil, Nigeria and finally Russia. His decision in the early 1980s to divert the bulk of exports to narco-traffickers in Mexico demonstrated the depth of his vision. The overwhelming business risk for Colombian narco-traffickers lies in delivering the merchandise across the US border and to a 'legitimate' client – that is, one who is not working for law enforcement. By establishing agreements with the Mexicans, Orejuela was unloading that risk onto them (and condemning northern Mexico to the same miserable fate as Colombia suffered). At around the same time, he established links with organised-crime groups in Spain, as well as the Mafia in Italy via Brazil. Most dramatic were the meetings between the Orejuela brothers' representatives and members of Moscow's Solntsevo Brotherhood on the thoroughly sinful Caribbean island of Aruba in the early 1990s. As the market for cocaine in the United States had reached the point of super-saturation, the collapse of communism was a gift from above for the Colombian cartels. Both the European market and the routes thereto could suddenly flourish.

The cartels that have emerged in the past thirty years are the phenomenon that corresponds most closely to the popular image of the organised criminal syndicate – that is, a vast, ruthless organisation bent on destroying Western civilisation. Once the sophisticated networks of Colombia appropriated the processing and distribution of cocaine from more modest industries in Peru and Bolivia, then cocaine did become a commodity that was handled by some of the largest criminal networks in the world. But contrary to popular perceptions, the Cali Cartel, like the other major cocaine corporations, was in fact highly decentralised. The cartel is a holding company, an agglomeration of small, flexible mafia groups that have differing stakes in the overall industry. The Orejuela brothers were unquestionably the most senior managers of this group, who conferred stability on the overall business environment and derived huge profits from its activities. The impact of their arrest and consequent removal from the trade only had a brief knock-on effect on the price of cocaine in the United States. This was occasioned by the struggle in the Cali region that followed the arrests as the smaller mafias making up the cartel jostled to seize the top spots that the Orejuela had vacated. Taking down an Escobar or an Orejuela is the stuff of law-enforcement legend, and rightly so. But in the case of cocaine, these spectacular operations do nothing to disrupt supply or demand.

It is now more than a quarter of a century since Ronald Reagan announced the Colombian cartels to be the prime target in a War on Drugs that the President redefined as a central national security issue for the US. And yet cocaine from Colombia is cheaper and easier to acquire in the United States than ever before. Billions upon billions of dollars have been spent in an attempt to root out an industry that has merely grown in size, in scope, in profits and in human sacrifices – tens of thousands of people have lost their lives; millions more have been shattered.

'By all empirical standards,' argued Alvaro Camacho, Colombia's leading academic researcher into US Narcotics Policy in South America, 'the War on Drugs has been a complete failure.' The execution of this ill-conceived policy, he and others claim, has frequently been exposed as farcical by the competing and contradictory interests of the CIA, the DEA and the state, whose squabbles have often made life for the narco-traffickers even easier than it might otherwise have been.

But Professor Camacho's most disturbing observation is that at most the cocaine industry accounts for just 3 per cent of Colombia's GDP. (Later the UN anti-narcotics chief assures me it is even lower, just 0.8 per cent). In Afghanistan, the United Nations estimates that since the fall of the Taliban, opium amounts to a staggering 57 per cent of GDP, rendering it impossible for the central government in Kabul to impose any effective control on the country outside the capital and the north. And that is despite the assistance of 19,000 heavily armed NATO-led troops. Far from cleaning up the scourge of cheap heroin on Britain's streets, as Tony Blair promised in 2001, the intervention has caused Afghanistan to become an epicentre of organised crime, insurgency and terrorism. The country now nourishes all manner of organisations, from the Turkish smack cartels through the despotic leaders of Turkmenistan and Uzbekistan, not forgetting al-Quaeda, whose prime source of income in the region is the Afghan opium trade.

Colombia's economy is more sophisticated and much richer than Afghanistan's. 'So that although the drugs only make up 3 per cent of GDP,' Professor Camacho points out, 'that is more than enough to sustain at least two private armies – the paramilitaries and narco-traffickers on the one hand, the guerrillas on the other.' Armies who for several years could keep 70,000 fighters permanently under arms.

The havoc that the cocaine trade wreaks on Colombian society is wildly disproportionate to coca's economic value. Bombings, massacres and motiveless killings perpetrated by all sides are well documented and frequently define foreign perceptions of the country (as I discovered when I tried in vain to insure myself before travelling there). But it is yet another army that inflicts the greatest damage on Colombia's moral capacity to emerge from the morass – an army of refugees. In 2004, Jan Egeland, head of humanitarian affairs at the UN, explained that Colombia's drug wars had resulted in 'the biggest number of killings; the biggest humanitarian problem; the biggest human-rights problem; the biggest conflict in the western Hemisphere'. He also warned that the Government in Bogotá had run out of funds to deal with the most dramatic expression of that crisis, the three million refugees driven out of their homes since the mid-1990s – the largest refugee population in the hemisphere and the third-largest anywhere in the world.

Guerrillas

In 1980, Susanna Castillo and her husband Ephraim used the few hundred dollars she had inherited from her father to buy a farmhouse with several acres of land in the Colombian province of Meta. The tiny village of San José lies to the north of the broad, meandering River Guejar. Beyond its banks, the serrated mountain range of La Macarena rises, while jostling with jungle that thickens southwards, home to thousands of unique plant and animal species. 'At the time there was no electricity, no roads to San José. There was nothing except malaria,' remembered Susanna, 'but we found the land was very fertile and we grew bananas and corn.' There she and her husband raised seven children, modestly prosperous in an unpredictable environment. Then in the space of two days, through no fault of her own, she lost her home and her livelihood and embarked on a wretched life as a refugee.

Mrs Castillo answers my questions patiently and precisely, but with no emotion, as I suspect the previous twelve months have drained most hope or expectation from her. We are sitting in the office of Roberto Sicar, the Ombudsman for *Tres Esquinas* (Three Corners), an unmappable agglomeration of shacks, huts and makeshift houses that accommodates an estimated 155,000 people, 80 per cent of whom are refugees. In a community the size of Cambridge or Bonn, there is no electricity and just a few punctured hosepipes that supply water.

Tres Esquinas is itself just a small part of Ciudad Bolívar, Bogotá's rambling *barrio* that spreads across the hills rising to the south of the Colombian capital. Sicar recognises that his job is quixotic. 'As far as the people here are concerned, I am the Colombian state,' he said with a gentle smile, 'even though I am actually funded by the United Nations. But there is little or nothing I can do for them.'

During the day, the economy in Ciudad Bolívar revolves around the construction of shacks for the newcomers. As dusk falls, women, children and the elderly hurry into their shelters as the nocturnal creatures emerge. 'We have identified three paramilitary groups and eight crime syndicates in *Tres Esquinas*,' Sicar says calmly. 'If I come here at night, I need an army escort. The syndicates are subordinate to the paramilitaries – they are the ones who really run the economy here, through cocaine and guns. They control everything and are an ersatz state. All I can do is help the refugees to fill out forms and write letters. And they draw their own conclusions about the capacity of the Colombian state and the capacity of the ersatz state.' The people of *Tres Esquinas* know full well where power lies in these dusty, ugly streets.

Opposite the Ombudsman's building, there is an office of the United Nations Development Programme. It is padlocked shut and looks as though it has been so for some time. The only other building is a spanking-new library courtesy of Plan Colombia, the $4.7 billion worth of assistance that the United States gave to Colombia over the first half-decade of the new century; 98 per cent of those funds were devoted to beefing up the Colombian armed forces' assault on coca plantations and left-wing guerrillas. I feel rather pleased for having uncovered one of its few civilian outlets. All the library needs now is to open (padlocked like the UNDP), a few books (there were none) and, most importantly, some people who can read (a rare species in Ciudad Bolívar).

Susanna Castillo does not need a library right now. As a recent recruit to Colombia's three million-strong army of refugees, she needs money, more space to live and access to water and electricity. She has bright-blue European eyes set behind sharp indigenous Indian cheekbones – like the majority of Colombians, she is mixed-race, a *mestizo*. Although forty-seven years old, the lines dug into her face add a good ten years to her age. 'When we first arrived there, we were able to survive off the income from the bananas and corn,' she continued. The Castillos were not obliged to pay taxes. The state simply did not penetrate that far into Colombia's interior. 'No tax collectors, no policemen and no post office unless you walked to Vista Hermosa, which was two hours away on foot.' And even in Vista Hermosa, the local town, where the Castillo family sold their crops, the pace of life was glacial.

This experience of living in a country without ever encountering its official representatives is common in underdeveloped countries. But Colombia is not underdeveloped. Rather, it is the country's geography that militates against the consolidation of state power in the country-side. Bogotá is a good example: pitched high in the mountains with poor transport links to the rest of the country, it is becalmed. Traditionally, power resided in the urban and coastal areas or the neigh-bouring rural lands – the economic centres have no access to Bogotá. Elsewhere, the interior remained untouched by the state and these boundless tracts of jungle often remain a mystery to this day. According to Sandro Calvani, the Italian who heads the UN anti-narcotics programme in Colombia, the effect of 'a large territory over which there was no state control at all for many decades has been profound. People have become accustomed to this, and still now there is a large part of the territory where there is no rule of law. So people have grown up here, knowing that they are Colombian, but without ever having come across the state in the form of police or justice.'

At first, this indifference to their existence did not bother the Castillos – quite the contrary. Their income proved sufficient to raise a family of seven children, five boys and two girls. The latter eventually left the village to marry, while the five boys remained, working the land for their parents. But as the 1980s turned into the 1990s, it was not the Colombian Government that began to interfere with their lives, but the impact of shifts in the global agricultural markets of which the family had no notion. Technological innovation and the 'banana wars' between the EU and America's fruit corporations were pushing down prices. Producers in areas like the Macarena were among the first to feel the effects, baffled as to why nobody was willing to pay the same prices as in the past.

Something else was happening in the Macarena at the same time. The Government's indifference was being steadily exploited by one of its fiercest competitors, the *Fuerzas Armadas Revolucionarias de Colombia* or FARC.

The FARC is not just any old ragbag guerrilla operation, conducting the occasional hit-and-run attack, or the bombing of shopping malls. With anything between 15,000 and 20,000 combatants, it is an organised military force that has attracted into its ranks men, women and children (with the emphasis often on the last two categories) across large swathes of Colombian territory. Since Manuel 'Sureshot' Marulanda founded the insurgent army in 1964, it has recruited members with ease from a large peasantry that has suffered systematic abuse by the more exploitative landowners and fruit companies controlling the agro-economy. Many landowners have never hesitated in employing thugs to assassinate those peasants who evince even a passing interest in political activity. Colombia is the least safe country in the world to indulge in trade-union work.

So for two decades the FARC grew impressively in size and influence, living off the produce from countless towns and villages where they operated; and where they did not enjoy that support, they had the weapons and the ruthlessness to persuade the peasants otherwise. The FARC has successfully inured itself to human pain and misery, an entry requirement for any organisation (whether state agency, rebel, drug trafficker or freelancer) aspiring to take part in Colombia's tragedy. When you introduce the cocaine industry as a catalyst to 150 years of bloody political struggle, this is hardly a surprise.

Powerful as the FARC became in the 1960s and 1970s, it was not able to halt the unstoppable tide of migration from the countryside into the cities. Like their counterparts everywhere else on the globe, Colombia's peasants were desperate to escape the poverty and violence of the countryside. The FARC's ideological appeal, stirring though it may have sounded to the dispossessed, could not compete with even a dim prospect of casual work in the *barrios* of Cali, Medellín or Bogotá. By the beginning of the 1990s, only 30 per cent of the population remained in the countryside.

Haemorrhaging its raw recruits and producers in this way, the FARC had to rethink its economic policy. So it decided to renounce its traditional

Chief Emmanuel Nwude – the biggest scammer of them all.

Nuhu Ribadu, head of Nigeria's Economic and
Financial Crimes Commission.

Nelson Sakaguchi – innocent dupe
or master criminal?

BC Bud – 6% of British Columbia's GDP.

David Soares – Albany's DA with a mission.

The blooming industry in the capital, Ottawa.

1985 – Fabio Ochoa (far left) of the Medellín Cartel and
Santiago Uribe (far right), brother of the current President.

The aftermath of Mia Casita in Jamundí.

Janneth Pachon – survivor of terror.

Mr. Pringle – the must-have accessory
for cyber criminals.

Protógenes Queiroz – the man who brought
down Lao Kin Chong.

The PCC strikes in São Paulo.

Mr. Agata – deputy boss of the
Sumiyoshi-kai in Tokyo.

PACHINKO!

'Let's drive the *Yakuza* out of the Nada-ward!' says this sign in Kobe.
Wolfgang Herbert, Professor of German and one-time *Yakuza* associate, remains sceptical.

'Face' houses near Fuqing in Fujian Province.

'To you, six dollars the lot!'

Su Hang Qi and her daughter: broken flotsam on the raging sea of globalisation.

indifference to Colombia's most notorious product and started encouraging the cultivation of the coca plant on the territory under its control. The logic was simple – a pound of bananas during the 1990s would fetch $1 on average; a pound of coca base (before the most expensive part of the refining process) was worth between $350 and $500.

At an anonymous shopping mall in Cali, I sit down for a beer with two senior members of the clandestine *Movimiento Bolivariano*, the FARC's urban wing. They are an elegant, educated and articulate couple, both doctors, but quite frank about their activities. 'We became engaged in kidnapping in the early 1990s soon after we had set up the cells here in Cali,' they explained. 'At first the FARC leadership was reluctant to allow us to become involved in this, but we were able to convince them that there was a war going on in the cities as well as the countryside.'

Like the other side, the FARC and the MB take the conflict very seriously, but are impervious to the consequences. 'We are not particularly interested in supplying people with drugs,' Lola explains, 'but the movement decided to engage with the *cocaleros* for financial reasons. But we do *not* process cocaine. The leadership merely taxes the peasants 10 per cent for its crop and in return provides a social-security network.' Police and military intelligence reports tell a very different story. They suggest that FARC's military bases are frequently situated close to the kitchens which process the coke and are more deeply involved in the trafficking than their supporters maintain. A dispassionate observer with access to this material, but who was nonetheless deeply sceptical of American policy in his country, described the FARC as 'organised crime in fatigues'.

It is difficult to verify the precise function of the FARC in the coke industry beyond the fact that it protects and encourages cultivation of the plant. That was certainly Susanna Castillo's experience. 'We did what everybody did then – we switched from bananas and corn to coca,' she continued. 'Actually we did not grow the coca ourselves, but we rented out our land to a *cocalero* and he grew the crop. He paid tax to the FARC and we paid tax to the FARC on the rental he paid us.' Rather touchingly, the 10 per cent that the FARC charges for every harvest consciously builds on the Church's tradition of collecting the *diesmo* or tithe.

This arrangement earned the seven-strong Castillo family about $2,000 a month – not a fortune inasmuch as six family members were of working age, but given that more than 50 per cent of

Colombia's population live on just $2 a day, it was a respectable figure.

In November 1998, President Andres Pastrana took an extraordinary step: in the hope of resuscitating Colombia's moribund peace negotiations with the guerrillas, he ordered the army and police to clear a
vast area of territory, roughly the size of Switzerland, in Meta and
Caqueta provinces. This left the FARC in complete control of what
became known as the *despeje* (cleansed area), which included most of
the Macarena as well as the land of the Castillo family.

Many Colombians have excoriated Pastrana retrospectively for establishing the *despeje*. They argue, not unreasonably, that this allowed the
FARC to consolidate its military base. They also point out that the cease-
fire did not dissuade the FARC from indulging in one of its major
pastimes of kidnapping people either for fiscal or for political ends. In
2002 as he was preparing to cede the Presidency to Álvaro Uribe,
Pastrana announced the end of the deal and warned the FARC that the
Government intended restoring its sovereignty over the region by force.

This was bad news for the Castillo family. While the *despeje* had
been in force, their business had flourished – the FARC left them
alone except when collecting taxes, and there was no prospect of the
bottom falling out of the coca market. But after President Uribe was
sworn into office, the Government announced its determination to
confront the FARC militarily and claw back the Macarena. Susanna
Castillo suddenly found herself on the front line of a merciless conflict.

'FARC became much more aggressive when manual eradication
was embarked upon,' explains the UN's Sandro Calvani. 'It was the
first time that we saw the FARC defend the crop as its safe-deposit
box was being attacked. If someone were to attack my pension fund,
I would also be aggressive. The crops in Macarena are where all the
funding for their operations comes from.'

'Things were getting worse through 2005,' Susanna recalled. 'In February
three children playing on a field were killed by a landmine.' The FARC
had started to lay quite a few mines in the region, as the Colombian Army
appeared to be preparing a serious offensive – the US Government wanted
to see some results for the billions of bucks it had been pouring into the
eradication programme and the war against the FARC. There was no lack
of political will to prosecute the war, but there was a legal problem: La
Macarena was a national park and therefore strictly exempt from

Washington's favoured method of coca eradication – the spraying of plantations with glyphosphate, a killer cocktail supplied by Dow Chemicals and
delivered in the field by DynCorp. How much of La Macarena's unique
flora and fauna would be eliminated along with the coca?

Instead, President Uribe announced a new plan, Green Colombia,
which would see the military provide cover to hundreds of peasants
sent into Meta to pull up the coca by its roots (in any case a more effective method of eradication than fumigation). This was a huge challenge
to the FARC – not only was the Government intending to move into
its area, but it was also bent on literally ripping up its source of income.

'It was about five-thirty in the morning, just as we were getting up,
when there was a huge burst of gunfire like thunder right on top of us.'
Susanna was describing the morning of December 27th, 2005, when a
400-strong detachment of FARC guerrillas ambushed soldiers who were
protecting the eradication operation. 'We just hit the floor and hid under
the beds. The fighting continued for two hours and we just remained still.'
Trapped in their village, the Castillo family sought refuge with a neighbour a little further from the battle, and here they spent three days. From
there they went to join the stream of the dispossessed in Ciudad Bolívar.
Susanna admits that her chances of returning to the farm, if it still exists,
are now minimal – instead she, her husband and five adult sons live in
two cramped rooms while during the day she learns to fill out forms.

At least Susanna and her family escaped with their lives. The soldiers
of the Colombian Army were less fortunate – twenty-nine were killed
that day, the bloodiest attack by the FARC in 2005 and further proof
that, for all the military beef served up by the US Congress in the
shape of Plan Colombia, the Government of President Uribe does not
have the wherewithal to defeat the guerrillas.

Paramilitaries

Massacres like the one in La Macarena leave a dangerous legacy for
local inhabitants. The FARC follow predictable guerrilla tactics: once
they have mounted a successful attack like the one on December 27th,
they then withdraw and begin preparations for their next surprise
attack, allowing the armed forces to assume again their precarious
control over a specified territory.

All too often, however, threatening bands of armed masked men follow in the wake of the military. These are the paramilitaries or *auto-defensa*. Like the FARC, they are not nice people. Within days of the Macarena massacre, the paramilitaries had assumed the vanguard role in sniffing out anyone among the civilian population in the area whom they suspected of being FARC collaborators.

In early April 2006, 26-year-old Eliades Pachon, his wife and their two young children were travelling by bus from Vista Hermosa south to Puerto Rico on the very edge of the Macarena National Park, where he worked as a mechanic. A mile or so before the village of Mattu Bambu, the bus was waved through one of the military checkpoints that had multiplied in the area since the December 27th murders. But in the village itself, the bus was again halted, this time by men wearing undefined fatigues. After ordering everyone off the bus, a masked man read out a list of names including Pachon's. 'They had a list of people, a physical list, and they appeared to be sorting out the passengers according to that list,' said Eliades's sister, Janneth. 'They called up another couple of people, including the guy next to my brother who was also wearing a blue jersey, and then the guy with the covered face shouted, "No – not him. Take the guy with the baby." He gave the baby to his wife and went with the guy who picked him out. They didn't take him where they had taken the first group, but down towards the river instead.'

At this point, Janneth's pretty, bright young face began to cloud over. I assumed that she, as a newly recruited NGO worker, was going to outline the general situation facing refugees. Her own story not only took me by complete surprise, but my Colombian friends listening with me as well. As the horror of her narrative unfolded, the entire company bit its collective lip in an effort to hold back the tears. 'My brother said, "Don't kill me – I'll give you anything you want, but please don't kill me!" As he was begging for his life, the man ordering him about took a machine gun from another paramilitary and shot him four times in the face.'

As the shots rang out, Janneth's sister-in-law begged the paramilitary leader to allow her to see her husband's body. 'If you want to die,' the *jefe* answered, 'you can go and join your husband. So if I were you I'd stay here and look after your children.' Eliades was one of four murdered that day in Mattu Bambu – one of several attacks on civilians in the area that followed the FARC murders in December.

Both Eliades and Janneth were members of the local committees that ran the towns and villages in the absence of any other authority. This is why they were listed as potential FARC sympathisers. This area is on the frontline between the FARC's *despeje* and government-controlled territory. Janneth insists that the committees existed purely to ensure that minimal services functioned in what was essentially a lawless area. The 28-year-old seems an unlikely revolutionary. A single mother of two children, she worked in Puerto Rico as the manager of a liquor store and a waitress at a billiard café. 'You have so many groups in the region; so many battles; so many confrontations with the civilians. Three doors down from where we lived, a soldier was killed in a clash with FARC people. The civilians just take their children and hide under a bed. We have nowhere to go, we have no support from anyone – we are entirely unprotected.'

She was able to escape the paramilitaries who hunted down her brother and take her two children to Bogotá, where she now works voluntarily assisting other refugees from La Macarena to find somewhere to live in the capital. She is also involved in what appears to be a vain battle to identify her brother's murderers.

When President Uribe promised President George W. Bush that he would redouble efforts to rein in the cocaine traffic, he faced one problem that towered above all others – the paramilitaries. This loose association of armed killers, infused with extreme right-wing views, acts principally as the militia of the drug cartels. But given their close personal and ideological ties to important parts of the Colombian military and their significant fighting role in the war against the FARC, they have long enjoyed both impunity and immunity for their role in the narcotics trade.

'*Auto-defensa* is not an enemy of the Government,' says Sandro Calvani, the chief of the UN anti-drugs office in Bogotá. 'They never attacked the Government. Instead they are fighting the terrorists, they are protecting people. They are enforcing the law. You'll find many places where police officers are enjoying beers with *auto-defensa* all over the country – there is no enmity between them.'

In areas like Chocó in the north-west of Colombia, the paramilitaries have 'cleansed' entire villages and towns in their efforts to secure cheap land where they can grow not only coca, but also large-scale palm plantations to cash in on the growing worldwide market for its oil around the world, and notably in the United States. These villages are as miserable as anything I witnessed during the Yugoslav wars: the peasants have had to leave in a hurry, sometimes in the middle of a meal, and some of the buildings have been levelled by the para-militaries to force the villagers to join Colombia's army of refugees.

The depth of the difficulties facing President Uribe became apparent in the autumn of 2005 when secret tapes revealed that the boss of Colombia's secret police, the DAS, had been trading and selling infor-mation to some of the most notorious paramilitary groups. The DAS chief and his deputy were forced to resign, but the President vigor-ously denied any involvement. Just as well, as the DAS stands accused of having handed out slush funds (provided by the US taxpayer through Plan Colombia) to armed groups who were not only responsible for killing civilians and trade-union activists, but who were also cultivating and producing cocaine before selling it to the United States.

Since money from Plan Colombia started flowing to the military, the DEA and some Republican members of Congress have been applying pressure on President Uribe to arrest the leaders of the paramilitaries and then extradite them to the United States. Already embattled in his war with the FARC, the President recognised that he simply did not have the resources to take on another enemy – armed, motivated and 30,000 strong – especially as this enemy was inextricably entwined with the military.

Uribe's solution to the paramilitary problem was the Law on Justice and Peace. By this, in short, the paramilitaries agreed to disarm, their leaders would hand themselves over to Colombian justice, but they would be exempt from extradition to America. Several thousand para-militaries have indeed disarmed and left the countryside, but only, according to UN officials in the *barrios* of Bogotá, to set up new crim-inal organisations in the slums of the major cities, where they have quickly established large networks to traffic narcotics.

Gringos

Like the FARC, like corrupt elements in the military, like the narco-trafficking bosses, the paramilitaries in Colombia seem unwilling and unlikely to atone for their devastating impact on society. The country registered a dip in the number of cocaine-war-related deaths in the two years after 2002, but, at the beginning of 2005, they started creeping up again. Since the advent of Plan Colombia, the number of acres of land under the cultivation of coca was down by several thousand. But thanks to improved techniques, the yield was up year-on-year. Having started Plan Colombia operating in just six provinces, the FARC finished the four-year period with active units in all but two. The evidence since the early 1970s is overwhelming: the combined policies of the United States and Colombian governments are failing in what they set out to do – they neither erode the power of the FARC, nor do they stop super-saturation of America and Europe with cocaine.

Since 9/11, the War on Terror has been the overriding priority of American foreign policy. The War on Drugs, by nurturing a huge and unmanageable criminal swamp in which all manner of undesirables roam freely, almost guarantees that the War on Terror can never be won. Those involved in the War on Drugs develop an extraordinary zeal and determination to prosecute it, whatever the cost. I was shocked when the UN's Sandro Calvani, a biologist by background, confessed that 'If somebody should tell me that they have found a new Agent Orange gas that kills all coca, but damages the environment very heavily, I would consider it.'

The War on Drugs not only turns biologists into advocates of toxic defoliation programmes, but over the decades it has also absorbed trillions of dollars – not just in the obscene profits it generates for the cartels in Colombia and Mexico or the Taliban and the warlords in Afghanistan, but in the incalculable sums spent on offenders around the world. These offenders are usually from underprivileged classes (and in the United States that means that more than 80 per cent are drawn from the black or Hispanic minorities). But they languish in jail in the prime of their productive capacity just when the Western economies are suffering a severe long-term shortage of labour.

If the consumption of narcotics in the Western world (the originator and prosecutor of the global model) had dropped by an appreciable amount (after almost half a century), then the supporters of the War on Drugs would have a credible argument for staying the course with this policy. But consumption has gone up and up and up.

Production has kept pace, and the price has gone down and down and down. If, however, the aim is to nurture the gangs, the hoodlums, the terrorists, the insurgents and the drug billionaires who can corrupt entire countries, then we must carry on regardless.

Ironically, it is Signor Calvani who offers Colombia a chink of hope for the future. Not because of anything concocted by the UN, the US, the Colombian Government, the FARC or anyone else, but because of the shifting drug culture.

> Cocaine has no future. Wherever amphetamines and synthetic drugs have arrived on to the market, like China, South-East Asia, Mexico, then there is always a big boom and it replaces everything, cocaine, heroin, the lot. It is a pill that looks like an aspirin and is much more user-friendly, it works fast and doesn't involve the paraphernalia of injecting or sniffing, a much better kind of drug – more dangerous, but it works. Here it has already started in Medellín. So the future is in the new drugs. The market will change and determine this. They don't need the narco-traffickers. The future will be completely different.

If it rescues Colombia from purgatory, then there are real benefits to this future.

CODE ORANGE

As I hand over my laptop to SuperGeek in an anonymous hotel room in downtown São Paulo, I ask him with as much authority as I can muster whether he wishes to use Internet Explorer or Mozilla Firefox. A polite smile is accompanied by a tone usually reserved for those with extreme learning difficulties.

'I'LL BE USING SOMETHING CALLED C-Y-B-E-R-S-C-R-I-P-T.'

And then.

'IT'S LIKE . . . mIRC.'

You may well ask . . .

I now know that CyberScript enables you to enter IRC (Internet Relay Chat). For some people, this system is as mundane as corn-flakes, but for cyber toddlers like me, IRC is an unknown, unexplored parallel world – a silent cacophony of virtual chatter inhabited by hackers, crackers, geeks, terrorists and security agents (among others). They communicate in languages which are recognisable on the page, as it were – English, Portuguese, Russian or Spanish perhaps. But syntax and vocabulary render the contents of these exchanges unrecognisable. Every step of the way, SuperGeek has to explain a term or an idiom, and still I must strain to get my head round the new concept.

SuperGeek – fresh out of nappies to my aged eyes – is everything you might imagine. His fingers on the keyboard mirror the virtuosity of the concert pianist, whereby hands, arms and mind meld together, enabling human and instrument to act as one. It is only minutes before others are attracted by his siren skills.

At my request, SuperGeek has sent a message over mIRC seeking a *laranja* or 'orange'. For reasons that neither the crackers nor the police are able to explain, an 'orange' is a go-between, a medium who can put living people in touch with their alter egos in the cyber world. More parochially, the orange's job is to turn stolen virtual money into hard cash. As such, these characters are pivotal figures in the world of cyber crime. A successful orange should move effortlessly in the esoteric world of the hacker while demonstrating the old-fashioned ability to bully, bribe, bamboozle or blackmail bankers and retailers into accepting ill-gotten credit-card and bank-account funds.

And we don't have to wait long before an experienced orange with the unusually simple handle of 'Bob' is offering his services. 'Portuguese isn't his mother tongue,' SuperGeek notes. 'Could be Spanish, could be English,' he adds. 'Could he be a copper?' I ask. 'Could be,' warns my friend. 'You never know.'

We explain to Bob that we have siphoned several thousand reals from a Banco do Brasil account and we need it in cash. 'No problem,' messages Bob. 'I can deposit it for you in a bank account. Or you can have it by DHL inside some magazines. Or I can transfer it abroad and you can retrieve it as remittances.'

Bob further tells us that he has contacts inside a couple of branches of Banco Bradesco (one of Brazil's biggest) and they can disguise any incoming transfers from credit cards or other accounts, no questions asked. He charges 50 per cent for the service, but will undertake the first transaction for free as a gesture of goodwill.

On this occasion, our several thousand reals from Banco do Brasil are not virtual, but imaginary. But they needn't have been. SuperGeek knows very well how you go about extracting millions upon millions of dollars from ordinary bank accounts because he was an intimate witness to one of the biggest heists in the short but lucrative history of Brazilian cyber crime, which culminated in a huge police sweep dubbed Operation Pegasus.

In late August 2005, a young man answered the doorbell to a small flat in São Paulo. Standing in front of him was the postman. 'I have a book to deliver for Max,' he said. The young man hesitated – this was not the same postman who had delivered letters to his address for years.

'There's nobody called Max living here,' he lied, thinking on his feet. 'You must have the wrong address.'

'But I have a parcel for him. It's very urgent.'

As Max closed the door, the postman tried one more time.

'It's from The Apprentice,' he called in vain.

'If I'd have accepted that parcel, I would have been arrested,' Max said later. On that day and the next, 114 people were arrested in seven different provinces of Brazil and in the capital Brasilia. All were taken for questioning on suspicion of involvement in the theft of around $33 million from bank accounts in Brazil, Venezuela, the United Kingdom and the United States. The investigation by the newly formed Federal Division of Cyber Crime police had been running for several months, having evolved out of two earlier cases – Operation Cash Net and Operation Trojan Horse.

Back in the São Paulo hotel, SuperGeek recalled the events that led up to the arrests. 'It all started when I was chatting with a few friends online about tech stuff,' SuperGeek recalled. His two closest cyber pals in the IRC chat room were young Brazilians, KG and Max, with whom he would exchange all manner of information about computers, but also about games and music. They were teenagers having fun.

'Every so often, this stranger called The Apprentice would enter the chat room and ask the same question, "Does anyone have any shells?" At first, SuperGeek, KG and Max told The Apprentice to get lost. They were a touch mystified as to why anybody would persist in trying to collect shells – programmes that enable people to interact with operating systems (the building blocks of most computers).

But The Apprentice was persistent, returning each time with the same question. 'Does anyone have any shells?' Finally, KG decided to investigate and agreed to enter into a private chat with The Apprentice.

For a month or so, KG disappeared. Max and SuperGeek attempted to contact him over Microsoft Messenger or IRC, but in vain. This is common in a culture that prizes anonymity above all else. Like most such online relationships, the friendship between the three cyber pals was fragmented and based on a minimal, yet intense, intimacy. They did not know where each other lived; what their socio-economic backgrounds were; or what they looked like. When somebody just disappears off the screen with no apparent explanation, you can't drop in on them at home to find out what's going on. And it is axiomatic that any virtual partner may be lying. Calibrating trust on the Internet

is even more difficult than in the real world. This uncertainty is both
the sword of Ajax and the Achilles heel of cyber criminals.

A month after vanishing, KG returned to the chat room with a
virtual swagger. 'The Apprentice and I have been working on something real big,' he told his two friends. 'And very worthwhile.' Despite
their irritation at both his disappearing act and his sudden reappear-
ance, Max and SuperGeek were curious to hear KG's story.

The shells that The Apprentice so prized, KG explained, were needed
to send emails. Lots of them – 50,000 in each batch. In order to stop
email servers from recognising these emails as spam, it is necessary
to hijack the shells from other people's computers so that the email
server cannot tell that the same source is generating them all.

KG revealed that The Apprentice would pay him $50 for every
1,000,000 emails he dispatched to unsuspecting PC users. That
amounted to a few evenings' work and, for a young unemployed
Brazilian like KG, this wage was a small fortune. KG now wanted Max
and SuperGeek to join in.

To speed up their work, they developed their own computer program
called GetMail, which was able to scan particular countries and servers
and download millions of email addresses. They then wrote a second
program called Remover, which cancelled any duplicate addresses. And,
finally, using the shells they had collected beachcombing the Internet,
they put together the lists of 50,000 emails a shot.

KG had already been doing this work for a month and evidently he
had performed his tasks well. In consequence, The Apprentice had
promoted him to the position of recruiter (cutting out the arduous
task of spam-list building), for which he earned a basic wage of $1,500
per month plus commission. So KG was on the second rung of a hierarchy that is almost impossible to map – learning from insurgency
and terrorist networks in particular, cyber criminals operate in cell
form and so each player only interacts with two or three colleagues.
The rest of the conspiracy is as obscure to them as it was initially to
the police.

Although only 14 per cent of Brazil's 188 million people are regular
Internet users (or *internauts* as they are known in Brazil), almost three-
quarters of these carry out the bulk of their financial transactions
online, which – along with South Korea – is thought to be the highest

ratio of users of Internet banking in the world; 90 per cent file their Internal Revenue returns online as well. Compared to the United States and Western Europe, Brazilian banks offer much wider services, with correspondingly more sophisticated security arrangements. For some years, bank customers in Brazil have enjoyed real-time transfer of money throughout the system. Clients have to overcome up to five different security hurdles in order to access their accounts. They have become used, for example, to onscreen keyboards activated by mouse clicks to circumvent Trojan spyware that monitors the strikes of physical keyboards. The banks were also the pioneers of dynamic fobs on which users receive constantly changing passwords. 'When you arrive in America from Brazil,' chuckles Rogeriot Morais, head of the Brazil operation of the global cyber security firm, ISS, 'and you see them still fiddling around with cheques, it looks very quaint.'

For the customer, Internet banking is seductively convenient. For the banks, it is a monumental money-saver as their labour costs have plummeted. For the light-fingered, it is an irresistible source of revenue. And for law enforcement, it presents a taxing challenge. Essentially, the Net cannot be policed without massive assistance from the private sector – even then, as a member of the Cyber Crime Unit in Brasilia remarked, 'We are always running behind these people. They get round new security blocks within hours of their insertion into a network.'

The Apprentice and his regiment of Pegasus spammers sent out a variety of emails to the addresses they had culled, containing one of two types of messages. The first, for domestic consumption, purported to come from one of the big Brazilian banks or from the Inland Revenue. These were simple 'phishing' emails, requesting that the customer fill in his or her details and return the email. The details, of course, would go to the scammers, who would then roam around the 'phished' bank accounts at will.

Still more insidious is the type designed for international consumption. Emails carrying messages like 'Someone loves you! Find out who!' encouraged the recipient to click on a hyperlink to a website. 'As soon as that screen came up, you had a key logger on your computer,' said SuperGeek. 'You were finished.'

A key logger monitors every stroke of your keyboard and sends back the information to whoever placed it there. Using that information, the cyber criminal is then in a position to extract your passwords, to enter your bank account and to clean it of funds. SuperGeek tells me that each batch of about 50,000 emails would guarantee The Apprentice about 200 infections – that is, 200 computers that the criminals could effectively control. Although representing a mere 0.4 per cent of the emails sent, this take-up allows the theft of phenomenal sums and explains the attractiveness of cyber crime. According to the Federal Police, The Apprentice and his dozens of co-conspirators got away with $33 million before Operation Pegasus put an end to it. The scam had only been running a few months and an even larger conspiracy from the previous year, 2004, had netted the criminals $125 million.

The era of the malicious virus that chewed up computer screens, destroyed your hard disk or directed you to vile pornographic websites is fast coming to a close. These attacks were the work of so-called 'ego-hackers'. They were designed to make the computer users' life a misery, as projects that had taken months or years were destroyed for the sake of an adolescent giggle. Now viruses, Trojan horses, worms and other malware go largely unnoticed. The sun has set on the age of the ego-hacker and the dawn is rising on the era of the criminal hacker or cracker. In 2003, '90 per cent of attacks were still the work of ego-hackers,' reported Peter Allor, the head of X-Force, the intelligence division of ISS, one of the world's biggest Internet security companies. 'Now that is reversed – 90 per cent of attacks are criminal and there-fore much more difficult to detect. They want to disguise the fact that they are out there. So when the Zotob virus provoked the crash of CNN's system in 2005,' he continued, 'we knew that the virus's designers had made a mistake – they had failed to update their virus to take account of a Microsoft update. That's a good thing – the criminals make mistakes too.' But not often enough.

With stealth becoming a guiding principle of malware, the ordinary computer user has become even more vulnerable than before. 'The only safe computer is one that is switched off,' I am assured by Kau, a Brazilian of Lithuanian parentage who specialises in testing computer security. 'Maybe you can check what's on at the local movies on the Internet, but any more than that and it is only a matter of time before you are infected, even if you are assiduous at keeping your anti-virus updated.' Standing proud next to Kau is a pack of sour-cream-'n'-onion-flavoured Pringles.

When he pops open the plastic top, instead of those annoyingly moreish crisps, he pulls out a copper wire with a series of silver disks placed at regular intervals. 'If we attach Mr Pringle to the laptop,' demonstrates Kau, 'then we immediately have a live directional antenna that can home in on any local wireless system.' For his research work, he has already hacked into the systems of several major companies in the centre of São Paulo (he is *not* a criminal). If that's what you can do with a tube of crisps and a bit of metal, just imagine what is possible with some really fancy gear!

But interestingly, it is not technology that inflicts the greatest damage in the cyber world. 'You tell me that the only safe computer is the one that is turned off,' retorts Marcos Flavio Assunção, a demi-god among the white hats (non-criminal good hackers) of Belo Horizonte. 'But what if I can persuade somebody to turn that computer on? Not so safe after all!' he beams. Marcos is explaining to me about what the cyber criminal and security worlds refer to as 'social engineering' – that is, the ability to influence people's actions. The most popular method of invading computers is through downloads and websites that many users find irresistible – music and pornography.

And here, dear reader (especially the men amongst you), is an important lesson: if you indulge in either of those two habits, stop it now if you value your privacy. Lesson 2 of Glenny's cyber gospel concerns emails: if you are not convinced both by the sender and the subject of an email (the computers of your closest friends can be invaded and transformed into part of a 'botnet' – that is, sending out illicit emails at the will of the criminal), then don't open it – just delete it. Among the most successful email-born viruses of all time was the I Love You virus, an assertion that brings out the irrational in even the most urbane among us. I was extremely fortunate as the first person to send me this email was an ex-girlfriend who nursed all sorts of feelings about me, but love was decidedly not among them. I deleted the email without further ado and spared myself a nasty infection.

It is not just your bank account that is at risk, your entire 'identity' can be seized, whereby somebody else rifles not just through your credit cards and bank accounts, but your social security number, your passport, and so on, to the point where if they commit a crime, a warrant may be put out for your arrest. 'In 2005, global losses attributable to identity theft stood at $52.6 billion,' Peter Allor of ISS told me. But, as he explained, although the spectacular identity thefts make the headlines, they are sometimes inadvertent. If you have a big 'data breach', as he terms it, 'then you get the Secret Service and the Feds on your back'. Much cyber-criminal activity is aimed at filching small amounts of money from large amounts of people. 'If I can get one credit card from you and I do a 25-buck transaction, will you notice? Will you report it? Will they do anything with it? $25 – no police force in the world is going to chase $25.' But if you take $25 from a million people, you will become rich.

Allor believes that a Manichaean, even apocalyptic, struggle drives his industry of cyber security. 'This is an arms race. I call it a sword-and-shield issue. In the underworld, they have an ever sharper sword – the malcoders – and you have to research it all to have a shield that can cover every thrust of that sword. If you can determine that something is not working properly, a vulnerability in your system, then you know you've got a big problem because if you've found it, you can bet the underworld will know about it soon – if they don't already. It now takes the underworld about forty-eight hours to sniff out a vulnerability. How long does it take a corporation to be made aware of that and find an update? The fast ones are about thirty days. The majority are running thirty to sixty days. And the home user? Are they even aware?'

ISS's Cyber Control Center in Atlanta, Georgia, is so reminiscent of the Bridge on the USS *Enterprise* from *Star Trek* that I almost expect a Klingon commander to appear on one of the vast screens that dominate the end of the room, and issue a sinister threat. In fact, the screens are reporting all manner of security alerts, attempted attacks and a frenetic blizzard of data, which means nothing to me. The nearest we get to a Klingon is the giant image of a CNN anchor, as ISS has a constant news feed in case a relevant story crops up. In front of this spectacular control panel sit maybe a dozen computer operators with the appropriate sprinkling of spotty adolescents, ponytails and Asian Americans who are silently warding off attempted attacks on ISS's corporate clients around the world by spotting and then shoring up vulnerabilities in their computer systems.

ISS is one of the leaders in the multi-billion-dollar Internet security industry that has flourished in the wake of the viruses and Trojans.

The company helped to reformulate the entire concept of computer protection – instead of going after specific viruses and spyware (which is how programs like Norton Anti-Virus function), they started examining the defence capability of individual programs or systems. In fact, they ape the hackers and crackers by sniffing out vulnerabilities in anything from Windows to entire banking networks. And X-Force is the virtual equivalent of the CIA, trying to penetrate the mindset and logic of the enemy. At times, Peter Allor's explanations of what X-Force actually does sound as mind-bending as the most impenetrable passages from Stephen Hawking's *A Brief History of Time*. 'You're familiar with Darknet, right?' he asks me. I shuffle and cough a little, not wanting to appear stupid.

'Errm . . . not terribly familiar, no . . .'

'Okay. Darknet is a set of IPs [Internet Protocols, for the uninitiated] that have never been addressed – they were never assigned anywhere . . . they're dark, so nothing should ever come out of them and nothing should ever be addressed to them. Well, we run a darknet and we have a nice set of contiguous IPs there, and so we see a lot of back scatter from across the Internet which is scanning and it shouldn't be there. So we take the information from grey nets and honey nets, which are waiting for things to come out, and we also crawl the Internet. Are you familiar with drive-by browsing?'

You know what? I think to myself, I'll save drive-by browsing for another day.

Obscure though their work might be, X-Force, ISS and similar organisations form an absolutely critical barrier, preventing the world from being swamped by viral infections, Trojans and spyware. But the shift from ego-hacking to cyber crime contains huge dangers.

Computer technology is advancing into every sphere of Western homes and businesses. No longer restricted to obvious gadgets like printers, scanners and ATMs, it is being built into telephones, televisions, cars, washing machines, vending machines, and more. 'If you find yourself in a hotel where hackers are holding a conference, stay clear of the elevators,' warns Allor, smiling. 'You'll never make it to the right floor – believe me it's happened.' There is nothing that a mischievous hacker enjoys more than telling a lift to go to the seventeenth floor when someone presses on the 33rd-floor button. Each of these peripherals (the gadgets hooked up to the central computer) has an IP address – that is, it has a separate cyber identity, which is then linked to other machines with IP addresses through a network. In a medium-size business, there will be hundreds of these units – and each of them is a separate portal through which an attack can take place.

Already businesses store data of incalculable value on their systems, but soon most people will be using Voice over Internet Protocol telephone systems for the bulk of their verbal communications. VoIP networks like Skype are increasingly attractive for offices as they reduce costs so dramatically. But what would happen if your business depended on telephone sales and somebody inserted a virus into the system to block the phones?

'Today anti-virus programmes are becoming ever less important because they can't protect you,' Amrit Williams pointed out. The thoughtful chief of security analysis at America's leading tech consultant, Gartner, Williams is concerned about the potential for destruction now that organised crime has lured the hackers away from mischief and into the underworld. 'Virus companies can only detect things that have signatures. Now cyber criminals are writing specific malware designed to attack a single company – be it Morgan Stanley, be it Visa or be it the BBC,' Williams continued. 'We recently came across a worrisome case where the Russian mafia was producing perfect copies of Windows with the plastic wrapping and everything. They looked perfect – but of course they had the spyware already loaded on them.' As Williams pointed out, it is not difficult for organised crime to insert such software onto the licit market as syndicates are especially practised at controlling distribution and retail markets.

It is not a coincidence that Russia and Brazil are world-beaters in electronic crime. Along with China, they form the top tier. The only country missing is India.

> With loads of money, the world is your oyster, you can do whatever you want whenever you want, all women are the same to a man with money, and the next day will dawn even better. The thing to do was to buy heaps of coke and go round chopping out lines for his friends . . . buy a flat in Copacabana, screw doctors' daughters, have a phone and TV and hop over

to the States from time to time like his aunt's employer. One
day he'd hit the jackpot.

Paulo Lins, *City of God*

It was soon after the millennium that Brazil started creeping onto the
radar of cyber security firms. With Russia and China, it now forms
part of a mighty triumvirate of the virtual underworld. It has earned
its place there for several reasons. Even if this, a curious confluence
of social and economic factors, were to change in the near future,
Brazil would remain a key centre of cyber crime simply because the
profit levels are astronomical. No other sector of organised crime can
match the growth rates of cyber crime, which are currently running
in the region of 25 per cent annually. Furthermore, the industry is
multifaceted, accommodating old and new crimes. Policing it is a
nightmare, even though in its mass form it is still extremely young.

In the legitimate world of computer technology, particular branches
'cluster' in certain geographical regions. Scandinavia has long been at
the forefront of cell- or mobile-phone technology, for example, while
California, Toulouse and Munich are leading bio-technology centres.
A variety of circumstances may contribute to the emergence of such
clusters – proximity to cutting-edge research institutes; tax-incentive
schemes and other government policies, local and national; significant
financial and lifestyle benefits for employees; and even serendipity.

*Snapshot of email 'harvesting' centres and spam targets, October 2006. São Paulo,
Beijing and Moscow are the chief farmers, Western Europe and the US the main
targets. South Korea and Bangalore (India's main techno-cluster) are also important.*

The clustering of cyber crime is the result of an equally complex mix. There are several prerequisites, but three are paramount: steep levels of poverty and unemployment; a high standard of basic education for a majority of the population; and a strong presence of more traditional organised-crime forms. Nobody fits the bill better than the so-called BRIC nations – Brazil, Russia, India and China. These are the leading countries among the emerging markets, the second tier of global power after the G8 (though politically Russia straddles the two). South Africa is regarded as a reserve player in the BRIC grouping, because although a regional giant like the others, it cannot compete economically. It also fails as a cyber-crime centre because its standards of education have yet to recover from the damage inflicted by apartheid.

Brazil, by contrast, fits the bill almost perfectly. Even in the *favelas*, various government and NGO schemes are steadily improving access to computers and the Internet. With social disparities and tensions akin to those in South Africa and Colombia, Brazil is well known for its high level of crime. Foreigners are warned to keep wallets well guarded and are told not to resist when confronted with a knife- or gun-wielding assailant. The *favelas* of Rio and other major cities mix extreme poverty with drugs, guns and violence – sometimes less than a mile from the most fabulous dwellings overlooking the beaches of Ipanema or Copacabana. It is this profound division that lies at the heart of Brazil's hugely powerful criminal culture, described with such biting accuracy by Paulo Lins. In his novel *City of God*, he details life in the eponymous grim estate in western Rio which in the 1960s drew its inhabitants, including Lins, from the inner city of South America's funkiest city with the false promise of improved living standards. Fernando Meirelles's Oscar-winning film of the same name freezes the blood with its evocation of violence and despair fuelled by the *favela*'s tribal rivalries and drug trade.

Rio's *favelas* produce some of the finest documentary films in the world, a testimony to the openness of the culture. This was the only country I encountered where not a single person asked me to turn off my tape-recorder when I spoke to them. Brazilians are fanatical communicators (witness the huge success of *orkut*, an equivalent of myspace.com in Brazil), and so it is easy to learn a great deal about the country (the dark and light sides) in a short space of time, especially in Rio.

But in the past decade, São Paulo has eclipsed Rio, becoming the great epicentre both of Brazil's crazed spurt of economic growth and the uncontrollable rise of its organised crime. Flying into São Paulo from the Atlantic towards its airport lying in the west is an unbelievable experience. No longer a city, but a megalopolis of twenty million people, from above it looks like an entire civilisation built from Lego and stretching beyond the horizon. But it is not like Chicago, Jo'burg or even London where huge skyscrapers gather tightly in a centre surrounded by sprawl. The skyscrapers appear on the outskirts and never stop, the *favelas* almost having to fight for their place in between them.

The economic force pulls in migrants not just from Brazil's poverty-stricken north-east and west-centre, but from all over South America and beyond, pumping out goods and services with a frenetic energy that Rio's inhabitants, the *cariocas*, sneer at (just as São Paulo's *paulistas* sneer at the *cariocas* for believing that the main aim of life is the pursuit of pleasure).

Despite the dire warnings regarding street crime, the centre of São Paulo, serviced by an excellent metro system, feels as secure and as modern as the centre of Madrid. It certainly doesn't feel like Crime Central.

But surrounding this urban vortex lies a network of prisons that are among the most overcrowded in the world. The conditions for the prisoners are atrocious and there exists a permanent state of low-level warfare among inmates, and between inmates and the warders. Two days after I had set foot in South America for the first time in May 2006, these prisons exploded in violence – right on cue. The uprising of the *Primeiro Comando da Capital* (PCC, the First Capital Command) was shocking in the bitterness of the violence it spawned.

Founded in 1993 by a hulk called Geleaio (Big Jelly), the PCC is one of the largest, most unpredictable and most dangerous organised-crime syndicates in the world. It can mobilise many thousands of members, who are recruited while stagnating in Brazil's crumbling jail system. The money available to the leading prisoners enables them to corrupt and subvert the warders, allowing them all manner of privileges, most critically mobile phones, which prison officers will permit inside the jail for a consideration of $300.

Its pampered, violent leaders can direct the tentacles of the PCC deep into the *favelas*, transforming the slums into training grounds for deadly drug warriors. In contrast to other major organised-crime groups around the world, the PCC does not seek to expand abroad, nor does it assiduously avoid law enforcement and detection. Instead, it occasionally and viciously confronts it. Its most determined and sustained attempt began in mid-May 2006.

At first, the *paulistas* appeared to dismiss the May events as an insignificant eruption of lumpen aggression. But on the first night of the unrest, the PCC demonstrated how powerful it had become in thirteen years of existence. Members tore through the streets of São Paulo slaughtering policemen and their civilian relations. Patrol cars, off-duty coppers sitting down to dinner, senior officers having a drink in a bar – all were targeted. Clearly, the PCC possessed significant intelligence, which they deployed ruthlessly as they ranged around the city on bloody parade, wielding machetes, machine guns and hammers. They set fire to dozens of buses and cars and threw up roadblocks. The marauding criminals moved around many areas, rich and poor, delivering an especial fright to the former, which are not used to the quotidian violence experienced by the latter.

The following day saw the zinging megalopolis stilled as the industrious population cowered inside its homes. Workers were too frightened to risk travelling on the city's vulnerable public-transport network.

Soon spokesmen for the PCC started cropping up regularly in the media, couching their reasons for rebellion within the cliché-ridden language of universal human rights, saying that they needed to draw attention to their plight. Their pleas were rather undermined by the brutality of their methods and, over the next few days, the many public prosecutors and detectives whom I met all said the same thing: 'This is a challenge to the police – they want to show us how powerful they are and that we must negotiate with them at all times.' Elizeu Eclair Teixeira Borges, the state Military Police commander, was more forthright at a news conference. 'This is war and we are not going to retreat. There will be more death,' he said.

What he did not say was that it was the police's turn to do the killing. After the initial mayhem resulted in almost 100 deaths, the police responded in the next two months by killing almost five times as many – and just as the prisoners were not too choosy about who they wasted, nor were the coppers. It almost began to look as though the 'Kumbaya' human-rights rhetoric that the PCC spokesmen had been using might not be so spurious after all.

Latent mob violence in Brazil lies nearer the surface than in its counterparts in Europe and Asia. This degree of paramilitary organisation among criminals, with the will and ability to confront the authorities, would be unthinkable in Moscow or Beijing.

My guide to the peculiarities of Brazil's extensive criminal landscape could not have been better informed. A judge and former chief of the National Drug Office in Brasilia, Walter Maierovitch is the most respected voice on organised crime in Brazil. In clipped, detail-laden sentences, he outlined to me the various factors that in his opinion have allowed the country to become the great centre of trans-national criminal operations, in particular linking the markets and production regions of southern Europe, West Africa and North and South America. He regarded the events of May 2006 as nothing less than a declaration 'of war on the State of São Paulo . . . Like fundamentalist terrorist organisations and the mafia, the PCC uses attacks and then goes into hiding, lulling authorities into a false sense of security.' The origins of the crisis lie in what Maierovitch calls the 'inhuman conditions' that pertain in Brazil's prisons, but he is nonetheless perturbed at the state's inability to counter the cancerous growth of the PCC.

The political response to the challenge of the PCC in May 2006 highlights a profound weakness in Brazil's system, which helps to explain why the country became a refuge for trans-national crime organisations during the 1990s. As soon as the PCC took to the streets, the government of President Lula offered to send in the army to quell the troops. The Governor of São Paulo province, who was from the opposition, rejected the offer as a provocation, saying that forces under his control were perfectly capable of dealing with the issue. It was hard to avoid the impression that both the federal and provincial governments were more interested in scoring political points than in dealing with the crisis.

As Walter Maierovitch pointed out to me, Brazil also suffers acutely from a problem that often dogs federal systems – duelling policemen. The animosity and jealousies that inform relations between the State

Police, the Federal Police, the Military Police (which have civilian jurisdiction) and the Special Forces are crippling. 'In the US, you have
regular difficulties between federal agencies like the DEA, the CIA and
the FBI,' Maierovitch explained, 'but at least it demonstrates that they
talk to each other on some level. With our federal system in Brazil,
there is no conflict because the provincial and the federal agencies
have no contact whatsoever with one another. And they certainly don't
do anything radical like share information,' he added with an ironic
shrug.

He ascribes the growth of the PCC and their equivalents, like the
Red Command in Rio, in the first instance to the profits they have
made from the drug trade. It was Maierovitch's job to sniff out drug
trafficking by the huge multi-syndicates that made Brazil their home
base in the 1980s and 1990s. Nonetheless, he insists that 'the War on
Drugs is a farce . . . And it looks as though Lula, our President, will
continue to bend to America's prohibitionist policy. However, there
are signs that Europe is continuing to distance itself from the UN
Conventions, which follow the American line. As the market leader,
the US's strategy of consumer reduction is a dead end.'

While the Colombians sent most of their cocaine to the US through
Mexico and the Caribbean, the supplies for Europe (via West and, later,
South Africa) were processed through Brazil. The presence of Latin
America's largest chemical industry in Brazil encouraged this growth,
as Brazilian narcotics traffickers did not have to import precursor
chemicals to turn the paste into powder (unlike their counterparts in
Colombia, Peru and Bolivia). But Maierovitch says they have been
greatly helped by the specific weaknesses of the Brazilian system of
policing and the profound levels of corruption met throughout the
judicial and political system.

Softly spoken with owlish features, Maierovitch first came to prom-
inence in the early 1980s when he assisted Giovanni Falcone in his
successful efforts to track down mafia fugitives from Italian justice.
Together the two men persuaded Tommaso Buscetta to return to Italy
and become a state witness in the so-called maxi-trial of the Sicilian
mafia's *cupola*, its secretive board of directors. This evidence eventually led to the conviction of some 350 senior mafia operatives in January
1992.

Falcone and his fellow magistrate, Paolo Borsellino, are the titans of anti-mafia law enforcers the world over. Murdered in Sicily within two months of each other, soon after the maxi-trial sentence had been confirmed in 1992, their deaths shook and finally toppled the old political establishment in Italy. Both men had worked on the assumption (quite correctly) that the major figures of the Sicilian mafia enjoyed protection among the highest political echelons of Rome.

Maierovitch reminisced about his dinners with Falcone and how they sought to protect the great *pentito* (informer) Buscetta from either assassination or suicide. (He very nearly succeeded in killing himself on the Brazilian judge's watch.) At first Maierovitch smiles when describing his late Italian friend, but before long he starts shedding quiet tears – a fitting tribute to Falcone (after whom Maierovitch named his Institute on Organised Crime), whose charisma and commitment to justice in the face of resistance from Rome's corrupt elite have made him a folk hero throughout Italy and among crime-fighters everywhere.

The Buscetta case was possibly the greatest success of Brazilian law enforcement in history. His extradition triggered a chain of events culminating in the maxi-trial and the murders of Borsellino and Falcone. The crimes of the mafia and the two deaths led to a popular revulsion with the Sicilian mafia, which has ensured that it has been in full retreat ever since. (Unfortunately the same doesn't apply to their cousins in crime, the 'ndrangheta, the Camorra and the Sacra Corona Unita). But while Maierovitch helped to inflict a devastating blow on the mafia inside Italy, Buscetta's arrest had little impact on the trans-national activity of the mafia's overseas diaspora, not least in Brazil. Along with Montreal, Rio and São Paulo had become home to the mightiest export and money-laundering syndicate in the world, devised and run by two families, closely related through marriage, the Cuntrera–Cuarana clans, known collectively as the Rothschilds of the mafia.

Ironically, the two families had fled from Sicily in the early 1960s to escape a fratricidal mafia war. In the military dictatorship of Brazil they found the perfect environment to set up in business. But their masterstroke involved moving into Aruba, the semi-independent Dutch colonial possession off the coast of Venezuela, during the 1980s. Aruba became renowned as the mafia's very own island. 'A magnificent washing-machine is sold here, its trademark is Aruba,' a despairing minister of Aruba's government warned in parliament. 'The machine is an Aruban–Colombian product, its model called Cartel. The brand is well known for its good performance in the United States and Europe. It is recommended by former ministers, members of parliament, owners of casinos, supermarkets, cosmetics manufacturers and importers of cars and batteries. The washing-machine fits everybody who has become inexplicably rich from one day to another.'

It was here, through the good offices of the Cuntrera–Cuarana families, that the Medellín and Cali cartels opened negotiations about the global expansion of cocaine with Solntsevo representatives from Moscow; with Bulgarian traffickers; and, of course, with countless Caribbean and Central American traffickers.

Some senior family members were arrested in Canada, others in Venezuela, resulting in deportations to Italy. But the grand old octogenarian, founder of the whole scheme, still lives unmolested a stone's throw from Copacabana beach in Rio.

It is an epic tale that Maierovitch tells. And implicit at every stage of his narrative lies the struggle between Brazil's astonishing exuberance and dynamism and its befouled institutions; a tale of a country whose people are deeply proud of their achievements and viscerally angry about the injustice and corruption encountered daily. Never underestimate, for example, the social cohesion that Brazil's status as the world's most gifted soccer nation confers on them. For many years, this was an important compensation for having to live in the shadow of Argentina. Brazil has now eclipsed its southern neighbour as the decisive economy in Latin America. But for all its growing wealth, the great heart of its economy, São Paulo, can be brought to its knees in a matter of hours by one of the most powerful and unaccountable criminal networks in the world. Dealing with the PCC and its associates would probably be more than a match for most police forces (even ones that were properly organised). In São Paulo, Rio and elsewhere in Brazil, the police and prosecutors I talked to were committed, smart and very hard-working. But deeply ingrained traditions of hierarchy and authoritarianism restrict their capacity to act. There are signs that this may be beginning to change, but when it comes to policing the trans-national threats that coalesce in and around its borders, the Brazilian police simply do not have the resources to manage. As

Maierovitch is detailing the permanent sense of crisis among Brazil's police and judiciary, he talks of crime in Brazil as a hydra – cut off one head and another two appear. I ask him for an example. He is quiet for a moment and then says just three words. 'Lao Kin Chong.'

Commander Protógenes Queiroz was going to take no chances this time. In late May, he flew his special unit into São Paulo incognito. The Director General of the Federal Police (FP) in Brasilia had chosen Queiroz personally to carry out the climax of Operation Shogun – or Operation *Gatinho* (Kitten), as the FP team referred to it among themselves. The easiest way to blow months of careful planning was to give the police in São Paulo advance warning of the impending raids.

'The first five officers arrived early, part of the Federal Police Tactical Operations unit, which is a special force we have,' recalled the urbane, but determined police chief. 'Any incoming aircraft would have aroused the suspicions of the São Paulo police. So my officers had a cover story: one of them came in handcuffs so it looked like a straightforward prisoner transfer.' To make sure that the real purpose of the mission remained secret, Commander Queiroz was also monitoring the São Paulo force. 'The head of the airport called the police superintendent, informing him: "An aircraft from Brasilia is arriving, with federal police officers." How many are they? "Four, bringing a prisoner."' Success – the ruse had worked.

Earlier that year, a commercial agent from São Paulo approached a Senator who was heading up a Parliamentary Inquiry into Brazil's rampant culture of piracy. The agent explained that his associate, Lao Kin Chong, a naturalised Brazilian from China in his early forties, was interested in assisting the Senator in his efforts to address this troubling issue. This was not wholly surprising, as Lao's activities were at the centre of the Inquiry. And the assistance the agent was offering was not designed to clear up these circumstances – it was in fact a very large bribe. The Senator agreed to meet Lao, but he also informed the Federal Police.

The main street in the São Paulo district of Iphegenia reveals the extent to which counterfeit goods are available to the consumer. Outside the shops, young men stand in front of boards with CD-Rom covers pinned to them – there is not a computer programme in the world they do not sell (all of them pirated), and I am able to buy for $2 a copy of the forthcoming Windows Vista, long before it is available on the licit market. Delighted by my interest, the vendor starts chanting in Portuguese, 'Don't Be an American Slave, Be a Patriot and Buy Fake Goods!' This commercial anti-Americanism helps to sustain popular support for the trade in illicit goods in Brazil and, indeed, throughout South America. Apart from the police and lawyers involved in the struggle against piracy, not a single Brazilian to whom I spoke considered the trade immoral. Minutes after my purchase, the street vendors' efficient system of lookouts has signalled that two policemen are scouring the streets. Within seconds, the stalls are packed up and the salesmen have been soaked up by the viscous sea of shoppers trying to crowd into the malls. Inside you can buy any type of electronic goods imaginable: cameras, iPods, laptops, real Sonys, fake Samsung, all piled higgledy-piggledy on top of one another. 'My friend, my friend,' they shout, 'please buy, very cheap.' They specialise in the generic fakes: a Microsoft keyboard that is in fact proudly produced by Krown Electronics; or a flat-screen TV by Semsin. But they all share one characteristic – Made in China.

Ismael, a seller of Lebanese descent (of whom there are many in South America), explains that they come in through three entry points: through the Bolivian border into the central province of Matto Grosso; via the north-eastern port of Natal; and above all through the legendary Ciudad del Este, the Paraguayan gangster capital suspected by American intelligence as a centre of al-Qaeda activity. It sits next to Brazil and Argentina in the so-called tri-border region. 'The bulk of Lao's goods arrived in São Paulo through Ciudad,' explains Pedro Barbosa, the prosecutor for São Paulo state with responsibility for the Lao case. 'And there was a lot of it.' Working with the Paraguayan authorities has its challenges. 'You must remember that 60 per cent of Ciudad's annual income is derived from smuggling,' Barbosa continues. 'We have one reliable contact with whom we liaise, but generally Paraguay is not a reliable channel.'

Barbosa explained that there had been several attempts to arrest Lao in the past, but all of them failed – 'That's why Protógenes Queiroz didn't tell anybody what he was doing that morning.' Lao Kin Chong began building his enormous empire, based around his shopping malls on the Avenue of March 25, in the early 1990s. He would import anything into Brazil, paying minimal (if any) taxes and flagrantly ignoring any rules of international copyright. Most of the patents and rights to this intellectual property reside with Americans and American companies, and the US Government takes its role seriously, pressing Brazil and similar recalcitrant nations to do something about piracy. Days after Lao's arrest, Jack Valenti, CEO of America's Motion Picture Association, excoriated Brazil's record on piracy as 'abysmal'. Describing the end of Lao Kin Chong's activities as the 'one bright spot' to a Senate hearing in Washington, he also claimed that in Brazil 'One out of every three tapes or DVDs is pirate. Our member companies lose an estimated $120 million every year in Brazil to piracy . . . Even in those jurisdictions where police have conducted raids, less than 1 per cent of all raids result in convictions.'

Lao himself has always kept his council, denying any wrongdoing and restricting his comments to one sentence on his arrest: 'This is a bad joke.' But he could not get around the fact that his commercial agent had offered the senator $1.5 million. Nor could he deny the video-taped evidence of the agent turning up with the first $75,000 in cash as a down-payment for the Senator's help in influencing the appoint-ment of a new São Paulo police chief. Once Lao was remanded in custody on charges of bribery and obstructing the course of justice, the Federal Police had a free hand to investigate his entire business dealings. Several of his relatives, including his wife, were arrested, and before long new charges of piracy and smuggling were preferred against him, ensuring that he will remain in jail for a long time.

When he was sentenced in July 2005 for bribery, the Federal Police and Queiroz in particular rightly patted themselves on the back for the success of an arduous operation fraught with risks. Lao was the most powerful and successful criminal businessman ever arrested in Brazil. But within a few months of his initial incarceration, Roberto Porto, investigator at the Chinese Organised Crime Unit of the São Paulo police, noticed something happening. 'Most of the Chinese working in the markets of São Paulo are illegal immigrants. They are unprotected and the last thing on their mind is to go to the police – they think as soon as they do, they'll be deported,' he said. 'So Lao Kin Chong gave them protection.' In São Paulo's Chinese community,

Lao was the state and the police. 'When Lao was arrested two years ago,' Porto continued, 'everyone lost their protection.' And that is when things for the Chinese of São Paulo started to get nasty.

Porto's office noticed that two groups were vying for supremacy. 'There is the Cantonese triad, Sun Yet On, and their competitors are from Fujian province,' he revealed. Both use much more direct methods to consolidate their influence. 'Both appear to send teams from China as enforcers. They arrive through Ciudad, but only remain here for a few months.' During this time, these SWAT teams of organised crime will intimidate, threaten, assault and, if necessary, murder anyone who fails to pay protection or who tries to shop them. 'Then, having done their job, they return to China or, who knows, somewhere else. We simply don't have time or resources to keep track of them.' Porto describes what happened to one of his few informers who was watched by the extortionists – the details are too vile to reproduce here, but the informant did not survive the ordeal. 'We don't have any Chinese-speaking officers, only interpreting services,' he lamented.

As I look around his spartan office with its dowdy sofa, fraying carpets and peeling paint, the enormity of the problems facing law enforcement in a globalised world is all too obvious. Even if Brazil's police forces were rationally organised, this country cannot afford the facilities and equipment needed even to monitor with any accuracy what people and goods are entering and exiting via its borders. The rapacious desire to trade, to buy, to sell, to make money long overtook any capacity of either the developed or the developing world to regulate how one trades and how one might ensure similar ethical standards across the world. One may denounce corruption in the developing world and the developed world alike, but in an age when billionaires stalk a globe on which 50 per cent of its people live on less than $2 a day, can one really be surprised that customs officers, policemen, judges, politicians and bureaucrats are often tempted?

Roberto Porto faces an even bigger problem, as I learned when I asked him whether he is able to cooperate with the Chinese police. 'I have no authority to deal directly with the Chinese police,' he explains, 'so I can only talk to the consulate here in São Paulo.' 'And are the diplomats there helpful?' I wonder aloud. 'They help the criminals we are trying to arrest,' he adds in a dead-pan voice. 'We ask for help in dealing with a particular case and they promptly hire lawyers on behalf of the people we are investigating.'

Wherever one looks in the world, Chinese citizens are soaking up the slack in labour markets. On my travels I have noticed that their ability to undercut the wages and the capacity for work in the licit sectors is mirrored very precisely in the illicit world. I have also noticed that the Chinese state, which clearly encourages the global wanderings of its labour force, does not differentiate between these two sectors. Whether in the overworld or the underworld, Chinese influence is growing at a remarkable pace. Early on, I had concluded that the future of the global shadow economy will be decided by the direction that China's engagement with the outside world will take. It was now time to travel west from Brazil to the East: a place where a new era of organised crime is dawning, just as another is struggling with an extended mid-life crisis.

PART FOUR

THE FUTURE OF ORGANISED CRIME

THE OVERUNDERWORLD

Early one Wednesday morning in the warm September of 1994, 54-year-old Kazafumi Hatanaka opened the door to his apartment while still in his pyjamas. Very little is known about his visitor that morning, except that he was unusually tall. The Japanese police deduced this because the single shot that he fired entered the front right temple of Mr Hatanaka (who was himself above average height) at a downward angle. It then exited at the lower left back of the skull, pausing but for a nanosecond to cause a massive cerebral contusion. Because the bullet had gone right through the head, the police report recorded a huge amount of blood surrounding Hatanaka's corpse when a neighbour discovered it at 7.20 a.m.

There were no obvious leads. Investigators found no evidence of a struggle inside the apartment, which suggests that Hatanaka might perhaps have known his assassin. Notwithstanding the mess, it looked to be a professional job. But there were neither eyewitnesses nor, at first, any apparent motive for the killing.

Two months later, it seemed the police's luck had turned. They arrested Tadao Kondo, a man with so rich a criminal pedigree that he would have done time for jaywalking. Apparently seized by a fit of conscience, Kondo had given himself up and handed over a .38 mil pistol to investigators. Ballistics then confirmed that this was the very murder weapon sought in the Hatanaka case. Kondo, a 73-year-old serial extortionist and thief, described how Mr Hatanaka had surprised him as he was carrying out an opportunistic burglary.

The police's initial delight at the ballistics report and confession soon turned sour. 'An opportunistic burglary?' the chief investigator asked rhetorically. 'On the tenth floor?' Surely if he was breaking and entering an apartment, Kondo would have chosen the ground floor, precisely to avoid someone like Mr Hatanaka catching him *in flagrante*, and to ensure a quick getaway? Then there was Kondo's height – the position of the body indicated that Mr Hatanaka was standing when shot. But Kondo was ten centimetres *shorter* than his supposed victim, which meant that he could not have fired the bullet down into the skull unless standing on a chair. All agreed that this was a cumbersome way to commit either robbery or murder. As the police questioned the suspect more closely, they concluded that the only details he knew of the case could have been gleaned from newspaper reports. He had no idea of evidence which they had held back from the media, but which the killer must have known.

After some weeks, Kondo admitted to having lied about the murder. In a revised, rambling confession he spoke of a group of men at an illegal gambling event, who had promised to resolve his debt problems if he were to take the rap for the hit on Hatanaka.

Gambling debts and the well-established practice of going to prison for a crime somebody else committed could only mean one thing: the killing was ordered by the *yakuza*, the largest and most meticulously organised protection racket in the world.

Hatanaka's murder sent a cold, cold shiver down the spine of the financial and corporate elites to which the dead man had belonged. And with good reason: since the early 1980s, *yakuza* groups had become very circumspect about resorting to violence. Even if they did, their targets were almost always competitors from their own milieu. But Hatanaka was not some low-life thug made good. He was a major figure in national and international finance, the boss of one of the key regional branches of Sumitomo Bank. As a board member, he was involved in the strategic decision-making of one of the world's three biggest banks. (The other two leading banks were also Japanese.) He had developed an unparalleled reputation in the company for managing large and difficult projects with a high rate of return. Why would the *yakuza* commission such a high-profile assassination as this and risk a huge crackdown on their activities?

To start uncovering the answer, first take a ride on the Shinkansen,

the Bullet Train. As it travels west from Tokyo, this magnificent engineering achievement passes through a visual cacophony of concrete,
metal and other man-made detritus. For hundreds upon hundreds of
miles, the Japanese construction industry has squeezed houses and
apartment buildings into unfeasibly small plots, sheltered under a
hideous web of thick, disorganised electric cabling. For the most part,
it is impossible to identify where one city ends and the next begins.
Indeed, I arrived in Kobe from Tokyo having travelled at more than
200 mph for almost three hours, with the slightly unreal sense of
never having left the Japanese capital.

This strip of land running from Tokyo to the Kobe/Osaka agglomeration is the most densely populated area of the world, cramming
more than 2,500 people into every square mile. Post-war Japan was
seized by a construction mania that saw anything old uprooted to
prepare the ground for the planting of the world's most extensive
concrete jungle. This reached its apotheosis in the late 1980s and early
1990s, during the period known as *baburu* – the bubble – a phenomenon that eventually changed the essence of Japanese society and its
self-perception. It certainly turned the centre of the country into the
most unrelenting urban landscape.

Two-thirds into my train trip through this Eternal City of the East,
my Bullet Train pulls into Nagoya, renowned as 'the sprawliest of the
sprawl'. In the middle of this sprawliest bit, there is a rare stretch of
lush parkland at whose heart sit two imposing mansion blocks –
Tsukimiga-oka, Sections A and B – which, if one leaves out the Sections
A and B, translates poetically (if disingenuously) as The Hill from
Where One Contemplates the Moonlight. And it was on the tenth floor
of Section B that Mr Hatanaka was murdered.

Not only did he live in the centre of the sprawl, but he had made
a significant contribution to its development – indeed, it was his role
in handing out huge loans that fed the construction frenzy in the
bubble that led to his murder. Or rather, it was his role in trying to
call in the bad loans after the bubble burst.

While losing patience with Mr Kondo and his false confession, the
Nagoya police had started looking into Mr Hatanaka's business dealings, to discover that he had been close to some notorious exponents
of land-sharking – the most ruthless business practice to emerge during

the *baburu*, and one that quickly produced a dizzy mixing of Japan's mighty corporate world with the proud *yakuza* underworld.

The chain of events leading up to Hatanaka's death in 1994 had begun nine years earlier, halfway around the world at the Plaza Hotel in New York. Ronald Reagan, under pressure from Congress, but emboldened by his ideological partner and friend, Margaret Thatcher, was now convinced that the world of international finance needed a big shake-up in order to usher in the regime of free trade that became known as globalisation.

Reagan's vision of free trade and of the liberalisation of international financial markets was coming under intense pressure from the Democrat-controlled Congress. The dollar was dangerously overvalued, especially against the yen and the mark, and this had enabled Japan and Germany to flood the American market with cheap imports. Above all, the US automobile industry was in serious trouble, incapable of competing with the smaller, cheaper and more reliable vehicles produced by their Asian and European competitors. By September 1985, Japan posted a record trade surplus with the US of $50 billion. Along with Congress's rowdy demands for restrictions to be imposed on Japanese goods, US authors published a spate of books warning how Japan was poised to take over as the world's number-one economy. One advertising campaign showed a compact vehicle above the rather ominous slogan 'Made in Japan – You're Not Laughing Anymore'.

President Reagan's insistence that Tokyo do something about its currency and its trade surplus came towards the end of a bad year for Japan. It had begun in late January with the sensational murder of Masahisa Takenaka, the fourth-generation *oyabun* (godfather) of the Yamaguchi-gumi, the Kobe-based *yakuza* group. Takenaka had only recently been elevated to the most senior position in what was the largest and most powerful organised-crime syndicate in Japan. Controlling more than 100,000 members, Takenaka could claim the title *capo di tutti capi nel mondo*. But unfortunately for him, the claim was undermined by a significant minority of his followers, a disgruntled faction known as the Ichiwa-kai. And late one January evening in northern Osaka, the Ichiwa hitmen murdered the *oyabun* in his mistress's apartment, along with one of his chief lieutenants. In the long modern history of the *yakuza*, such a provocative attack was unprecedented.

Over the next two years, large parts of Kansai (western Japan) were rocked by the most bloody *yakuza* war on record. Hundreds of members and associates of the Yamaguchi-gumi and the Ichiwa-kai fell victim to carefully coordinated hits.

Manabu Miyazaki was on the run from the police during the Ichiwa wars. As his portly frame settled into an armchair at one of Tokyo's poshest hotels, he told me in vivid terms how nerve-racking life as a fugitive had been at that time. '*Yakuza* guys I met in Osaka right after Takenaka was killed were all thirsting for blood. "It's different this time," many told me. "I'll either get killed or end up in jail."' Miyazaki, known by the title of his riveting biography, *Toppamono* (Wide Boy or Wiseguy, freely translated), continued with a broad, warm smile, 'Local tabloids splashed big reports under headlines like *Yamaguchi-gumi Determined to Exterminate Ichiwa-kai*. Underneath would be a little box near the bottom of the page labelled *Today's Yama–Ichi War Scorecard*, with a daily tally of deaths, serious injuries and light injuries, broken down by category.'

The public despaired both of the *yakuza* behaviour and the apparent inability of the police to do anything about the violence (in fact, the police had an interest in seeing the Yamaguchi-gumi eviscerate itself and were happy to stand back and watch the spectacle). Japanese culture, which so prided itself on social concord, was being publicly humiliated by thugs and an incompetent police force.

At home the *yakuza* were running amok, and abroad anti-Japanese sentiment was growing in the United States. A malaise descended over Japan. Tokyo resented Washington's insistence that it open its domestic market to American goods while reining in exports to the US. But it reasoned that if it did not cooperate, the backlash against Japanese interests in America would be even more damaging. The coincidence of the *yakuza* civil war and sustained American economic and political pressure on the Tokyo Government convinced many Japanese that the harmonious age accompanying the country's remarkable post-war ascent was coming to a close. They were right. It was. But not quite in the manner that most imagined.

On September 22nd, 1985, together with the governors of their respective central banks, the Finance Ministers of the G5 gathered in the banqueting rooms of the Hotel Plaza on New York's Fifth Avenue under conditions of strict secrecy. In order to bring down the dollar against the yen, James Baker, the new Treasury Secretary, realised that there would have to be a massive sale of dollars on the currency markets by central banks. This flew in the face of Reagan's 'the-market-regulates-everything' approach, but everyone buckled to the demand. (There is much more that is managed in globalisation than its authors and advocates care to admit.) In the final communiqué, Japan agreed to resist protectionism and begin the 'steady implementation of the Action Program announced on July 30 for the further opening up of Japan's domestic market to foreign goods and services', as well as the 'intensi-fied implementation of financial market liberalisation and of the yen, so that the yen fully reflects the underlying strength of the Japanese economy'.

In Tokyo, the view prevailed that as America emerged from its reces-sion with the aid of a weakened dollar, Japanese growth would slow down. Within twelve months the yen had indeed strengthened and a deep gloom spread across the boardrooms of Japan. Resentment towards the United States continued to grow, along with the percep-tion that Tokyo had been bullied into sacrificing a successful economic policy. The Government felt compelled to act to combat this percep-tion and so it lowered interest rates and eased open the money supply.

Business started to borrow money. Lots and lots of it.

The unexpected consequences of this move included the unlikely marriage between the *zaibatsu* (Japan's Godzilla-like corporations – Mitsubishi, Mitsui, Hitachi, et al.) and the *yakuza*, pulling them both out of the doldrums of the mid-1980s into one of history's greatest and most destructive money-making ventures.

'Around the end of 1987, we noticed something odd was going on,' explained Raisuke Miyawaki, the founder of Japan's Anti-Organised Crime Squad. 'At the time, I was working as a special adviser to Prime Minister Nakasone, and the economic figures we received from the central bank didn't seem to add up. Something strange was happening with the money supply, but we weren't quite sure what!' Nobody from the PM down had anticipated the sensational outcome of the Government's monetary policy – the stock market shot into the strato-sphere like a rogue firework, fizzing, sparkling and mesmerising on its unpredictable path to the heavens.

The boom in Japan's financial markets was of such intensity that, as one economist noticed, 'Every investment seemed to make money, and speculators were quick to jump on any new development. When American physicists announced that they had achieved cold fusion in the laboratory (a claim later shown to be unproved), eager Japanese investors ran up the share prices of firms that had any sort of relationship with potential cold-fusion processes. In retrospect, it appears that by year-end 1988 the Japanese stock market was in the midst of a full-fledged bubble.'

It was not long before the extraordinary speculation on the Nikkei found its way into the property market. Financial corporations and banks wanted to transfer the notional money of the stock-market bubble into hard assets, and property was the best bet.

Soon the vortex of speculation started to consume the existing housing stock, and so the banks and big corporations started looking for new land to develop. But the post-war construction mania had ensured there were no empty spaces on which to build. To make way for the glistening-new bubbly buildings, existing owners or tenants would have to move. And if they didn't want to, someone would have to persuade them: enter the Sharks.

'It was also around then that I remember seeing for the first time the big, burly men in black suits hanging around Tokyo's fanciest hotels,' remembered Miyawaki, the Anti-Organised Crime Tsar. He is an unusual man. Even by Japanese standards, he comes across as exceptionally polite and respectful. But most strikingly, Mr Miyawaki talks, and talks frankly, unlike the majority of cops and ex-cops in this country. Most prefer to sweep the presence and role of the *yakuza* under the carpet. Miyawaki believes they represented, and still represent, a serious threat to social stability. In the late 1980s, he was among the few to alert Japan to the implications of the burgeoning friendships between gangsters and businessmen. 'What worried me was that I could see these men were lunching with the most unlikely business and finance leaders. The corporations wanted to buy land in clusters, big plots,' continued Miyawaki, 'but things didn't always go that smoothly. A lot of people didn't want to sell, and so the companies and banks turned to muscle – the *yakuza*.'

First, the *yakuza* would offer financial inducements for tenants to leave their apartments, while negotiating with the owner to buy the land. And if either the tenant or the owner refused to budge, then the *yakuza* would issue verbal threats or a physical warning. (One of the most common and tasteless entailed spreading human faeces in and around the desired property). Those who remained stubborn then ran the gauntlet of *yakuza* intimidation. In its mild form, this might involve the notorious sound trucks (audible to this day in Tokyo), which would park outside a property and blast frenetic political rhetoric from huge loudspeakers, rendering life impossible for the targets. The final stage of intimidation was of course physical assault and murder.

Toppamono or Manabu Miyazaki, the Wide Boy, was never actually a member of the *yakuza* despite growing up as the son of an *oyabun* or godfather. But in his colourful life, he has been involved in all manner of *yakuza*-style activity, including land-sharking, and he makes no bones about it. With a mischievous grin across his broad face, he shakes his head as he relives those heady times:

> With hundreds of millions of yen flying around, each day passed in a haze of Dom Perignon and Rémy Martin . . . During a land speculation I helped out with in Tokyo's Kanda district, where an elderly couple lived in a shabby house, the old woman we negotiated with on behalf of her sick husband stubbornly refused to pursue the matter, leaving us nothing to go on. 'The old bitch is making things difficult because she wants more money,' we naturally concluded. 'Okay, let's double the offer!' Twice the original amount was stuffed down her throat. As it turned out, the old woman wasn't holding out for more. She only wanted to let her husband, who had terminal cancer, die in the house . . .

The banks, the corporations, the politicians (who were soon in the thick of it) were making tens of billions of dollars in speculative deals. At first, the jamboree seemed to confirm that a superior form of capitalism had evolved from Japan's peculiar culture. With the price of land doubling every month, nobody seemed to notice the wholesale removal of thousands of unwilling, disenfranchised residents from their apartments and houses. This could only happen because the core institutions of the Japanese state and economy were content to work hand-in-glove with organised crime at the expense of ordinary citizens.

It did not take the *yakuza* long to figure out that their role as policemen to this shameful larceny was a modest ambition. If the big corporations and their political cronies were making money hand-over-fist by speculating on land, why shouldn't the *yakuza*? Japan's legal and illegal worlds were steadily becoming indistinguishable, and nowhere was that distinction more fuzzy and impenetrable than at the Sumitomo Bank.

Sumitomo was Japan's second-oldest corporation, tracing its beginnings as a purveyor of medicines and books back to the early seventeenth century. Its banking division was established in the late nineteenth century, and by the mid-1970s it had developed a reputation for turning around the fortunes of declining corporate dinosaurs like Toyo Kogyo, the truck manufacturer, or Asahi Brewery. In 1984, it sought to expand beyond its main base in the industrial heartland of Kansai – Osaka, Kobe and Kyoto – by purchasing Heiwa Sogo, a relatively small bank, but one that had a high concentration of branches in Tokyo, where Sumitomo had a relatively weak presence. Heiwa Sogo also carried a lot of bad debts – *yakuza* debts, many of them from the senior members of the Yamaguchi-gumi.

But it was the takeover of Heiwa Sogo, masterminded by the Sumitomo President, Ichiro Isoda, that catapulted the bank into the world's top three. The international banking community and the Japanese Government showered Isoda with awards for his achievements, and Sumitomo revelled in the speculation of the late 1980s.

One of the bank's subordinate companies, Nagoya Itoman Real Estate Corporation, became a vehicle for Sumitomo's strategic land purchases in Tokyo, and Mr Hatanaka of Sumitomo Nagoya became ever more closely involved with this operation. What Hatanaka may not have known is that a fellow Itoman board member enjoyed a close business relationship with Takumi Masaru, the *wakagashira*, or deputy godfather, of the Yamaguchi-gumi. As the champagne flowed, Itoman's board lost its head, embarking on a shopping spree for artworks as collateral for dubious loans. Paying vastly inflated prices, often directly to the *yakuza*, Itoman squandered about half a billion dollars of its capital, and police estimated that about half of this ended up in the coffers of the Yamaguchi-gumi.

The exposure of Itoman in July 1991 led to the disgrace and resignation of Ichiro Isoda, perhaps Japan's most respected international banker until this point. Sumitomo's headquarters gradually put the screws on Hatanaka to call in some of the horrifically bad loans he had sanctioned. But, as many corporate figures discovered after the bubble had burst, a lot of their most eager customers had no intention of paying up, least of all the *yakuza*. By now Hatanaka was hopelessly compromised – many of his Nagoya associates were also associates of the mafia, and the Nagoya police finally concluded that he had pressed one of them too vigorously to make good on a loan.

Not surprisingly, the police were never able to clear up exactly which of his clients Hatanaka had upset so grievously. But his murder, along with several other attacks on prominent corporate executives (including the murder of Fuji Film Corporation's Managing Director) provoked Japan's cowed government into taking the unprecedented step of writing off the bulk of the major banks' and mortgage companies' bad debts. In effect, Japanese taxpayers underwrote the excesses of the bubble period, subsidising the obscene money-grabbing in which both the *zaibatsu* and the *yakuza* had indulged. The post-bubble period was soon known as the Heisei recession in Japan, referring to the age that began with Emperor Akihito's accession in 1989. Abroad it was more usually dubbed the *yakuza* recession. This was unfair – the *yakuza* was the junior partner in this venal cavalcade, albeit a truculent and dangerous one. But it certainly highlighted how profoundly well rooted the *yakuza* are: they are not an ephemeral force, but an institutionalised element of Japanese society.

It was appropriate that the underworld and surface world should find their common interest in real-estate speculation – the corporations are inveterate speculators. And construction is, if not the heart of *yakuza* business, then certainly its lungs.

'All these guys here in Kama are dependent on the *yakuza*,' says Django, my guide around Kamagasaki, where the poorest and most desperate people in Osaka seek jobs as day labourers. In front of us stands a line of poor, huddled masses – some of them certainly Chinese and Korean, undoubtedly a few *burakumin* (Japan's underclass born into caste discrimination), and others whose lives at some point took a downward spin. Unshaven, sometimes toothless, acquiescent, they are lining up in front of the Kamagasaki Labour Exchange, a bleak grey monument to bureaucratic functionalism. Gone are the endless flashing lights, the digital advertising and the incessant electronic noise that characterise so many urban areas in Japan – this long line of the dispossessed hardly makes a sound in the twilight. 'We are waiting for the buses to take us to the homeless hostels where we can sleep,' one exhausted man explains. 'Not everyone gets a place,' he adds, which means those who don't will have to chance their luck sleeping underneath the railway arches next to Kama.

'Eighty-five per cent of the labour agents here are *yakuza*,' my friend Django continues. 'You have to arrive at about 5.30 in the morning when they come around and pick out the best.' Django started here as a labourer at the end of the 1980s when the bubble ratcheted up the demand for new buildings. 'It was easier at that time, of course, because there was such a demand for construction workers,' he recalled. 'The only criterion you had to fulfil was a working knowledge of Japanese.' We walk down the dingy streets of Kama, past the tiny hotels where the more successful labourers find a bed for $10–15 a night. Past the new police station, which looks like a fortress – all part of the post-bubble image that the police are now doing something about the *yakuza*. That particular illusion is quickly shattered when, in this otherwise dingy area, we chance upon two immaculate, grand red-brick buildings with blacked-out limos parked outside. 'The only change is that since the 1992 anti-organised crime law, the *yakuza* aren't allowed to mount plaques outside the buildings with their names and symbols.' Django stops briefly. 'See that guy at the crossroads? Careful how you look at him. He's *yakuza* – acting as lookout for a gambling den.' And as we walk by, a little door opens to reveal a dark circle of mah-jong players.

We stroll into the bar on the corner. On seeing us, the clientele – a smoky mixture of workers, drunks and outcasts – lets out a huge cheer. Behind the narrow bar, the landlady has hung pictures from a calendar depicting famous tourist destinations: London, New York, Prague, Cairo and other places a few light-years away from Kama. In place of the usual plasma HD screen is a cumbersome old TV from the 1970s on its last legs, but still pumping out Japanese music videos. In general, the cliché holds that the Japanese maintain a stark social reserve, but such considerations are brushed aside as the landlady beams excitedly at Django while placing some raw fish and tofu in front of us. She grabs the telephone and calls her friends. 'Django's here. Come on down!'

Django hasn't stepped into this bar for five years, but he is greeted like a football star returning to his childhood home. The assembly becomes riotous when he picks up the microphone and sings along to an all-time *yakuza* karaoke favourite about two 'brothers' and the inevitable themes of trust, loyalty and death. As his sonorous bass growls out the tale in Osaka working-class dialect, his T-shirt rides up his forearm to reveal the tail of a blue dragon tattoo – that forked tip is enough to warn people.

Over a couple of suckers of raw octopus, Django told me of his first encounter with his old *yakuza* mentor, Ken-chan. 'I walked in and he was staring at me. This is very important in that scene – it is very macho. They are always checking out how much of a man you are. It's done in subtle ways, as well as in more obvious physical ways. I had no problem about people staring at me because I knew how to calibrate the return stare.'

Although slight in build, at eighteen years old Django was a national junior karate champion. 'People involved in martial arts probably don't like to hear it, but the way the martial-arts business here in Japan is organised, it is like the *yakuza*: the *dojos* [schools], the training, how the *sensei* [teacher] relates to his students. The *sensei* has complete say, and the students are supposed to be enormously deferential. In Japan when the *sensei* steps out of the *dojo*, he will have the same way of swaggering with the students. They must carry his bag and so he makes his position very obvious and public. Even the way they greet and the way they talk is very close to *yakuza* language.' Django's facility with the habits of the martial-arts world was decisive in persuading the *yakuza* to trust him.

Ken-chan befriended Django and showed him around the food stalls of Kama. 'I control all of these,' Ken-chan explained as the mama-sans who ran the joints handed over their cash.

'I never once saw one of them do this unwillingly,' Django insisted. 'While this was a protection racket, it was also a protection service. Nobody would ever touch one of Ken-chan's stalls without the most severe consequences. And when the police are unable or unwilling to do their job, you need somebody like Ken-chan looking after you. If there was the slightest hint of trouble – unruly customers, unpaid debts, brawls, harassment of waitresses – the mama-sans would call Ken-chan and his boys would be down like a shot to sort it out. They all insisted that the police are absolutely useless. Ken delivers what he promises – this is a real service.'

Before long, Ken-chan was taking Django on his collection rounds around a much more significant revenue source – Namba, one of the biggest entertainment districts in Osaka.

'We'd go in, he'd call the mama. We'd have a drink. We would sing a song or two on the karaoke and, while I was chatting to the waitresses, he would go behind the counter and the payment was made. It was done on an amicable basis – there was no tension, no reluctance, it looked to me like business as usual. Of course, we weren't on our own; he would have his young goons with him, rather bulky guys, two or three of them. Some had shaven heads, missing pinkies or gold chains, so it was absolutely clear who was visiting.'

On one occasion Django left a bar in Kama with two drinking buddies to take the subway home. His friends were jumped on by two others from the bar, who claimed they were owed money. As the fists were swinging, Django's two friends screamed for help, 'Come on, karate boy. Help us! Use your strength!' Django didn't move. If he failed to come to his friends' aid, it would mean breaking the bonds of loyalty – they would never speak to him again. But Django had no choice: he could not get involved, as it would have threatened his entire livelihood and existence in Japan.

This was because Django was not Japanese, but a university professor born and raised in the most unlikely *yakuza* recruiting ground of Bregenz, capital of Austria's most westerly and chintziest Alpine province, Vorarlberg, which sits on Lake Constance close to the German and Swiss borders.

Leading a double life, Django (or Wolfgang, to give him his real name) was lecturing at the Goethe Institute in Osaka by day, while at night he hung out with Ken-chan, who liked to introduce him as his international associate. 'I have to say what was revealing and shocking is that I felt a real affinity to this world,' explained Wolfgang, who is exceptionally honest about his life with the *yakuza*. 'And maybe it was due to karate and this swagger, this feeling like a real man. But the greatest shock to me was when I realised that we were walking down the street – four, five of us maybe – and of course I was in the middle and I saw how ordinary people on the street perceived us. They averted their gaze and many had real fear in their eyes. And I have to say that, yes, in some sense I felt comfortable with this proud walking, with everybody showing respect. And one evening, I saw in myself how corrupt and corrupting this feeling can be.'

One of Austria's leading sociologists and Japanologists, Dr Wolfgang Herbert researched his doctorate by immersing himself in Osaka's underworld. He belongs to a new breed of researchers, who in the past fifteen years have completely transformed academia's understanding of and approach to organised crime. Along with colleagues in Russia, Western Europe, South Africa and the United States (and doubtless elsewhere), Wolfgang has revealed a huge amount about the culture, ambition and economic motivation of major criminal structures.

These young researchers also have one other thing in common – they have a bible to which they invariably refer: *The Sicilian Mafia: The Business of Private Protection*. Written by Diego Gambetta, Professor of Sociology at Oxford University, the book condensed several key ideas about organised crime that had been floating aimlessly about academia for many decades into an utterly convincing theory about the mafia. Instead of regarding the mafia as bullies for whom violence is the be-all and end-all, Gambetta argues that the mafia is involved in the business of protection:

> To define the mafia as 'the industry of violence' is open to misunderstanding. Violence is a means, not an end; a resource, not the final product. The commodity that is really at stake is *protection*. It may be argued that ultimately protection rests on the ability to use force, but it does not follow that it coincides with it . . . There are people who find it in their individual interest to buy mafia protection. While some may be victims of extortion, many others are willing customers.

Gambetta has also separated the core mafia activity – protection – from those criminals involved in trading. The mafia can operate in legal markets, as Ken-chan does, offering protection to genuine businessmen and -women like bar owners in Kama and Namba, but they also operate in illegal markets: a drug dealer will require some protection in order to ensure that his buyers or sellers do not renege on a deal. In order to understand and hence combat organised crime, it is important to recognise the distinct activities involved.

Gambetta highlights the extreme difficulties involved in carrying out fieldwork in this area. 'Scholars,' he notes drily, 'do not like to waste time with uncooperative sources who refuse to talk and, alternatively, they do not like to be shot.' But several acolytes around the world, like Wolfgang in Osaka, have taken up the challenge. Not only has this work begun to locate the economic and social role of the mafia in societies across the globe, but their work is teeming with observations that have rarely been included in classical criminology studies.

At the moment when Wolfgang suddenly realised that he was *enjoying* being a *yakuza* associate, 'It was instantly clear to me why young Japanese guys who do not have any other means of making a career get hooked by this lifestyle. They will do everything for their *yakuza* mentors because their ego has been bloated in a unique way. All of a sudden they are somebody big and powerful, just by walking in a group of *yakuza*. If we think about, say, Koreans or people without any education, society has been shitting upon them for a long time and suddenly they ain't being shat on. And they need no qualifications, it is almost effortless. So emotionally for them it is not only this feeling of being something important, but having found a group where they are at home. I felt the psychodynamics of it quite intensely.'

The good doctor could feel himself being overcome by the intoxicating aura of power that surrounds the *yakuza*. But he also found the tension of leading a dual life ever harder to bear, and eventually he concluded that he must kill off 'Django', his own Mr Hyde.

The Namba is a rather tired arcade with little shops squeezed between the pachinko parlours, the giant temples to Japan's collective commitment to compulsive gambling. Just a decade ago the teenagers drifting through the Namba with red and blond dyed hair and Gothic clothing were both exotic and provocative, a challenge to Japan's carefully calibrated social sensibilities. Now ubiquitous and mundane, they nonetheless act as an important reminder of the changes triggered by the collapse of the bubble and the cultural impact of globalisation.

At the far end of the arcade, the teenagers thin out and the noise from the pachinko halls recedes. In the corner of yet another bar with the standard attributes of karaoke, raw cuts of primeval sea-dwellers and alcohol, a quiet man sits hunched in the corner. He could be an ageing hippy. In fact, he is one of the most senior tattooists to – among others – the Yamaguchi-gumi.

Like most established organised criminal communities, the *yakuza* have a complex mythology about their origins, their founding purpose and how this has developed and modernised. The *yakuza* cultivate an ur-image of the samurai, going back to the Tokugawa shogunate of the early modern period. In fact, their genesis was messy and on the whole less romantic, drawing on (among others) traditions of the itinerant trader and the gambler. The very meaning of *yakuza* is revealing. A composite of the slang for 8, 9 and 3, it refers to a set of mah-jong tiles, which at first sight looks like a winner because it adds up to twenty but, under specific rules, is in fact worth zero. The *yakuza* have traditionally drawn a large number of recruits from those on the margin by dint of their birth, in partic- ular Koreans and the *burakumin*. The latter comprise an underclass whose status was defined centuries ago by their professions: those who worked in abattoirs or in some capacity with 'faeces and flesh'. It is a prejudice that infects Japanese society to this day. 'On the surface,' Wolfgang interprets this for me, 'the *yakuza* are ostenta- tious, dramatic and recognisable like the winning card hand, but underneath they feel shunned like zeros.'

Apart from those who have lost their little fingers, the most osten- tatious mark of *yakuza* membership is the tattoo. Nothing so cheap as 'I ❤ Yamaguchi-gumi' across the biceps, these tattoos are breath- taking representations of gods, animals, warriors, mythological crea- tures or women, often intertwined in dramatic pose, imprinted on the body through millions of tiny pinpricks. Aside from the considerable physical pain, a *yakuza* tattoo has significant social and psychological implications. And of course the tattooist has to make sure that the customer walks away content – the last thing he needs is an unhappy *yakuza* on his books. 'The skin has several layers,' explained Horitsune II, the master tattooist, 'but in order for the image to be retained and reproduced by the body, the ink must reach about the third or fourth layer. The problem is that the thickness of the dermis varies at different parts of the body – you have to know every inch of the body if you want to do a proper job.' Sipping a beer, Horitsune II exudes the quiet concentration of a watchmaker. He clearly regards his work not as a profession, but as a higher craft. 'I don't tattoo just anyone who walks in here,' he continued. 'Taking on a tattoo is a serious business and so I spend a lot of time in consultation with the client to ascertain whether they are ready for it.'

The painting of a full-body tattoo takes between one and two years (or several years, as Horitsune jokes, if the *yakuza* recipient is in and out of prison), and it can cost more than $10,000. In a society where procedure and hierarchy are pervasive, the *yakuza* 'families' invest their rituals with greater importance than any comparable organisations in the world. Loyalty to a 'family' should be lifelong (although one may on request negotiate an honourable discharge, albeit for the possible sacrifice of a little finger), and, as with the mafia, the commitment supersedes one's obligations to blood relatives. Betrayal and gross insubordination are capital offences. The tattoos are a physical reminder of one's vows. They also serve as an effective warning to outsiders and competitors. Of course, this extreme loyalty can have horrific consequences if the family structure breaks down, as its logic requires a fight to the death. The Yamaguchi–Ichiwa war was an internal family matter, hence the intensity of its violence.

Ten to fifteen years ago, 90 per cent of Horitsune's clients, he explained, were *yakuza*. 'Nowadays, it is 50 per cent civilians and 50 per cent *yakuza*. And of course most of the civilians are young adults who see tattoos as a fashion accessory rather than as a sign of loyalty and commitment.' Certainly the cultural breakout of the younger generation in the 1990s and its sudden experiment with individualism represent a huge change for the country, which until the 1980s clothed its citizens in the uninspiring uniforms of school and work from birth till death. But that statistic also reveals something about the *yakuza* and their current situation. 'The bosses would always pay for their soldiers to be tattooed,' sighed Horitsune, 'but frankly it has become too great an expense for many of them – that's why my *yakuza* trade is going down.' Things aren't quite so rosy these days for the *yakuza*. They remain a core element of Japanese society, but since the collapse of the bubble they have faced unprecedented challenges to their authority, both from their enemies at home and, increasingly, from foreign rivals who are beginning to squeeze their economic base. Like the rest of Japan, the *yakuza* are encountering some difficulty in adapting to a globalising world.

Through much of the twentieth century, the *yakuza* may not have been as popular as their members like to believe, but they were influential. Their status as outsiders was always paradoxical. While the *yakuza* 'families' emerged in large degree from lumpen classes, they were often attracted to and supported extreme right-wing nationalist ideologies, and in the interwar years they were used by both government and business as effective strike-breakers. When the United States occupied a devastated Japan at the end of the Second World War, it was the *yakuza* who within days of surrender were resurrecting the country's economy with the establishment of a vibrant black market. The Americans tolerated and often collaborated with the *yakuza*, just as they accepted the assistance of the Sicilian mafia in establishing order throughout southern Italy after the 1943 Sicily landings. The mafia developed decisively corrupt connections with the Christian Democratic Party that dominated Italian politics during the Cold War. Similarly, the *yakuza* struck up an intimate relationship with the key factions of the Liberal Democratic Party (LDP), which dominated Japanese politics during the same period, but unlike the Christian Democrats survived the fall of communism and, despite some hiccups, still runs the country today.

The bubble – when the *zaibatsu*, the LDP and the *yakuza* all joined forces to realise what one commentator dubbed 'the great transfer of wealth' – was no aberration. It was merely the country's crony capitalism assuming its highest form for a blowout that lasted five years. This begs the question as to how the *yakuza* were ever able to occupy such an exalted position in Japanese society. Contrary to popular assumptions, they did not shoot, extort or bribe their way to the top: they are, bizarrely, a product of Japan's legal system.

'Traditionally, of course, the *yakuza* have always been involved in prostitution and gambling. Everyone more or less accepted this state of affairs, and that accounted for the bulk of its income,' says Yukio Yamanouchi. 'But in the 1960s, it started getting involved in civilian affairs and this soon grew to be one of its greatest revenue sources.' The chirpy Mr Yamanouchi is in an excellent mood. After a number of years in the wilderness, he has recently been welcomed back as the chief lawyer to the Yamaguchi-gumi after his old friend, Shinobu Tsukasa, was chosen as the sixth-generation *oyabun* of Japan's largest crime syndicate. This is like having a lawyer in the US who introduces himself breezily as *Lawyer to Don Antonio Soprano of the New Jersey Mafia Corporation*. Yamanouchi explains how failures in the legal system provided the *yakuza* with their opportunity. 'This move into civilian affairs began with the collection of outstanding debts. If anybody went to court in order to get a debt paid, it would take an eternity and, if judgement was finally passed down in a case, it often resulted in nothing. The *yakuza* are able to offer a much quicker solution to the problem.'

It was a law passed in 1949 that caused these sorts of frustrations with the judiciary. In order to discourage the use of litigation, which was felt to be divisive and contrary to the spirit of *wa* (harmony) that underpins Japanese society, the post-war Government ruled that only 5,000 lawyers would be permitted to graduate from the Legal Research and Training Institute in Tokyo every year. The great majority registered in Tokyo and Osaka and sought comfortable and lucrative positions working on behalf of one of the *zaibatsu*. Few were interested in representing members of the public, and before long the entire judicial system was clogged up with civil cases that made the deliberations in Dickens's *Bleak House* look reasoned and swift by comparison.

'It was only a short step before people realised that they could use the *yakuza* for resolving a host of things – they have since developed a close involvement with all manner of transactions in the property business, of course; but they also act as bankruptcy assessors; in anything really where the courts ought to be responsible, like insurance claims after car accidents,' outlined Yamanouchi. By the late 1990s, the consequences of Japan's policy on legal training were jaw-dropping by international comparison: Germany had one lawyer for every 724 head of population, Britain one for every 656, and the United States one for every 285 citizens. In Japan, there was one lawyer for every 5,995 people. Basically, the mafia occupies a huge segment of Japan's *de facto* legal system, which is, of course, what some people observe about lawyers in the US.

In its core activity, the *yakuza* are not only a privatised police force; they are a self-contained judicial system as well – criminal syndicates as cops, barristers, judge and jury.

Two interest groups are – if not entirely unhappy with this situation – at least ambivalent. The first is the general public. Though their demand for law enforcement and conflict resolution is what keeps the *yakuza* in business (and in many cases, the *yakuza* provide a good and efficient service), members of the public are unable to contest the outcome of a dispute mediated by *yakuza* if they believe it to be unjust. Yamanouchi is very frank about the regard in which his *yakuza* clients are held: 'You know, they have become so closely involved in civilian affairs that for some ordinary people their presence and behaviour have become a real burden. That's why the 1991 law was so well received in public.'

The Government felt able to pass the Law Regarding the Prevention of Unjust Acts by Organised Criminal Syndicate Members in May 1991 because public disquiet about the *yakuza*'s involvement in the bubble had led to a real slump in the *yakuza*'s image. The law's focus also enabled the Government to shift responsibility for the bubble away from the primary culprits, the *zaibatsu* and the LDP, and onto the *yakuza*.

Although designed to clip the *yakuza*'s wings, the Law contained some astonishing features that illuminate how the Japanese mafia is in fact an institutionalised element of this democracy. It stipulated that all the families or associations must annually submit their membership lists to the police, both full members and candidates. When I asked the lawyer Yamanouchi whether this confers legal status on members of the organised criminal syndicates, he leaned back in his chair, pondered the question and then averred, 'Yes, it does.' So the *yakuza* enjoy the unique status of being a legal and an illegal entity simultaneously.

Every year, the police White Book informs the public on the

fluctuation in *yakuza* membership and what type of activities particular families indulge in. The Law also forbids the *yakuza* for the first
time from displaying their symbols on the doors to their offices,
although it is still perfectly legal for them to have offices. 'After the
Law was passed,' said Mr Yamanouchi, 'the police told the Osaka Bar
Association that I was no longer permitted to print the phrase Legal
Counsellor to the Yamaguchi-gumi on my business card. But apart
from that – it hasn't affected me too much!'

The gold standard of anti-organised crime legislation is the RICO
Act (Racketeer Influenced and Corrupt Organisations Act). Passed by
the US Congress in 1970 and thought (apocryphally, some say) to be
named in honour of Edward G. Robinson's character in *Little Caesar*
('Is this the end of Rico?' he asks rhetorically while breathing his last
in the 1930s classic), it took ten years before a mafia boss was actually convicted under RICO. Since then, however, it has proved more
effective than any other policing tool against organised criminal syndicates. Using RICO, prosecutors do not have to prove specific crimes,
merely that individuals are involved with groups that follow a criminal pattern. This breaks the defensive wall erected by criminal bosses
whereby foot soldiers take the rap for their superiors' crimes, enabling
the Feds and district attorneys to smash much of *Cosa Nostra* in the
United States during the 1980s and 1990s.

The Japanese borrowed from RICO, but then diluted it. *Yakuza*
bosses can now be held accountable for the sins of their subordinates,
but the police will only use this in order to exercise a measure of
control over *yakuza* affairs – they are not out to destroy them. 'The
earlier economic relationship, when the *yakuza* could bribe the police,
that is now unthinkable,' explained Yamanouchi. 'Furthermore, the
police are much more confident about moving against the higher
instances of the families. My chief client, Mr Tsukasa, for example, is
in custody at the moment for a trivial matter. The reason behind this
is because the Yamaguchi-gumi is moving from its traditional home
in the west and into the east of the country. If successful, this would
greatly increase its power. The police are trying to clip its wings, not
destroy it.'

It is hard to underestimate the influence and standing of the
Yamaguchi-gumi. At the top of a quiet residential street in Kobe's

fashionable Nada district, a wooden sign stands proud: 'We Will Keep Organised-Crime Gangs Out of Nada!' A few yards further down past houses that are uncharacteristically spacious by urban standards, there stands a cutesy grey-and-white hexagonal building at the top of a side street – the local police station. Grrrr! The mouse roars. Fifty yards down the street from the mouse hole, there are discreet fortress walls around a garage door of grey corrugated metal. Cameras and security lights are dotted everywhere and, should anyone succeed in scaling the wall, they would also need to contend with a roll of matted barbed wire. As I walk past the headquarters of the Yamaguchi-gumi, my luck is in and, as if reproducing a scene from *Thunderball*, the metal starts to roll slowly upwards, revealing a line of five men standing ramrod-straight in light green uniforms and sunglasses. Behind them is an elegantly manicured lawn and in the distance a passable imitation of a Renaissance Italian courtyard. As I stand gawping, their eyes settle on me and, having no letter of introduction, I move slowly on. One Yamaguchi soldier ushers a big man with even bigger sunglasses into the driver's seat of one of several limos parked in the drive and it screeches out before the grey metal drops again, locking away the secrets of the Yamaguchi-gumi once more. Good luck, Nada-ku police – you've got your work cut out.

Since 1991 the police have registered a significant consolidation of *yakuza* power into just three families – the Yamaguchi-gumi and two Tokyo-based groups, the Sumiyoshi-kai and the Inagawa-kai. The 1991 Law enabled police to weaken or eliminate many of the smaller *yakuza* associations and so, to protect themselves, several have affiliated with the Big Three. Since the millennium, the Yamaguchi-gumi has been extending its influence ever deeper into Tokyo, taking advantage of a simmering feud between sub-groups of the Sumiyoshi and Inagawa, which sporadically breaks out into murderous violence. By 2005, Yamaguchi-gumi accounted for 45 per cent of Japan's 'designated' gangsters, according to the police White Book, and when Shinobu Tsukasa was named the sixth-generation *oyabun* in July that year, police began warning of the possibility of a major gang war breaking out.

Yakuza leaders themselves downplay the prospect of a war between the Big Three. 'We have cordial relations with the Yamaguchi-gumi,' says Mitsunori Agata, Deputy Chairman of the Sumiyoshi-kai, Tokyo's largest criminal syndicate. 'We have great respect for them and we think they are an effective operation.'

The slight reserve I detected in Agata-san's response was explained three months later in February 2007, when a leading young Sumiyoshi-kai man was gunned down by members of a Yamaguchi-gumi affiliate in Tokyo. For several days, Japanese newspapers speculated furiously that the country was on the brink of the mother of all gang wars between Yamaguchi-gumi and Sumiyoshi-kai. Then news leaked that the Yamaguchi affiliate had paid a substantial sum (estimated at around $1.3 million) to the Sumiyoshi-kai group as blood money. Behind the drama, however, is the economic reality that Kansai (western Japan), the Yamaguchi-gumi's base and traditional hunting ground, is lagging behind eastern Japan economically. This is what lies behind the Yamaguchi-gumi's eastward drive into the capital. Contracting markets still have the potential to trigger a major conflagration between the two big groups.

In public, all the major *yakuza* figures remain admirably circumspect in their pronouncements, not wishing to provoke unnecessary bloodshed. In his late sixties, Agata has been through a lot in the *yakuza* world: rebellion against a stern middle-class father in post-war Japan; doing time for a murder he did not commit; a ruthless streak that propelled him to leadership of his gang, the Blue Dragons, around Shinjuku station; his recruitment by a Sumiyoshi-kai operative; and then building a protection racket around Kabuki-cho, one of the toughest and most contested turfs in Tokyo.

Now in his cosy, cluttered room where no more than three people can sit cross-legged, Agata-san insists to me that his methods have changed – the *yakuza* now stress the importance of diplomacy, violence is a final and always undesirable resort. 'We hold a meeting on the twentieth of every month with all the families and associations in eastern Japan and we resolve our differences through dialogue,' he continues. 'The Sumiyoshi-kai does not seek conflict, but of course if anybody attempts to encroach on our territory, then problems will ensue . . .'

There is no question that since the Yamaguchi–Ichiwa war in the 1980s and the collapse of the bubble in the early 1990s, there has been a significant reduction in *yakuza* violence. The key to an effective protection racket as run by the *yakuza* is less the actual deployment of violence as a sanction than the credible *threat* of violence. Too much violence is bad for business – it draws heat from the police, opprobrium from the public and the media, and can lead to retaliation. All these take a heavy toll on the *yakuza*'s *raison d'être*: making money.

On the edge of Kabuki-cho, Tokyo's main red-light and gambling district, lies the highest concentration of *yakuza* offices anywhere in the country. As one of Tokyo's most important bosses, Agata has two offices and he still observes the *yakuza*'s traditional symbolism: he reveals a magnificent dragon tattoo across his chest and proudly shows me the DVD of the ceremony (theoretically illegal) at which he was elevated to Deputy Chair. These days, however, *yakuza* bosses like Agata are as much harassed senior managers as they are traditional gangsters. When he speaks of the recruitment crisis facing the *yakuza*, we drift surreally into the discourse of Human Resources wonkery. 'Like all organisations, we are facing problems encouraging young people to join,' Agata said, explaining the impact of Japan's fabled ageing society on the *yakuza*. The country currently registers the lowest birth rate in the world, so the *yakuza* are competing with all legitimate businesses for members. 'For young people there are many more attractive and lucrative trades to go into nowadays,' he continues, 'so we as an organisation are now ageing – too many chiefs, not enough Indians, frankly. The most effective way for us to respond to this is to point out that we are a family, and this is very attractive for young lads who maybe don't spend as much time with their own family. This is something that is lacking in society.'

But for Agata, as for many of the *yakuza*'s management class, their main headache recently has been the police – not in the shape of any crackdown on the families, but because of pachinko, Japan's national sport.

Just around the corner from Agata's office is a five-storey pachinko building. A visit allows you to revel in the profound otherness of Japan. On every floor row upon row of bright blue, red, yellow or green pachinko machines splutter, crackle, zing and trill as an army of seemingly brainwashed people, of both genders and from all classes and age groups, send dozens, hundreds, thousands of little balls into an upright slot machine. These contraptions gobble up most of the balls (¥2.5 each), but some fall into special holes. These trigger three revolving wheels in the centre and if, when they stop, the symbols match, the machine pays out more balls. Neatly stacked around the more successful players are baskets full of little balls, which represent winnings that sometimes run into thousands of dollars. Hyper-polite young men and women in toytown uniforms smile and provide the addicts with more balls to feed the machines and their habit.

The sheer size of this industry and the fanaticism of its devotees are hard to comprehend. Pachinko machines colonise whole high-rise buildings like mechanical spores, and players remain biologically attached to their machines for hours on end. Having accumulated a treasure chest of little balls, the player is permitted to exchange them for goods – insignificant gifts, dolls, cigarettes and the like. The player is then permitted to exchange these goods for cash at a separate kiosk, which must be out of sight of the main pachinko hall. This bizarre accounting ritual, known as *santen hoshiki*, emerged in order to circumvent Japan's laws on gambling, which is itself strictly illegal. But while pachinko *is* gambling, it is in fact strictly legal and has an annual turnover estimated at about $300 billion, twice the value of the entire Japanese automobile industry, and somewhere in the region of the total global narcotics market!

Until the 1991 Law, it was not only the *yakuza* that were making money out of pachinko: traditionally Korean businessmen and their syndicates controlled large parts of the trade, while Chinese gangs also took a cut from the *santen hoshiki* kiosks. There was so much money that all three were able to help themselves to a piece of the action without getting in each other's way. But after the 1991 Law, the police themselves started muscling in on the *santen hoshiki* system – often retired policemen backed by their working colleagues. And so by bureaucratic fiat, the police have largely requisitioned the *yakuza*'s most important legal business for their own ends. It's an unorthodox crime-fighting strategy, but an effective one. *Yakuza* bosses like Agata-san can barely contain their indignation: 'They are trying to take over a business that generates enormous amounts of money, so all of a sudden we have been deprived of these huge revenue streams. All these retired policemen came in and robbed from our banks, so all this black-market money is now going into their fat pension funds!'

In Kabuki-cho, snapping turtles and puffer fish (the ones with fatally toxic organs) compete with misty-eyed prostitutes and escort boys for the punters' attention. In Tokyo's most famous entertainment district, there are four activities: eating, drinking, fucking and pachinko. Occasionally, there is a murder or two.

On my stroll around the district, it looked like business as usual. Soliciting clients for sex has never been easier or more clinical for the workers and procurers of Kabuki-cho. The client has merely to walk into a small room. In the middle stands a single table and telephone; on the walls are illuminated posters advising of establishments offering a variety of ethnicities. After selecting a favourite, the client calls on the special phone and before long a courteous guide will lead him off to his chosen fantasy. Japanese men are keen on Caucasian women, which perhaps explains why 70 per cent of Japanese visas issued to Russian women in the past ten years have been 'entertainment' visas, and why Japan receives more trafficked Colombian women than any other country. Foreigners are unlikely to be offered Japanese women, as it is widely held that 'Westerners are hung like horses and disease-ridden'. But there are plenty of Chinese, Burmese and other Asian women on offer to satisfy the seedy curiosity of the Western male.

Kabuki-cho's best restaurants are hidden down impossibly narrow side streets, up rickety wooden stairs and then through low doorways. Gangsters seem to colonise at least one table in the small room that characterises each joint. Everyone understands the rules – no staring and no loud talking.

The Parisienne, slightly gaudy but somehow endearing, was a favoured hangout for the foot soldiers of the mob. All kinds: Korean, Taiwanese, Chinese, north-easterners, Shanghaiese and Japanese. Early on Friday evening, September 27th, 2002, two heavies from the Sumiyoshi-kai swaggered down the stairs and into the bar area. They closed in on a group of mobsters from the Chinese mainland and demanded money. The rent for that area had gone up. As the discussion became heated, one of the Chinese unexpectedly pulled a gun and fired. The first *yakuza* fell dead on the spot; the second was badly wounded and was losing consciousness as the Chinese fled.

Two and a half years earlier, the Governor of Tokyo, a right-wing rabble-rouser, Shintaro Ishihara, had issued a chilling warning to the capital's residents. 'Crimes in Tokyo are getting more violent,' he thundered. 'If you ask who is committing them, they are all *sangokujin* [derived from the derogatory wartime term for Koreans and Chinese]. In other words, foreigners . . . who have entered illegally and remain in Japan are the criminals, is that not so?'

Statistics clearly refuted Ishihara's hysterical claims. But opinion polls suggested that many in Tokyo agreed with them. And that was the point – he intended to tap into a suppressed fear that has started to erupt sporadically through the skin of the Japanese psyche.

Japan has largely recovered from the bubble and the devastation it wrought. But for the first time since Hiroshima and Nagasaki, many Japanese feel uneasy about an external power – not the United States this time, but China. Visiting Tokyo, one can almost feel the deep pulsing boom of economic growth from across the East China Sea, like the approaching footsteps of a new Godzilla. Is this adolescent giant benign or malignant? Until this question is answered, Godzilla excites and terrifies in equal measure. Both Japan and Taiwan benefit substantially from being nestled so close to the twenty-first century's new economic superpower. But the political implications of change remain opaque. Speaking at a closed session of the World Economic Forum in Davos in 2007, a senior Korean corporate leader articulated the fears of all China's neighbours. 'I am very impressed with Hu Jintao and the current Chinese leadership,' he said, 'they are good and honest partners and I like doing business with them. But what happens if we get a different, more nationalist leadership in China – we will all be worried and afraid.' Being close to the outer edges of the economy, the *yakuza* have sensitive antennae that are often able to pick up changes in the environment earlier than others.

Yet in contrast to most major national criminal operations, the *yakuza* do not travel well. When they venture abroad it is not to make money, but to have fun. In the 1960s the prohibition on gambling in Japan led them to visit Korea, the Philippines, Thailand, Taiwan,

Hong Kong and Macao in search of casinos and cheap sex. Their quest coincided with a huge influx of American men into eastern Asia, involved in the Vietnam War. But this group, too, when they left the battlefields of 'Nam, went looking for nearby brothels. The regional criminal economy that the Americans and Japanese fostered has since expanded hugely, embracing consumers (almost exclusively men) from the subcontinent, Europe, the Middle East and parts of Africa. But the *yakuza* did not seek to establish overall control of this trade. They certainly invested heavily in the legitimate tourist trade, purchasing hotels, restaurants and other facilities, but the selling of protection and the use of violence was left to the Chinese, the Thais or the Filipinos.

This is not to say they did not take some pride in using US business opportunities to launder the vast amounts of money accrued from the bubble and the more traditional criminal activities of gambling, prostitution and trafficking in methamphetamine (eastern Asia's drug of choice long before it hit the US). They bought into leisure facilities across the western United States, but especially into Hawaii and Las Vegas.

Nobody would admit this publicly, but many Japanese derive some satisfaction from the knowledge that the *yakuza* is eating into the licit economy of Pacific America. While proclaiming their dependency on each other in economic and security matters, US–Japanese relations are misted by an unspoken mutual cultural suspicion. Congress has expressed this most forcefully in a report on Asian organised-crime activity in the US, after the FBI had indicated its difficulty in combating the *yakuza* because Japan's police were dragging their feet: 'Anemic Japanese law enforcement efforts against *Boryokudan* gangs have had an adverse impact on the United States,' according to the report. 'The executive branch should negotiate formal and informal agreements with Japan to improve law enforcement cooperation and intelligence sharing. In addition, the State Department should amend current visa regulations to make *Boryokudan* membership an independent basis for denying a visa.'

To this day, the *yakuza* enjoy laundering their cash through the US. But their business remains concentrated at home. In contrast to the Sicilian mafia, which in the last fifteen years has taken some heavy blows in the domestic arena, the *yakuza* continue to enjoy a powerful and lucrative position inside Japan, so there is less incentive to expand abroad.

But as more mainland Chinese enter Japan as legal and illegal labour migrants, so do the triads and other Chinese organised-crime operations expand their influence in the country. In 2003, a senior official at the National Police Agency in Tokyo told a researcher that clashes between the *yakuza* and the Chinese gangs were proliferating. He explained this as the consequence of a 'conflict over turf and the low price that Chinese assassins charge for the job. A Chinese gangster will do three jobs for the price a *yakuza* will charge for one.' Just like everyone else, the *yakuza* are worried about the influence and strength of Chinese organised crime in Japan.

The notorious murder at the Parisienne brought swift retribution from the *yakuza*. 'After the two Japanese were killed, Chinese clubs were fire-bombed,' recalled Agata-san, whose patch as a senior Sumiyoshi-kai boss includes part of Kabuki-cho. 'Faecal matter was spread all over them and I think some dead Chinese were found lying on the rail tracks. That's the last we heard of them . . . Nobody has been arrested yet and we don't know who the Chinese were. Nonetheless, the *yakuza* sent a clear message that if you mess with the mafia, then this is what you get. I think the message was well communicated.'

What is less well advertised is the symbiotic relationship between the *yakuza* and Chinese gangs in cities like Tokyo, Yokohama and Osaka. Increasingly, the *yakuza* outsource the punitive deployment of violence to Chinese gangs. 'The mainland Chinese don't care about this,' a Taiwanese businessman, who travels low under the radar screen as he moves between China, Taiwan and Japan, explained. 'If they are caught, they face a short spell in jail and then deportation. Then the snakeheads bring them right back here. And the *yakuza* will go out and commission them again.' The implication of this is extraordinary – the *yakuza* are combating their recruitment difficulties provoked by an ageing society and the declining prestige of their organisation by subcontracting Chinese groups to carry out the least attractive and riskiest part of their business.

When I ask the old *yakuza* hand, *Toppamono*, whether he thinks

Chinese organised crime has come to represent a long-term threat to the *yakuza*, his smile broadens into a smirk. 'Let me put it like this,' he says, 'if I was a broker I'd be telling my clients now to move out of *yakuza* stocks and start investing in the triads!'

THE FUTURE OF ORGANISED CRIME

Another sip of delicate green tea. Another pause. Then another whispered explanation. 'Behind Chen Kai there was a shadow. A dark shadow. This is an invisible force, a dark force here in Fuzhou and it did not operate behind Chen Kai alone. You only see the shadow when it strikes – then it is too late.'

Talking in metaphors is central to the experience of China. The invisible shadow conjured up by a cautious businessman in Fuzhou catches the sense of unease that is common to all police states. Unlike most police states, however, China has made room for a rampant culture of conspicuous consumption that obscures the presence of the shadow. As 'the richest man in Fuzhou', Chen Kai had sophisticated instruments for tracking the capricious moods of the shadow, and so perhaps he had less to fear than most.

Until his arrest on May 16th, 2003, he was on top of the world. Good-looking, tall and in his early forties, he sported a diamond-encrusted watch. And Chen could survey the capital of Fujian province from atop his glitzy entertainment complex, the Music Plaza, or from the penthouse suite at his luxury apartment development, Triumphant Gardens, the most expensive real estate in the city. Or, indeed, from any one of the other hotels, restaurants and housing estates he owned.

A few months earlier, Chen had welcomed Song Zuying in person when she performed at the Plaza. China's most glamorous singing star and a Grammy nominee, Song had followed the path already travelled by many of the country's glitterati to the Plaza's stage door. Chen's generosity was fabled – he was happy to shell out up to RMB 200,000

($26,000) for a half-hour performance. And the Music Plaza was the place to be seen.

As in many parts of China, the money and celebrity also attracted the distinctive blacked-out cars with a K or an O registration, denoting senior Party and Security officials respectively. The Chief of Police and other big shots would regularly join in an evening of gambling, supplemented by bottles of vintage mao-tai liqueur and Hennessy XO champagne cognac, served by some of the joint's 200 hostesses.

Nobody from Chen's village in nearby Minhou County could have dreamed that his career might develop so spectacularly. Born just after the Great Leap Forward, Mao Zedong's murderous programme of agricultural reform, Chen grew up during the Cultural Revolution, a living nightmare for most of China, characterised by fear, intimidation, starvation and butchery. From 1959 to 1976, hundreds of millions of Chinese shared a single goal: survival. Tens of millions did not make it or were so damaged by the state-inflicted violence that their lives were barely worth living. This was especially so in Chen's poor community in Fujian, on China's east coast. Mao Zedong suspected this backward province of harbouring all manner of class traitors and counter-revolutionaries, and so for three decades he neglected the region as a punishment for suspected thought-crimes and recidivist bourgeois habits. Perhaps it was to compensate for Mao's vindictive behaviour that China's great reformer, Deng Xiaoping, chose the city of Xiamen in southern Fujian as one of the first Special Economic Zones (SEZs) in the early 1980s to inspire local entrepreneurs in thawing out the economy, which had been frozen solid by the Maoist ice-age. Agog at the success of the Xiamen experiment, Fuzhou's local bosses soon opened up the provincial capital as well. Deng did not confer the honour on Fujian by chance – 80 per cent of Taiwan's people trace their roots back to Fujian. By opening up this province, Deng hoped to attract huge investment from Taiwan to the mainland. And he was proved right.

Chen's peasant father took advantage of the new opportunities. 'He started his own business, transporting goods into Fuzhou from the surrounding countryside with a hand-pulled cart,' said Mr Jiang as he took a tea break at a small tile shop, Wild Goose Ceramics. By the standards of the time, Mr Jiang observed with a smile, this made him a master entrepreneur, the equivalent of a Harvard MBA. We drank our tea in small gulps and stared at the huge blue mansion, now empty, that Chen had built for his mother and father. Although Chen is still alive – probably – his ghost already stalks all Fuzhou.

Chen graduated from his father's laborious trade of hauling vegetables and such like to selling carpets door-to-door. He accumulated enough capital to rent a shop where he sold electronic goods. This was in itself revolutionary. In the early 1980s, the state still told most Chinese what profession they would pursue and where. Choice was both precious and rare. Generally life was unutterably boring. 'There was nothing – nothing to buy, nothing to do at the time,' said the photographer and businessman, Wan Sui. 'Shops selling anything but the most basic goods barely existed and so Chen stood out.' Traditionally, Fuzhou boasted a bigger selection of consumer goods than almost any other part of China. In the 1980s, it was the only place you could buy blue jeans, for example, and people would come to this province from all over the country for a pair. The reason for Fuzhou's relative diversity was one of the many reasons why Chairman Mao so despised its people. A hundred miles from the port of Fuzhou lies Taiwan, the nationalist thorn in communist China's flesh. If Taiwanese smugglers made it across the small stretch of water to the mainland, they landed in Fujian. Apart from proximity, Fujian province and Taiwan are linked by language – they speak the same dialect, and even those who hail from Shanghai or Beijing must strain to understand a single word the Fujianese are saying.

Days after Deng announced his cautious economic reforms thirty years ago, dozens of fishing boats from Taiwan and Fujian were meeting in the sea halfway between the territories to exchange money for cassette recorders, which were then sold by men like Chen. And his experience in electrical goods led to his first big break – securing the exclusive concession to sell Hitachi colour televisions in Fuzhou. These were the first colour TVs to hit China and the concession opened the door to considerable wealth. Before long, Chen was investing in larger shops before becoming a pioneer of Fuzhou's entertainment industry.

In the early 1990s, a shy young man, Xu Li, took a shine to one of Chen's girlfriends. Despite his charisma, Chen was not a great womaniser and he magnanimously acceded to Li's request to start dating the girl. Soon afterwards, Li introduced Chen to his father – Xu Congrong. Xu grew very fond of Chen and before long he had pronounced himself Chen's godfather. A blessed embrace for Chen, it turned out, as Xu Congrong was the chief of Fuzhou's Public Security Bureau. The marriage of Chen's restless entrepreneurial spirit to Xu's power as the province's most senior law-enforcement officer was happy and fruitful. It spawned one of a new breed – the Political Criminal Nexus (PCN), a profoundly corrupt relationship between the local tycoons and party leaders. The Chinese Government has watched perplexed as these mischievous offspring grow across the country. Beijing feels threatened by the PCN, 'mainly because it is eroding the authority of the Chinese Communist Party (CCP)', as Ko-lin Chin, America's foremost expert on Chinese organised crime, has argued. 'In other words, for the Chinese Government, the PCN is first a political issue and second a criminal-justice issue.'

But it is also a matter of economics – the PCNs create a lot of wealth, and in Fuzhou the golden years began. Under Xu's protection, Chen Kai started importing slot machines into his clubs. Gambling is strictly illegal in China (with the jaw-dropping exception of the former Portuguese colony of Macao). Except under Mao, however, that has never stopped most Chinese indulging in the habit with an industrial zeal. As the gamblers of Fuzhou fed the machines, the coins fell out the other end into Chen's pockets. In November 1997, Gu Wei, a reporter with the newspaper *Fuzhou Evening*, published the only story ever written on the trade. It was intended as the first in a series, but after a gunman fired shots into Mr Gu's front room, he chose discretion over valour and dropped his interest in the subject. Meanwhile Chen kept on making money and shrewdly investing the profits in the Chinese businessman's most important commodity – influence in the Chinese Communist Party.

This arrangement is not peculiar to Fuzhou. 'The only people you are afraid of in this country are the Party or the Police – nobody else. So you *have* to keep them onside,' explained Paul French, a British businessman living in Shanghai. 'Nobody gets rich here by being 100 per cent clean,' he continued. 'I'm not 100 per cent clean and nobody else is. If we did everything by the book, nothing would ever get done'.

The Government, or more precisely the Party, maintains this close control over its citizens because it is frightened. Like its imperialist predecessors in power, the CCP nurses a visceral fear of the chaos that could ensue were its authority undermined. The anarchic collapse of the Soviet Union struck terror into the hearts of China's bureaucrats, and a possible repetition in the Middle Kingdom keeps them awake at night. They have located multiple sources whence this chaos might burst forth: the PCNs; peasant unrest; fragmentation along provincial and regional lines; mass social and religious movements like the Falun Gong cult; excessive foreign influence in the economy; democratisation; or a significant economic downturn. While all these threats to Party authority are real, some are more remote than others. The Party's ability to assess and handle potential disruption lies at the core of the debate among China's elite and sinologists worldwide as to where China is heading and what its impact on the rest of the globe will be. Yet frequently the Party discovers that in capping one source of disruption, it simply diverts the flow of latent chaos to a second, adding to its force in the process.

The futurology of China is hence an uncertain science. As perhaps its primary concern, however, the CCP monitors social unrest in the impoverished countryside. If it fails to provide sufficient new jobs every year for the rural masses streaming into the coastal cities in search of work, or if the staggering gap in wealth between town and country continues to widen, then the disappointed peasants are perfectly capable of shaking the foundations of regional Party power. In the last five years, the number of peasant riots has risen spectacularly to roughly 80,000 per year and they continue to proliferate. These outbursts of discontent can be serious, involving the wrecking of local government offices and the lynching of officials. In spring 2007, the BBC's James Reynolds visited Zhushan deep in central China after news had filtered through of one such riot; 20,000 protestors had taken to the streets after the local privately owned bus company exploited its monopoly by doubling the fares. Buses were overturned and burned before the authorities mobilised the military and riot police. On arrival, Reynolds described a town under martial law. A few weeks before this, the Government in Beijing had relaxed restrictions on foreign journalists, allowing them to travel anywhere in the country without prior permission. Nonetheless, within a matter of hours of his arrival in Zhushan, Reynolds was detained, interrogated and then expelled from the town.

In the short term, China uses military force to quell this growing pattern of rebellion, but in the long term it seeks to counteract peasant unrest by creating tens of millions of jobs every year to placate the legions of impoverished rural workers. To this end, anything is permissible. 'It doesn't matter whether the cat is black or white,' mused Deng Xiaoping when he was explaining the need to introduce economic reforms in the 1980s, 'it only matters if it catches mice.' It doesn't matter how China runs the economy, as long as it makes money.

Deng realised that for the Chinese to make money required dumping the traditions of central economic planning, and so for twenty-five years (and especially since the early 1990s) the Government has afforded the provinces considerable autonomy in their economic policy. Their confidence in exploiting this exposes an important myth – China is not a huge monolith moving inexorably towards global domination. Indeed, economic change is fragmenting the country, highlighting its tremendous cultural diversity; reinventing rivalries and alliances; and heightening the tension between 'the centre' (Beijing) and 'the periphery' (everywhere else).

Having established their independence from Beijing, provincial government and businesses devote much energy to warding off the capital's interfering ways. They are much more comfortable than Beijing with the Political Criminal Nexus as both a system of governance and an economic strategy: the local elites can feather their nests and deliver the requisite job quota demanded by the centre year after year. 'It doesn't matter whether the mice are black or white,' as Deng's saying has now been paraphrased, 'as long as they avoid the cat.' The provinces may be as corrupt as they wish in making their money, as long as Beijing doesn't catch them red-handed.

Once Deng Xiaoping had given his blessing to economic experiment, a truly wild version of capitalism quickly swept away decades of stagnant socialist planning in the SEZs, especially in the south of the country. Entrepreneurs could manufacture and sell anything they wished if there was a market. All they needed was to find their *baohusang* or 'protective umbrella', whose spokes were local Party bureaucrats able to reduce business risks by signing licences or stifling the curiosity of regulatory bodies. The cost of the umbrella was high, but could be paid in a variety of currencies. 'If we ran into a senior CP official,' explained a European businessman in Fuzhou, 'we might have bought them an apartment; we might have bought them a car; we might have arranged a scholarship for their son or daughter to go to the Sorbonne, Heidelberg or perhaps Oxford.'

Mysterious events can curtail the careers of Communist Party officials without warning or explanation. Once expelled, they must survive on a measly pension that cannot keep pace with inflation. In his perceptive novel, A Case of Two Cities, Qiu Xiaolong relates the gripping fictional tale of a PCN that straddles Fuzhou and Shanghai. Contemplating a difficult interview with a powerful Party official, Qiu's hero, Chief Inspector Chen (no relation to Chen Kai!), reflects on the pressure of public service and money in China:

> Chen understood why a large number of Party cadres were unable to resist the materialistic temptation. As Dong had implied, the system was far from fair. As a hardworking chief inspector, Chen earned about the same state-specified salary that a janitor in the bureau did . . . Once he had seen a Ming-style mahogany desk in a furniture store. It took him five or six months to save enough money for it. When he finally went there with the sum, the desk was long gone.

The logic for both bureaucrats and policemen is inexorable: they have to leverage the money-makers, be they businessmen, criminals or both, while they are able. And even if they are not inclined to corruption, pressure from their peers will usually change their mind – a single mouse cannot survive in a house of cats. Chinese officials invest billions of dollars every year across the globe as personal guarantees against enforced retirement or, worse, a political purge. The latest vogue for both businessmen and Party officials is for their children to be born abroad, preferably in the United States, so that the youngsters are eligible for American citizenship. Because the relationship between bureaucracy and business is corrupt and not accountable to an independent judiciary, the Political Criminal Nexus creates an environment in which weeds and flowers alike can bloom. The more poisonous varieties draw the immediate attention of the head gardener: criminal groups prone to violence or fomenting public disorder usually attract swift police intervention. In stark contrast to Russia in the 1990s, the Chinese state has fiercely resisted ceding its monopoly on violence to private organisations.

Until 2003, Fuzhou's PCN was rampant – Chen Kai's friends in high places included the Mayor and Deputy Party Secretary of Fuzhou and the most senior members of the Party Consultative Committee. Even when Chen's main protector, Xu Congrong, retired, he was able to appoint his successor as police chief to ensure that Chen's economic dominance was not interrupted. Over a ten-year period, Chen paid out tens of millions of dollars in bribes, securing influence throughout the entire administration.

Fuzhou is no ordinary provincial capital – it is the centre of one of the globe's biggest illegal operations: the trade in Chinese migrant labour. Squeezed by a rapidly growing population and high rural un-employment, more than half a million Fujianese were smuggled abroad between 1985 and 1995. Around one-fifth of these landed on America's eastern seaboard and headed for New York, including most of the 286 souls who swam to New York's shore from the *Golden Venture*, run aground in 1993 after its human cargo had finally mutinied after months of mistreatment. In São Paulo, in Belgrade, in Berlin, in Dubai and in South Africa, the Fujianese have either established or come to dominate the Chinese communities. The province's distinct dialect is steadily eroding Cantonese as the lingua franca in many Chinatowns around the world. Brooklyn's Eighth Avenue began as a Cantonese settlement, but in just six years since the millennium, immigrants from Fujian have come to make up almost 50 per cent of the popu-lation.

It is the snakeheads, or people-traffickers, who make it all possible. These men and women pump people relentlessly into boats, planes and trains to replenish what has now become the biggest retail trading and migrant labour network in the world. And in return the migrants pump remittances and capital back into Fujian. They also reduce the unemployment rate in the province. Let there be no doubt – the snake-heads enjoy the tacit backing of the authorities, both thanks to the rules of the PCN and because, further up the political food chain, it is not in Beijing's interests to disrupt the trade. The local authorities are brazen in their support for emigration, some styling themselves as part of a 'New Overseas Chinese Area'. They even organise classes instructing aspiring migrants in 'general knowledge about foreign countries (legal affairs, customs, local conditions abroad) and training in sewing, cooking, and trading', as Frank Pieke, a leading Oxford scholar on Chinese migration, has observed.

The Government in Beijing completes the virtuous circle of profit by placing all manner of tax and financial incentives for overseas Chinese to invest back in the mainland. There are no awkward questions asked about the money's origin, which goes some way to explaining why the two biggest sources of capital invested in China are Hong Kong and the British Virgin Islands!

Fuqing, fifty miles south-east of Fuzhou, is just another million-strong city that has sprung up unbeknownst to the rest of China, let alone the outside world. Fuqing exports two main commodities: car windscreens (it supplies 90 per cent of China's needs) and labour migrants. In the city centre, preposterously garish skyscrapers overwhelm the unprepossessing residential blocks of the communist period. The showpiece is the enigmatically titled Surefar Enjoy Hotel, adorned by hundreds of reflective copper windows, a reminder of how post-communist arriviste chic always has a surprise in store. The more outrageous the architecture, the more prosperous the city, and there is a lot of cash in Fuqing. The snakeheads, conveyors of men and women to their Yankee dream, generate much of it.

But it is the rural settlements around the major cities like Fuqing that offer the most astonishing testimony to the adventurous spirit of the Fujianese. In place of rice and tea, the Fujianese peasant has planted houses. Not shacks or cutesy cottages, but five- and six-storey neo-classical monsters financed by their earnings overseas. Hundreds upon hundreds are dotted around the Fujianese countryside – the majority contain just one family who occupy only a single floor. Many are completely empty. These are the most ubiquitous and grand manifestations of 'face' in Fujian. Regardless of one's personal woes, 'face' dictates that one must project one's achievements in as ostentatious a manner as possible. As a foreigner, it is nigh-impossible to pay a restaurant bill if dining with an indigent in China, because all would regard this an unacceptable loss of 'face'. And so, in order to show their 'face' to the outside world in all its pomp, the labour migrant of Fujian cultivates houses.

The seeds of this strange fruit are scattered by the snakehead. It is the snakehead who enables the unemployed to escape rural poverty and have a shot at making it big somewhere in the world. Whole villages or communities club together to pay for the trip. It costs $20,000–70,000 (depending on the émigré's destination) to send a single person abroad. Once the nominated worker has arrived at a foreign location, he or she is expected to work all hours for the benefit of those who have pooled their savings to pay the snakehead.

In the West, the moniker 'snakehead' has a pejorative ring to it – snakeheads are popularly portrayed as evil, manipulative crime bosses, exploiting the misery of China's despairing poor by sending them to a labour hellhole in some god-forsaken part of the world. Cases that conform to this image – the *Golden Venture* off New York, the Dutch lorry in Dover with its payload of dead men, and the Morecambe Bay cockle-pickers' tragedy – are in fact the exceptions that prove the rule. Snakeheads are not triads – the criminal outfits based in Hong Kong that are classic mafia protection and extortion rackets, as well as traders in illegal goods. Nor are they linked organisationally with the syndicates that dominate Taiwanese politics, like the United Bamboo Gang. Rather, they are effectively travel agents who include illegal entry to a third country in their service remit.

In the US, the Department of Justice floated an idea of offering an amnesty to illegal Chinese immigrants who would testify against the snakeheads. 'When the DoJ came to me with this idea,' explained Professor Ko-lin Chin in New Jersey, 'I said, "You've gotta be crazy!" These snakeheads are regarded as heroes by the illegal immigrants. They pay the fee quite happily – there is no coercion. The snakeheads are heroes, not villains. The last thing the migrants want to do is turn these people in – they want to thank them!'

*   *   *

We will never know what Lin Guo Hua thought of the snakehead who flew him to Belgrade. The Serbian capital witnessed the fastest growth of any Chinatown in the world during the late 1990s, despite Serbia's status at the time as an international pariah. Slobodan Milosevic had cultivated the Chinese leadership after the imposition of economic sanctions on the former Yugoslavia in 1993. This included lifting Serbia's visa requirement for Chinese citizens: the snakeheads could now fly planeloads of would-be migrants close to the heart of Europe. No more dodgy boat trips; no more expensive negotiations with Russian and Ukrainian policemen. No more setting up safe houses in Bucharest or dodging police in Budapest. Wham! Fly to within 250 miles of the European Union's borders and receive a friendly welcome. The infrastructure was up and running within weeks – at Belgrade's administrative offices, bilingual signs were posted in an attempt to assist the Chinese seeking to smuggle themselves into the EU. A bubbling Chinatown flourished among the tower blocks at the end of Yuri Gagarin Street in New Belgrade. As I wandered around this cacophonous retail madhouse, it was clear that – unlike most Chinatowns – the traders had no interest in penetrating the local Serbian market (ridden by hyper-inflation, gangsterism and poverty): they were servicing the itinerant Chinese with final provisions for their journey north and west. This is where many of the fifty-eight men who suffocated in that Dutch lorry at Dover in the summer of 2000 first touched European soil, before being taken across Slovenia into Austria and then up to Rotterdam.

Milosevic, of course, knew perfectly well why the Chinese were arriving every day in their hundreds. It was his way of sticking two fingers up at the EU for Brussels's hostility towards him. The Chinese Government knew this as well, because it does not view the snakeheads as criminal, either. By exporting labour, the snakeheads extend China's influence around the world and contribute to the economy, both by alleviating unemployment and by sending money home. Others who celebrate the snakeheads (often tacitly) include the European, American and Middle Eastern businessmen and -women who revel in the unstinting work ethic of the Chinese, which comes at a bargain price. The consumer also benefits (albeit unwittingly) because the cost of labour drives down prices and extends choice.

So if all parties derive profit from the work of the snakeheads, should they not, perhaps, be legalised? And why are they so excoriated in the West?

The snakeheads are smugglers, not traffickers. They do not, on the whole, fix up jobs in the country of destination – they get you there and then it is up to you. Victims of labour-trafficking are kidnapped or duped by traffickers in league with employers, who intend to enslave or coerce the migrant labourers. The snakeheads who arranged the travel plans for the ill-fated cockle-pickers who were swept out to sea from the beach at Morecambe Bay in Lancashire had nothing to do with their employment. They conveyed them to the United Kingdom as they had agreed – no more and no less. And few Chinese are forced into overseas labour contracts; they enter into them willingly. The illegality of labour-smuggling lies in the illogicality of globalisation. The EU (the United Kingdom, Ireland, Spain and Italy in particular) is desperately short of labour. By 2050, Europe's median age will have risen to fifty – only Japan is ageing faster. As Europeans get older, they place an ever greater strain on the generous welfare state systems that became the continent's hallmark after the Second World War. But because they are also having ever fewer children, the workforce able to sustain the welfare system through taxes is shrinking.

And so Europe is faced with a choice: either its citizens rediscover the joy of reproductive sex, or they allow more people from outside into the licit labour market. Few Europeans objected to the opening of markets in far-flung places to enable the export of their goods, services and capital as globalisation took hold. But they have proved stubbornly reluctant to accept the quid pro quo of labour movement *into* Europe. The governments of the EU find themselves trying to balance the disparate interests of two powerful forces: the populist media that warn against the 'swamping' of indigenous culture by immigrants; and the urgent entreaties of business, which needs cheap labour to survive in a ferociously competitive global market. At a European summit in Helsinki in 1999, Prime Ministers from across the continent pledged to cooperate in developing a managed immigration policy to introduce some order into this unholy mess. Eight years later, even the most experienced observers of Brussels's arcane bureaucracy have yet to register any verifiable sightings of the policy in action – and so, for shrewd entrepreneurs like the snakeheads, opportunity continues to knock.

By its very nature, it is impossible to ascertain the level of illegal migration, but Britain is generally regarded as the favourite destination for migrants seeking work. Throughout the 1990s and 2000s, the long-term impact of Margaret Thatcher's economic reforms ensured that there were plenty of low-paid jobs available in Britain as the service and construction sectors boomed. In the retail sector, supermarkets demanded produce in much larger quantities than before, as Britain aped the megastore patterns familiar in the United States (but rare elsewhere in Europe). Farmers and food-processing companies looked abroad for the army of labourers prepared to undertake the miserably repetitive and physically shattering work of picking and sorting produce for low pay. The decline of trade unions and the rise in affluence of the indigenous population enabled employers to drive down wages in these industries for the predominantly immigrant workforce. Outside of Starbucks and McDonald's, the only time immigrant workers came to public attention was either when they committed a crime or when they died in gruesome circumstances.

Although the Fujianese dominate the Chinese communities in southern Asia and helped to establish new Chinatowns in places like Budapest and São Paulo, in Britain they came up against one of the most entrenched communities, the Cantonese from Hong Kong, whose pedigree stretches back to the nineteenth century. Unable to assimilate into this community, the Fujianese were pushed to the margins, where they became prey to some of the most unscrupulous employers in the country – the gangmasters. And this was the misfortune of the cockle-pickers in Morecambe Bay. Of the nineteen who drowned there in February 2004, sixteen came from Fuqing and surrounding villages.

'He called me just a few hours before he drowned,' sobbed Su Hang Qi quietly. 'He told me about the cockle-picking, and how he hated the job and that it was badly paid. He said he received £5 for one bag of cockles, but that he would have to carry on if he were to receive his back-pay. Guo Bing Long called his wife, my friend,' Su continued, 'from the beach as they were drowning. "The water is up to my chest," he told her, "the bosses got the time wrong. I can't get back in time!"' He was still talking as the water engulfed them.

In her early thirties, Su now brings up her daughters in two rooms of a rundown cottage twenty minutes from Fuqing. She has no electricity, one gas ring and occasionally secures work at a local restaurant washing up. 'I still owe RMB 300,000 ($40,000) and I am paying interest on this,' she continues. Her nine-year-old clings to her side looking frightened and sorrowful. On her fleece is written a message in English: 'I miss you my friend.'

Su and Mrs Lin, whose husband also drowned, are quick to exonerate the snakehead who transported their menfolk. 'This is simply supply and demand,' Mrs Lin says briskly. 'Our husbands and cousins wanted to travel to England and they provided that service.' They insist that the snakehead (or 'the boss' as they call him) only demanded the money once their husbands had confirmed their arrival in Europe and the UK. But I sensed they protested too much when I enquired whether they had been in touch with the boss since the accident. 'I never met him. I never saw him,' said Su nervously. 'I only know his bank account and, after I paid him, I didn't have any contact.' I was convinced the two women were holding back, frightened of retribution, should details about the snakehead leak out.

It is only by accident that Mrs Lin revealed how the smugglers had threatened her husband with violence if he complained about his treatment. Snakeheads regularly use violence against clients who don't pay up. Most have associates living in Chinatowns the world over to enforce this, if necessary. The journeys are uncomfortable, uncertain and frightening at best. At worst they are fatal. The snakeheads are not nice people and they are involved in organised criminal activities. Nonetheless, the migrants whom they smuggle are clients more often than victims.

They are not disposed, of course, to hand out compensation to their clients if things go wrong, as at Morecambe Bay. The two widows, Mrs Su and Mrs Lin, cling desperately to the fanciful notion that the British Government will compensate them so that they can escape the misery of a hand-to-mouth existence defined by huge debt. Their creditors refuse to believe that London has not granted them compensation. In reality, they have abandoned hope – flotsam on the turbulent seas of globalisation and crime.

JAMES B. COMEY, the United States Attorney for the Southern District of New York, and DUAN DAQI, Police Liaison Officer for the Ministry of Public Security for the People's Republic of China, announced today that 25 defendants have been indicted in Manhattan federal court for being members of a massive heroin-trafficking organisation that smuggled more than $100 million worth of Southeast Asian heroin into the United States from 2000 to the present. At present, 20 people have been arrested, both here and overseas . . .

The joint statement by Comey and Daqi in May 2003 was triumphant. They had arrested the 125 Gang's four top leaders – known in the heroin-smuggling trade as The Untouchables. The quartet's nickname was not just an ironic homage to Elliot Ness, purported nemesis of Al Capone. The No. 1 Untouchable, Wong Kin-Cheung, had boasted they would never be caught. The Untouchables were the masterminds of the 125 Gang, named after stubby Mr Wong's great weight, 125 kilos (275 pounds). Wong had first come to the attention of US law enforcement in 1989 for his role in a drugs network run out of Manhattan's Chinatown. Arrested and convicted, he was sentenced to four years in jail followed by deportation to China after he had completed his sentence in 1994.

Back in Asia, Wong secured Hong Kong citizenship for himself, but commuted between Britain's colonial territory (until it came back under the jurisdiction of the mainland in 1997) and Fuzhou. In Fuzhou, Wong set up his own nightclub, the Huamei Entertainment Co., which is located a few hundred yards from Chen Kai's Music Plaza. According to Chen's business partners, the relationship between the two men was cordial. Using Fuzhou and Hong Kong as his two headquarters, Wong established links with heroin wholesalers among the rebel Shan tribes in eastern Burma, the world's second-largest opium-growing region after Afghanistan. A significant part of the resistance to Burma's foul military junta is financed by two less-than-salubrious trades: trafficking in heroin and trafficking in women, the former servicing addicts throughout the world, the latter servicing primarily the tens of thousands of Western men visiting Thailand every year for cheap sex. The opium is grown in the Golden Triangle, much of which is in Shan-held territory. The failure of Western policy in Afghanistan since the intervention of 2001 has ensured that the Central Asian country has outstripped all other poppy-growing regions in the world. But thanks to the liberalisation of trade between Burma and China, the Golden Triangle has also experienced a revival of its opium tradition.

Until 1949, China had been a major grower, consumer and exporter of opium. But after Mao Zedong's communist takeover in 1949, the industry was eradicated as the Party constructed an effective and ruthless police state. Opiates disappeared from China for forty years, but as Deng Xiaoping's economic reforms accelerated in the early 1990s, the drug in its modern form, heroin, began creeping back. By 1998, the Shanghai Annual Police Review reported that drugs-related crime was up 250 per cent over the previous year. This reflected a trend visible across the country, but it was especially resonant in Shanghai, China's first port and second city, because of its pre-war history. Shanghai in the 1920s and 1930s was an international treaty city that was used by imperial powers to manage trade in and out of China. It was divided up into different zones or concessions, each run by a European power and the United States. Along with Chicago, it was also the largest centre of criminal activity in the world. Thanks to the organisational genius of Du Yueh Sheng, known by all as Big-Eared Du, the Shanghai triads were consolidated under his group, the Green Gang, whose history became intimately linked to the rise of Chiang Kai-shek as the head of China's nationalist movement. Just as political parties in Eastern Europe and the Soviet Union fused with crime groups to finance themselves after the fall of communism, so did China's political movements (including the Communist Party) fund themselves through crime in the 1920s and 1930s.

Where Al Capone rose on a tidal wave of illegal liquor, Big-Eared Du developed Shanghai as the largest centre for the sale and global distribution of opium from the Golden Triangle. Even more than gambling and prostitution, opium was Shanghai's trademark, reinforcing the port's separateness from the rest of China, and notably from its great rival Beijing. Although the Green Gang opened tentative negotiations with Mao and the Communist Party in the late 1940s in anticipation of the coming political earthquake, no agreement was reached. Once the revolution triumphed in 1949, Mao succeeded in destroying the influence of the Shanghai triads. Organised crime that had exerted such a profound influence on Chinese history in the nineteenth and twentieth centuries was obliterated as a social and economic force for three decades. The triads, the entrepreneurs of rebellion and collaboration in the name of profit, and whose name implied the harmonious balance between Heaven, Earth and Man, were eradicated. The traditions and structures survived in the colonial remnants, Hong Kong and Macao, but also in Chiang Kai-shek's Taiwan and the Chinatowns of South-East Asia and Europe. Some have argued that the destruction of Shanghai's triads was one of Mao's monumental achievements. Others have countered that to do this he turned the Chinese state into one of the most powerful criminal instruments ever devised, a killing machine that has the blood of forty million people on its hands.

Mao's legacy remains palpable in Shanghai: the triads have not returned since the liberalisation of the country's economy. But heroin has made a forceful comeback. It returned with the millions of migrant workers that Shanghai needed to construct its hyper-modernist skyline. From their cramped, miserable quarters in squalid districts like Xuhui, the peasantry – often illiterate and already with a heroin habit picked up in the villages – have been building the new Shanghai's skyscrapers at frenetic speed. Thanks to his astonishing documentary series, *Shanghai Vice*, British director Phil Agland has given an excellent insight into how seriously Shanghai's police forces now view the issue of the heroin trade and what an immense challenge it presents. The chief of the Criminal Investigation Unit, Li Rui Ping, reported that by 1999 hundreds of pounds per month were entering Shanghai to supply local addicts. This suggests ferocious rates of drug dependency. 'There are two networks that supply heroin to Shanghai,' he continued. 'We haven't penetrated them yet, but these rings are very sophisticated.' One network transports heroin from the far west, Xinjiang province, which borders Kyrgyzstan and receives its heroin from Afghanistan. The other comes up through the Burmese border into southern China. Both pass through the central distribution centre of Guangdong, the major Cantonese city. Here not only are prices low, but levels of police corruption are high. In one dramatic sequence of *Shanghai Vice*, the Shanghai police mount an undercover sting in Guangdong without alerting the local police because – as they openly admit – their Cantonese colleagues are so corrupt they would tip off the heroin-wholesalers immediately.

The Shanghai police are frank that, with these levels of corruption and limited financial resources, it has been extremely difficult to infiltrate the new decentralised crime networks that have spread across the country. In the drugs trade, they wield one very blunt but intimidating instrument: the death penalty. The courts can order the execution of anyone found with just 50 grams (1¾ ounces) of heroin, or long periods of imprisonment for possession of less. 'China has plenty of state-run rehabilitation centres,' as one commentator noted, 'but they function more like prisons and treat drug users like criminals. Some addicts even find it easier to buy drugs from crooked guards inside the detox centres than on the streets. Not surprisingly, the failure rate at these facilities is alarmingly high: relapses are estimated at between 70 per cent and 90 per cent.'

Chinese jails are now being clogged up by vulnerable users. The big dealing syndicates who have sufficient cash not just to bribe police forces, but to establish their own intelligence and counter-surveillance operations, are netted less often. The Intelligence Division of the US drug-busting agency, the DEA, has now reported that 'Many individuals and criminal organisations involved in drug trafficking are increasingly arming themselves with automatic weapons and grenades to protect their drug shipments from theft by rival organisations. Many firefights occur along the Burma–China border, where larger drug shipments are more prevalent. Traffickers also arm themselves to avoid being captured by the police, and some smugglers are better armed than the local police forces. Furthermore, many traffickers believe they have a better chance of surviving a firefight than the outcome of any legal proceedings.'

The emergence of armed groups inside China and around its borders threatens, of course, to undermine the state's monopoly on violence and is therefore regarded with utmost seriousness by the authorities. This may have influenced Beijing's deliberations when it agreed in 2000 to permit the creation of the first-ever joint DEA–China Public Security Bureau operation. The Chinese have a long history of suspicion of outside powers, which was heavily reinforced by their experience as major victims of imperialism and colonialism in the nineteenth and twentieth centuries. For Beijing to sanction a joint police taskforce that saw DEA agents operate on Chinese soil was a hugely telling decision, which symbolised China's deepening relationship with the outside world. Operation City Lights was set up after a DEA informer working in Manhattan's Chinatown told his handler that the 125 Gang was exporting heroin to the eastern seaboard from Fuzhou. After an operation that lasted a full two years and encompassed not just China, Hong Kong and the US, but India as well, the Federal Government was understandably pleased that the arrests of The Untouchables and the 125 Gang, led by Wong Kin-Cheung, involved:

> unprecedented cooperation between the DEA, FBI, Bureau of Immigration and Customs Enforcement, the New York City Police department, together with the People's Republic of China, and the Hong Kong Special Administrative Region. This represents the first coordinated dismantling of a narcotics-trafficking organisation by the United States, the People's Republic of China ('PRC'), and Hong Kong in history.

One of those picked up in the Fuzhou swoop on May 16th, 2003 was none other than Chen Kai, 'the richest man in Fuzhou'. He was arrested on suspicion of having laundered drugs money on behalf of Wong. To the outside world, Chen's arrest was largely meaningless – he was an unknown accessory of the 125 Gang. But in Fuzhou itself, the news provoked panic among the local administration. Xu Congrong, the former chief of police and Chen's main protector, fled the country for the United States, where he quickly lost himself among the Fujianese of New York.

It was not long before the focus of the investigation into Chen Kai switched from narcotics to corruption. The leading figures from a Political Criminal Nexus in China always attract jealousy and hostility, especially from those bureaucrats who are excluded from their network. But whistle-blowers are few and far between in China – exposing corruption is a very risky undertaking. Unless you can gain the confidence and ear of an official with more clout than the one you are trying to nail (and that means finding someone influential in Beijing), campaigners against corruption have in the past usually found themselves demoted, publicly humiliated and even imprisoned. The trick is to wait until the PCN is genuinely vulnerable. When Chen Kai was arrested, some fast-thinking official got the message to Beijing that this went even deeper than money-laundering. 'Once Chen Kai was arrested,' the tea-sipping Fuzhou businessman explained, 'then his enemies in Fuzhou moved very quickly to alert the Party Disciplinary Committee.'

The purge began with eight senior officials being placed under house arrest, including Song Li Cheng, the deputy Party boss in Fuzhou. By the end of December another seventeen were taken in for questioning and charged with corruption. Two years later on and 'We still hear of people being arrested,' said the businessman. 'So many have been arrested that we stopped counting and barely notice it any more.'

The rot ran so deep that President Hu Jintao, the most powerful man in the country, personally ordered the dispatch of thirty investigators to Fuzhou in April 2004. The President also requested that he be informed of all developments in the Chen Kai case. The team from Beijing started their work by dismissing the most senior anti-corruption official in the city (who had allegedly secured an apartment in Chen's luxury Triumphant Gardens complex).

Eighteen months after his arrest, Chen Kai was finally tried at the Intermediary Court in Nanping, a provincial town in Fuzhou. (It was reasoned that there was a high chance of any proceedings in Fuzhou being nobbled, either by Chen's allies or by his enemies.) But there was a surprise in store when the charges were read out. There was no mention of the laundered drugs money. The accusations of bribing officials were relatively minor. Instead, Chen's main crime was the running of a brothel. Nobody in Fuzhou disputes that prostitution rackets were part of Chen's empire. Indeed, at the Baihe Hot Springs Hotel where I stayed, and which was part of Chen's operation, there was no question that the massage and hot-springs parlour on the fourth floor was nothing other than a knocking shop. Chen's guilty verdict shocked nobody, but the city was stunned to hear that he was sentenced to death for the crime. 'If you execute everyone in Fuzhou involved in running brothels,' said a friend of Chen, who, like everyone else, was insistent on remaining anonymous, 'then you'd wipe out half the city.'

Chen protested against the sentence, and by law his appeal should have been heard within two months of the original sentencing. 'But we have heard nothing since then,' said the friend. 'We don't even know if he is alive or dead. But there are a lot of people in the city administration who will be relieved if he is dead.' Chen Kai was no angel, but his conviction and death sentence for running a brothel looks suspiciously like a state-sponsored murder, designed to keep the details of the PCN firmly beyond the public domain.

The case of Chen Kai does not suggest that China is an especially dangerous or crime-ridden place. Chinese prostitutes, for example, rarely have to pay off a pimp. In Shanghai, sex workers openly negotiate their own price with Westerners in bars that are well known to the authorities as pick-up joints. As long as there is no violence, nobody interferes. Street crime is very low by comparison with Taiwan or Hong Kong. But Chen's case does highlight that, in the absence of the rule of law, corruption renders the distinction between legitimate and criminal business opaque and sometimes completely obscure.

Within China itself, this has developed into a political problem for the Party, whose authority is threatened. But it becomes an even greater headache when projected onto the international stage, because of America's determination to stamp out the most widespread crime in new China: counterfeiting. Of course, counterfeiting in China is not about currency (that is the speciality of North Korea), but about goods. If it is popular anywhere else in the world, you can bet that within months somebody will be producing a counterfeit version in China. No one fakes it like the Chinese. And no one is more determined to enforce intellectual property law, or copyright, than America.

Most megalopolises like São Paulo, Mexico City, Istanbul and Cairo have a history stretching back hundreds, if not thousands, of years. Twenty years ago, Shenzhen had a population of several thousand and was no more than a few scattered villages. From the gentle agricultural pastures of northern Hong Kong, you can now cross into a twelve-million-strong giant of hyper-malls, factories, tower blocks and work, work, work. Shenzhen on the Pearl River delta is the gateway to the new China, having formed a profoundly dynamic symbiotic relationship with Hong Kong. One of the original Special Economic Zones, not only has Shenzhen become the blazing vanguard of China's future, but it has even rescued the former British colony from decline by throwing it a lifeline of economic opportunity. If there is a market niche, the entrepreneurs of Shenzhen will sniff it out and fill it.

Mo Bang Fu, a Chinese journalist who has travelled to Chinatowns throughout the world, explained how it works. 'I went to Dubai recently,' he said. 'There is a river and there are all these little boats heading for Africa packed with mountains of products. All the products are made in China. They are like little capillaries coming off the veins, feeding places like Sudan, feeding places like Iran despite the American embargo, feeding places like the DRC, feeding Zimbabwe – feeding both established markets and those that other traders cannot be bothered to supply. They ship very cheap things to Dubai and to Africa – there is very little added value; maybe it's a bra; maybe it's little plastic things for the kitchen. So, to bring it from China to Dubai and then Dubai into Africa, how could you make a profit once you take the shipping costs into account?'

The goods are shipped from the world's cheapest miscellany goods markets, like Yei Wu near Shanghai or Shenzhen. Mo explains how China's economies of scale enable their traders to produce goods at one-tenth of the price found elsewhere. 'And they will push down the price to a point where nobody else can be bothered to compete,' he concludes. That same day, I watched a report on BBC World Television demonstrating how manufacturers in Egypt had given up producing the souvenirs sold in Cairo and at the Pyramids – they are now almost all shipped from China.

The world economy has never experienced a change comparable to the release of 1.25 billion people's energy that followed China's renewed reforms in 1991. From accounting for less than 1 per cent of global trade in 1990, China had become the world's third-largest trader by 2004, outstripping Japan and only lagging behind the entire European Union and the United States. Analysts at the World Trade Organisation predicted that its 6.7 per cent of global trade in that year would top 10 per cent within a decade. In its 2007 Trade Policy Review of China, it also pointed out that in the course of this ten-year expansion, the country would need to create yet another 100 million jobs. China's economies of scale mean that it can already compete in any industrial sector, and before long in most service sectors, too.

But with China, there is one major problem that is visible more or less wherever you travel in the country. As I prepared to cross the border from Shenzhen to Hong Kong, I was funnelled through a long marketplace selling all manner of knick-knacks. I could not judge many of the Asian products on display, but the Rolexes and the DVDs were as bent as a three-dollar bill. Even so, the fake DVD market has now attained such levels of sophistication that some fake brands advertise themselves as 'genuine fakes' – that is, 100 per cent reliable copies made from master tapes. They have developed this branding to ward off competition from even cheaper DVDs. As a consumer, I soon deduced the reason. In Shanghai, the traders I bought from would slip the DVD into a player in-store to prove before I purchased it that the DVD was studio quality with English dialogue or subtitles. Such a facility was not available in Fuzhou, and as a consequence I picked up a copy of *Night at the Museum* with dialogue only in Russian or Ukrainian (good practice for me, but a huge disappointment to my nine-year-old son) and of *Volver*, whose English subtitles bore no relation to Pedro Almodóvar's heart-warming story about a single mother, but instead told a preposterous B-movie spy story.

But the DVD store that fascinated me most was on the border between Shenzhen and Hong Kong – not because of the quality of the fakes, but because the goods were laid out in one of the country's most heavily policed customs zones. Customs officers were indeed strolling by unconcerned as I was purchasing counterfeit DVDs for less than a dollar a piece (all for the purposes of research, of course). Being offered a fake DVD by a Chinese trader is an everyday experience in many parts of the world. But in China, if you want to show 'face' to the outside world, you can be much more ambitious. Why bother buying a Mercedes-Benz when you could buy a Geely! A quarter of the price of a Merc, but physically almost identical. And the fervour for faking it doesn't stop there.

In January 2004, the two German engineering and electrical giants, Siemens and ThyssenKrupp, watched proudly as their Maglev train, the Transrapid, left Shanghai's Long Yang Station for its inaugural commercial journey to Pudong airport. The Transrapid's electromagnetic technology enabled this remarkable train to complete the twenty-mile journey in just under eight minutes, travelling at a top speed of 270 miles an hour. It is the fastest ground-transportation system in the world. But it was expensive. When the Chinese announced a possible 85-mile extension to the tourist destination, Hangzhou, they received a shock when the German consortium put a $6 billion price tag on its construction.

One December evening in 2004, CCTV cameras were monitoring the maintenance depot of the Transrapid in Shanghai when they recorded the unexpected arrival of a team of Chinese engineers. They began measuring, weighing and testing the entire train. Within a year, China announced it would be building its own high-speed Maglev train. Before long, the German Foreign Minister, Frank-Walter Steinmeier, had become involved in the row, and the German press accused China of having stolen the technology and pirated German know-how on an unbelievable scale. Siemens and ThyssenKrupp were faced with a dilemma. Although the Transrapid was a huge project, they were bidding for other major investments in China as well and opted to tread very cautiously. Furthermore, Shanghai is the only world showcase for the Transrapid and the consortium needs cordial relations with the Chinese to show off the achievement to other prospective customers. Eventually, a compromise was reached whereby 90 per cent of the new trains would be manufactured in China under German supervision. Nevertheless, it still represents a huge loss to the consortium.

There is nothing the Chinese will not copy. Whether it is Swedish bathroom fittings; spare parts for aircraft; furniture; non-toxic paints (the fakes made, of course, with highly toxic materials); foodstuffs; clothes; or even an entirely new set of adventures for Harry Potter, such as *Harry Potter and the Crystal Turtle* – anything that is produced is fair game for the Chinese counterfeiters. The European Union Commission estimates that fake goods around the world are worth between $250 and $500 *billion* a year. Of these about 60 per cent originate in the People's Republic of China – 20–25 per cent of exports from China are counterfeits, while 85–90 per cent of products sold in the domestic Chinese market are fake.

Intellectual property theft has assumed centre stage in the relationship between China, on the one hand, and the world's other three main trading powers: the EU, the US and Japan. The last two (the US in particular) advance two arguments when they demand that the

Chinese Government does something about it. First, they insist it is unfair for counterfeit-manufacturers to derive profit from goods into which they have invested no development or marketing capital. Second is the issue of safety. This began to exercise the Government in Berlin after German customs confiscated $200 million worth of counterfeit goods in 2003, among which they discovered spare brake pads for Volkswagen vehicles. While the spares look authentic, they are invariably cobbled together in a hurry – safety is not a primary concern of the counterfeit-manufacturers, and the brake pads have the potential for transforming their host vehicles into death traps. Although refreshingly entrepreneurial, the producers and retailers of these goods are organised criminal syndicates.

Since being admitted to the World Trade Organisation in 2001, the Government of China has rapidly introduced the core legislation required to combat intellectual property theft. Three serious issues, however, ensure that implementation is a different matter. First, although China is a one-party police state, its various police forces suffer from shortfalls in funding, as well as from huge inefficiencies and corruption. Second, the Government is reluctant to launch a concerted campaign against counterfeiting companies that employ an incalculable number of workers who might otherwise be on the streets. And finally, the Political Criminal Nexuses that run the provincial economies are even less interested than central government in playing by the book, even if it means alienating Western partners.

The expansion of global trade that has accompanied China's rise in the past two decades has undoubtedly assisted in lifting tens of millions out of poverty – this is a monumental step forward for China and other emerging economies. But the rush to trade has left the world's ability to police and monitor trade flows in a mess. The World Trade Organisation is supposed to ensure fair play and as free an exchange of goods as possible around the world within existing rules. But noble though its aims are, in practice the WTO just holds the ring as a group of prize-fighting countries use their muscle and guile to secure as great an advantage as possible at the expense of others. In the blue corner, a tag team defending unfair subsidies shapes up to the producers of counterfeit goods in the red corner. Naturally, the weak and defenceless take quite a bruising in this arena.

In 2007, the desperate failure of the Doha Development Round of world trade negotiations, whose aim was to smooth out such conflicts and contradictions, suggests that trade disputes will become ever more bitter in the coming years. China's imperative to create jobs through exporting goods means that the temptation not to clamp down on fake produce will remain high, especially as their ability to police the trade is limited.

Individual Western companies have found that China's Public Security Bureau is a weak, inefficient, corrupt and unwilling partner. So increasingly they are turning instead to the many foreign and domestic business consultants now found throughout the country. Companies engage these consultants for all manner of services, chiefly to negotiate a passage through the Scylla and Charybdis of the national and local bureaucracies. But frequently they charge them with the task of tracking down clandestine operations that are aping Western brands. By painstakingly building up a raft of contacts – in the police, in Western trade missions and in local contacts in the Communist Party (not to mention investing in their futures), some consultants like Paul French and Matthew Crabbe's Access Asia in Shanghai can arrange for raids to be mounted with the collaboration of local law-enforcement agencies.

'We have to find the factory,' explains French. 'We have to do the due diligence. Then we get the court to issue the raid order and then we get the cops – we get on well with the Shanghai police. The problem is they have to tell the local police, who may or may not inform the people we want to raid. So we send an advance guard to the factory and then go to the police. If you work with an American brand, the consulate will send somebody to the courts and on the raid. Then we go in, Rambo-style, kick down the doors and seize the goods. But piracy is only a civil offence in this country. We can fine them, but we can't put them in prison and in a couple of days they've opened up somewhere else.'

China allows these private law-enforcement agencies to operate, but under strict supervision – and the muscle work is usually left to the police. Cracking down on opportunist enterprises churning out Louis Vuitton bags for the tourist market is enervating work, as they seem to breed like rabbits. Still, they are vulnerable to rough policing if the local authorities are genuinely committed. But bigger and more troublesome enterprises are now springing up in several parts of China that are not so easily cowed. The Empire of Counterfeiters is beginning to strike back and the strength of the Dark Side is gathering at an alarming rate.

Travelling inland south-west from Xiamen in southern Fujian province, the road begins to rise. As one climbs ever higher, the vegetation becomes less verdant, the trees more craggy. The constant business of China's cities recedes in favour of a Confucian quietude. In November 2006, a young officer from TMAD (the Tobacco Monopoly Administration Department) was on road-block duty when he spotted a motorcycle with a driver and pillion passenger heading in his direction at speed. The TMAD, which is a crack law-enforcement unit, spends much of its time in these mountains, which are notorious for hosting huge factories that are buried underground (literally and metaphorically), producing counterfeit cigarettes. The young officer, tough and fit, put out his hand, gesturing to the bikers to slow down. As he did so, the pillion rider took out a machete from under his jacket and brought it down with immense force on the officer's arm, severing the limb completely. Although his colleagues immediately drove him to the nearest hospital an hour away in Xiamen, surgeons were unable to reattach his arm.

The TMAD established which village the attackers came from and approached its elders with the request to hand them over. The elders refused to cooperate with the investigation and, in consequence of the attack, the TMAD has dismantled the road-block programme, which had been hailed as a major initiative in the plan to neutralise some of the most powerful gangsters in China. The aim had been to identify the whereabouts of a large underground factory that had been producing American and Japanese brand cigarettes.

The region in southern Fujian is called Da Shan (Big Mountain) and it is home to some of the biggest and most lucrative counterfeit factories in the world. These facilities, built deep into the mountain, produce millions of cigarettes a day, which are then either introduced onto the huge Chinese domestic market or taken by containers around Asia, over to the United States and beyond. Health concerns and legislation aimed at reducing smoking in the United States and Europe may have dented tobacco companies' profits in the West, but in China and Asia, it's party time! As Asians sample smooth Virginian blends in ever greater numbers, these exceptionally lucrative cowboy operations of Da Shan employ whole villages and communities to undercut the market with their inexpensive and ever improving fakes. In doing so, of course, they also undercut the Chinese Government's income from sales tax on tobacco, and it is a measure of how seriously Beijing takes the problem that in the China State Tobacco Monopoly (CSTM) and its armed wing, the TMDA, it has created probably the most effective police force in the country.

This is not quite war, but something close – the illegal tobacco producers have developed their own intelligence networks, which monitor the activity of the CSTM and customs officials. Law enforcement loses several officers or private-sector workers a year to the illegal cigarette producers and, when the CSTM launches a raid, it does so with a mighty paramilitary force. 'What if I were to take a drive around Da Shan as a tourist to see what I could find there?' I asked one operative involved in battling the baccy mafia. 'You can go there,' he replied, 'but you won't be coming back.'

One man well known both to the baccy mafia and the Chinese police was Tung Yan Yuk, aka Tony Tung, who had started life as a fishmonger north of Xiamen in Fujian. In the late 1990s, Chinese police issued a warrant for his arrest and for that of his two younger brothers. They were charged in connection with tax evasion and cigarette smuggling to the tune of RMB 600 million ($78 million). One of the brothers was caught and imprisoned indefinitely in 2001, but Tony and the second brother got away. According to a confidential intelligence report on Tung, he no longer visits either Hong Kong or mainland China for fear of arrest. But he is happily ensconced now in Singapore, from where he controls one of the biggest counterfeiting and container empires in Asia. Every month, police believe that:

> Tung's cigarette-smuggling enterprise alone ships between 20 and 50 40-foot container loads of international brand-name cigarettes each month. The cigarettes generally are collected and consolidated in Singapore and then shipped through Manila and Subic Bay to the port of Currimao, Ilocos Norte, in the Philippines, bound for China either directly or via

Vietnam. Tung owns or controls three container ships, as many as seven ocean-going tankers, and an unknown number of other vessels that he employs to smuggle cigarettes and fuel oil from/to Taiwan, China, the Philippines, and possibly elsewhere in East Asia.

Many of the details of Tung's operation came to light when the Philippines National Police organised a raid against his Forietrans factory, where hundreds of millions of cigarettes were being manufactured illegally. This was a tough job: 'Tung's factory – where he made the half-billion sticks of counterfeit Mild Seven – was in Pampanga, north of Manila,' reported one operative involved in the raid. 'This town is part of the legislative district represented by Congressman Mikey Arroyo, the son of President Arroyo.' Investigators discovered what they had long suspected: evidence showed that Tung was paying off legislators in Taiwan and that he had established links with a factory in North Korea's miserable little free-trade zone, Raijin, that was also feeding counterfeit cigarettes into the retail chain.

In criminal terms, these links to North Korea are disturbing. This tawdry state has almost realised the totalitarian dystopia imagined in George Orwell's 1984. Stalin himself might have blushed at the cult fashioned by the Kim dynasty, whose self-regard grows in inverse proportion to the misery it has spread among the people. Millions face a daily battle against starvation as their leaders gorge themselves on a surfeit of imported luxury foods. To fund their lascivious lifestyle, Kim Jong-Il and his acolytes have turned North Korea into a major hub of the shadow and criminal economies in Asia. North Korea is renowned as the world's largest producer of virtually undetectable counterfeit $100 bills (the so-called 'supernotes'), and much of its pharmaceutical industry is devoted to the manufacture of methamphetamines to keep up with demand in Japan. According to sources in the CIA, a major Russian criminal developed a healthy trade in fissile material with North Korea during the 1990s.

More recently, North Korea has discovered the profits to be made in counterfeiting goods. Like the Chinese, its people are willing to turn their hand to anything, although they have proved particularly adept at producing fake cigarettes.

North Korea's emerging reputation as a counterfeiter is grist to the shadow economy's mill because it brings the country ever closer to China's grey zone. Yet North Korea's engagement with the global criminal economy has an unexpected positive side-effect. It paradoxically makes Asia a more stable place: the deeper North Korea is sucked into China's economic orbit, the greater the influence that Beijing exerts over Pyongyang. Beijing is not interested in a rogue nuclear neighbour acting unpredictably in a region where things are changing very quickly.

China's emergence as a regional superpower with aspirations to reprise this role on a global stage has shuffled the security pack vigorously in Asia. Tensions between China, the two Koreas, Japan, Taiwan and Russia, which until recently appeared abstract, are taking on more concrete forms. The most immediate concern both to the United States and to the big regional players – China, Japan and South Korea – is North Korea's emerging identity as a dysfunctional nuclear power. Japan and the US have also expressed disquiet about China's growing impact on the security of the entire Asia-Pacific region. Essentially, the days of the United States overwhelmingly defining the security parameters of Pacific Asia are coming to a close.

This has already led to nervousness born of uncertainty, but China's rise and its hunger for economic growth also demonstrate a profoundly stabilising effect on many of its smaller, volatile neighbours.

China's economic drive, both as a producer and as a market, is spilling over into transitional neighbours like Vietnam and the Philippines, but also into more settled countries like Thailand. It is encouraging growth throughout the region. Even the once-isolated economies of countries like North Korea and Burma are beginning to mingle in an ever more intimate manner with China's. In the critical case of North Korea, the United States's policy of confronting the government in Pyongyang with angry rhetoric and implicit threats may prove much less effective than the slow, steady absorption of North Korea's economy by Beijing. (The Middle East, where two other members of the Bush-appointed 'Axis of Evil' are located, signally lacks a stabilising power like China.)

China can muster immense influence in North Korea, if it feels so inclined. The outsourcing of production to North Korea is not restricted to fake cigarettes. North Korea produces goods even more cheaply than China, and some of the wares that we find in Western stores marked Made in China are in fact Made in North Korea. Rather than threatening to bomb North Korea, the Chinese are very sensibly slowly transforming it into an economic vassal.

And thanks to perhaps the most egregiously silly programme instigated by the Bush Administration's War on Terror (although there is stiff competition for this award), those goods Made in North Korea often have a swift and untroubled passage straight to Los Angeles or New York.

After 9/11, Washington decided it would have to beef up its port security; 90 per cent of the world's commercial traffic is transported in containers on the high seas. 'In 2001, US Customs processed more than 214,000 vessels and 5.7 million sea containers,' according to a customs statement. The four largest foreign ports of departure for the US were: 1) Hong Kong; 2) Shanghai; 3) Singapore; and 4) Kaohsiung in Taiwan. And so it was decided by Commissioner Robert C. Bonner that 'A proactive stance by Customs in screening sea containers will significantly contribute to the agency's overall efforts to secure the borders against dangers that might be introduced through commercial traffic.' The Container Security Initiative (CSI) was born.

Testifying to Congress a few months later, Bonner outlined that 'The specific purpose of CSI is to prevent terrorists from using cargo containers to conceal nuclear weapons or radiological materials. With CSI, we are partnering with foreign governments to target and screen high-risk containers for nuclear and radiological materials using technology before the cargo is shipped to US ports. The targeting aspect of CSI involves using sophisticated automated targeting technology to identify high-risk containers, those that may contain terrorist weapons or even terrorists.'

All very exciting. And so Bonner dispatched teams of US customs officers all over the world to the ports which signed up to the CSI – those ports that refused, of course, would lose out to competitors also trading with the United States, and so most were prepared to join in this global extension of US power. Once the containers have been screened in Shanghai or Kaohsiung, they have gone through the Green Channel and are effectively already in the United States.

The great majority of customs officers dispatched around the world have never worked abroad and only a very few speak foreign languages. In Kaohsiung, Taiwan, one of the biggest foci of the CSI, not a single customs officer speaks Mandarin, let alone the Fujianese dialect of Taiwan. And so in order to ascertain which containers might be containing nuclear material or not, they depend upon customs offi-cials from the local port. 'These people are the most susceptible of all to bribery and corruption,' explained a senior Hong Kong police officer. 'And so far as we understand, if you are not carrying nuclear mate-rial, if you can succeed in getting your container selected for examin-ation in Kaohsiung or Hong Kong, then you are home free! It is an ideal way to smuggle any manner of goods into the United States.' And any number of those goods originate in North Korea.

I asked the journalist Mo Bang Fu whether the corruption and deceit inherent in China's political and economic life were not in danger of corrupting the world trading system. 'Two hundred years ago, people from England came to Shanghai,' he began to admonish me. 'These were not your fabled "English gentlemen"! They were pirates! Just as the British pirates came and raped our shores, so there may be pirates out there with the Chinese traders of the present day. But when the market reaches a certain scale, the worst practices will fall away and something that *demands* regulation and an adequate regulatory mech-anism will emerge.'

If Mo Bang Fu is correct in his assumption, then governments around the world may be able to stem the growth of the global shadow economy and the powerful dose of instability that it injects into our lives. But if we fail to construct an adequate regulatory mechanism – that is, some form of global governance – then organised crime and corruption will combine with protectionism and chauvinism to engender a very unstable and very dangerous world.

EPILOGUE

As consumers, we are all involved – often unwittingly – in the shadowy world of trans-national organised crime. Food prices have plummeted in the West as a proportion of the household income in the past fifteen years. Illegal and trafficked labour has driven down the costs in the agricultural industry, and in Britain inflation has been kept at acceptable levels in part due to the low wage paid to migrant workers.

In 2005, Italian scientists measured the River Po for a chemical derivative found in urine only after cocaine usage. The highly accurate procedure recorded that the five million people in the Po valley were consuming almost 1^1/$_2$ tons of the drug every year. This is *twenty* times previous estimates, which were based on haphazard collations of statistics from sociological studies (as with smoking and drinking, users generally underestimate the amount of cocaine they consume, if they are prepared to admit to the habit at all). The white powder still regularly graces the tables of white middle-class professionals at dinner parties in Berlin, London and New York. By using prohibited narcotics, consumers are not only contributing to huge criminal profits, but they bear indirect responsibility for the trail of blood that marks every stage of its journey.

When I was a student in the 1970s, it was considered completely unacceptable among my peer group to visit a prostitute. Yet today, educated young European men think nothing of flying to Estonia or similar Eastern European destinations on stag weekends, where hiring prostitutes is all part of the fun. The profits from these activities derive from the willingness of individuals to break the law or cross social taboos to satisfy their own desires.

But whatever benefits ordinary citizens may derive from organised crime in terms of lower food prices or indulgence in recreational drugs, they are at risk of losing in other areas of criminal activity. A huge second-revenue source for criminal syndicates is theft, either straightforward larceny or through deception. Cyber crime now threatens all of us and, thanks to the ever-greater use of computers in every area of our lives, this even includes people who do not go online. Cyber crime has witnessed an astonishing growth since the millennium and represents perhaps the greatest challenge for public law enforcement worldwide. Cyber police suffer from both poor funding and a lack of qualified personnel.

Perhaps the most attractive profession for modern trans-national criminals involves taking money from governments. Smuggling goods with high rates of tax is the oldest form of organised crime and remains popular today in industries such as the illegal cigarette trade. But the ability to move money and goods in huge quantities at great speed has also encouraged new forms of crime, especially those that exploit discrepancies in tax regimes around the world. The profits offered by taking advantage of these loopholes are staggering. Europe's most vigorous criminal industry between 2002 and 2007 was 'carousel fraud'. This involves gangs importing goods into the European Union, or between EU countries, and illegally claiming the VAT, or sales tax, on these items before re-exporting them. The EU reported in 2006 that it could not put an exact figure on the fraud, but estimated that the exchequers were losing at least $100 *billion* a year to these fraudulent schemes. The arcane nature of fraud and its status as a 'victimless' crime (nobody suffers direct personal injury by the theft of taxpayers' money) boosts its popularity along with the extraordinary sums it can earn.

The move into large-scale financial crime has been assisted by what has happened on the global financial markets since their liberalisation in the past two decades. In 2007, with GDP at around $50 trillion, the consulting firm McKinsey estimated that the world's financial assets were now three times that figure. Even more dizzying and frightening is the figure of $300 trillion that is accounted for by 'derivative' securities. In lay terms, the vast sums accruing to the world's largest banks, hedge funds and private equity firms are the result of ever more arcane speculation on the performance of markets around the world.

Successive financial meltdowns have demonstrated that the level of risk associated with these activities is much greater than was predicted.

In the summer of 2007, the collapse of the so-called US sub-prime mortgage market gave the world a hint of how closely this structure resembles a house of cards. When tens of thousands of Americans with low credit ratings could no longer keep up with the rising interest payments on their homes, financial institutions around the world showed signs of buckling. Central banks in the EU, Japan and Australia, and the Federal Reserve in the US and Japan's Central Bank, pumped more than $150 billion of taxpayers' money into global markets to ward off a greater collapse (roughly the same amount that the beleaguered taxpayers of the EU shell out annually to carousel-fraud criminals). BNP Paribas was among the world's grandest institutions to confess that it was unable to calculate exactly how many hundreds of millions of pounds it had lost in consequence.

This last admission reinforces the urgent need for greater regulation in the financial markets: in a world where legitimate institutions are unable to account properly for their dealings, the ability of criminals to launder their money through this merry-go-round of speculation is greatly increased. The Caymans, British Virgin Islands and all the other offshore banking centres are the back door through which criminal money can enter the legitimate, if increasingly opaque, money markets. Western governments could close this anomaly overnight if they took decisive action, making money-laundering a significantly trickier prospect. But they don't. And the deeper the involvement of shadow funds with the licit money markets, the harder it becomes to follow the cash, which is the key to the successful policing of international organised crime.

Politicians are fond of talking tough on law and order. In June 2005, the then British Prime Minister, Tony Blair, urged the European Parliament to focus on 'cross-border intelligence and policing on organised crime; developing proposals to hit the people and drug traffickers hard, in opening up their bank accounts, harassing their activities, arresting their leading members and bringing them to justice; getting returns agreements for failed asylum seekers and illegal immigrants from neighbouring countries and others; developing biometric technology to make Europe's borders secure'.

The need for strong, well-equipped law-enforcement agencies to combat organised crime is axiomatic. But appeals like this, which offer solutions based on the greater engagement of the police or military alone, betray a profound abdication of political responsibility. They are the product of unimaginative politicians who lack either the vision or the interest to address the great structural inequities in the global economy upon which crime and instability thrive.

It is not globalisation in itself that has spurred the spectacular growth of organised crime in recent years, but global markets that are either insufficiently regulated, especially in the financial sector, or too closely regulated, as in the labour and agricultural sectors. In the 1990s, we witnessed the beginnings of a global regulatory regime of the financial markets that held out a hope: there was a chance that we might establish a grip both on the partially regulated licit economy and on the entirely unregulated shadow economy. Since the millennium, however, a hostile United States, an incompetent European Union, a cynical Russia and an indifferent Japan have combined with the unstoppable ambition of China and India to usher in a vigorous springtime both for global corporations and for trans-national organised crime.

TEN YEARS ON

When researching *McMafia*, I quickly appreciated that organised crime values many of the tools used by people working in the licit economy, not to mention the people themselves. The leaders of criminal syndicates have always, where possible, cultivated relationships with politicians, businessmen, lawyers, journalists, civil servants and the members of other key professions who, for one reason or another, are open to cooperation, intimidation or bribery. Paltry salaries for public servants have often proved an invaluable aid to organised crime. Above all, organised crime and its proceeds mingle with respectable businesses and individuals in the deliberately obscure backwaters of money laundering and offshore banking, where the proceeds of corruption, tax evasion, pyramid schemes and criminal enterprise flow beyond the grasp of revenue services and law enforcement.

However, while it wasn't hard to identify this murky confluence, I failed to anticipate just how warmly elites around the globe, including in the most influential capitals, have since embraced the culture, the techniques and the morality of *McMafia*. Planet McMafia has become so tightly entwined with the world of finance, politics, the law and its enforcement that it is often impossible to distinguish between them. I would even argue that the world of organised crime, the rapid deterioration in our economic prospects and increasing political instability are closely connected. Money from multiple explicitly criminal sources has been funding licit enterprises on an ever grander scale. We have observed it in real-estate transactions in New York and Miami, to mining ventures in West Africa, across the collapse of Greece and to the sale on world markets of oil extracted in territories under the control of the Islamic State. In all instances, oligarchs, organised crime bosses and their collaborators, in both the private and public sectors, have made billions of dollars at the expense of tax payers and law-abiding citizens.

On 15th September 2008, not long after *McMafia* was first published, the Lehman Brothers investment bank collapsed, triggering a shattering crisis in global capitalism that had been brewing steadily over a twenty-year period. Eight years later, political classes across the Western world and in several key emerging markets were left reeling by a mighty backlash in the shape of unpredictable populist anger. No event symbolised this more acutely than Donald Trump's election to the presidency of the United States.

While this anger was clearly directed against a potpourri of policies which political and economic elites had promoted as part of an agenda of globalisation, remarkably – with the exception of one or two cases – the monied classes got away with it scot-free. Perhaps most inexplicably, inequality within and between countries continued to sky-rocket, despite having already reverted to levels similar to those seen in the sixteenth century. In early 2017, Oxfam published a report detailing that the world's eight richest men – six Americans, a Spaniard and a Mexican – controlled as much wealth as the poorest 50 per cent of the globe, that is to say 3.6 billion people.

The impact of the crash and the practices that led to it are troubling. Even given the immense and growing influential trade in illicit goods and services, traditional mafias, even if they united in a SMERSH-like body, would still not be capable of inflicting the staggering economic and political damage wrought by the collective efforts of Western banks, hedge funds and Enron-style corporations. Such 'legitimate' institutions have achieved this by persuading, cajoling or bribing successive governments, especially in the United States and the UK, to permit their outrageous speculation for personal and institutional gain. Together they fashioned an unforgiving black hole at the centre of our financial galaxy. In 2008, these activities resulted in the global economy crossing the event horizon of recession and impoverishment. The Masters of the Universe retreated into their McMansions and McYachts to leave weakened and incompetent governments to extract the balance from hard-pressed taxpayers. Meanwhile, the leaders of groups from Wachovia to the Royal Bank of Scotland suffered at most a rescinded knighthood and perhaps one or two fewer dinner invitations. The global oligarchy barely noticed a blip in the staggering progress of wealth accumulation.

Democracy has proved fragile in many regions, with autocrats seizing upon economic uncertainty to consolidate their position in countries across the world, including China, Russia, Hungary, the Philippines, Thailand, Turkey and South Africa. In the most established democracies, entire ideologies – most notably European social democracy – have been in headlong retreat while angry populism in various guises appears to have risen from the dead. The European Union continues to face an existential crisis which has already led to the comprehensive political and economic breakdown of one of its members, Greece.

It is hard to imagine that Brexit and Trump would have succeeded without the decision of British and American governments to hand out billions to save banks whose criminal recklessness came within a few weeks of bringing down the global financial system. Barely a week goes by that we don't learn of some story or other of gross malfeasance, whether in the most advanced democracies, autocracies or hardened dictatorships.

Paradoxically, perhaps the most egregious example of an elite gorging itself on public money with the aid of criminal practices offers a real glimmer of hope that such practices may not be sustainable in the long run.

Travel for three miles west along the Esplanada dos Ministérios in Brasília (where most of Brazil's federal ministries are housed), then hang a left, then a right and you will come across the Ale petrol station.

Behind the sixteen pumps, which dispense fuel to some 3,000 vehicles a day, stands a string of small shops for the convenience of motorists. One is the dry cleaners where Brasília's civil servants drop off their suits in the morning before picking them up in the evening. The adjacent shop, Valotur, is also a laundry. But it cleans something else: money.

In March 2014 a police investigation of Valotur opened, looking into the laundering of profits from all manner of gangs, from drug dealers to counterfeit goods smugglers and beyond. This was a run-of-the-mill anti-organised crime operation and the suspects were well known to the cops. Most had previous convictions for a variety of offences and the investigators were expecting to pull up a few weeds and toss away the offenders.

But as they started pulling, they found that these weeds had inexplicably long, tough roots. They followed them as they led all the way back down the Esplanada dos Ministérios. By the time they were being properly unearthed, these roots were sufficiently thick to rip down entire institutions of state, not to mention two of the largest companies in all of South America.

Operation Car Wash, named after the Ale petrol station and its Valotur currency exchange outlet, was the beginning of what, to my reckoning, is the largest corruption scandal in the history of the world, involving the laundering of at least $50 billion dollars.

At the time I was working in Brazil and living in Rio de Janeiro's largest favela where tens of thousands of families eke out a life of subsistence in cramped, dangerous and unhygienic conditions. I followed the events of Operation Car Wash with increasing disbelief. For many years a majority of the country's most senior politicians had colluded with the most powerful businessmen in order to embezzle money from the state and their companies on an astronomical scale. As millions of Brazilians struggle to afford a minimal standard of living, their law-makers, judges, businessmen and lawyers were showering themselves with luxury condos, imported high-end vehicles, private jets, Swiss bank accounts and holidays abroad. The state oil company, all major construction companies, the food industry and part of the mineral extraction industry were complicit in the scheme, handing over billions in bribes to ensure that politicians would do their bidding in Congress and in government.

According to the main investigating magistrates, the fraud reached right up to the president, Michel Temer, and cut swathes across the Senate and the Lower House. As they pulled still harder at the roots, it brought state governors tumbling down, along with their wives, their friends and the richest men in Brazil. As a consequence of a routine investigation into known launderers of the proceeds of organised crime, Brazil has collapsed into a political, economic, social and constitutional crisis of epic proportions.

When I first started investigating the drugs economy in Rio's favelas in 2012, I had lunch with an experienced journalist from the city. He said, 'You shouldn't have too much difficulty dealing with the narco-traffickers. They're relatively harmless. Now, if you were to investigate the construction firms, like Odebrecht, then you'd be dealing with a serious mafia. Then I'd be worried for your life!'

In March 2016, Marcelo Odebrecht, the Chairman of the epony-mous construction firm, the largest in South America, was sentenced to 19 years and 4 months after being convicted on charges of corrup-tion, money-laundering and the formation of a criminal organisation. Yet it went deeper still. The World Cup of 2014 and the Rio Olympics of 2016 were constructed on the most rotten of foundations, with corrupt deals being conducted more or less in plain sight; the legacy is that Rio de Janeiro is bankrupt and consequentially sinking into a mire of violence and broken public services.

Brazilians are well acquainted with the culture of corruption, which has been a feature of the country's statecraft since the days of Por-tuguese colonialism. So while they were angry when the revelations concerning the Car Wash investigation began to emerge, they were not in the least surprised.

They were, however, profoundly shocked that for the first time in Brazilian history, the perpetrators of grand larceny and corruption were being held to account. It was hard to believe that the country's highest court, O Supremo Tribunal Federal, was actually insisting on the interrogation and detention of some of the most powerful people in the land. The federal police were resolutely searching premises and arresting their social superiors. And the magistrates were ferreting out every little scrap of paper proving the existence of the transfer of huge sums across borders and currencies. For the first time in over 100 years since the founding of the Republic, the organs of state oversight were actually carrying out their job as envisaged in the constitution. The commitment on the part of the criminal justice system to go after the richest and most corrupt members of a society represents a fundamen-tal break with the past.

The Brazilian events are, however, what is known as a 'prosecutors' revolution' where the barrel of bad apples is thrown onto the dung heap but the management of the orchard remains unchanged. In order for

Brazil to throw off the colonial legacy of egregious criminality, which its pampered elite regards as a birth right, the country will require a thorough political and constitutional reform. Don't hold your breath.

Nonetheless, the Car Wash investigation points to a wider phenomenon too: crime and corruption may still be rampant across the globe but we are also seeing a fight back against this behaviour.

While I may not have fully appreciated the attraction of the McMafia culture to unscrupulous movers and shakers, in both *McMafia* and in a later book, *DarkMarket*, I certainly did anticipate the other structural shift in global crime: cybercrime.

Law enforcement sometimes prefers to talk about the 'digitalisation of organised crime.' This, they argue, embraces two things. The first is pure cybercrime, activities that can only exist as an intrinsic part of networked computer systems such as DDOS attacks or ransomware. The second is cyber-assisted crime, i.e., the enhancement of traditional criminal activity such as drug trafficking through the use of computers, much in the way that licit businesses do.

For two decades, traditional organised crime and cybercrime were quite distinct. Even less than ten years ago, a Swedish cybercriminal described to me how he had tried to interest his father's organised crime operation in Malmö in online credit and debit card fraud. 'I told them that the returns were much higher and the risks much lower,' he explained to me, 'but they just couldn't get their heads round the technology. They preferred to stick with what they knew best – extortion, robbery and protection rackets.'

His response hinted at the gulf that divided old-style crime and the new world of criminal hackers: the use of violence. In the world of mafia organisations, if you can't deploy or credibly threaten intimidation, you don't make the starting grid. Violence is the *sine qua non* of traditional organised crime. But in cybercrime, the physical is not an issue: you can hatch a crime in Kazakhstan with your victim in LA while organising the cash out at an ATM in Dubai.

As a consequence, cybercrime has attracted perpetrators with a wholly different social profile from the hitmen of Sicily, the *sicarios* of Pablo Escobar or the fingerless enforcers of the *yakuza*. They often start very young as gifted computer users who love to explore the far reaches of the Internet and networked computer systems. More experienced cybercriminals monitor the activity of youngsters with aptitude on the Dark Net and recruit them by gently enticing them into criminal activity – although this process begins before the young hacker has developed a mature moral compass.

As I got to know cybercriminals around the world, I discovered that a minority conformed to the stereotype: geeks with limited social skills and, much more commonly, without any track record of thuggery. They do exist and their technical ability is often astonishing. Nonetheless, actual hackers only make up a small minority of those involved in cybercrime. A hacker is simply somebody who has acquired an advanced understanding of computer science and coding. They usually demonstrate an elevated ability to identify weaknesses and vulnerabilities in the system. Hacking should not have the pejorative overtones which the practice has acquired. Instead, one should qualify hackers as being either Black Hat, Grey Hat or White Hat. Those coders who write malware and release it into the 'wild' are definitely Black Hat. Meanwhile, the front line of cybercrime is usually waged by 'social engineers' – modern confidence tricksters who persuade you to do things on your computer which you will later regret.

Younger members of traditional organised crime are, of course, digitally literate and its members have come to understand that embracing technology can lead to spectacular profits. In one case, a Dutch–Turkish group engaged in importing cocaine from South America persuaded or cajoled two techies to hack into the port of Antwerp and to manipulate the unique nine-digit PINs that every seagoing container is allotted. Using this they were able to digitally mark the containers with cocaine as having been cleared by customs.

This emerging fusion between traditional organised crime and cyber comes at a time when malfeasance on the Internet has reached new levels. In early May 2017, the WannaCry cyber-attack launched against computers running Windows around the world caused ferocious disruption and sent governments into panic. The impact of cyber-attacks was becoming ever greater. In the two years prior to the WannaCry ransomware attacks, the CEO of Sony Pictures had been forced to resign after the publication of email exchanges which *inter alia* referred to the movie star, Angelina Jolie, in unflattering terms. The many clients of

Ashley Madison, the website for people seeking extra-marital affairs, froze with fear after their names were released online.

WannaCry was quickly followed by another attack of ransomware: NotPetya, as it was called. Both proved that a country's infrastructure might also be at the mercy of relatively unsophisticated hackers. It was a malignant harbinger of future disasters but one which nonetheless gave us crucial pointers as to how we might mitigate their impact.

The key aspect to both attacks was EternalBlue, the vulnerability used to transmit the ransomware. In both cases, once a single computer was infected, the rest of the network was defenceless. Microsoft failed to spot this bug but it didn't escape the eagle eye of America's mighty digital spy agency, the NSA, the creators and guardians of this vulnerability, which it was doubtless stockpiling for use at some future point. Unfortunately, they turned out to be poor guardians, as it and other hacking tools were stolen by a mysterious group, The Shadow Brokers. The speed of transmission and reach of the EternalBlue worm accounts for the devastation of the WannaCry and NonPetya attacks. Microsoft's Brad Smith went as far as to say that 'an equivalent scenario with conventional weapons would be the U.S. military having some of its Tomahawk missiles stolen.'

The targets of the WannaCry attack were equally important. Although it may have been pure coincidence, the assortment of targets was of such variety that one might think they were cherry-picked intentionally to demonstrate power: the National Health Service in the UK; rail transport in Germany; telecommunications in Spain; banking in China; and government (the Interior Ministry no less) in Russia. If the attack had also brought down a major utility somewhere, it would have scored a royal flush of hits on the so-called Critical National Infrastructure.

We have entered a brave, but frightening, new world.

That doesn't mean that old-style McMafia activities have taken a back seat. They continue to expand and develop their networks and businesses on an unprecedented scale. I cannot give comprehensive details here so I restrict myself to one of the trades I cover in Chapter 9, Black and White. It is a crime which has assumed terrifying proportions in the last decade. It is also a peculiar business as it often seems like a crime against evolution itself.

During a conference on organised crime I attended in The Hague in late 2016, a South African ranger showed the audience a video that took us completely unawares.

From a distance, the large animal looked as though she was enjoying some well-earned repose. But as the camera slowly zoomed in, it became clear that this majestic rhinoceros in early adulthood was in considerable distress. She was lying immobile on the ground. A bullet from a hunting rifle had lodged in her back.

There was worse. Her face was a horrendous mess. The men who shot her had hacked off her horn while she was still fully conscious, leaving a huge cavity where a puddle of congealed blood had pooled. On this occasion, the rangers found her too late and her life would end in excruciating pain as it ebbed away over a period of many hours.

The consequences of transnational organised crime are often grim. But few are as upsetting as those associated with the illegal trade in endangered wildlife which has accelerated dramatically since I published the first edition of this book. Rhinos and elephants have been joined by lions, tigers, turtles, sharks, rays and pangolins on the list of species whose existence is now threatened by the demand in East Asia for their body parts to be used either as decoration or medicines.

In 2007 South Africa registered 13 illegal rhino deaths. By 2014, that figure had skyrocketed to 1,215: an increase of 9,246 per cent. Enhanced protection measures have helped to reduce this number but it still stands at over 1,000 deaths per year. Given that 70 per cent of the world's 30,000 rhinoceroses live in South Africa, these statistics describe a fast track to extinction for one of evolution's most majestic creations.

Poaching is frequently carried out by impoverished South Africans and Mozambicans who risk their lives at the hands of rangers and soldiers. They will be paid a month's salary for each rhino horn, maybe $150. But the markup on the product starts rocketing when the middlemen get their hands on the body parts. They then dispatch these products to Vietnam, primarily for sale to Vietnamese and Chinese clients. When the horn reaches this market, it will fetch between $90,000 to $100,000 per kilogramme.

But while China has made strenuous efforts to curtail the trade in illegal rhino horn, the government in Hanoi has been less rigorous. The Vietnamese gangs behind the trade use a variety of circuitous sea routes to deceive law enforcement. Ten years ago the market in Vietnam for rhino products was insignificant. But after it became the main conduit for illegal sales to Chinese citizens, a local market around Hanoi developed. This mirrors one lesson of the drugs trade – countries across which illicit products transit soon develop their own habit.

Elephants are also faring badly in Africa as traders seek out their tusks for ivory products. In the Great Elephant Census released in 2016, researchers found that across Africa there were now 352,000 elephants remaining. This may look a healthy number compared to the rhinos but the stock is being depleted by 30,000 animals a year. Given that a century ago Africa was host to some 20 million elephants, it's clear the danger that humans pose to the species is extreme.

The ban on the sale of ivory, which most countries around the world support, remains relatively uncontroversial as a way of protecting the elephant. But rhino horn is not a tooth extension like the elephant's tusk. It consists primarily of keratin, a variety of the substance that strengthens hair and fingernails in humans. As such the horn grows back if it is harvested carefully.

Many of South Africa's private rhino owners have been arguing that they should be allowed to sell licensed horn that has been surgically removed. In April 2017, South Africa's Constitutional Court upheld a challenge to the moratorium on the domestic sales of rhino horn. The owners argued that a legal market would satisfy demand in East Asia without threatening the species. Some conservation organisations, like the World Wildlife Fund, claim that this will merely inflate demand. Whoever is right, time is not on the rhinos' side.

The rise in the trafficking of endangered wildlife species was not a development I anticipated. Along with people smuggling, this has been triggered by the increased demand for these illegal commodities in countries like Laos and Vietnam, rather than being indicative of a fundamental shift in the nature of organised crime.

It is not all gloomy. Awareness about the threats posed by organised crime and corruption has grown. There is now a growing body of individuals, institutions and government departments determined to shine a light on the many dark recesses of the world. The concerted action taken by police and magistrates in Brazil is a case a point.

Despite the challenges that the Internet has posed to traditional print media, there has been a remarkable flowering of investigative journalism. The Organised Crime and Corruption Reporting Project, Pro-Publica and, above all, the International Consortium of Investigative Journalists have dug ever deeper to expose how politicians, diplomats, arms dealers, criminals, bent lawyers and bankers exchange information, techniques and their ill-gotten gains as far away as possible from responsible institutions of state.

There have been some major takedowns – most importantly because of its global profile, FIFA was exposed as the organised crime operation that it truly was. There is still much more to be done in the area of global sport organisations but the international bodies responsible are finding it increasingly difficult to keep their skeletons in the closet.

Thanks to the Panama Papers and investigators like Nicholas Shaxson, the author of *Treasure Islands*, a book exposing how tax havens operate, we know much more about how criminals and corrupt politicians squirrel away their cash and try to anonymise their dark money. There has been huge regulatory pressure on big corporations, especially those in mineral extraction, to increase their transparency, forcing them to desist from corrupt practices. There has been a pushback against important anti-corruption regulation in the United States since the election of Donald Trump, but the next elected president is likely to come under considerable pressure to reinstate a regime of close scrutiny.

Another major area where we are witnessing steps in the right direction is in drug law reform. It is perhaps both ironic and appropriate that much of the impetus for this is coming from the country whose drug policies have for so long held so much of the world in their thrall. Individual states in the United States, starting with Colorado and Washington state, but now including California, have been legalising marijuana for recreational use.

In January 2018, Colorado will have had legal marijuana for four years. Not only has Western civilisation not yet collapsed, but the state government has enjoyed a windfall in tax revenue. In 2015, this amounted to an extra $78 million dollars for health and education programmes, which is double the taxes collected on alcohol sales.

Change is also palpable in South America. Most countries there have now decriminalised drugs for personal possession. They are simply fed up with bearing the brunt of exceptional violence directly caused by the persistence of the US's war on drugs. The battle to end this senseless war with its murderous consequences is not yet over, but it has at last begun in earnest.

Perhaps most importantly there is now a general agreement in democracies that organised crime and corruption represent a fundamental threat to the smooth functioning of our political systems. If we are going to overcome the multiple challenges facing the world in the next few decades, we have to place crime and corruption, alongside climate change, resource depletion and inequality, at the top of the list.

Misha Glenny, 2017

NOTES ON SOURCES

The primary source material for this book emerged from nearly 300 interviews which I undertook between May 2004 and April 2007. Many are quoted here but those which are not have still contributed vitally to the text. However, in addition to these interviews I have referred to countless articles and studies and a number of important books.

The key criminological study informing this work is Diego Gambetta's *The Sicilian Mafia: The Business of Private Protection* which, I believe, has transformed our understanding of organised crime. On the Sicilian mafia, I would also recommend Peter Robb's stunning *Midnight in Sicily* and the partial autobiography of the former mayor of Palermo, Leoluca Orlando, *Fighting the Mafia and Renewing Sicilian Culture*. *The Shadow Economy: An International Survey* by Professor Friedrich Schneider and Dominik H. Enste has laid the groundwork for our growing ability to quantify the shadow economy.

There are also several valuable general studies of the rise in organised crime and the shadow economy. Moises Naim was the first to identify the true significance of trans-national organised crime in our globalising world. Jeffrey Robinson's *The Merger* contains fascinating details on some of the global crime networks. See also *Gangster Capitalism: The United States and the Global Rise of Organized Crime* by Michael Woodiwiss, and in German *Die Barbaren kommen: Kapitalismus und organisiertes Verbrechen* by Jean Ziegler.

Chapter 1

The work of Yovo Nikolov and other journalists from the Sofia news-paper *Capital* has been especially helpful in this chapter, as have several monographs produced by the Centre for the Study of Democracy in the Bulgarian capital. I have also drawn on the memoirs of Dimitur Ivanov, *Sesti Odel* (Sixth Department), and *Afera* by Bogdana Lazarova.

Chapter 2

There has been a great deal published in the former Yugoslavia on this subject both in books and magazines, as well as in some academic studies. The only material in English is the important series on the cigarette trade published in 2002 by the Croatian magazine *Nacional*. This was based partly on interviews with some of the players but also on Croat Secret Police sources (so it comes with attendant health warn-ings). In German, see Norbert Mappes-Niediek's *Balkan-Mafia: Staaten in der Hand des Verbrechens – Eine Gefahr für Europa*. The most inter-esting book in Serbian is Milos Vasic's *Atentat na Zorana* which looks at the background to Djindjic's assassination. There is important mater-ial in all major Serbian news magazines and in Montenegro's *Monitor*.

Chapters 3 and 4

There are two crucial English texts that deal with the Russian mafia: Vadim Volkov's *Violent Entrepreneurs: The Use of Force in the Making of Russian Capitalism* and Federico Varese's *The Russian Mafia: Private Protection in a New Market Economy. The Oligarchs: Wealth and Power in the New Russia* by David Hoffman is a masterful account of the power behind Yeltsin's throne. Stephen Handelman's *Comrade Criminal: Russia's New Mafiya* was one of the first books to document what was happening in Russia. Olga Kryshtanovskaya's research is indispensable. In Germany, the works of Jürgen Roth are probably the best introduction to the narrative of the Russian mafia. *Der Oligarch*, his biography of Vladimir Rabinovich, is one of the most useful and detailed explanations of the social psychology of this rare but hugely influential breed. Many of the Rabinovich quotations in my book are from this text, although I also interviewed Rabinovich myself. See also

Roth's *Die Gangster aus dem Osten*. In Russian, I have used Artyom Tarasov's *Millioner*, the autobiography of Russia's first millionaire, as well as an interview with him. Alexei Mukhin's various books are vital chronicles of the emergence of individuals and groupings, especially *Rossiskaya organizovanaya prestupnost i vlast*. See also *Tenevaya Rossiya* by Lef Timofeev and Igor Klyamkin. The only book in English dedicated to the murder of Gongadze is *Beheaded: The Killing of a Journalist* by J.V. Koshiw. See also Global Witness's report *It's A Gas*.

Chapter 5

The late Robert I. Friedman's *Red Mafiya: How the Russian Mob Invaded America* details how some of the links between the Russian mafia and Israel developed. It is a rip-roaring read but needs to be taken with a pinch of salt in parts. There is no comprehensive study of the growth of organized crime in Israel, although Mark Galeotti, the British scholar, has written about it in various publications. *The Global Political Economy of Israel* by Jonathan Nitzan and Shimshon Bichler is a very useful introduction to the shifts that have taken place in Israel's economy over the last two decades.

Chapters 6 & 7

Material on Dubai beyond the journalistic is scarce but *From Trucial States to United Arab Emirates* by Frauke Heard-Bey is a superb introduction to the modern history of the UAE. On money-laundering, John Kerry's report (chiefly penned by Jon Winer) into the BCCI scandal is a seminal text, but see also *The Outlaw Bank: BCCI* by Jonathan Beaty and S.C. Gwynne, Nick Kochan's *The Washing Machine: How Money Laundering and Terrorist Financing Soils Us*, and the more academic *Chasing Dirty Money* by Peter Reuter and Edwin M. Truman. On the relationship with terrorism see *Terra Inc: Tracing the Money behind Global Terrorism* and the National Commission's *9/11 Report*. The UK-published *Journal of Financial Crime* and *Journal of Money Laundering Control* are also very useful.

On Bombay and the bombings of 1993, by far the best source is Hussain Zaidi's *Black Friday: The True Story of the Bombay Bomb Blasts*.

There are countless articles and studies on Dawood Ibrahim and his network published in India and elsewhere. In addition, the several Bollywood movies that take the Mumbai underworld as their theme are worth viewing.

Chapter 8

The two most useful books for understanding crime and corruption in Nigeria are Karl Maier's *This House Has Fallen: Nigeria in Crisis* and Daniel Jordan Smith's *A Culture of Corruption: Everyday Deception and Popular Discontent in Nigeria*. Equally valuable are the writings of Chinua Achebe and Wole Soyinka.

Chapter 9

The best resource for anybody trying to understand crime in South Africa is the Institute for Security Studies (www.iss.co.za), which offers superb intellectual resources. The most riveting and illuminating book is Al Lovejoy's *Acid Alex*, while Ted Leggel's *Rainbow Vice* and Jonny Steinberg's *The Number* are also very important. See also *Crime Wave: The South African Underworld and its Foes*, edited by Steinberg. For the diamond and coltan trade, the most important source is Global Witness and their path-breaking reports, as well as Douglas Farah's *Blood from Stones: The Secret Financial Network of Terror* and (with Stephen Brown) *Merchant of Death: Money, Guns, Planes, and the Man Who Makes War Possible*, about Viktor Bout.

Chapter 10

Two books are very revealing about Canada, British Columbia and the politics of crime. *Bud Inc: Inside Canada's Marijuana Industry* by Ian Mulgrew is the first; *Angels of Death: Inside the Bikers' Empire of Crime* by William Marsden and Julian Sher is the second.

Chapter 11

There are three highly readable texts on the cocaine industry of the past two decades. The first is Dominic Streatfield's excellent *Cocaine: An Unauthorized Biography*; the second is *Killing Pablo* by Mark Bowden, and the third is Ron Chepesiuk's *Drug Lords*. Finally, in Spanish there is the masterful *Los jinetes de la cocaína* by Fabio Castillo which is easily available in various forms on the internet.

Chapter 13

On the modern *yakuza*, start with the classic *Tokyo Underworld* by Robert Whiting, but don't miss *Dogs and Demons: The Fall of Modern Japan* by Alex Kerr or *Yakuza: Japan's Criminal Underworld* by David E. Kaplan and Alec Dubro. Peter Hill's *The Japanese Mafia: Yakuza, Law and the State* is essential to understanding how the *yakuza* has developed since the end of the Cold War. *Toppamono: My Life in Japan's Underworld* by Miyazaki Manabi is available in English in Japan and the US. In German, the most fascinating book is *Japan nach Sonnenuntergang* by Wolfgang Herbert.

Chapter 14

There is a wealth of material on China but the starting point must be the academic papers and reports written by the Rutgers University academic Ko-lin Chin. See also *The Dragon Syndicates: The Global Phenomenon of the Triads* by Martin Booth, and *Tongs, Gangs and Triads: Chinese Crime Groups in North America* by Peter Huston. *The Triads as Business* by Chu Yiu Kong is also important. For material on 1930s Shanghai refer to *Old Shanghai: Gangsters in Paradise* by Lyn Pann. Otherwise, the two best-written introductions to what on earth is going on in the Middle Kingdom are James Kynge's *China Shakes the World: The Rise of a Hungry Nation* and Duncan Hewitt's *Getting Rich First: Life in a Changing China*. Both are equally illuminating but for different reasons.

ACKNOWLEDGEMENTS

The research and writing of this book have occasionally presented me with daunting challenges. I could not have overcome these without considerable help. This book has thus enabled me to work with some wonderful people around the world. I cannot acknowledge them all here and a significant number have asked me not to mention them. They know who they are and many thanks to them.

Over the past several years, I have been privileged to participate in annual discussions hosted in Greece by the leader of Pasok and the former Foreign Minister of Greece, George Papandreou, and Ada Papandreou at the Symi symposia of the Andreas Papandreou Foundation. My most sincere thanks to both of them and to George's vision.

Many participants at the symposia have been generous with their time and knowledge in helping me frame this project but I must single out four in particular whose friendship has sustained me through thick and thin. Alex Rondos was the inspiration behind an initiative to promote reconciliation between the peoples of Eastern Kosovo, South Serbia and northern Macedonia, through which I learned for the first time in detail about the overwhelming social and economic importance of organized crime in this region. Richard Parker has always been patient in answering queries on the political economy of the post-communist era, and the banking industry in particular. Ivan Vejvoda is a masterful observer of the Balkans and one of the region's most distinguished representatives. Mark Medish not only willingly shared his knowledge and experience but also assisted me in reaching several instances that would otherwise have been impossible, not to mention providing accommodation in Washington. His influence on this book is considerable.

Juliana Ruhfus researched much of the Nigeria chapter for me *in situ*. Her reporting was tenacious and illuminating, and she deserves great thanks. Vesna Vucenovic has combined tireless backup support with welcome optimism. Ted Braun and Melissa Llewelyn-Davies were honest and encouraging critics of the text. Thanks also to Chris Harrison for his help. Juliet Sydenham, Tamara Glenny and Paddy Glenny assisted as usual in a variety of ways. Thanks also to Ralph Glenny for the photo. Neil Belton and Colin Robinson have provided friendship, advice and laughter over many years.

In Bulgaria, Ivan Krastev and Ognyan Zlatev were unfailingly cheerful in the face of my numerous demands on their time, knowledge and contacts. I would also like to thank Boyko Borrisov, Jeremy and Katy Hill, Iain Stewart, Dessislava Gavrilova, Vessela Tcherneva, and special thanks to Yovo Nikolov. In Serbia, Braca Grubacic has been a great friend and ever-willing source. I also wish to thank Dejan Atanasijevic, Milos Vasic and Spomenka Vejvoda. In Macedonia, thanks, as always, to Saso Ordanoski and Güner Ismael, whose knowledge of corrupt networks is almost unparalleled. Roman Kupchinsky in Prague was most generous in sharing his expertise on Ukrainian and Russian matters. The John Smith Fellowship Programme and several of their fellows provided me with invaluable help in several parts of the Soviet Union. In Moscow, my particular gratitude is reserved for Tessa Szyszkowitz and her family for putting me up and providing me with so many insights. I also wish to thank Yelena Rubin, James Hill and Alexei Mukhin. In Ukraine, Olga Bondaruk was forever willing to undertake great challenges. I also wish to thank Alexander Radovic, Roman Olearchuk, Helen Fawkes, and Alexei Stepura. In the Czech Republic, I wish to thank an old friend, Oldrich Cerny, and Jan Zvelebil. In Moldova, thank you to Eugen Burdeliini, Stella Mocan and Alina Budeci. In Kazakhstan, I would not have got anywhere without the support and assistance of Shannon Crownover and Christopher Pala in Almaty. I also wish to thank Artur Shakhnazarian and Oksana Martinuk in Atyrau.

In Israel, my particular thanks go to Alon Farago. I wish further to thank Professor Menachem Amir, Alexander Gentelev as well as Orla

Guerin and everybody at the BBC offices in Jerusalem and Gaza City. In Dubai, Julie Studer provided sterling support as did Ashfaq Ahmed. I also wish to thank Driss Mekkaoui, Najib Bencheriff and Ron Bagnulo.

It was my greatest fortune that Vikram Chandra kindly introduced me to Hussain Zaidi in Mumbai. Hussain is without peer as a student of Mumbai and India's organised-crime groups, and he opened all the crucial doors to his knowledge. I would also like to thank Mrinmayee Ranade.

Justice Malala was an exemplary mentor in South Africa. Special thanks to Suzanne Lang for introducing me to the work of Al Lovejoy. I was then privileged to meet Al himself, whose wit and intelligence I greatly admire. Thanks also to Nick Dawes, Jonathan Lang and Justine Lang.

Special thanks go to my Canadian publisher in Toronto, Sarah MacLachlan of Anansi Press, and Noah Richler, and also to Merito Ilo.

In Washington, my thanks to Robert Gelbard and Jaime Jaramillo-Vallejo, as well as to several others who prefer to remain nameless. In Colombia, my sincere thanks to Juan Pablo Morris, and to Landa Acevedo in London. In Brazil, I owe a great debt to Emily Sasson Cohen, Ana de Andrada, and of course Caboclo Sonhador. I would further like to thank Tony Smith, Marcos Flavio Araujo Assuncao, Fabricio, João Salles and my publisher in Brazil Luis Schwarcz.

In Japan, I was very lucky to work with David d'heilly and Shizu Yuasa. Before I left Britain, I received important guidance from Peter Hill. In Tokyo, Velisarios Kattoulas was a lifesaver, while in Osaka Wolfgang Herbert offered me profound insights as well as a great night out.

Thanks in China go in the first place to Rui Huang. I could not have managed without the friendship of Lindsey Hilsum as well as Betty Du and Max in the Channel 4 office. Thanks also to James Kynge and Paul French in Shangai. Ko-lin Chin at Rutgers University gave me an essential grounding in the subject before I visited China.

My thanks as well to the remarkable team at Global Witness, in particular Charmian Gooch and Alex Yearsley. And thanks to Alex for putting me in touch with Gary Busch, who has been most generous in sharing his experience and material. The European Stability Initiative team, led by the indefatigable and disarmingly intelligent Gerald Knaus, has been consistently ahead of the field in explaining the rational relationship between society on the one hand and organised crime and related phenomena on the other. I also wish to express my gratitude to Federico Varese for sharing his knowledge and material.

In London and New York, I would like to thank my editors, Will Sulkin and Dan Frank, whose enthusiasm and belief in the project have sustained me throughout. Their editorial comments and guidance have had a significant impact on the final version of the book. I would also like to thank the staff at The Bodley Head and Knopf, particularly Dan Hind, Fran Bigman, Rebecca Carter, Drummond Moir and Lily Richards.

Clare Conville, my London agent, has been a close friend for thirty years. Her input into the genesis of this book was uniquely important and she proved a wonderful calming influence, particularly when the going got tough. I cannot thank her enough. Much gratitude also to my New York agent, Michael Carlisle, for his drive and commitment.

My greatest debt goes to my wife, Kirsty Lang, to whom this book is dedicated. She assisted me in every aspect of researching and writing this book, and kept me afloat when I was in danger of sinking. She is an exceptional woman in every respect and I am very fortunate.

And finally, my love and thanks go to my three children, Miljan, Alexandra and Callum.

INDEX